'PINKOES
AND
TRAITORS'

'PINKOES AND TRAITORS'

The BBC and the nation, 1974–1987

JEAN SEATON

P

PROFILE BOOKS

First published in Great Britain in 2015 by
Profile Books Ltd
3 Holford Yard
Bevin Way
London WC1X 9HD
www.profilebooks.com

ISBN 978 1 84668 474 6
eISBN 978 1 84765 916 3

Text design by *sue@lambledesign.demon.co.uk*
Typeset in Dante by MacGuru Ltd
info@macguru.org.uk

Printed and bound in Britain by
Clays, Bungay, Suffolk

The paper this book is printed on is certified by the © 1996 Forest Stewardship Council A.C. (FSC). It is ancient-forest friendly. The printer holds FSC chain of custody
SGS-COC-2061

CONTENTS

To
ASA BRIGGS
with respect, gratitude and affection

ILLUSTRATIONS

ILLUSTRATIONS

TIMELINE

Date	Events	BBC
1922		BBC founded as 'British Broadcasting Company Ltd' under John Reith
1927		BBC incorporated under Royal Charter, with the motto: 'Nation shall speak peace unto nation'
1932		'Empire Service' begins; forerunner of World Service
1933		Informal 'vetting' of BBC staff by Security Service begins
1937		First TV outside broadcast: George VI's coronation
1938		Arabic is first foreign language to be broadcast
1939	*World War II begins*	'Empire Service' renamed Overseas Service
1945	*World War II ends*	*Woman's Hour* first broadcast
1954		David Attenborough first presents *Zoo Quest*
1956	*Suez crisis*	Alasdair Milne produces crucial interview with Anthony Eden as prime minister
1957		BBC Natural History Department founded in Bristol
1958		Radiophonic Workshop founded
1960	*Margaret Thatcher first writes to the BBC as backbench MP*	Sir Hugh Carleton Green becomes director-general
1962	*Cuban missile crisis*	Prime minister Harold Macmillan alerted to Russia climbdown by BBC Monitoring report while chairing war cabinet in Admiralty House.

1964		*Play School* is first programme broadcast on new BBC2 channel; *Top of the Pops* starts
1965		David Attenborough becomes controller of BBC2; Overseas Service renamed 'World Service'; *World at One* begins
1967		Paul Fox becomes controller of BBC1; colour television starts
1968	*First civil rights march in Londonderry televised*	Alasdair Milne becomes controller of Scotland
1969		Charles Curran becomes director-general; David Attenborough becomes director of Programmes; *Civilisation*, by Kenneth Clark
1970	*Conservatives win election*	Listening to the BBC World Service becomes an offence punishable by prison in Pakistan
1971		*Yesterday's Men*; *The Old Grey Whistle Test*; first 'World Music Prom'
1972	*First British soldiers on the streets of Northern Ireland; 30 January: 'Bloody Sunday'; William Whitelaw is first secretary of state for Northern Ireland*	Largest number of complaints received about violence of coverage of Northern Ireland, leading to new guidelines; *Ways of Seeing*, by John Berger; *Newsround*
1973	*Sunningdale agreement proposes power-sharing for Northern Ireland; commercial radio begins*	Margaret Thatcher suggests Michael Swann as replacement for Charles Hill as chairman; Alasdair Milne becomes director of Programmes; first report on women in top jobs in BBC; *That's Life* begins long run

1974	*Labour win election; responsibility for broadcasting moved to Home Office; Roy Jenkins becomes home secretary; Merlyn Rees becomes Northern Ireland secretary; Protestant workers' strike wrecks Sunningdale agreement; Portuguese revolution*	Bryan Cowgill becomes controller of BBC1; *Porridge*
1975	*Sex Discrimination Act; Employment Protection Act*	A *Guardian* journalist describes the 'BBC's god-like authority' on both sides of the Vietnam conflict.
1976	*Inflation at 26 per cent; IMF called in; Harold Wilson resigns as prime minister, to be replaced by James Callaghan; Merlyn Rees becomes home secretary; Roy Mason becomes Northern Ireland secretary*	John Birt and Peter Jay publish report suggesting a 'bias against understanding' in TV news reporting; Alastair Hetherington (former *Guardian* editor) becomes controller of Scotland; *When the Boat Comes in*; *Brimstone and Treacle*; *Multi-Coloured Swap Shop*; *I, Claudius*
1977	*Royal Jubilee*	First of three short-term licence fee increases imposed; Bill Cotton becomes controller of BBC1; Ian Trethowan become director-general; Annan Report
1978	*'Winter of discontent';* The Times *ceases publication for a year*	Second of three short-term licence fee increases imposed; Georgi Markov of the Bulgarian Service dies after poison attack on Waterloo Bridge; *Young Musician of the Year* first broadcast

1979	*Scottish devolution referendum fails;* *Conservatives win election after Labour lose no-confidence motion forced by Scottish nationalists;* *Margaret Thatcher becomes prime minister;* *William Whitelaw becomes home secretary;* *revolution in Iran;* *Soviet invasion of Afghanistan;* *most strike days since General Strike of 1926*	Third short-term licence fee increase imposed, lasts two years; Wesley Kerr is first black general trainee to be appointed; last edition of *Tonight* carries interview with INLA member who claims responsibility for murdering Airey Neave; *Life on Earth;* *Tinker Tailor Soldier Spy;* *Question Time* begins; *Not the Nine o'Clock News;* *Testament of Youth;* *Antiques Roadshow;* *Churchill and the Generals*
1980		Lord Howard becomes chairman; *Newsnight* begins; first *Children in Need* telethon; *Shock of the New*, by Robert Hughes; *Ireland, a Television History*
1981	*Riots in Brixton and Toxteth;* *wedding of Charles and Diana;* *Rupert Murdoch buys* The Times; *ITV broadcasts* Brideshead Revisited; *SDP founded by the 'gang of four'*	Alan Hart becomes controller of BBC1; *The Borgias;* *Bergerac;* *Hitchhiker's Guide to the Galaxy;* *The Lord of the Rings*
1982	*Falklands War;* *Channel 4 and S4C begin broadcasting*	Alasdair Milne becomes director-general; *Boys from the Blackstuff;* *The Young Ones;* *Rough Justice*
1983	*Unemployment reaches 3,224,715;* *Conservative re-election with increased majority;* *Labour's election manifesto described as the 'longest suicide note in history';* *Leon Brittan becomes home secretary*	Stuart Young becomes chairman; Brian Wenham becomes controller of Programmes; SDP founders Roy Jenkins, David Owen, Bill Rogers and Shirley Williams defend BBC in Parliament against Conservative accusations of treachery; *Blackadder;* *Breakfast Time* begins; *An Englishman Abroad*

1984	*Miners' strike;* *IRA bomb Grand Hotel in* *Brighton*	Michael Grade becomes controller of BBC1; all of Shakespeare's plays commissioned; Michael Buerk's report on *Six O'Clock News* on famine in Ethiopia watched by Bob Geldof; report on women in the BBC by Monica Sims; *The Living Planet;* *Maggie's Militant Tendency;* *The Thorn Birds;* *Lenny Henry Show*
1985	*Douglas Hurd becomes* *home secretary*	First televising of the whole of *Last Night of the* *Proms* – second half becomes an international hit; *Live Aid;* *Real Lives* on Northern Ireland; *EastEnders* begins; *Edge of Darkness;* Security Service vetting of BBC staff revealed in *Observer* story
1986	*US bomb Libya; Norman* *Tebbit complains to BBC* *about Kate Adie's reports*	Marmaduke Hussey becomes chairman; Peacock Report; John Tusa becomes director of World Service; *Casualty;* *The Monocled Mutineer;* *The Singing Detective;* *Childwatch*
1987	*Ronald Reagan abolishes* *the 'Fairness Doctrine'* *which had obliged US* *broadcasters to provide* *'honest, equitable and* *balanced news'*	Michael Checkland becomes director-general after Alasdair Milne forced to resign; Jonathan Powell becomes controller of BBC1; Alan Yentob becomes controller of BBC2
1988	*'Broadcasting ban' imposed* *on reporting in Northern* *Ireland*	
1989	*Berlin Wall comes down;* *end of Cold War*	

INTRODUCTION

WHEN IT GOT IT RIGHT the BBC metabolised Britain by airing the nation's virtues and gnawing away at what it had botched. It hunted out the voices of the less powerful and alternatives to fashionable arguments and steered them alongside those of the established and influential. It bestowed recognition on people and problems that might otherwise be ignored – including the mad aunts and errant teenagers in the national family group. But that was not all; while all views had to be treated courteously, the BBC, as a public service, had also to test the evidence that supported them. Impartiality was not passive between truth and falsehood.

The BBC had to attend to the nation as it got up and as it went to bed, when it celebrated Christmas and on an ordinary weekday evening. It needed to be sensitive to the public when it was worried, but supply life-enhancing silliness in the right place. The Corporation also needed to fathom the deeper temper of the times. If the BBC had a duty to showcase and polish up the crown jewels of British culture, it had an equal obligation to wash as much of the nation's dirty linen as it could find, out there on the street. Finally, it had to find a way of taking the mickey out of the whole damned lot.

This book starts in 1974, where Lord Briggs's last great volume of the BBC history ended. It ends in 1987 with a convulsive moment: the resignation of Alasdair Milne, the director-general, just before the fall of the Berlin Wall. It was a tumultuous time of uncomfortable, relentless overturning of expectations and ways of life, which tested the BBC severely. The seventies were characterised first by a melancholy apprehension of national decline and frozen inertia, and then a panicked disorder. Inflation spiralled out of control, wreaking havoc on the nation and institutions such as the BBC, and defying the Labour government's battle to control it. Yet by the eighties Britain was being remade at a furious pace on a triumphant new model, as an ebullient, get-rich-quick, something-for-nothing culture emerged. The iconoclastic Conservative government attacked, and yet in the very last instance also protected, the Corporation.

At its best the BBC followed John Stuart Mill in believing that however self-evidently true an argument seemed, 'if it is not fully, frequently, and fearlessly discussed, it will be held as a dead dogma, not a living truth'.[1] Rather than allowing the strongest opinion to triumph, it saw views as affecting each other, listening and reacting, undogmatically and cheerfully. Endowing important things with vivid life was the BBC's central task. The probing interview, conducted by Robin Day, William Hardcastle, Brian Redhead, Joan Bakewell, John Humphrys or Ludovic Kennedy, was an interrogation of power in direct descent from enlightenment scepticism. The freedom of expression it embodied was a profoundly British construction – one which aspired to widen the national conversation.

Indeed, by the 1970s the BBC had helped to define Britain. Yet 'Britishness' had to be a co-production bubbling up from the life people lived, not imposed. The BBC's attention to the audience's pleasures gave it access to an unrivalled range of British life, through *Gardeners' World*, *Question Time* and *Play School*, *Woman's Hour* and Michael Parkinson's chat shows, as well as *Dad's Army*, Radio 1, *The Good Life*, *Just a Minute* and *The Proms*. In representing the nation these programmes were pillars of the BBC's part in the unwritten constitution, holding things to account and describing decencies.

Although more directors-general have come to bloody ends than is generally recognised – leading the BBC is an intensely political and exposed task – Milne's dispatch was traumatic, and connected to the tornado of national re-engineering going on around it. By the late eighties the BBC was all too often the story, vulnerable to new commercial and political models, its capacity to exercise political balance tested by three great Conservative election victories, an unelectable opposition, and the emergence of a new third party. Old sentimental certainties fell. Traditional restraints on the power of the government no longer worked. An independent civil service, the trade unions, even the media, wrote Ben Pimlott, had been reduced by the late eighties to 'a state of quivering sycophancy'.

The period has coherence, ending at a time of intense agitation within the BBC and a fraught relationship to a sharp, frequently hostile yet reinvigorating political climate. Partly because previously closed state papers have become available, however, this book also reinterprets BBC history over a longer period. It ranges over longer timespans because some of the issues that jostle urgently forward in this period have not been investigated.

The Corporation inevitably got things wrong in the seventies and eighties, left things undone, and the fulcrum of balance shifted. It did not always question its own ideas, or the conventions of the moment, enough. It became defensive and arrogant. It was late to the new 'dry' economics that were to reshape the world (except in the brilliant *The Money Programme* on BBC2 and in *Analysis* on Radio 4). But when it blundered, people could demand that it try harder, which was part of its glory, as it was 'ours'. It was not easy getting the right balance. Bitter battles raged in BBC Scotland during a period of devolutionary passion. England had voted in a Conservative government in 1979, but Scottish voters had not. Which version of the nation did the Corporation represent to whom, when a BBC principle was that it should tell the same story at home and abroad? Sometimes telling the truth offended people and unleashed attacks on the Corporation, sometimes the BBC temporised, which was also damaging. The BBC needed to be managed from the 'top', creatively independent at the 'bottom', but remain an ensemble. In a contentious period when the pressure of divisive events bore down on it, many throughout the Corporation believed passionately in its values, but disagreed about who had the right within the BBC to define them. Nevertheless, this clash produced some fearless programmes full of the energy of inquiry. As decent political systems were distinguished from malign ones by the frankness of the discussion they conducted with themselves, however demanding, the BBC had to be an engine of level-headed realism, as well as a box of delights.

Crises, arguments, disagreements, gloom and doom are a prominent feature of the world of archives and memories; the BBC in any case thinks through the way forward by poring over the runes of past car crashes. Like generals fighting the last battle it sometimes gets it wrong, or even worse it can sometimes forget itself. The seventies and eighties were terrible and exciting for the nation as well. But this book equally tries to examine the carefulness that was needed to make great programmes. Because, beside the *Sturm und Drang*, the BBC went on day in and day out, tending to the everyday pleasures of living – the life of its audience.

In the World Service the BBC was also outward-facing as one of the world's great objectivity traders. It was a precious gift to international intelligence, avidly followed by people hungry for truth but trapped in oppressive states, in a period when the Cold War was still alarmingly hot. After the fall of communism (shortly after the end of this book), it was greeted all over the former Eastern bloc with the same moving gratitude that had met it across occupied Europe at the end of World War II. The World Service served British self-interest, not by crassly echoing the work of government in expressing British policy, but by putting into practice hard evidence of British values in action. Government cuts had to be managed, and an absurd Labour plan (from young female Turks at the centre of government) to reduce the World Service to an anti-communist propaganda rump had to be fought off. Yet the World Service and Monitoring (the nation's ears to the world) were equally important for the knowledge they transferred back into Britain, by sensitising the entire insular political system to the nuances of how the world beyond was behaving and thinking. The World Service helped us see our place in the world better.

AUDIENCES

Broadcasting was then a mighty behemoth, forging powerful collective experiences, the common coin of everyday life. Everyone watched or listened to the same programmes at the same times in the same places. Vast audiences gathered together routinely every evening to watch the news. Before audiences became fragmented, over 20 million watched the more nail-biting episodes of *EastEnders*. This capacity to mobilise attention allied with the BBC's values of independence, impartiality and quality, adding an authority to the experience, was eyed warily and avidly by politicians and commercial rivals. BBC accountability was measured in audience pleasure and attention, within which education and information were embodied. It treated children as citizens in waiting. It is no wonder that objectivity and impartiality were bitterly disputed. In command of such great unifying force fields of public attention the BBC had to be responsible, and win the battle about being seen to be responsible.

Nevertheless, audiences had to choose to spend their time with the BBC. They could always switch off, switch over or kick a football in the park instead. So the Corporation had to win and woo. Sometimes different parts of the BBC were reacting differently to the same impetus. In the febrile eighties, when it was sometimes out of step with the national mood, other parts of the BBC were able to express that mood in sometimes surprising ways. In 1979 a nation apparently in headlong economic decline watched David Attenborough's *Life on Earth*, gripped by a story of the ruthless evolutionary extinction of redundant species (or the adaptive capacities of small entities with long histories). In 1984, *Live Aid* released the immense energy of popular culture for charity. It was a BBC news story about Ethiopia which galvanised Bob Geldof into action. Then the BBC provided, almost miraculously in such a short period, the organisational agility to translate Geldof's evangelical mission into a global concert that was a kind of activism, releasing the power of young people all over the world who wanted to give to others. It had an impact at the heart of government, mutated charities from small- into large-scale enterprises, changed lives in Ethiopia, and started a long and still unresolved debate about the relationship between politics and need.

DOWN WITH THE BEEB

And the BBC had to continually review the borders of political power. The lines drawn in the sand that protected its editorial independence were always having to be remade, by choices made at all levels of the Corporation, but also out in governments. The habits and principles that mattered were reiterated in documents, but more importantly they lived in programmes. This book is concerned with how, in practice, an independent institution was preserved. It was a matter of enduring structures, principles, everyday decisions, but even more than in the civil service, for example, it was also a matter of characters, taste, aesthetics, hunch, insight.

Politicians had often pressured the Corporation. It was a quite proper part of democratic negotiation in a representative democracy, however much it rattled the BBC at times. What mattered was how the BBC assessed each case and dealt with the pressure. Sometimes it had been a very grown-up conversation. Occasionally there had been fair, but at other times improper, political attacks on the Corporation. Then, as always, the press had rampaged, audiences had complained, groups had agitated. Sometimes prime ministers had been out of order: after the Suez crisis in 1956 there were threats to cut the licence fee in revenge for perceived BBC failures.

In the seventies and eighties, however, for the first time since it was founded, the very existence of the Corporation was in question. Confrontation steadily escalated. Behind the backs of the British public, both Labour and Conservative governments considered a radical move. Labour planned to abolish the licence fee by bringing the Corporation within general government expenditure. It was so controversial that relevant papers were marked 'Secret' and their circulation restricted. The plans were backed by a coalition within cabinet of the Labour left from Tony Benn, who thought the BBC governors 'undemocratic' and the licence fee an unfair poll tax on the poor, to the prime minister James Callaghan on the right. (They agreed on little else except that they should 'do' something about the BBC.) This would have made the BBC a 'state' broadcaster, competing head-on with health, education and defence for funds. Indeed, Labour came in practice, if not in name, very close to doing this when it gave the BBC three inadequate licence fee settlements, eked out year by painful year. 'Tethering' the BBC to the government by annual and inadequate licence-fee settlements was driven by a desperate, ultimately successful attempt to grapple with inflation, and there was a strand of political exasperation with the BBC as well. But while Labour ministers may have been morosely convinced that the BBC was biased against them, they saw that as a failure in delivering values they agreed with – not as an indication that the values were wrong.

The challenge from the new Conservative administration, elected marginally in 1979 and triumphantly in 1983, was more fundamental. For the first time the legitimacy of BBC values as well as their practice was directly contested. The government in the short term calmed licence-fee negotiations by taking the 'permanent revolution' out of them. But the arguments that the licence fee was a state handout inimical to free expression, that funding by advertising and greater 'choice' between channels would be more democratic, that impartial news values were a deception and 'responsible national interest' a better value, that to articulate opposing views was biased and sometimes treacherous, that the BBC was part of an establishment that needed to be re-engineered for the sake of the nation – all these arguments were combined with continual agitation about the Corporation. In addition, the BBC was expected to restrict its output to the elevated, because entertainment was intrinsically commercial. Its spending was seen as profligate, its plays political, its standards of taste and decency out of touch with the public, or coarsening to public taste. This was a strongly held, coherent attack on the Corporation's founding principles. The BBC had imposed on it governors who were actively hostile, not merely properly critical. Some Conservative ministers regarded the threat with disquiet. The Corporation seemed helpless in the face of this onslaught. Milne understood the political threat, but the great programme maker failed to understand the more fundamental challenge.

There are more uncomfortable aspects of the BBC which hardly appeared on the charge sheet drawn up by politicians at the time. Its relationship to security, which was complicated and largely defensible, was one; how women fared within the BBC another. By the seventies a new generation of women was thundering through the BBC, but encountering a world that seems quite alien now. They had tremendous working lives. Their story is exemplary of how disadvantaged voices have to struggle and how institutions have to be reinvented. The BBC had been a progressive employer and always knew its female audiences mattered. But the story of women at the top of the BBC is more complicated than a happy story of progress. These energetic young women helped bring the contemporary world into being. More perturbing was the sexual exploitation of other, younger, less middle-class, less articulate women (who belonged to the audience) by BBC and other media 'celebrities', above all Jimmy Savile. But all of these unsettling realities need to be understood within the context of the times: mores were different. Other institutions too failed to identify what was happening within them.

However, throughout the period the BBC also made wonderful programmes, made hard decisions, and above all explained a complicated world to the British public. Many of the wilder complaints against it now seem misjudged. On occasions they were driven by commercial and political animus that needed to be resisted. What is striking is that many of the programmes that caused the most controversy, from Dennis Potter's plays to *Real Lives* and *Tumbledown* (a play about the Falklands), have become iconic.

WARS

Conflicts in Northern Ireland and the Falklands War were the backdrop to the seventies and eighties. Unlike the remote wars of choice of the nineties and after, these conflicts were deeply felt, consequential and alarmingly unpredictable. In different ways they remade the nation. Faced by deep divisions in the public, the BBC, with its accumulated authority, and governments struggled separately to define the national interest and shape perceptions. The BBC brought another dimension to public understanding of the events that would reshape the United Kingdom – in the public interest, but challenging to government. Throughout, it was in the front line of the Cold War, which produced its own abrasive disagreements. Yet both governments and the BBC in desperate times were doing their best.

The grinding and seemingly unfathomable urban and domestic conflagration in Northern Ireland produced a new kind of violence, threatening ordinary people and prime ministers in unprecedented ways. The possibility of a more profound fracture of civilisation was so imminent at times that the word 'war' itself was too dangerous to be used in public. Yet something close to a civil war raged throughout the period of this book.

As ministers flailed about, attempting to impose order amidst escalating intercommunity violence, catastrophic mistakes were made. The BBC, the messenger carrying unpalatable stories, was often blamed. Much that it did, exposing abuses, learning to find audiences across a fractured community, representing real power on the ground anchored to the primacy of accurate news, brought it into headlong confrontation with the British government. The evidence reveals that Labour considered an extraordinary intervention in the ownership of commercial TV to make it more compliant. And Labour formed a nearly lethal informal coalition with the Conservatives against the BBC. Explosive rows about programmes blew up from nowhere – not least because experience in Northern Ireland was becoming so removed from that at the metropolitan centre. But the evidence shows too that civil servants mostly fought the imposition of a broadcasting ban for over a decade, and William Whitelaw was talking to the IRA earlier than was previously known.

Did the BBC get the conflict wrong in part? Yes, as did the military, the police, local and national politicians, civil servants, paramilitaries and the security services. The toxic impact of the continual threat of violence was hard for a democracy to manage. The BBC paid a high price for arriving at a proper policy of creating a mature, informed debate in the end. It drew lines around accuracy that helped create a shared public space.

If Northern Ireland ground on painfully slowly, a constant threatening drumbeat, the Falklands War was fast, furious and risky in a different way. Mrs Thatcher's political future depended on it and something sulphurous in the relationship between the Corporation and the government was set going by it. When it started the nation was divided; when it ended in victory there was a shift in national temperature. For men like Milne, it was perhaps an incomprehensible imperial hangover. But although it had been blundered into, the principle of self-determination was contemporary. The military margins were excruciatingly tight, and this led to censorship, when the BBC could instead have been a trustworthy confidant.

The BBC won the reporting war on the front line with model journalism. The world went on listening to the World Service – because it remained the best, most accurate source of information. The Corporation lost the home front over the transformation of political fortunes, it was late to a change in national mood. As the new director-general, Milne was horribly damaged by a confrontation with braying MPs. But government papers show that the incomparable Sir Frank Cooper, permanent secretary in the Ministry of Defence, was battling No. 10 as much as he was the BBC. Peter Snow was accused of treachery for calling the troops 'the British' on a brilliant new invention called *Newsnight*, leading to unprecedented attacks from a triumphalist nationalist popular press, but it turns out that he was following established government policy in doing so. The press continued the attack, accusing the BBC of reporting information that led to the death of a heroic soldier; but the briefing came from a government minister.

The answer to the problems raised by the Falklands was that the BBC needed more secure management at the top, and had that been in place, the government ought to have told the Corporation more. The prime minister emerged remade, as did the nation, but accused the BBC, which had a duty to reflect dissent, of putting impartiality before patriotism. The BBC believed impartiality served the nation, and the World Service served the national interest by telling the truth.

While the BBC and the government slugged it out in public, they also cooperated in private and in the public interest over bigger issues – planning for the threat of Armageddon after a nuclear attack or the collapse of order. Because of this, BBC staff were vetted. When this story first emerged in 1985, even the Corporation was unable to understand its own history. Now recently declassified papers overturn the account known then. The decision by the BBC, until Milne became director-general, not merely to accept but to argue for *greater* vetting of its staff was partly protective: when the Corporation was being routinely accused of infiltration by opponents of the state, official clearance proved it was not. The Corporation was also the communicating part of the security state. BBC engineers were in the front line of the Cold War battle for hearts and minds in eastern Europe – a conflict the BBC helped decisively to win. Yet the offices of the DG and the chairman were regularly swept for bugs throughout this period, revealing a dark anxiety about surveillance and mutual suspicion between the BBC and the government. Nevertheless, even as it rowed with it, the government was also relating to the Corporation.

MONEY, MONEY, MONEY

Did the BBC waste money? Mrs Thatcher thought that as a flabby public service it must do. John Birt, later director-general, had a clear analysis of its inefficiency and reorganised and reinvested money in news and production. He remade the Corporation and helped in a challenging way to save it. But the evidence is more complicated. Birt's reforms after 1992 would not have been possible without the foundations laid by Michael Checkland, one of the quiet heroes of this book, who replaced Milne as director-general in 1987. He was dismissed as a 'grey' accountant, but rarely by those who worked with him. He was clever, decent, unassuming, strategic, always completely in charge of his domain, and had BBC values in every bone. His steady rise through the BBC mirrored the importance of managing money as the economy buckled under inflation. Checkland helped the BBC beat over-mighty unions with an audacious plan, before Conservative legislation made such approaches easier. He plotted to make money and spend it better. In the Acorn computer, for example, the BBC combined technical expertise with public outreach. The idea came from the bottom of the BBC – the parts of engineering and programme-making that related to the public – backed by Checkland at the top. It combined a cheap and easy-to-use computer with brilliant programmes that helped people use and understand it, and it went around the world. It made money for the Corporation and produced a generation of computer scientists.

The licence fee was the cornerstone of BBC independence, enabling it to spend money creatively, and not to government diktat. The BBC sometimes made flops, but they were a proper part of the creative process: *Fawlty Towers* failed to find an audience on first showing. Defending the licence fee depended on spending public money well, which Checkland began to sort out, as well as explaining its legitimacy. In the end it was the Peacock Report, set up by the Conservative government apparently to demolish the licence fee, which saved it, and furthermore articulated a new justification for the BBC.

MARGARET THATCHER

Inexorably at the centre of what became a broader mood of confrontation with the BBC was the formidable Mrs Thatcher. Papers in the BBC archives, going back many years before she became prime minister, and never examined before, show her bouncing on to the BBC stage as a new MP brimming over with her splendidly particular self. As Bernard Ingham, her devoted press secretary, said, in a myth-making but accurate perception, she needed 'lead weights not rocket boosters'. The Corporation never managed to steer itself into a more comfortable relationship with her; maladroitly it fell into the trap of being defined as an 'enemy'. At numerous levels within the BBC they discussed what to do for her, with her, how to ration her appearances on Savile shows, how to check her capacity to wipe the floor with interrogators. Armed with Finchley, her constituency, she bombarded the Corporation with articulate complaint, leaving it floundering. Yet her attitude towards it was contradictory. She was observant of proprieties and devoted to public service broadcasting, but she did not hesitate to seek approval from Rupert Murdoch for her suggestion for a new BBC chairman. Everyone agrees about it. No one, then, apparently found it odd.

Another, perhaps related, factor was a sharp change in the climate of press opinion. It was partly that the reinvented popular press was on the whole in favour of Mrs Thatcher (and so also defined the BBC as an enemy), but also that the Corporation was in a larger way seen as a commercial competitor. 'Had Northcliffe and Beaverbrook [the mid-twentieth-century press barons] seen the BBC as a rival in the same way,' said the BBC's historian Asa Briggs of the foundation of the BBC, 'then the Corporation would have been strangled at birth.'[2] Meanwhile, many others who were hostile to the BBC attacked its practice and constitution as a more acceptable substitute for attacking its existence.

WORRY

The Corporation was characterised by anxiety. It did nothing casually. The worry that made great programmes and reinterpreted the careful principles that kept the BBC honest had to go from the top (if it was working right) to the bottom. The structures and bureaucrats that shaped the BBC in a larger way were there to make the everyday problems of who should speak and how things should be done what mattered, clearly based on shared BBC values. The creative processes and delicate wooing that led to Alec Guinness's great performance as George Smiley in *Tinker Tailor Soldier Spy* are displayed in a riveting set of BBC papers, including a subtle and brilliant correspondence; they were the product of the attentive intelligence of BBC managers working in enabling structures and in values evolved through time. Another version of the same values could also play out in rapid decisions in the middle of terrible news dilemmas: decisions to broadcast an interview with a Provisional IRA spokesman at a raw moment, choices about pictures, decisions about what to broadcast into Iran as a revolution rolled. Of course, News and Current Affairs, being transformed by technology in this period, were driven by one morality – get the story out. They could be devious. But the capacity to protect the freedom of speech that was the purpose of the Corporation became too easily muddled when the BBC was under attack.

Yet, at the same time, other 'deep structures' of BBC intelligence were functioning exceptionally. In this book, for the first time, the creative originality of Attenborough's transformative series *Life on Earth* is dissected forensically. The extent of its revolutionary ambition and the processes behind its production are explored. Attenborough exemplified public-service BBC, running great swathes of television in a distinguished career. In turn, the BBC made possible the Attenborough that the public trusted devotedly. *Life on Earth* was determined by Attenborough, yet could not have happened without decades of highly professional dedication to considering nature in the BBC's western region in Bristol, investment in science at the very heart of BBC programme-making, and the assembling of a team of passionate experts. The series emerged triumphantly out of rows and clashing principles, tactfully bound together by Attenborough as leader.

Meanwhile a programme like *Grange Hill* caused a riot of public and official complaint. It dealt with gritty life in an urban comprehensive school and had been deeply researched. It tackled uncomfortable issues about teenage sex, drugs, rock 'n' roll, racism, bullying. The 'taste and decency' fundamentalists (who were going to cause the BBC political grief later in the decade) immediately attacked it and it was demonised in the popular press for leading the nation's youth astray. But 'as the press launched into us and No. 10 was complaining loudly to the DG,' said Anna Home, the director of children's programming, 'the Department of Health became very interested – after all we were tackling just the issues they were concerned with, but better than they could.'[3] And *Grange Hill* was popular. The BBC did not do government campaigns. It did not accept direction about what issues it should take up or how to do them. It brought separate, careful intelligence to the reality of the nation's condition.

In difficult times, the BBC needed to provide everyday fun, such as the extravaganzas of delight embodied in a *Morecambe & Wise* show. Being popular was fundamental to the BBC – as it had to serve everyone. It did so by inventing a triumphantly successful soap, *EastEnders*, full of melodrama and matters of real public interest. Nurturing entertainment was tough and holding the line over taste demanding in a period when mores were altering (as they do continually). The nation lapped up stories. The BBC put great and trivial, comforting and challenging narratives into people's homes like a Homeric bard. In doing so, it involved its audiences in reflecting on their own situation and in understanding the different lives of others. At the same time, the BBC made programmes – *Panorama, 24 Hours, Newsnight* – that reinvented the news in ways that put the beleaguered British public in charge of their own story. Through all of these, and making children's programmes and pop music shows, the issues of balance, fairness and serving the public were encountered and assessed. BBC mandarins and the shock troops of producers and programme makers tried (and sometimes failed) to find the lines that distinguished what the BBC as a public service broadcaster ought to do from the things it ought not to do. The BBC had principles. Did it apply them, did it betray them? The BBC survived, and some of its saviours were surprising.

The story of survival emerges from the electrifying process of matching the BBC's point of view with that of others, especially politicians and civil servants, seen from state papers, memoirs and interviews. The problems that beset the BBC and the nation, whether small or chronic, are recorded in BBC papers that are witty, literate and, in pre-FOI days, frank. State papers are equally honest and reveal the camaraderie of government. Watching both sides plot and plan is riveting and at times surprising. The security services wanted fewer BBC staff vetted, the BBC wanted more; the civil service fought the broadcasting ban for nearly twelve years, while the Treasury had little truck with constitutional niceties, trampling over BBC decisions. Ministers in Northern Ireland *were* derailed by BBC stories, and *they* did discuss how to influence individual journalists. The political classes can often be seen struggling with intractable problems against an obdurate Corporation. Quite frequently they are both right – but partial.

Another revelation is the view of the Home Office, then the ministry responsible for the BBC, with its powerful ministers and experienced, able civil servants. When Mrs Thatcher intervened in the constitutional conventions that had guarded the Corporation's independence from government, William Whitelaw cashed in his loyalty to the prime minister to protect the BBC. The Home Office (amid gnashing teeth, real rows, occasional fury and plots) often came to the BBC's aid like a knight in shining armour. Home secretaries could be infuriated by the Corporation, but were often vigilant within government in protecting sacred BBC territory. They were holding lines drawn in the sand of public life that gave the BBC its unique independence, because such demarcations seemed vital to British integrity.

MONARCHY

The BBC stoked and reflected attitudes towards another institution that marked British exceptionalism: the monarchy. Both the BBC and the monarchy combined a commonly misunderstood constitutional role, an obligation to the entire nation and public spectacle. The BBC had helped form the contemporary vision of the monarch: a shifting contract with the public based on charity and image rather than power. The Corporation's royal files and interviews in the Palace, compared with BBC accounts, offer a snapshot of a relationship that was vital but tested during the eighties.

BBC outside broadcasters, equipped with ethical values and a capacity to compose emotions from the raw material of events, understood how to put together a satisfying royal show. They depended on a delicate collaboration with the Palace. BBC papers show the monarchy, especially Prince Philip, sculpting the construction of the broadcast royal image. At the heart of the story is the glittering royal frenzy that was the marriage of Prince Charles and 'Lady Di'. The Corporation's planning of an emotional feast for the public was one of the trapdoors that slammed down on the couple at its centre. If Brian Hanrahan managed (as wily journalists do) to get a scoop, if there was mayhem at the fireworks before the wedding (which went unreported at the time), perhaps the most remarkable fact was that the entire outside broadcast team, seeing Diana weep at the rehearsal, kept the secret, making sure that the pictures did not reach the newsroom. BBC Outside Broadcasts were the trustworthy guardians of a young woman's mood. Yet later, as the royal marriage tragically collapsed and royal fortunes wavered, the BBC often failed to apply all of its institutional intelligence to the gathering crisis.

By 1987, faced by a racing, apparently uncontrollable set of crises, everything the BBC did came under political attack. Great plays caused rows, not such good plays caused rows, the non-broadcasting of plays whose quality is disputed caused rows. There was a bleak atmosphere of panic and crisis, fantasies of plots and real plots. The director-general, Alasdair Milne, was forced to resign. Yet despite all the threats the Corporation survived. It did so because it largely told audiences things they recognised to be true. It brought them programmes they loved and showed them an image of their lives that made them thoughtful, but also cheered them up. It respected and listened to them, and even in hard economic and political times made them feel proud of their realism. It explained the world and in making it comprehensible made it less alarming. It offered them the incomparable reporting of a Charles Wheeler. Although 'saving' the BBC would take time, the Corporation survived the onslaught because it mattered, made a difference and was defensible.

George Orwell wrote, 'If liberty means anything at all, it means the right to tell people what they do not want to hear.'[4] The BBC paid a high price for trying to put this demanding standard into practice. Yet it survived because informing, educating and entertaining the public meant that it was held dear. Perhaps because the only institutions that people love are those that touch the imagination.

I

MRS THATCHER AND THE BBC:
THE CONSERVATIVE ATHENE

THERE IS A DISPUTE among historians about when Margaret Thatcher became her true 'Thatcherite' self. She bustled into power after the 1979 election with the largest swing since 1945 as the first woman prime minister in any industrialised country. However, her relationship with the BBC shows her as the Athene of British politics. Like the Greek goddess of wisdom, born fully formed from the brow of Zeus, the Mrs Thatcher seen in the BBC's archives sprang forth in 1959 as a newly elected MP, armed with values, a social analysis, a keen appetite for argument, reproval, and a strong sense of the BBC's prejudices and failures. From the start it is a peculiarly focused intelligence. Her views of the Corporation were confirmed by experience. Colin Shaw, a wise and emotionally astute BBC Secretary, wrote after a bruising encounter with her: 'She is a proud and difficult lady and needs a particular kind of wooing.'[1] Despite taking her seriously from the first encounter, despite libating her with the gift of public exposure, despite a strong-minded independence from her that she might have respected, the BBC haplessly confirmed her worst suspicions about public service broadcasting. It was like a rabbit caught in the eye of a ferret.

Most British prime ministers have been sensitive to criticism from the BBC, an organisation which they are held in part responsible for. Brian Griffiths, who worked with Mrs Thatcher closely on broadcasting in No. 10, said she 'was utterly devoted to public service'.[2] This did not stop her querying the very building blocks of the BBC: the licence fee, the obligation to broadcast to the nation, and the nature of 'impartiality' versus 'the national good'. She passionately believed two contradictory things: that the BBC ought to be more elitist, exercising ever higher 'standards' as it shaped public behaviour and attitudes; and that it needed exposure to the brisk winds of market competition, preferably by replacing the licence fee with advertising revenue. She wanted a BBC changed beyond recognition.

Mrs Thatcher crashed through taboos and provoked a savage, bemused humour which captured something of her power. Dennis Potter, the great television dramatist, described her at a Conservative party conference, demonstrating something of the misogynist hostility she encountered: 'She kept her glossy head tilted at a rather too carefully alert angle, and occasionally made small pawing gestures with her hands in a manner which reminded me of everyone's favourite celluloid bitch Lassie. "Oh look – she wants us to follow her."'[3] The BBC, however, had a hidden asset that would, in the fullness of time, prove valuable. Patricia Hodgson, a junior Open University producer, first met Mrs Thatcher in 1976 when the new Conservative leader arrived at a Crossbow dinner organised by Hodgson. A grand affair, it brought together every living leader of the Conservatives – Alec Douglas-Home, Harold Macmillan, and an Edward Heath early in his bruised 'Easter Island-faced' sulk. Hodgson dispatched a chap to chivvy Heath out of the Gents, as she had been warned that he would try to be the last to enter the room in order to upstage his successor. Mrs Thatcher, in cream silk, greeted the young Hodgson, in a cream silk cocktail dress, through gritted teeth, 'But you said you'd be wearing blue!' The dinner was fortuitously timed, coming on the evening that Harold Wilson announced his unexpected retirement. Attention focused on Mrs Thatcher, the new Conservative leader. Heath, from one side of the table, bellowed ever louder at Macmillan, who was deaf, that he must be part of the plan to get rid of Mrs Thatcher, and that he, Heath, would see him about it the next day. The new leader ignored Hodgson, whom she was sitting next to, ate nothing and spent the meal anxiously rewriting a speech. After giving a lacklustre performance, Mrs Thatcher prostrated herself, kneeling, at Douglas-Home's side, nervously seeking reassurance.

Although she had ignored Hodgson she had not failed to notice her. The next day, Hodgson received a handwritten note from Mrs Thatcher, apologising for being so distracted and asking her to dinner. It was an entirely typical personal kindness. From then on, Hodgson and Mrs Thatcher would meet for an annual lunch or dinner in London or Chequers. Milne shut this channel of communication down when Hodgson became BBC Secretary. However, wearing the wrong dress had given a young Open University producer a personal link to the prime minister-in-waiting.[4] Throughout the BBC's turbulent conflict with Mrs Thatcher's No. 10, one person at least within the BBC, as Hodgson moved up the Corporation, was known by the prime minister to be 'one of us', a connection that was to help save the BBC.

Mrs Thatcher saw the arts and broadcasting as industries that ought to be managed like any business, regarding any protection from the 'market' as inimical to freedom of expression. Talent, she argued, 'let alone artistic genius – is unplanned, unpredictable, eccentrically individual. Regimented, subsidised, owned and determined by the state, it withers.'[5] This philosophy was formed by her perception of the state-censored culture of communism. She told Woodrow Wyatt, 'There has never been a justification for the existence of the BBC. It was formed during an authoritarian mood following World

Holding power to account:
Mrs Thatcher, the prime minister, and Robin Day in 1980

War I. Justifications for state broadcasting ... are identical to those used in Communist and other dictatorships for state monopoly of the press.'[6]

FINCHLEY AND THE UNWRITTEN CONSTITUTION

Her Finchley constituency was Mrs Thatcher's bedrock, and a fertile source of engagement with the BBC. Early in her parliamentary career she called the Corporation to account over a constituent's protest about anti-Semitism on *Any Questions*. The director-general, Hugh Greene, answered immediately and personally that there had been a slip on the programme. He said that the *Any Questions* team was 'firm and unanimous' in its distress at the incident and opposition to such a view: 'Anti-Semitism is not a question on which the BBC is or should be impartial.'[7] Over the next five years there was gathering traffic between Mrs Thatcher and the BBC around family values (BBC lack of support for), anti-commercialism (BBC bias in favour of), vulgar programmes (BBC broadcasting of), the advantages of advertising funding (BBC hostility to), and political bias (BBC's airing of any opinion not shared in Finchley).

In 1969, Mrs Thatcher asked the new director-general, Charles Curran, to give a talk to the Finchley Council for Christians and Jews on 'The role of the BBC'. It was a bracing encounter. 'When we met', he wrote, 'we had an interesting exchange about the obligations of the BBC in matters of programme policy, particularly as they concerned the standard of national life.'[8] Finchley believed that the BBC needed tighter legal regulation. Curran took the responsibility of educating Mrs Thatcher seriously, sending her a careful reply including an extract from a 1964 letter by the chair of the governors, Lord Normanbrook, to the Postmaster General, reminding him that it was the BBC Board of Governors (not him and certainly not the government) who were responsible for maintaining due impartiality over controversial subjects, and that 'so far as possible the programmes for which they are responsible should not offend against good taste or decency, or be offensive to public feeling'.[9] It was also a reminder of the BBC's special status, regulating itself, unlike ITV, whose standards were laid down in law.

Curran included an extract from the Canadian parliament's 1967 discussion of broadcasting, which argued that 'sporadic interference' by politicians would only damage the capacity of broadcasters to 'fairly and squarely' take responsibility in the national interest.[10] He concluded with a quote from Adlai Stevenson (perhaps, on reflection, the über-liberal of American presidential politics was not best placed to win Mrs Thatcher over). 'Freedom', Stevenson had asserted, 'demands infinitely more care and attention than any other system. It puts consent and personal initiative in the place of command and obedience ... How are we to defend freedom if, for the tyranny of external control, we substitute the clattering, cluttering tyranny of internal aimlessness, confusion of ends and fuss?'

Curran added his own interpretation of the BBC's purposes in an unusually explicit defence of the Corporation's, and indeed the nation's, unwritten constitution.

Good broadcasting is a practice not a prescription. In my view, traditions are more important in this respect than written documents, and I think that in this the BBC reflects the general character of British constitutional life. We depend more on the atmosphere in which we live than on the rules which come into existence as a result of the codification of that atmosphere.

He went on to defend the Board of Governors because, if the members are chosen well, 'it is a more flexible instrument for interpreting the public mood than any written document could possibly be'. The governors moulded the human capital of the BBC by appointing the director-general and nearly sixty other positions in the Corporation: 'these people set the tone at the BBC'. Writing down an obligation to preserve standards in national life or the integrity of British institutions would in fact be damaging. The Glorious Revolution, 'on which so many of our civil liberties are founded', would not, he argued, have taken place if such prescriptions were codified. Curran was articulating the BBC's capacity not merely to reflect and change with the temperament of the times, but also the BBC's primacy in challenging and holding other British institutions up for public inspection.

Mrs Thatcher sent a handwritten reply to Curran: 'I have digested your letter thoroughly,' she wrote, and proceeded to rebut Curran's arguments thoughtfully like the lawyer she was. The Thatcher radical was already forming – not yet a monetarist but not a conventional Conservative either. Curran had argued that the BBC was successful if it reflected the variety of public opinion. She replied, 'I do not think it is sufficient to say that your objective is to present a full and wide range of opinions in the country today. This seems to me to sidestep the responsibility you have by taking refuge in what on the face of it is an attractive concept.' Mrs Thatcher wanted the BBC to shape and mould attitudes – to lead the nation, not represent it. At the same time she suspected them of doing this subversively, leading 'in the wrong direction for the nation'. She finished with candour (or pride): 'You may have gathered that tact is not my strong point when I start discussing things with busy people. May I say finally (and it is a liberty) that I should be happier if you weren't quite so sure all is well.'[11] Curran sent her another educative lecture by Lord Normanbrook, asked her to come and see for herself how 'senior colleagues are preoccupied with the practical aspects of the problems we have been discussing', and warned her of the danger of the imposition of formal regulation.

Throughout her parliamentary career there were perpetual skirmishes with the BBC. She was incensed by a BBC series for schools, designed to get 'less academically able' teenagers talking about the problems they faced, in which John Peel, the presenter, had criticised marriage as 'an artificial device which tends to destroy relationships'.[12] She complained about the effect of television on children, bad language, violence among the young, and bias in favour of trade unions. Her Finchley constituents worried that Arab spokesmen had too much airtime.[13] Later she complained about a drama series, *When the Boat Comes In*, starring James Bolam, set in the North-East of England, about the impact of the 1930s industrial collapse in the region, and said that although she had not seen it, 'Conservatives did not like it'. When George Howard, chair of the governors, protested that he was a Conservative from the North who enjoyed it, she retorted 'not a typical one!' A programme about the Angolan government's employment of mercenaries distracted from what really mattered, that it was facing a Marxist rebel force. When the director-general accepted that the BBC had 'missed the point', she retorted that the BBC was not in business to miss points. Mrs Thatcher dismissed the BBC's claim that over time they had cumulatively told the right story, saying getting 'a' story wrong was not excused by getting 'the' story right. She had argued that freedom of information, and consequently the independence of the BBC, was threatened by union pressure; the free flow of information 'was perhaps of much greater importance than the right to a closed shop'. She worried that individuals who stood out against unions were not given proper recognition by the BBC.[14]

Mrs Thatcher saw broadcasting in Cold War propaganda terms, as a force shaping behaviour in a Manichaean struggle between good and evil. The BBC agreed, and believed it participated by stretching the variety of views and serving the whole British public. A Reithian commitment to providing imaginative excellence and fostering virtue also remained important in the morality of news and programming in general. Mrs Thatcher thought that BBC programmes led to copycat riots (after Brixton in 1981), gave terrorists publicity, and were politically motivated. She asked, 'if television in the western world uses its freedom continually to show all that is worst in society, while the centrally controlled television of the Communist world and dictatorships show only what is judged as advantageous to them – how are the uncommitted to judge between us?'[15] She thought, as many did, that broadcasting had an immediate and direct impact on behaviour.

Heat was also rising over how the BBC spent its money, the fact that the licence fee 'was not a choice but something that everyone was obliged to pay':[16] she also thought that the BBC had too many people working for it and was complacent. By 1971, when she had become the secretary of state for education, she was determined to appoint Bryan Forbes to the BBC's Schools Broadcasting Council. He was a considerable film-maker, who was producing the Conservative Party political broadcasts, but with no experience of or interest in schools. By now the BBC was more familiar with her style. Curran wrote in a slightly weary memo, 'we shall have to decide in what terms to tell her that this is none of her business'.[17] Forbes 'seemed to us wholly unacceptable in an impartial body'. She also claimed that BBC interviewers let politicians off the hook. Perhaps, Curran concluded, she meant they let the wrong politicians off the hook.

One consistent theme was that she 'regretted that the BBC's independence should rest only on convention'.[18] The BBC's unwritten constitution needed 'entrenching' in law. The BBC was anxious about attempts to regulate it, seeking always to retain a fluid independence. Mrs Thatcher believed the independence was being exercised irresponsibly. She viewed the market as the discipline that brought institutions into line. She believed that the BBC, unlike everything else, needed *more* regulation. She also concluded from BBC meetings, with governors and management and programme makers, that they were united in its defence against her. What was the use of such boards? she asked. They had become creatures of the broadcasters, not their rulers. The sense that the BBC needed root-and-branch reform was in her mind from the fifties and reinforced by the eighties.

Where did Mrs Thatcher get her ideas about broadcasting from? She was not the kind of mother to rush home for *Play School* with the twins. She listened religiously to *Farming Today* and kept a wary ear on the *Today* programme – presented by the admitted Labour sympathiser Brian Redhead, who she assumed ran it for 'socialist propaganda'. On Saturdays at about ten at night, she told the Board of Management, she tried to find something to watch – but there was never anything worth seeing. She did enjoy, however, Stakhanovite that she was, late-night schools programmes, which 'were really excellent'.[19] Ingham said he only saw her gripped by television twice: on the occasions of Nelson Mandela's release and the siege of the Iranian embassy.[20] Denis Thatcher, however, was a keen rugby, football, golf and cricket watcher, and Chequers, said Nigel Lawson, 'had a chintzy television room that was Denis's snug'.[21] Carol Thatcher said, 'I grew up listening to "But he's a socialist!" whenever Denis disagreed with anyone on television, as if describing some common criminal.' Denis assured John Cole, the BBC's political editor, that the entire management of the Corporation were Trotskyists. He was tickled by the 'Dear Bill' satirical letters in *Private Eye*, written by Richard Ingrams, ostensibly from Denis to Bill Deedes. They were uncannily accurate: one 'letter' about the BBC went: 'Dear Bill, I keep telling the Boss, if ever there was a state-owned industry ripe for privatisation, it is that nest of Pinkoes and Traitors at Shepherd's Bush.'[22]

As Mrs Thatcher rose through the political system the BBC tried, and failed, to get to grips with her. On one programme, when she was education secretary, she was exposed to articulate and angry teachers, during a teacher's strike that damaged schools for a generation and degraded the standing of teachers for decades. It confirmed her hostility to the teaching profession. Although she was 'friendly' afterwards, said John Tisdall, a BBC political adviser, it was an optimistic spin on a bruising event.[23] At a lunch with the governors she said that the aggrieved teachers had not represented 'the Country' as she did, and had been a typical example of the Corporation's secret political agenda. A cautiously firm letter was dispatched: 'I am not including our own assessment of whether they were satisfactory or not since I don't want to prejudge the issue,' said Michael Swann, then the BBC chairman. 'But perhaps when you are less busy you could consider which programmes you felt went wrong and why? I want to pin down things that went wrong and see if anything can be done to make sure that they don't go wrong again.'[24] Meanwhile her office wanted the right-coloured flowers to be part of any set she appeared on. (Blue hyacinths would be 'suitable', went one request, as Mrs Thatcher would be wearing strong blue.) The Board of Management discussed whether this was bias and concluded that as long as Jim Callaghan was offered whatever he wanted – 'a harvest festival arrangement perhaps, a kind of Constance Spry right of reply' – it would be permissible.[25]

She was hawk-eyed for breaches of balance. A programme in the *Open Door* series, made by the Free Palestine Group, seemed to be partial. Her constituents complained that the programme gave no right of reply. Indeed, the idea of the series was to open broadcasting space up to non-mainstream groups and opinions, and for them 'to say what they want to say in their own way'. Although the BBC selected organisations with a careful eye to balance across the series, it was an innovative attempt to permit partisan, minority expression. Skilled assistance in putting the programmes together was given by the BBC's Community Programme Unit, and the series was edited by Giles Oakley, a punctilious broadcaster who anguished over getting it properly balanced. The problem, or indeed the glory, of *Open Door* was that editorial control was handed over to the groups being broadcast. Viewers accustomed to the BBC's editorial responsibility for content were at first affronted. Mrs Thatcher was incensed at one made by the Anarchists, who had fun describing the defence of Heathrow as a way of softening up the population with 'tanks on the streets', and the army in Northern Ireland as imperialist oppressors. In contradiction of the founding principles of anarchism it ended by giving the address of Anarchist headquarters for viewers to apply for membership forms. Mrs Thatcher's constituent said, 'This was the final straw ... when anyone has declared they are going to set fire to your house, is it usual to hand him the box of matches? This is what the BBC has done!'[26] The director-general pointed out that both the Scouts and the anti-union organisation 'Freedom under the Law' had also had programmes in the series. 'We take care', he assured her, 'not to allow the programmes to promote a political party or to pursue an industrial dispute. *Open Door* allows for dissent and a generous interpretation of free speech.'[27] Mrs Thatcher saw this as a classic example of a weighty principle being used to disguise insidious betrayal.

THE WRONG SORT OF CHAP?

Perhaps the problem was BBC chaps? They did not seem able to charm her. Everywhere she turned in the British establishment she met a tolerant, faintly dismissive club. The relaxed, jokey, allusive style, the affectation of doing things well without trying, the view of politics as a game, all expressions of male culture, 'were alien to her'.[28] Mrs Thatcher relished situations when she could feel the edges of her 'outsider' status, and the BBC had allowed itself to become – in her eyes – a classic example of establishment pomposity. She worked furiously hard, was happiest with her red boxes, and cultivated an image of superhuman energy. Percy Cradock, who had remained impressively cool in charge of the British embassy in Peking when it was attacked during the Cultural Revolution (no doubt useful training for life in No. 10), wrote, 'One of my most abiding memories is of her coming down the steps from her flat to the study in Downing street, exactly on time, beautifully turned out, with every sign of positive anticipation of a good discussion on some particularly ugly international situation.'[29]

BBC chaps: Mrs Thatcher being shown how to use a computer to gather news, 1987.
Ron Neil seated at bottom right, with Martin Lewis behind him

As she became a minister, then leader of the opposition and then prime minister, she increasingly made her views of the BBC public, in Parliament, in speeches, in interviews and in occasional off-the-cuff responses to questions. She set up a special Cabinet Committee (Misc 128) which she chaired to consider broadcasting policy. As well as Bernard Ingham, her pugnacious and effective press secretary, she appointed a series of No. 10 advisers on media policy. The BBC was not as hostile to her as she seemed to need it to be. Ian Trethowan, the director-general who succeeded Curran, was a conservative, and there was a group of passionate, independent-minded more right-wing bureaucrats like George Fischer and Ian McIntyre who certainly understood that the mood of the nation had shifted. Michael Checkland and his resources team completely shared her view that the unions were out of control. Sir David Nicholas, who ran ITN, had a wife 'who worshipped Mrs T'. But Percy Cradock summed her up: 'She was intensely feminine, making rapid, instinctive judgements on people, reacting well to certain kinds of men, losing few opportunities of commentating on male weaknesses and inadequacies.'[30] She was impetuous, combative, would jump to conclusions. Ingham said, 'She positively liked to take people on – "not our friends" – she would say after a meeting. But above all she was absolutely serious about policy.'[31]

As a not very secure leader of the opposition she refused numerous invitations to appear on BBC programmes, turning down *Today* (27 times), *Analysis*, *World at One*, programmes on religious belief, *Woman's Hour*, *Question Time*,

*1979 'Swingometer': David Butler, Angela Rippon,
David Dimbleby and Robert McKenzie*

interviews with Robin Day, and a proposed *Panorama* special on her.[32] For the
BBC it made maintaining political balance difficult, and they thought that as a
potential prime minister she needed to be tested for the British public. 'She kept
herself for the big stuff,' her office told the BBC, her 'shadow home secretary
could for example speak on hanging'. Small-scale guerrilla conflict flared all over
the country. Sometimes local BBC reporters may have been too pushy, but she
was abrasive, especially when she was trailing Callaghan in the polls. In Carlisle,
she treated reporters to a lecture on media failings and then refused to give BBC
Radio Carlisle a prearranged interview; in Aberdeen she turned her back on a
hapless BBC reporter who had been waiting all day; in Medway the BBC local
radio producer, Langley Brown, described her as the 'Ice Matron', and claimed
on air that she had yet again refused to do a BBC interview which had been
cleared locally and with her campaign manager. It was, he said, another incident
for the BBC file. The story bloomed in both the local and national press: 'Riddle
of Beeb's "File on No-No Maggie"', said the *Sun*'s front page.[33] The BBC went
into overdrive apology mode: 'This was not only thoroughly unjustified, but it
was impertinent.'[34] Brown was suspended,[35] which in a delicious twist led to the
local Medway Conservative Party petitioning the BBC on his behalf, while Mrs
Thatcher told the BBC that she had not been at all offended.

Was there a file? Yes and no. The BBC kept a scrupulous record of political
appearances to ensure 'a proper audit of balance is kept'. There may have
been no file of 'refusals', but her performance and refusal to perform were

discussed in meetings at all levels of the BBC. Her appearance on *Sixth Sense*, a radio programme in which sixth-formers interrogated people in public life, was dissected. The sixth-formers had given James Callaghan a rough ride, but on this occasion the children 'had become "Thatcher-fodder" rather than the other way round'. She was so eager to appear on Jimmy Savile's *Jim'll Fix It* or his Radio 1 and 2 shows that the governors thought they ought to 'ration' her appearances as she should have to face 'hard' questions as well.[36] Meanwhile there was a hopeless attempt to engage her socially. She never refused dinners or lunches, but visits to the BBC rarely went well for the Corporation: 'A regal progress,' observed one critic of a similar set of trips around Whitehall, 'which legend has it left several of her shattered hosts bobbing like driftwood in her wake.'[37] Meetings with Mrs Thatcher were not for the faint hearted – or the badly prepared. She had normally read all of the papers, probably in the middle of the night, and although she could be charming and was personally and privately considerate, at meetings 'She will frequently launch a ferocious attack', observed Sir Michael Butler. 'She expects ... advisors and officials to defend themselves with equal vigour.'[38] More successfully she was invited to one of the regular 'Bushmen' dinners with the aristocracy of the World Service: Alexander Lieven, controller of European Services, Austin Kark, David Witherow and others. They patronisingly told her, as it was an 'all-male' club, they had had to make a concession for her; she wrote warmly thanking them afterwards: the keen Cold War antennae of Bush House suited her.

Meetings with the governors confirmed her view that they had been 'captured' by the BBC. Meetings with the Board of Management confirmed her view that they were self-interested. Although she ruled out grant-in-aid as a way of financing the Corporation during one 'gruelling' lunch, 'she pressed us hard on the subject of advertising, particularly on Radio One', and she did not accept the argument that this would be the 'thin end of the wedge'.[39] The trouble was that 'wet and waffly' was a fatal judgement. 'The BBC', said Ingham, 'was the wettest and waffliest of the lot.'[40] If she had found the BBC of Curran and Swann wanting, the BBC of Milne – badly prepared, awkward – confirmed her worst suspicions.

Even without the abrasion of Northern Ireland she arrived in power in 1979 with firm views that had been polished over the years. Broadcasting and the BBC were overmanned, underperforming, out of control, supine in the face of union threats, undermining the nation's morale, badly managed by inadequate governors, fat for want of commercial competition, and disguising systematic political bias as impartiality. She wrote in her memoirs:

> Broadcasting was one of a number of areas – the professions such as teaching, medicine and the law were others – in which special pleading by powerful interest groups was disguised as high-minded commitment to

Jumpers and pearls: two pioneers, Mrs Thatcher and Sue MacGregor

some greater good ... The idea that a small clique of professional broad-casters always knew what was best and that they should be more or less immune from criticism or competition was not one which I could accept.[41]

WHITELAW MAGIC

Yet the election of the Conservative government brought immediate relief to the BBC, even if it was seen differently later. The frenzy around the licence fee began to calm down the moment Mrs Thatcher appointed William Whitelaw as the home secretary. He spread his special Willie balm and the BBC and British public service broadcasting were to owe him a large debt. He said, 'The organisation of the BBC and IBA ensures standards which are the envy of other countries,' and the whole system 'was a remarkable compromise' for which he had great admiration.[42] Whitelaw was anxious to settle the question of the Corporation's long-term financing.[43] He assured the BBC that he supported the licence fee and was aware of the dangers of advertising. From the first meeting, Whitelaw 'had been agreeable and courteous as one would expect', but had said it would not be easy, 'indeed it would be difficult', to get the BBC the licence fee it wanted. Whitelaw warned the governors that the question of the licence fee 'raised more heat' than almost any other subject, but he believed that the national utility of broadcasting was guaranteed by leaving it in the hands of the broadcasters and declared 'his intention to do the best he could for the BBC in relation to the overall economic position of the country'.[44]

With bold vision Whitelaw implemented the Annan Report's recommendations for a new commercial public service broadcaster: Channel 4. Its remit was an inspired extension of public service broadcasting: to reach new and minority audiences with original content financed by a levy on the hugely profitable ITV, which forced the commercial broadcaster to invest in more unusual content. It opened up a market of independent production. 'Air and opportunity began to flow in broadcasting,' said Anthony Smith, a charismatic BBC producer and one architect of Channel 4.[45] Whitelaw got the BBC the best licence fee agreement he could, even if it was only for two years. More significantly, and with considerable adroitness, in 1981 he renewed the BBC Charter and Licence, the founding constitutional document, cosmetically altering it but enshrining the BBC's independence in it. In contrast to Labour's annual deals, Whitelaw gave it the longest renewal it had ever had: fifteen years (perhaps to put it beyond the prime ministerial career of Mrs Thatcher).

Whitelaw's 'apparently guileless charm' was accompanied 'by a razor-sharp shrewdness'.[46] His relationship to Mrs Thatcher had evolved. She had backed Curran into a corner at one of Whitelaw's Christmas parties, complaining about the BBC. When Curran's wife asked Whitelaw to save her husband 'from the clutches of that woman', Whitelaw had said: 'Not her again. She's always shouting at somebody.'[47] John Chilcot, his private secretary, recalled him lying on a sofa in the Northern Ireland Office after a venomous debate about the media in Northern Ireland waving his legs (and tiny feet) in the air, saying of his own Conservative Party, 'Oh they are so ghastly, so ghastly.'[48]

By 1979 Whitelaw had assumed his posture of loyal indispensability to the prime minister. Ian Aitken, one of the great left-wing commentators of the period, argued that Whitelaw 'believed he could exercise a moderating influence over the wilder flights of [Mrs Thatcher's] radicalism', but his 'emollient effect' on the prime minister 'cannot alter the fact that the rather unpleasant Britain created by the Thatcher revolution is almost as much a monument to him as it is to her'.[49] One of the trophies Whitelaw secured, however, in return for rock-like loyalty, was the integrity of the BBC and the British broadcasting system.

Mrs Thatcher thought that the BBC was smuggling partisanship under a cloak of impartiality. Her views were strongly expressed yet contradictory. More fundamentally the licence fee was threatened by a coherent liberal economic argument. Rationalising expenditure, creating sources of income, battling the unions and articulating a new case for the licence fee would decide the BBC's fate in the most existentially challenging period since its inception. Yet the range of political attack, the Corporation's internal disorder at times and the failure to understand the shift in ideas brought it perilously close to a turning point.

THE LICENCE FEE AND BBC INDEPENDENCE: MONEY, MONEY, MONEY

GIFT TO CITIZENSHIP

The licence fee, set by governments, paid by everyone to receive broadcasting, was the foundation of the BBC's uniqueness. It secured the economic and political independence that the BBC's reputation and value depended on. Financial and political autonomy had to be sustained by a myriad of small proprieties in a mysterious, visionary piece of British constitutional engineering. The matter of who had the right to define the national good was contentious, and the BBC's independence required constant tending by politicians, civil servants and citizens. Programmes were part of the unwritten British constitution. *Gardener's Question Time, Blackadder, Yes Minister, The Proms, Morecambe & Wise, Woman's Hour, Grandstand, Panorama* and *The News* were the reason for the licence fee. They were also ways of showing the nation to itself, with a dusting of the stardust of impartiality added. The BBC had to be seen to deliver on the duties imposed by the privilege of spending the licence fee. It was not a nationalised industry, nor a commercial enterprise, nor a utility.

The licence fee was a gift to citizenship. It made the BBC responsible to the *whole* British public, not just the bit of it with commercial clout that advertisers liked; not just the bits that were usually in power, or were the right age, or in the right place or with the views that everybody chased. This direct relationship with the public came at a cost: people did not like having to pay more for it. Defending the licence fee was vital. The Corporation had longer-term purposes than any government. It sailed over them, and this sometimes rankled with governments struggling with stubborn problems. Nevertheless, in a representative democracy the bond with politics was strong – a tense but proper relationship rather than a damaging constraint. Civil servants frequently protected the niceties that preserved the functioning of an impartial, independent institution. Yet the argument for the licence fee and the existence of the BBC itself had to be made with increasing rigour in changing circumstances. It took much of the seventies and some of the eighties for the BBC to recognise that it had to reshape the case.

Festering alongside political arguments lay the more damaging accusation that the Corporation managed people and money fecklessly. It could be portrayed as arrogant and out of touch, with a self-righteous sense that it deserved special dispensation. Governments and the public were suspicious as to how a big organisation that they met on a daily basis spent their money. A BBC Secretary said, 'You can say no to politicians, but you should not frustrate them.'[1] The BBC was to spend a decade more or less doing that. It was too much in the news, becoming the butt for a particular sense of disgruntled anxiety about the nation.

Confrontations with politicians sometimes had surprising outcomes. Harold Wilson moved broadcasting from the Post Office to the Home Office in 1969 in order to keep a beady eye on it. He believed a big department was less likely to be 'captured' by broadcasters than a small one. Yet the move helped the BBC. It was now the responsibility of Home Secretaries, big cats in the cabinet jungle, who became proprietorial about broadcasting. Roy Jenkins, Willie Whitelaw, Merlyn Rees, Leon Brittan and Douglas Hurd were important ministers with a powerful department behind them. The new Broadcasting Unit in the Home Office 'thought that broadcasting was definitely "theirs"'.[2] So although there was always the Treasury to deal with, full of confident Scrooges with little time for cant about culture and values, the case for the licence fee and reasonable finance for the Corporation was accepted, at least in principle, during the seventies, and had strong ministers and strong departments guarding it. But, according to Douglas Hurd, 'setting the level of the BBC licence fee never goes away. Everyone was always in a state about it.'[3]

The public did not understand that the licence fee paid for many things that were national requirements. From planning for nuclear threats and disasters to supporting the nation's vital transmitter system and setting engineering standards, the BBC was part of a national infrastructure. In a different mood, direct involvement in education from preschool to the Open University was part of a historic mission that went back to the Corporation's origins. The Corporation had set up and run nationally and internationally important archives, from the world's first (and leading) collection of birdsong and animal film, to the most comprehensive musical score archive in the world, as well as the written archives in Caversham, which set a model for the role of broadcasting in national history. The BBC played a vital role in the European Broadcasting Union, and paid by far the largest dues to it. Charles Curran, a former director of the External Services, fluent in French and German, 'moved with ease and enjoyment in international broadcasting circles'.[4] The EBU was important for broadcasters in the front line facing the Eastern Bloc when the Cold War was raging throughout this period. The World Service, a key vehicle of British impact abroad, and BBC Monitoring, the ears and eyes of the nation,

Charles Curran: the first Catholic, grammar-school-educated director-general

were subsidised by the domestic Corporation. In ways the public had little understanding of, the licence fee had national purposes rolled into it.

Yet between 1974 and 1987 both Labour and Conservative governments threatened not merely to cut the licence fee but to abolish it. Never since 1926 had the basis of the BBC been so insecure. Labour threatened to replace the licence fee by a 'grant-in-aid', direct payment from government as part of the spending round each year. The government knew that it was an unprecedented thing to consider and never directly discussed its plans with the BBC, let alone in public. Such a change would have made the Corporation a 'state' broadcaster, competing head-on with education and health for funds. The World Service was financed by just such an arrangement without it leading to political control. But as Gerard Mansell, the World Service's shrewd and engaging director, said, it was 'out of a politician's hearing and was out of mind'. If the domestic service was to be financed in this way, the political pressure would be 'unbearable'.[5]

WAGE GRAB

In 1974, Labour came back into power with a fragile minority government led by Harold Wilson. It promised to replace the spectre of Edward Heath's 'Dark Age', with its 2 million people out of work, loss of 5 per cent of the economy in less than a year,[6] unheated offices, dark streets, striking miners, three-day week and, most disturbing of all, television abruptly shutting down earlier each evening. With another election later in the year looming, the government attempted to replace confrontation with what the new prime minister called a 'bit of peace and quiet'. Yet, in the summer of 1974, the BBC behaved towards renegotiating its finances with blithe irresponsibility. It put its own interests first, and appeared to do so behind the government's back.

In a speech that his biographer Ben Pimlott compared to the first chapter of Genesis, Wilson described himself as bringing order out of chaos. On their first day in office, Labour ended the miners' strike, by Wednesday the lights were going on again, and on the fourth day they imposed rent control.[7] Labour's soothing, if vague, 'Social Contract' was its alternative to the Conservative government's 'autocratic and bureaucratic' system of wages restraint. The new government wanted lower wage settlements, and in return would offer price controls and some improvements in social benefits. It was an attempt to make Britain more equal, and to 'bring the unions back on board'. But in the brief moment between the end of the Conservative's compulsory pay restraint policy and the start of the Labour voluntary agreement, the BBC awarded weekly paid staff a 20 per cent wage increase and 'regraded' many of them – reclassifying jobs at a higher level to get around pay restraints – by arguing that the workers were doing new, more skilled work.

Even worse, the BBC was the first part of the public sector to break the government agreement, and gave the Home Office just two hours' warning. Roy Jenkins, the new home secretary, was 'hopping mad' at the BBC for making him look ignorant.[8] Then, after breaking the wages part of the Social Contract, the BBC demanded a higher licence fee and more money, driving a tank through both sides of the new government's economic policy. Wilson was incandescent, suspecting that the Corporation's actions were motivated by political animus against him. He had been distrustful of the BBC since *Yesterday's Men*, a 1971 programme which he believed, with some justice, had made a mockery of him and his shadow cabinet. During the 1974 election, he complained that 'a lot of BBC people had pursued him around the country and come between him and his supporters'.[9]

The wage agreement bred a suspicion about frankness that lingered behind cross-party mistrust of the Corporation for years. The beleaguered yet robust chancellor, Denis Healey, although a passionate defender of the World Service, called the BBC 'self-interested and devious'. Jim Callaghan's hostility to the BBC, based on its failure to take his concerns about violent imagery seriously when he was home secretary, was reinforced by a sense that the Corporation had been misleading when he took over as prime minister in 1976. The Treasury was still referring to the BBC's duplicity four years later: 'The BBC is not our most reliable of customers: there is a strong feeling of grievance that salaries ... have got out of line ... again.'[10] The wage increases damaged the licence fee claim and undermined trust. Headlined as 'BBC Busts Social Contract First' in the *Daily Mail*, and 'BBC Breaks Government Policy' in the *Mirror*, it came to seem typical of Corporation Olympian disdain.

At the time there was a row going on, as there usually was, about reporting in Northern Ireland. The Corporation 'bleated', said Wilson, that it had done only what many other institutions had done in rushing to make pay awards when threatened with strikes, that ITV had awarded far more, earlier, that the BBC had made significant cuts – late-night television finished earlier, fewer hours of afternoon broadcasting, the reduction of BBC2, overall production costs reduced by nearly 10 per cent. Finally, 'feebly', it argued that no one had told them not to. BBC managers trooped into the Home Office for a dressing down from Roy Jenkins. They were careful not to defend the wage increases.[11] The BBC chairman, Michael Swann, an abstemious Wykhamist, told Jenkins, the bon vivant home secretary, that the Corporation had already acted with resolute speed, cutting back on entertaining 'of all kinds. If Mr Jenkins or anyone else goes to Lime Grove now he will ... find not more than three staff having drinks with him.' They would be offered only beer or wine, though as a concession '*he* may get the hard stuff'. Swann, in one of the few minuted reflections on a vigorous part of BBC culture, drink, said that BBC staff had a lifestyle which was a fusion of journalism and show business, working extraordinary hours under great pressure on fixed salaries, mischievously adding 'my observation of the House suggests that it's not altogether different there'.[12]

Presumably BBC hairshirts kept mutating into silk ones, as later Harold Wilson, Jim Callaghan, Tony Benn, Barbara Castle, Norman Tebbit, Bernard Ingham, Cecil Parkinson and Margaret Thatcher reiterated complaints about the lavish supply of alcohol in green rooms. The BBC had to balance getting visitors into the right frame of mind against the opportunity to demonstrate austere values: menus were consequently intensely political. In 1977 a great dinner was held in the Guildhall to celebrate the BBC's fiftieth anniversary. It was meant to fix the BBC in the heart of the nation's establishment and remind politicians of its enduring importance. But, according to the *Financial Times*, 'it struck the wrong note of grandeur'. Later Curran had said that conspicuous consumption of anything was the wrong message to send out at that moment.[13]

Jenkins had laid out what were to be the main criticisms of the Corporation for the next decade: the BBC was too bureaucratic; it was not making the same effort to deal with inflation as other organisations; it must be 'seen to make ... retrenchment'; it ought to absorb more of the increased costs without complaint; it was unwise to advertise how much some 'blockbuster' programmes had cost. Jenkins told the BBC not to 'cut programmes the public was fond of'.[14] Ominously, he warned that 'there was pressure from some of his colleagues to resort to direct funding of the BBC'. The BBC replied that the Treasury had imposed an unrealistic inflation estimate on it, cuts had already taken a significant slice of the BBC's income,[15] and that without a new licence settlement the BBC would have to reduce the hours of television. 'The home secretary said that, speaking for himself, he would not regard this as an intolerable burden on the British people.'[16] Jenkins was sending a set of warning shots over the BBC's bow, but also showing them the pressures he would be answerable for. It was urbane and accomplished, never remotely questioning the existence of the Corporation.

Harold Wilson was in a different mood, wanting to replace the licence fee, which he saw as a regressive tax, endowing the BBC with large sums of money at the beginning of a funding cycle and encouraging 'the tendency to over-lavish expenditure'.[17] He considered appointing a different 'kind' of director-general, just as he had appointed Lord Hill to be BBC chairman from ITV, and even breaking the service up. Wilson set up the Annan Committee to review the BBC and ITV, and a Royal Commission to look at the press. Jenkins persuaded Wilson not to do anything about the structure of the licence fee until Annan reported.[18] The Corporation slashed all developments in the first half of the coming year,[19] determined to sell more programmes abroad, and decided 'to scrutinise practices right across the board (e.g. use of cameras, construction of scenery, location work abroad, film ratios and so on)'. Telling the public that they had made cheaper programmes – as Labour ministers seemed to want – was not an appealing strategy. The BBC was, after all, in the entertainment business. 'Am I supposed to announce that there are less layers of net in dancers' dresses as an economy measure?' complained the head of Light Entertainment.

The Treasury was not impressed, believing the BBC to be 'in the hands of grown up children with unlimited pocket money'.[20] The wage settlement had presented the Treasury with a fait accompli. Perhaps the next licence fee would have the last pay settlement taken out of it punitively and retrospectively, or they could cut grant-in-aid to the World Service instead, 'So that the BBC does not have a surplus to play with?' And in 1976 that is precisely what the government did, making the World Service renegotiate its funding, year by debilitating year, despite the exigencies of the Cold War. The Treasury had little time for the decorous veils of separation; they just thought of the BBC as a single unit of spending.

INFLATION

The BBC knew that its relationship with governments over money was likely to get harder for both sides to manage, because politicians loathed having to raise the licence fee. Indeed, for all of their complaints about escalating costs, the change from black-and-white television to the more expensive colour licences had given the Corporation a growing income without any need to return to Parliament (or the public). This quietly sustained independence just as Northern Ireland was hotting up. As the British public turned inward and homeward, colour television spread from 1.5 million homes in 1972 to 11 million in 1978. By 1978, however, many who wanted a colour TV had bought one, making future increases in the licence fee inevitable. Between the first radio licence fee in 1922 (at 10s.) and the £6 charged for the combined TV and radio licence in 1971 there had been only six increases in 50 years. Negotiations had been conducted behind closed doors, a courtly minuet between politicians and the Corporation, with everyone understanding the need to avoid proximity to elections. But between 1976 and 1985 there were as many licence-fee rises as in the entire previous history of the Corporation.

The arguments came during the most perilous economic crisis since the 1930s. Inflation in 1975/76 had shot up to a precipitous 26 per cent. The government was running out of capacity to borrow money and there was a run on the pound against a drumbeat of industrial unrest. In contrast to the BBC, ITV could spend, spend, spend. Its revenues outpaced inflation, rising 25 per cent a year in the late 1970s.[21] Pay differences between ITV and the BBC were accelerating – a cameraman working for ITN would earn nearly a third more than his equal at the BBC. By 1976 the Corporation needed a 50 per cent rise in income to bring it back to the 1970 level.[22] ITV could make better programmes, starve the BBC of resources, or outspend it. In the regulated television world, competition for quality, and not merely the largest audiences, was built into the way the IBA allocated licences for commercial broadcasting. Thus competition was fierce, and, by challenging the BBC over quality as well as finances, ultimately saved the BBC. But ITV had lavish finances to pitch against the BBC.

The fact that the BBC, unlike the nationalised industries, was a success, making programmes that everybody watched, made no difference: 'Here they come again, mink caps in hand ... The Corporation is short of money. It has old movies to buy and the staff bar at Shepherd's Bush to maintain,'[23] said the *Evening News*. A formidable range of papers attacked the BBC on their front pages, even as they carried stories based on its programmes elsewhere. The *Daily Mail* was reinventing itself as a sinuous political beast. Although *Mail* readers watched more BBC than readers of any other newspaper, it was resolutely hostile to the Corporation. The *Sun*, bought by Rupert Murdoch in 1970, used aggressive TV advertising and the coy leer of Page Three Girls to overtake the *Mirror* in 1978 as the largest-selling paper in the country, with a circulation of 4 million. But it was also acutely in touch with a shift in the nation's mood as desperate times led to a more punitive reaction in its key, Southern audiences.[24] In the 1970s, *Times* leader writers would talk confidentially with the director-general and chairman, not always agreeing, but building consensus about the national interest. Influential *Times* columnists, such as David Wood, took the BBC seriously. But after Murdoch bought the paper in 1981, reopening it after a year's closure forced by the print unions, *Times* leaders attacked the Corporation not just for its practice but as an idea.

Later the editor of the *Sunday Times*, Andrew Neil, would write Murdoch's chillingly brilliant speech at the Edinburgh Television Festival condemning the BBC: 'For 50 years British television has operated on the assumption that the people could not be trusted to watch what they wanted to watch, so that it had to be controlled by like-minded people who knew what was good for them,' he said, putting Sky and News International on the populist side against the entrenched establishment of what he called 'top people' who had 'bitterly opposed commercial television and supported government monopolies'. The BBC (but ITV and C4 as well) had restricted the freedom to broadcast, and was 'not compatible with mature democracy'. The lecture perfectly articulated a new case against the BBC. The Corporation failed to provide any sophisticated intellectual answer to the Murdoch position. Michael Grade said that Murdoch's forte was to 'parlay newspaper power into political advantage, then to use this political clout to gain even more commercial advantage'.[25] The Corporation was slow to deal with this new atmosphere.

After Charles Hill, who had upstaged Curran, retired in 1973, Curran had emerged as an authoritative director-general conspicuously in control of the BBC. He was part of the most effective double act for a decade, with Michael Swann as chairman. Curran said that the secret of BBC success was 'competent integrity', something he embodied. His personal secretary said that he 'made work, in the good sense that he was tireless and went out to find things that had to be dealt with – he was always thinking ahead'.[26] So how did Curran and the governors get the calculation of paying staff more and appealing for an increased licence fee so wrong? From the BBC's point of view, it had to ask for more money because it was in alarming new waters – running out of cash before the end of the life of a licence fee for the first time.[27] The licence fee was 'front-loaded', generous at the beginning of a settlement, tight at the end, and inflation destroyed any savings. The BBC was well aware of the political dangers of having to return to government as a mendicant too often.

Curran argued (rightly) that continuing uncertainty about BBC income made planning impossible: 'Miserly financing militates against economy in the not very long run.'[28] He believed that 'in the public service', where broadcasting was provided because government demanded it, 'the first requirement was to define the nature of the service itself', and then work out from this 'the amount of income necessary to provide that service'.[29] This assumption was now challenged, first by a desperate Labour government facing financial turmoil, and later in a philosophical clash with the Conservative government.

British matrons began to stockpile lavatory paper – an issue earnestly debated on *Woman's Hour*, 'creating unnecessary panic', according to the Home Office. 'I must dash,' said a housewife in the sitcom *George and Mildred*, 'and get my shopping before the pound slides again.' Amid dark talk of Latin American-style runaway inflation, there was a broader sense of moral malaise. Inflation was especially damaging for the BBC as the greater part of its expenditure was on wages.[30] Between 1976 and 1979, because of Labour's prices and incomes policy, negotiating the licence fee was a permanent struggle. It became a populist issue in the increasingly hostile press. Yet at a time of financial turbulence, controlling such a visible organisation mattered to the government as well: the BBC was seen as exemplary. It was not treated fairly.

As he asked for more money Curran also believed that the Corporation could pride itself on comparative frugality and efficiency. On a similar income to ITV, which had only one television channel, the BBC ran two television channels, national production centres in Ireland, Scotland and Wales, more than twenty regional broadcasting centres (of international significance in the West Country and Manchester), four national radio networks – BBC Radio 1, 2, 3 and 4 – twenty local radio stations, and the World Service.[31] The BBC produced one hour of television more cheaply than any other European broadcaster. In 1975 each hour of broadcasting cost less than it had in 1965, and the amount spent on employing outside contributors was cut. Moreover, the Corporation could not rationalise expenditure in the same way a commercial broadcaster might. Providing broadcasting signals for audiences was treated like a utility, not on a commercial model. The responsibility was to make broadcasting accessible to everyone at the same time, not just to build transmitters for economically viable dense urban audiences. And the BBC had to make the kinds of programming (for children, for example) that made social, not direct economic, sense.

Yet the Corporation could not be separated from the nation's plight. Knowing that the pound had to fall, but that this would stoke inflation, Denis Healey remarked, 'I had mixed feelings, like the chap who saw his mother-in-law go over Beachy Head in his new car.' Every attempt to control BBC expenditure was overturned 'when inflation appears to hold the reins'.[32] Foreign news costs quadrupled in six months. Covering the Montreal Olympics (where Princess Anne was competing) cost six times the original budget and had to be bailed out at the last minute. Inflation altered the BBC's relationship with the wider creative world. The BBC had never paid musical performers the commercial going rate – arguing that it gave them a reach that compensated.

In 1975, the BBC paid guest musicians the same fee as it had in 1947, the year of greatest post-war austerity.[33] It was raised from £200 to £900 in 1975, and to £1,250 in 1976. Yet the first rank of conductors were still getting £3,000–£4,000 for concerts outside the BBC.

Even high-minded but market-savvy intellectuals like Noel Annan, and the literary critic Denis Donoghue, demanded to be paid more: 'The willingness of some men of distinction to do something for the sake of the old firm is not something we should trade on indefinitely.'[34] Tony Palmer, an influential young freelance producer and writer, complained to the BBC, 'For your information, your <u>weekly</u> rate is less than my daily rate.' He had gone on working because of 'loyalties' to staff on the programme, but not to the BBC itself.[35]

HUB

During the seventies the BBC was leaching skilled staff. In one month alone, twelve make-up artists left the BBC for Thames TV, where they would earn £1,400 more a year. Each had cost £10,000 to train. The Corporation became the training hub of the entire broadcasting industry; the only way it could fill positions 'lost at the top' was by 'pulling more in at the bottom'.[36] Camera and sound technicians were departing 'in droves'. Rumours spread of videotape editors being paid up to £100,000 at ITV.[37] In the autumn of 1977, fourteen programmes were cancelled because the Corporation had lost too many technical staff to deliver them.[38] For the first time the BBC could not recruit enough engineers: 60 per cent of those offered jobs turned them down because they could get better pay elsewhere. Engineers were brought out of retirement to fill the gaps.[39] Ian Trethowan (the future director-general) said the 'corridors of Broadcasting House seemed empty'.

In 1977, budgets were slashed again: programmes were repeated; the number of minstrels in *The Black and White Minstrel Show* reduced; *Woman's Hour* budgets were slashed by a quarter, although radio was far cheaper than television; orchestras were eyed hungrily as they were so costly to run; two new thrillers were put on hold; and there were proposals to shut BBC2. In the past, negotiations over the licence fee had taken place behind closed doors[40] (once after the director of Finance had 'hopped on a bus' and sorted it all out in an afternoon at the Post Office headquarters).[41] But now the BBC responded to the crisis by going public. Jolyon Dromgoole, the bracing new Home Office official in charge of negotiations, said crisply that the BBC wished 'to let the world know they are asking for a licence fee increase',[42] as the chairman and the director-general took to the airwaves to push the Corporation's case. Not that a hesitating appearance by Curran on *What's My Line* was likely to sway the nation.

UNIONS

To open any BBC file from the seventies and into the eighties is to step into an alien and deeply puzzling world, where Machiavellian strategising about the unions comes before everything else. The mayhem around pay forced all workers to become involved in industrial action. Groups with industrial muscle, or just an accidental stranglehold over a vital moment in the production process, distorted the relationship between reward and contribution. 'In spite of everybody's best efforts the situation tended to get worse', said Roger Chase from Finance (later one of Michael Checkland's new breed of resource managers). It raises the intriguing problem of why so many people were prepared to take action. Then it seemed perfectly normal; now it looks admirable at times, like madness at others.

Fans knew that groups mimed on *Top of the Pops*. The reality was odder still. They mimed to a performance recorded in a BBC studio earlier, squaring the union requirement that the show would not deprive musicians of the right to be paid to play live music. Stars like David Bowie were paid the union rate of £12 per hour to create a tape of their own records. The Buzzcocks, a radical 'post-punk' Manchester band, refused to cooperate with the playacting, their lead singer standing frozen and mute in white mime make-up on screen. This rebellion actually damaged their careers, fans apparently accepting the conventions, insofar as they understood them. There was a famous Musicians' Union official, known as Dr Death, who would preside lugubriously over the BBC studio recording to make sure there were no tricks, as groups frantically tried to recreate the sound of their hit record in the three-hour session allotted to them. Queen managed to put together an extraordinary live performance of 'Killer Queen'. Other groups got the union official drunk, and surreptitiously substituted new tapes with original recordings. Once the tape had been sorted out, bands had to be careful what they did during the mime. Plugging in your own guitar might lead to a walkout. The charade behind the charade was surreal.

Play School, the visionary daily programme focused on providing even the most deprived toddler with developmental skills, was brought to a standstill as unions fought over whose job it was to turn the hands on the programme's clock. It had to be plugged in by an electrician, but who could turn it on? The electricians argued with props workers, whose job included time cues. For a number of weeks there was no clock. Duncan Thomas, another of Checkland's henchmen, finally persuaded the electricians that it was a prop. The dispute went public. In a 1979 dispute that affected a *Blue Peter* appeal the striking cameramen donated their salaries to the appeal – enough money to buy nearly one thousand hoes. The show's redoubtable producer, Biddy Baxter, thanked them. Another action threatened *Crackerjack*, but because live

Play School in 1975: Johnny Ball, Carol Leader and Derek Griffiths. It took two different unions to turn on the Play School clock, so a demarcation dispute stopped it

audiences would be upset to miss the trip, the strikers agreed to put the show on – but not to screen it.[43] Demarcation disputes were contagious: a lamp-post was 'scenery' and had its own attendants, but the lamp itself was a prop, with a separate band of retainers. The two were assembled by a third group of craftsmen. One manager said there was a 'dispute based on the premise that Hessian palm trees were scenery but glass fibre trees were props'.[44]

The new mood of militancy had hit the BBC on 11 October 1969 when Yvonne Littlewood, the only woman producer in the all-male world of Light Entertainment, was making the *Petula Clark* show with her regular studio crew. The pattern was simple: having set up in the morning and rehearsed in the afternoon, the production team would break for dinner at 6.30 and return at 8.00 for the live broadcast. On this evening the crew (with whom Littlewood had worked on fifteen previous shows) simply did not come back after dinner. It was a startling betrayal of the principle that the show must go on. Littlewood was in shock and Pet Clark burst into tears. Roger Chase called it 'a dramatic and deeply significant event', shaking the Corporation from the top to the bottom.

The madness was linked to the government's piecemeal attempts to arrest inflation through pay restraint. Denis Healey said, 'Adopting a pay policy is rather like jumping out of a second-floor window: no one in his senses would do it unless the stairs were on fire. But in post-war Britain the stairs have always been on fire.' Disputes were rational in the sense that securing monopolies and fixing pay for specified tasks helped workers in unstable times; but collectively the system produced injustices. Labour's voluntary Social Contract, then a statutory prices and incomes policy, followed by Jack Jones's flat across-the-board financial cap, were attempts to get the unions to agree to binding commitments and to control inflation. The BBC's instinctive reaction was to protect broadcasting at all costs. It embarked on a huge jobs and skills regrading exercise. Designed as a one-off solution, it would become a decade-long guerrilla war. The rigid grading system, matching pay and skills in an inflexible hierarchy, caused problems as new technologies came thick and fast to newsrooms and broadcasting. People saw every change in their work as an opportunity for 'regrading' as this allowed their pay to rise. If one job was 'graded up', this led to demands across the Corporation from other workers that their work had to be reassessed. It created anomalies that continually needed to be sorted out.[45] The film sound recordist's job description ran to 27 pages because every detail of a job had to be specified. In 1976, Personnel dealt with 476 regrading claims; the next year this shot up to 872. (And they did it all with only one new member of staff: Personnel's productivity had doubled.) Staff in jobs close to the 'pinch' points in production were the most militant, and last-minute walkouts were used increasingly cynically. Television Centre, a huge factory of programme-making, was especially vulnerable. As Curran said, 'Today's *Today* programme is of no use tomorrow.' While craft unions and the whole support staff could get their pay increased by threatening strikes and getting their jobs reclassified, the professional journalists and BBC managers were in a much weaker position. With the ink hardly dry on the early version of this dance of regrading in the 1970 Conditions of Service agreement, copies of a telling cartoon by BBC correspondent Michael Sullivan circulated among BBC managers.[46] It showed a reporter like Sullivan with broken-down shoes and stubble, working alongside a sleekly clad cameraman – a parody of a fat-cat trade unionist. It pointed to a decade's turmoil ahead.

If grading was one tiger unleashed by the 1970 agreement, overtime was the other. By 1977,[47] there were 33 film cameramen, 44 assistant cameramen, 47 film recordists and 37 film lighting assistants doing more than 400 hours of overtime per year, 87 of them more than 800 hours. The following year, some of the weekly paid staff were doing 25 hours a week throughout the year in this way, amounting to over £3,000 for some scenery carpenters and painters.[48] A worry was that reporters, whose own salaries were frozen but who were accompanied on stories by staff whose wages were racing ahead because of overtime, would in the end refuse to work beyond their official hours and bring news to a halt.[49] In February 1976, some cameramen could earn more than their own supervisors and even the head of Filmic Operations.[50]

The overtime culture seeped across every area. *Newsnight* had to negotiate an emergency ad hoc overtime deal in the middle of the Falklands War, when

'And this is my reporter': a cartoon by the BBC journalist Michael Sullivan

everyone on the programme was working round the clock on a new show that was making itself a vital and intelligent part of the schedules. In 1978, a highly secret memo (on pink paper for limited circulation) pointed out that the BBC Conditions of Service meant that a cameraman on assignment in Africa got £3,000 in overtime, while the reporter, ostensibly in charge, got nothing.[51] Effort and reward were disconnected. Employers tried to get around pay restraint by offering payment in kind. BBC canteen charges were reduced (though not as much as at Thames TV, where workers would ask for steak for lunch, and when asked how they wanted it would answer 'raw' and take it home for supper). Prices in BBC bars became very attractive to drinkers, and staff were offered interest-free loans.

BBC management and unions danced a deadly quadrille, each side knowing its steps. There were clear levels at which disputes could be settled, from the local and proximate, through national disputes and then beyond that to ACAS for independent conciliation. As time went on there was a deliberate strategy to push disputes up the system. Warnings, suspensions and formal notifications were tactics to avoid walkouts, with the message: 'We're going to refer it up, now carry on working.' For the unions, application of pressure could deliver concessions later. A florid array of formal, informal, official, guerrilla, unofficial, local, regional and national disputes spread out.

By 1975, trade union negotiators were said to be 'playing a game of pass the parcel, in which the size of the parcel seemed to increase each time around, as one wage settlement exceeded another, but the real weight, in real money, stayed the same'.[52] Responsible union leaders understood the problem. Len Murray, the general secretary of the TUC, said he would be in meetings in which people were voting for 30–40 per cent wage increases, but over a cup of tea would say in alarm, 'You have got to do something ... we can't go on like this.' Denis Healey called it 'irresponsible lunacy to ignore the fact that wages were the main cause of inflation'.[53]

The BBC's own unions, especially the Association of Broadcasting Staff, were well aware of the irrationality of the system. The ABS began during World War II as a staff association, with members across the BBC, cleaning ladies, technicians, journalists, engineers and senior managers, all unusually in the same organisation. Within the ABS previously, 'discussion about one sector's interests could at least always be seen to have knock-on effects elsewhere in the Corporation', leading to a more balanced view of conditions and pay.[54] Unlike ITV, however, the BBC refused to allow the ABS the right to set up a closed shop, and would have gone off the air rather than allow its independence to be infringed.[55] So the ABS lost members to other unions, membership of which was a precondition for working for ITV – which paid better.

The roll call of industrial disputes in the seventies was exotic. One tactic was to 'black' programmes – if one union was in dispute it would call on reciprocal agreements and the other workers in the other unions would join it on strike, making it impossible for management to work around the action. In 1976 alone, 45 programmes were blacked out in the London broadcasting operation and countless more around the regions. In 1977, the television broadcast of the A Song For Europe competition (to choose the UK's entry for the Eurovision Song Contest later in the year) was blacked out, although the radio broadcast, presented by Terry Wogan, went ahead. Later that year, the BBC had a sneaky contingency plan for a Dutch TV crew to help run the Eurovision Song Contest in the event of a strike. The strike took place, and the plan saved the broadcast – although it was an unpleasant occasion and incensed the unions. Also in 1977 new computers were blacked by the unions, which banned anyone working on them, and managers 'were happy to put it to arbitration' rather than 'let equipment worth £1½ million lie idle'. A new system bought to cover elections was blacked, as was the new internal electronic distribution system, even though in both cases the unions had been involved in the proposal to introduce the new equipment. One group wanted 'danger money' for the screens, to cope with threats 'ranging ... from a supposed reduction in the procreative powers to eyestrain'. Union pressure stopped the computers bought to report the independence referendums in Scotland and Wales from even being unpacked.

The use of freelance camera crews (when no one else could get to the story in time) on stories in Hong Kong, Nicaragua and the Lebanon led to walkouts and the shocking threat that crews would 'black' individual journalists: this would have been censorship. Electricians and engineers would 'pull the plugs' on equipment minutes before broadcast. When a rigger was dismissed on the spot for punching a manager, there was an official strike of all BBC riggers. Electricians in Scotland went on strike over a new generator; electricians in Manchester over manning a new studio; an electrician's demarcation dispute threatened scoreboards at cricket, football and European musical competitions. One dispute lingered on from the Christmas holidays because some groups had got £234 for working 'unsocial hours' and other groups £400, and the NUJ wanted everyone to get the higher amount.

THE THREE WISE MEN

As genuine cuts began to bite, the Corporation set up an internal inquiry to work out where they should fall. The result, known as the Three Wise Men report, was led by Dick Francis. It suggested that the BBC 'outsource' various services such as catering, cut some central departments, and keep an eye on staffing. Nobody took much notice of it. Alasdair Milne said that many of the proposed cuts looked 'cosmetic'. It was Michael Checkland who began to grapple with BBC costs, knowing as he did that the Three Wise Men report had no muscle to deliver its recommendations. Appointed in 1969 as the BBC's first 'total-cost accountant', Checkland worked in the outlands of the Corporation. He created a redoubt within the empire, transforming how the BBC spent money and used resources. With his loyal team, Checkland altered the way the BBC did business: rationalising, simplifying and changing management style from the inside.[56]

A slow and steady cost-cutting revolution took place. While the number of staff had barely changed, by 1979 the BBC was producing 20 per cent more broadcasting with the same staff. The BBC knew there was a paradox: Dick Francis said at a Board of Management meeting that one of the BBC's problems was that 'it was poor but not that poor'. Curran agreed; it was hard to plead poverty when they were expanding in some areas.[57] The government thought the BBC could try harder. Meanwhile both left- and right-wing Labour backbenchers thought that the licence fee was unjust, costing poor people more than rich ones: Jack Ashley and Roy Hattersley campaigned loudly. BBC computer boffins had ingeniously solved Ashley's difficulty (he was profoundly deaf) in following parliamentary debates. Ashley wrote a warm letter of thanks to the BBC – but it did not stop him complaining about the licence fee.[58]

All politicians had a niggling suspicion that the Corporation's much-vaunted impartiality was a masquerade. Jim Callaghan, after he became prime minister in 1976, spent a morose afternoon comparing the Corporation's coverage of government and opposition policy, and concluded that it always favoured Conservative policy and was instinctively small-'c' conservative 'on

Michael Checkland: the man who transformed getting and spending in the BBC

every issue that matters'.[59] Labour prime ministers often felt that they got a better deal from ITV. Meanwhile Peter Shore turned angrily on the BBC's new parliamentary reporting for paying disproportionate attention to loud, unrepresentative, left-wing MPs.[60]

The Labour government saw the Annan Report as a way of doing something about both the governance and financing of the BBC. Callaghan said in cabinet in 1978 that he 'wanted to split up the BBC. There is too much power concentrated in the hands of the director-general.' Annan considered putting all public service television (commercial and BBC) together, which would have abolished the BBC as an institution. Tony Benn had previously attempted to sack all of the Board of Governors because they were undemocratically selected, and was by the mid-seventies at the height of his ascendancy in the Labour Party – ceaselessly building his power base among activists. In a cabinet discussion of the Annan Committee, Benn 'made a superb attack on the BBC, equating it with the medieval Catholic Church, controlling thought from a middle class, establishment position'.[61]

There was a sense on the Annan Committee that the Corporation was powerful and closed, its inner workings inscrutable and private. Swann said, 'Lord Annan seemed genuinely puzzled about the way in which the BBC actually worked. Mr Fuller [Roy Fuller the poet] observed that he was not the only one.'[62] The report proposed that the BBC take complaints more seriously, and criticised BBC journalism for being 'conservative, timid, following rather than leading'. Although this criticism was resented, it encouraged BBC programme makers, especially in Northern Ireland, to take risks.

THE NOOSE: ONE YEAR AT A TIME (1977–79)

In 1977, as the government dealt with the indignity of IMF cuts and industrial militancy, it imposed on the BBC the first of three hand-to-mouth licence-fee settlements that were to last for one year only. No one called it grant-in-aid but in practice it was. Thus Labour came close to tying the BBC into general expenditure without a fig leaf to protect political independence. The Home Office was proposing to put the BBC in the red at the beginning of the licence fee period, to cover already-committed broadcasting costs. The BBC felt it was treated worse than other public services: 'There has been no increase in licence fees for three and a half years. Is there any other commodity or service which has stood still in price for this period?' complained Curran.[63]

In 1977 and 1978, the BBC's response was to go public. The governors demanded a marketing campaign to dispel the myth that the BBC was expensive. They would publicise proposals for cuts, and even the Home Office, battling the Treasury on the BBC's behalf, thought this a good idea.[64] The governors thought that the Corporation's problems were to do with how it presented itself, rather than how it managed itself. Curran was coming up for retirement. The BBC had lost more able potential directors-general than it had to choose from. The wonderful Paul Fox had left for more power and more money at Yorkshire TV; David Attenborough did not want the job; Gerry Mansell was seen as too much a radio insider; Milne was too young; Baverstock had blotted his copybook and gone to ITV. Looking around, they noticed Ian Trethowan, who had started as an ITN presenter before becoming a BBC administrator, and had close Conservative contacts. Treating him like a queen bee grub, the BBC began to feed Trethowan on royal jelly – deliberately moving him from Radio to Television to give him experience of the whole Corporation. They thought the BBC needed a more persuasive public face.

By now, government was considering such a damaging settlement that the Home Office papers on the licence fee were marked 'Secret'.[65] The BBC's debt was growing by £3 million each month, and when it hit its borrowing limit it would have no money for day-to-day broadcasting. The proposal was to give the Corporation another inadequate one-year licence fee settlement.[66] Officials understood that this was politically explosive. 'If the licence fee is henceforward to be another mechanism used by the Government to hold down general prices,' said a Home Office memo, 'theories about the independence of the

BBC may begin to look rather tattered.' There might have to be a fundamental reform of the whole basis of BBC funding – direct funding for some services, or advertising, or more borrowing.[67]

The Home Office and the Treasury had given evidence to the Annan Committee supporting the licence fee, and longer-term settlements rather than frequent increases, as a matter of principle.[68] But government survival was more urgent than principle. The Home Office was told not to consult the BBC because the decision was so sensitive. Merlyn Rees, the home secretary, sent a formal letter to the chancellor saying that 'on this occasion alone' he was prepared to countenance a one-year settlement[69] despite 'the strains this might impose upon the relationship between the BBC and the Government'. He glumly noted that the BBC reaction would be to leak further stories and cut programming so that 'the Government took all the blame'.[70]

Remarks by the chairman, Swann (who knew nothing of the Home Office thunderbolt), that the BBC did not now expect to be quite as deeply in debt led Denis Healey to say it was not 'an organisation in desperate financial straits'.[71] Indeed, the licence fee was becoming a tool for a desperate government driven by short-term political needs.[72] Ministers knew that in the necessary and frantic attempt to cut increases across the board in the fight against inflation the BBC, a very visible body, was being treated unfairly.[73] The governors decided to write a 'calm and constitutional registration of the principle that the licence fee should never be seen as part of annual expenditure' and to say how dismayed they were by yet another short settlement.[74]

The *Guardian* carried a report[75] that the government was going to abandon the one-year settlement. An infuriated home secretary blamed the BBC,[76] who replied that as they knew nothing about the proposal the leak must have come from inside government.[77] *The Economist* helpfully reminded its opinion-forming readers that the BBC was the cheapest broadcaster in Europe.[78] Trethowan was duly appointed director-general in early 1978, and he and Swann went on the offensive, writing articles in *Ariel* (the BBC's internal magazine), *The Times* and the *News of the World*.[79] Swann told an audience at the Royal Television Society that an increase of almost a third would be necessary to compete with ITV.[80] The BBC continued to receive a broadly positive press. Favourable pieces appeared in *The Times* and the *Sunday Telegraph*: Peter Knight in the *Sunday Telegraph* noted that administration accounted for only 3 per cent of television expenditure. The Corporation had been doing some 'careful briefing' but the climate was more favourable.[81]

Perhaps, said the Treasury, a public row with the BBC could be avoided if they were promised a longer settlement next time?[82] Denis Healey told the prime minister that an increase in BBC funding would destroy his counter-inflation policy. Privately, ministers worried that any increase would be defeated by the government's own backbenchers, because it would hurt those on low incomes.[83] In a tense exchange, the home secretary said that because the Corporation 'will see their independence as at stake, they will ensure any row is public'.[84] The only way to control the BBC was to give them a very small increase, and hope that the discipline would work. The Treasury relished endless negotiations with the Corporation; 'the BBC will have to accept in effect annual financing'.[85]

The Treasury's next suggestion was so extreme that it was also kept secret.[86] It proposed to make the Corporation live hand to mouth, receiving portions of the licence fee on the 15th of every month, the day before its debt repayments peaked, or even smaller fractions weekly. The idea that the BBC could plan, or retain independence, when it was on a monthly leash was a mark of the fevered desperation in government. Meanwhile the BBC was approaching the limits of its borrowing powers. Could it go bankrupt?

Then 'out of the blue' the Treasury ordered the 'minimum increase to cover inflation'.[87] So in 1978 the BBC was again bound to the government. A special cabinet committee known as GEN 152, put together to discuss the BBC's licence fee, duly met on 16 November, and there the Treasury won the day completely.[88] The BBC was awarded another one-year settlement far lower than they wanted. On the same day, ITV announced it had outbid the BBC to secure exclusive rights to league football. It felt like 'a deliberate and unmistakeable indication of the Government's ... intentions in relation to the BBC', said Trethowan.

WINTER OF DISCONTENT

During the 1978 'winter of discontent', it felt as if the unions were behaving not just irresponsibly, but callously. For the first time, badly paid public service workers in local government and the health service, who had lost out in the spiralling wages competition, went on strike. The consequences of their strike nevertheless felt like a betrayal of the very foundations of civilised life. Peter Shore, secretary of state for the environment, said in a BBC interview, 'very few people ever imagined that the Welfare State – set up to care decently for everyone – would have descended into such collective barbarity'. As putrid rubbish spilled over the streets, and rats swarmed through Soho Square, Liverpool gravediggers and crematorium staff went on strike, producing sobering images of temporary mortuaries filling up with corpses for six days in a row on the *Nine O'Clock News*. 'They Won't Even Let Us Bury our Dead' was the *Daily Mail* headline, and Norman Tebbit said, 'The sheer viciousness and nastiness of unions such as NUPE in the hospital service was displayed day after day on every television screen in the land.'[89]

The BBC was heading towards Christmas with looming union problems. Not only was it being forced to borrow money just to keep broadcasting going, but a great accumulation of pay anomalies looked as if they would come to a head with strikes. One solution had been to send pay disputes off to independent arbitration; but how would pay awards be funded? The atmosphere was changing. Staffs across the BBC, from carpenters to news editors, were now threatening action at Christmas. The Board of Management knew 'that we were very vulnerable, salaried staff were feeling very aggrieved and the craft unions were on the move'. Management could ask for their borrowing powers to be increased, but that would ultimately compromise their independence. In a labour-intensive industry such as broadcasting, the obvious course was to shed jobs, but this would bring no financial benefit for months. The director of Finance advocated seeking an interest-free loan from the Treasury.[90] The Home Office turned these ideas down. The BBC was being forced deeper into debt and could not deal with an imminent crisis at a point in the year when the unions knew they had maximum power.

In a delicate pre-election period, however, with a rising sense of panic and ungovernability, the last thing the Labour government needed was blank TV screens over Christmas. Nor did it want to increase the licence fee just before the election that was inevitable in the spring. Depriving the nation of its Christmas viewing (at a time when 96 per cent watched on Christmas night) would have been dramatic evidence of a world in turmoil. Under pressure from the Treasury to cut capital investment along with other spending, the BBC threatened to stop building a new generation of UHF transmitters for colour TV – some in the constituencies of 'vociferous MPs' where reception would have been badly affected.[91] With devolution looming, the Home Office pointed out to the BBC and the Treasury how important it was to give Scotland and Wales the best possible service. As the winter crisis deepened, Denis Healey saw that Christmas viewing had to be protected. Yet Healey had begun to wrestle inflation under control and – perhaps inevitably – bothering about BBC proprieties mattered less than getting a grip on the economy.

Then, at an extraordinarily convenient moment, the Post Office 'found' a windfall of £6 million to pay the BBC. It had, so it said, miscalculated what it had collected from the licence fee. 'This had apparently resulted from an abnormality, quite without precedent, in the functioning of the licence fee issuing system.'[92] It remained unexplained a year later. The transmitters were reprieved. Of course, in the case of a national civil emergency – which the strikes seemed to herald – any government would have needed to communicate with the nation via the BBC. A BBC need and a government priority coincided. A new pay settlement was reached with large numbers of staff. The unions did not strike over Christmas, and the ratings were spectacular. Bill Cotton plucked a schedule out of the air that suited the mood of the times – mild, funny, distracting – with the skill of a great showman. Yet a worm was turning within the BBC. Anyone thoughtful knew the dangers of a permanent revolution of monthly negotiations over money.

In January 1979, the Labour government faced an imminent election and it was politically impossible to irritate the British public by raising the licence fee to cover what it demanded the BBC deliver. The ghastly merry-go-round of negotiations kept turning. The Corporation was forced farther into debt; its borrowing limit was raised from £30 million to £100 million. By March the BBC was running a deficit of £14 million and the overdraft interest payments were at more than £600,000 a month. Swann was appalled: 'by forcing the BBC to stay in deficit the government had committed it to paying £1½ million of public money in bank interest. This was crazy.' More threateningly still, the award of a new BBC licence and Charter, which gave the Corporation the right to broadcast and set the terms under which it was to do so, was extended by only three years. Or, as the Treasury official Shirley Littler put it, 'the government had decided to extend the life of the BBC until the end of July 1981'.[93]

The Labour government had come very close to abolishing the licence fee in practice: a desperate expedient at a time when inflation threatened to politicise BBC finances. For the Corporation, disputes had also become too political and threatening. In 1979, when Mrs Thatcher was elected, Donald Gratton, head of Educational Broadcasting, called in all of the union representatives and warned them that the Conservative victory marked a turning point. For the first time in living memory there would be an argument about the right of the BBC to exist at all. Yet the BBC was also about to be transformed from the inside.

MICHAEL CHECKLAND

As he ascended the Corporation, Michael Checkland left new structures behind him. In 1980, he had been appointed director of Resources, beside the programme supremo, the director of Programmes. This new position demonstrated how important managing money and the production process had become, but was also a testament to Checkland's capacity as an enabler. His position was unique in the BBC's history. By 1983 he had a place on the Board of Management. By 1985 he was deputy director-general and in 1987 he became director-general. His strategic moves from the technical wings to the centre of the political stage were watched beadily by senior BBC producers, who would meet periodically for vast meetings in a TV studio. One said, 'we used to watch as Checkland moved closer and closer physically to the centre of the room'.[94] People would gossip about it afterwards, reading the runes for where power lay. Nigel Willmott wrote that his recent elevation to the board was 'a signal to intensify the struggle against inefficiency and over-manning, which has bedevilled public service broadcasting'.[95]

Checkland knew that overmanning had not been dealt with, that despite cuts there was still waste, that distortions produced by union power had grown, and that the BBC weakened itself by asking government for more money too frequently. Scarce revenue had to stretch around the new things the BBC needed to do, such as breakfast and afternoon television. Between 1979 and the early 1980s Checkland began to put in place a new strategy: his vision was probity, efficiency, better management, people talking to each other, and professional exploitation of BBC products to put money back where it was needed – in making programmes. He built a team of loyal and able men who went out to grapple with how the BBC spent and made money – as well as tackle the unions and reinvent management. 'We went through a lot together,' he said.[96] Checkland, unlike Milne, backed people up. The man who would succeed him as director-general, John Birt, called him 'conscientious, good, honest, helpful, Methodist, hard working'. He was a lean, modest man of impeccable integrity and great acumen. Yet he was, said Birt, 'a small "c" institutional conservative, the Gorbachev of the BBC'.[97]

Checkland wanted to push the production process to its limit. But it was not until after 1982, when the independent sector was created to serve Channel 4, that a market in production emerged, and consequently the possibility of establishing proper prices. The BBC was always balancing the expense of the internal resource against the likely expense of an industrial dispute, until Checkland and his team grasped the nettle. Before 1982, any British broadcasting company, said Dick Bates, might control costs, but it wasn't until the market developed that you could 'compare and control'. Producer 'choice' was the next logical phase. Checkland argued forcefully for using independent producers to drive down costs, but Milne was dismissive.

Having seen the failure of previous attempts to cut costs, Checkland assembled the people to undertake a rigorous analysis of how the BBC was spending money, and the machinery to ensure that cutting took place. He replaced 'the officer class' from the civil service or the army, who had previously run the personnel department, with a 'grittier', more professional breed of managers with industrial experience. Becoming deputy director-general finally provided him with the reach he needed. His 1985 'Black Spot' review of resources, which audited everything the BBC did, 'struck fear into the hearts of BBC executives'. Roger Chase, Bill Dennay and Derek Thomas already knew how the BBC worked and where cuts might be made. The more important thing was to re-engineer the BBC's resources back into programme-making.

So having reformed how the BBC spent money, Checkland tackled how it made it. 'Enterprises', which sold BBC programmes abroad, was an amateur Corporation backwater, used to park failed managers. It produced mid-Atlantic programmes and, ridiculously, paid tax on profit. As money got tighter, individual programmes had made mistakes: *Panorama* made a programme with money from World Vision, an American charity, which compromised it. Occasionally a programme would be damaged by badly negotiated co-producers' demands: Americans interfered in the production of *Tender Is the Night* and ruined a subtle adaptation by Dennis Potter with clumsy casting.

In 1979, Checkland appointed a new chief executive to Enterprises, and hived it off into a separate company. A useful consultation with Deloittes helped them think through the new model. Satisfyingly the 'profits' of the new company plummeted; consequently it stopped paying so much tax and channelled licence-fee-generated income back into programme-making. Enterprises made sure that programmes were sellable first by ensuring that the rights were clearable ('getting them not to use a Beatles song because we would never get the rights – please make a cover') and standardising the BBC contract system so that individuals, such as Terry Nation, the creator of the Daleks, could not block the exploitation of their creations.[98] Enterprises moved to become important internal co-producers and BBC programme makers would go to them early in the process, rather than at the end.

The American market was large and the BBC was not making enough money out of it. Time Life, the BBC's agents in America, were sacked, as they 'weren't trying hard enough', and a new distributer, Lionheart, formed. In 1985, the BBC bought out the company, quadrupling revenue from America. The BBC collaborated with European broadcasters as well, at a time when public service television, in countries such as Italy, was strong and independent. Reiner Moritz from German television was keen on music and arts programmes, but slow to pay: Checkland finally received one considerable cheque in the lavatories of Covent Garden. 'It meant that Munich was investing in BBC programmes.'

Enterprises tackled the *Radio Times*, the magazine with the biggest circulation in Britain, protected then by a quite improper monopoly on publishing schedules, which meant you had to buy it to know what was on television. Checkland recruited James Arnold-Baker to run it with a remit to double turnover and profits. They wrenched the publishing and distribution back from Robert Maxwell, who had the rights, revolutionised the production, introduced colour and prepared the magazine to survive in the open market. They axed *The Listener*, 'which lost a fortune', but which had provided an intelligent venue for discussions of things that mattered to the BBC. They got *BBC Wildlife* back from another publisher, started programme-related magazines such as *Gardeners' World*, *Top Gear* and the *Good Food Show* – all of which were very popular. Previously, the book of the programme appeared 'in time for the repeat', as producers were often the authors and their first task was to get the programme made. Yet the books of *Life on Earth*, and Delia Smith's cookery courses, had great commercial potential. So Enterprises set about getting the whole broadcasting product synchronised. Delia's books became runaway successes.

Enterprises was never involved in casting or scripting: 'they weren't there to wag the creative dog – they were there to make the dog possible'. But they became good at pre-selling programmes. As they saw ideas coming down the line, they negotiated the co-production finance of nearly all the big drama and factual series – the ones the BBC always proudly pointed to as significant broadcasting achievements. Cunningly, faced with selling 37 Shakespeare plays – some made brilliantly by Jonathan Miller and Trevor Nunn, others 'horrible', said Chase – they stipulated that broadcasters had to buy them all. Only the 'Shakespeare mad' Japanese showed the lot.

Indeed, BBC Enterprises created the home video market in the UK, after four years of tough negotiation with the Musicians' Union and Equity. There was a hard battle over pricing, with the BBC wanting to keep videos cheap so as to make a market with a large base. In the end, £9.99 was agreed upon. By 1987 the BBC was selling more videos in the UK than the Hollywood studios. It seized opportunities coming out of technological developments. To coincide with a large government adult literacy scheme in 1982, and several related BBC programme series, the BBC worked closely with Acorn to produce a reliable and easy-to-use computer. By 1984/85 half a million of these Acorns had been sold, mostly to schools. The tightly framed merchandising deal brought in a substantial sum. The project was an example of the BBC making links between programming and new technology, and of close collaboration with a government that was elsewhere berating it. The BBC worked with electricity companies to use the long-wave signal to switch on people's meters at very slightly different times of day, so that power stations could come on sequentially, saving fuel and avoiding overloads. None of this sounds like 'core' BBC work, but it all made money by exploiting spare BBC capacity in the interests of the central task – 'making programmes'. The BBC was managing and centralising how it used resources with a more commercial eye.

In 1979, there was the first BBC Showcase trade fair in Brighton. European buyers in hotels and conference facilities were invited to look at new BBC programmes in revolutionary video-viewing booths. It was the biggest broadcasting sales event in the world run by a single organisation: the moment the BBC made clear that it was serious about trade. The event raised the Corporation's profile as well as increasing sales by 25 per cent. But not every kind of taste could be satisfied. When Will Wyatt gave a lecture about sex and violence on television, after a long debate European buyers concluded that British television was far too violent and not sexy enough.[99]

But ambitions to manage the BBC more rationally were limited by the blinkered reaction of the Board of Management and Milne to Conservative Party intentions, and by union power. Everyone knew something decisive had to be done. In the late seventies, BBC staff laughed when the BBC boasted of its efficiency in public.[100] Corporation philosophy that the 'show must go on' had undermined attempts to deal with the unions, which, like newspaper unions, understood precisely how to exploit the imperative of a commodity with no shelf life. Checkland moved to unite BBC management behind hard and potentially painful action. The *Financial Times* reported, 'Keeping programmes on the air at any price is no longer the first priority.'[101]

SHOWDOWN

Duncan Thomas, a large, cheerily forceful man, was given the job of sorting out the BBC's most intransigent union problem – Scenic Services (set building, moving and management) – over a lunch with Checkland in 1980. He was known as 'Kamikaze' by his colleagues, one of the 'self-selected hard men among the BBC's line managers'[102] by the unions, and 'a gutsy manager' by Checkland, who gave him a two-page letter analysing the problems, and told him 'do what you need to – I will back you up'. The lunch led to the Scenic Services dispute – the BBC's Wapping. By dealing with the most obstinate area of industrial practices (known in broadcasting more offensively as 'old Irish practices'), it changed the weather of industrial relations in the Corporation. Before it, union disputes escalated. After it, they eased away.

By 1980, insiders could see a simple pattern to BBC industrial conflict. Unions with the least personal investment in making programmes, the heavy lifters of the great 24-hour machine of scenery shifting in Television Centre, workers with the least specialist skills, the carpenters and the general electricians, were most likely to disrupt production. Close behind them were the skilled electricians, cameramen and sound recordists. It was called militancy, but was really just a 'recognition of industrial strength'.[103] The National Theatre and the English National Opera had similar problems and failed to solve them. ITV's problems were more focused on technical staff and, since commercial TV revenues were increasing, it did not care as much and bought them off with money.

Computer technology made skills like graphic design increasingly important in programme production, but the relationship between skills and rewards was growing ever more estranged. 'You could have a construction worker getting more money than a graphic designer when their skill levels were in the opposite direction.'[104] Over the previous decade the BBC had conceded – usually in the face of a strike or unofficial action – a mad patchwork of agreements. A minimum of six men were needed to unload a lorry and all 'unloading' was designated as 'overtime'. Fixed shifts were manipulated mercilessly so that most work fell outside them, while rotas for overtime were run by the unions.[105] A 'Studio Standby Agreement' meant that each studio had a carpenter, a painter and a construction operative sitting around but not permitted to help out if there was an emergency in another studio.

The first dispute blundered into Duncan Thomas's web three days after he started his new job. It was the right crisis, in the right bit of the BBC, and was just the kind of dispute that the public would back the BBC in solving. A large outside broadcast was planned for the Queen Mother's eightieth birthday in St Paul's Cathedral. Two camera towers were to be built of scaffolding, clad with plywood and painted to look like stone, 'so that as the cameras panned across to show the Queen Mum as she entered the Cathedral, you wouldn't notice that there were these ugly camera towers'.[106] These would normally have been built by the scenic carpenters and painted by the scenic painters. This time, however, the scaffolders had put up the plywood cladding. When the carpenters found out 'that somebody else had done the work which they regarded as theirs, the scenic painters in solidarity with their brothers wouldn't paint it'. They arrived in Thomas's office to tell him that the existing cladding had to be taken down, and that unless they were given the work of replacing it themselves, they would stage a walkout and picket the cathedral, to prevent the cameramen and other technicians from working. The Palace was not informed. Thomas 'had a bit of a set to', said that he was not prepared to waste BBC money, and refused to take the towers down. The union's national officer, Stan Ogden, was called in – one of the 'old-fashioned trade union officials who believed that if you made an agreement you were bound by it' – and Thomas was encouraged because he could see that Ogden was embarrassed by the local union action. Thomas issued an ultimatum: if the scenic painters refused to paint the existing towers he would sack them all. The towers were painted and Her Majesty's celebration was broadcast to the world.

A new routine emerged: the unions would make an unreasonable demand, Thomas would refuse it, the unions would threaten to stop a programme, Thomas would suspend them, and then 'the rest of their brothers would walk out and threaten the rest of the shows'. Sometimes, when the unions estimated they were not going to be successful, they 'would back off, we would reinstate the men and everything would go on as normal for a while'. Although union membership was between 50 and 60 per cent, it was more like 100 per cent in the craft areas. Thomas said, 'I was a platoon commander at the front [where] people were not being rewarded for what they did. People were being rewarded for what they could grab.'[107]

Conservative legislation made the process of restoring sanity easier. First, the 1980 Employment Act provided government funds for union ballots. Later, the immunity for lawful picketing was narrowed, rights to secondary industrial action were reduced, as was the definition of a trade dispute. But legislation provided no way of dealing with the sediment of years of concession and compromise in agreements about working practices. By 1983 Thomas had reviewed working conditions in Scenic Services and found 57 agreements that were merely 'income generators'. Elsewhere in the Corporation there had been a steady renegotiation of such contracts: basic pay was raised in exchange for a loss of overtime and a loosening of inflexible job demarcations. In September, a serious clash occurred over demarcation, which led to nearly four hundred members of staff being suspended. They were eventually reinstated, but no concessions were made and management welcomed the publicity.[108]

Thomas had spent two years attempting to arrive at an agreed new settlement. It came to a head in the fortnight before Christmas 1983, at twenty negotiating sessions with the scenic unions. But on Christmas Eve 'they had pulled the plug on every one', including those they had made concessions on in the autumn. Thomas and Checkland both knew that the unions would threaten peak Christmas programmes so left the issue. But in January, management issued an ultimatum – it would implement the changes to pay and agreements on 14 February 1984, with or without the agreement of the unions. BBC managers understood that they were heading for a major strike, that they were breaking agreements because the other side would not negotiate with them. They were prepared for it, as civil servants were prepared for the miners' strike.

Nineteen eighty-four was a year of confrontations, most famously between the government and the National Union of Mineworkers. In 1979, when Mrs Thatcher came to power, unemployment was less than 1.2 million, but by September 1985 it had reached 3.1 million.[109] This formed the background to desperate yet suicidal union conflicts. There was a battle with the print unions over production of the *Radio Times*. The National Union of Journalists (NUJ) attempted to get David Dimbleby, who owned a local newspaper where he was having union problems, blacklisted, and to black programmes such as the *Budget in March* if he appeared. This was political interference with the BBC's editorial independence and was resisted fiercely.

On 14 February 1984, as Thomas's deadline was reached without agreement, Scenic Services workers walked out. The strike spread through the BBC's own union, the ABS, disrupting all television and some radio production. Television Centre and Broadcasting House were picketed. Union leaders could see that management had chosen their fight and intended to win, threatening the role of trade unions within the BBC. They privately believed that they had 'no chance of winning an arbitration and therefore management would have its way in the long run'.[110] On the first day there were 171 on strike, by the fifth 750,[111] and with a wider wildcat support of several thousand workers. Programmes tottered and fell. *Play of the Month, Marti Caine* and *The Kenny Everett Show* sank.[112] *The Time of Your Life* and episodes of *The Young Ones* disappeared.

By March the unions were handing out flyers to the studio audience of *That's Life*, saying that the BBC was wasting a good deal of public money by this dispute and that 'it ought not to spoil your enjoyment of the show'.

The set had not been changed for three weeks, and did not belong to *That's Life* anyway – it had been used for a previous Leo Sayer series. There was some intimidation, although Thomas said cheerfully that the doors of his BMW were glued shut only once.[113] Checkland's people managing the strike met with programme planners twice a day. The strategy was to keep live programmes going but accept losses to recorded ones. 'It was quite hairy,' said Checkland, but for the first time the whole BBC management was united. Late in February, the unions urged Bill Cotton, the head of Television, to sort out the mess, which they said was made by Thomas. Cotton's response was to send a letter to everyone saying that this time, for the sake of the BBC, management had to win.

Meanwhile the long-running dispute with the NUJ over payments for the use of the new technology, Electronic News Gathering, had escalated dramatically on 12 January, when the union had called a mandatory meeting at 8.30 p.m., and walked out. For the first time, the *Nine O'Clock News* – 'seen by management and unions at the BBC as an important symbol'[114] – had not been broadcast. John Foster of the NUJ identified the new mood in the BBC in a letter to the *Guardian*,[115] saying of the determination to continue to use Dimbleby for their budget special, 'Perhaps it's just part of their new macho policy towards all BBC unions or else penance to the government over *Panorama*.' He was referring to the 'Maggie's Militant Tendency' programme, which had been broadcast on 30 January. He seemed blind to the reality that the unions' improper attempt to control who appeared on screen was also a threat to the Corporation's independence.

When the unions refused a new deal,[116] Cotton escalated the conflict by warning staff that they were in breach of their contracts and would lose their jobs if they continued. There was an angry mass meeting in Television Centre. Management knew that the strike was bankrupting the unions. The BBC's more sympathetic union, the ABS, had been forced to amalgamate with the film industry union NATTKE. The BBC unions did not have the resources to sustain a drawn-out strike.[117] They relied on the lightning walkout.[118] Tony Hearn, the wily new head of the new amalgamated union, said that 'if the BBC had ever decided that it had had enough and was prepared to suffer the loss of a few days' programmes, it could beat us hands down'.[119]

After twelve weeks of disruption, Cotton threatened the scenic workers with the sack. A week later, 600 of the strikers who had not returned to work were sacked and asked to return their BBC identity cards. It was a symbolic moment. On 4 April, in response to Cotton's action, 2,000 staff at Television Centre walked out. BBC management did not attempt to cover for them and the screens went black. BBC1 was off the air for 24 hours and management did not blink. Checkland said, 'it was a terrible day for all of us. We'd devoted our lives to this organisation.' But it worked. The dispute came to a swift end and industrial relations in the BBC were never the same again. Working agreements were rewritten across the Corporation, new skills were flexibly rewarded, strikes and walkouts disappeared from the BBC landscape. It was not merely a question of victors and vanquished: both management and unions recognised that the brinkmanship of the recent past had been destructive. Meanwhile at ITV, its main union, the ACTT, had just won 'golden time' – three times the normal rate for extended periods of overtime on making commercials.[120]

It was one thing for the BBC to successfully reform industrial practices, quite another for it to be seen to be doing so. Reporting was slow as the press went on doing what they liked doing best, berating the Corporation: in the *Evening Standard* for being run by unimaginative bureaucrats; in *The Economist* for chasing ratings and being downmarket; in the *Spectator* for being incorrigibly snobbish, anti-market and anti-British.[121] George Gale in the *Daily Express* might have been expected to approve of a victory over restrictive practices, but instead wrote, 'The BBC has over 700 scene shifters. What on earth are the scenes these shifters are forever shifting around? By the BBC's own reckoning, it could do without 189 of them. It has been having an industrial dispute on the matter.'[122] He went on to call for the break-up of the Corporation. After the strike ended, Conservative MP Christopher Chope wrote to Milne, complaining of the pay settlement that accompanied the end of the dispute but saying nothing about the redundancies.[123] When the BBC asked for a licence fee increase that December, *The Times* complained about rising staff numbers; the *Daily Mail*[124] about BBC management failing to control 'spiralling costs'; and the *Daily Express*, in a front-page opinion column, said that the BBC 'now has more scene shifters than Cecil B. De Mille',[125] not letting the fact that he had been dead for 25 years, or that the Corporation had just reduced its numbers, get in the way of a telling phrase. Between 1983 and 1984, the number of people employed by the Corporation went down from 30,000 to 26,000.[126]

CHALLENGING THATCHER

John Birt, the director-general who succeeded Checkland in 1989, would argue that the financial model Checkland introduced was neither radical nor strategic. Birt had inherited a system that still suffered some of the distortions of the period of industrial turmoil. He argued that the BBC's financial inadequacies were also the consequence of psychology and an entrenched view of 'how' it expected to do things. People behaved as if the BBC was 'different', which it was, but that view had become allied with a relationship to resources that was neither defensible nor efficient. 'BBC Wales was run like a small navy and the head of it thought of himself as the admiral,' said Birt. Wales wanted outside broadcast vans parked outside the office, not because it was using them, but as a status right, an outward sign of dignity. Birt said that the BBC got into so much trouble because it had no capacity to think ahead. Sometimes it dealt with issues with success and sometimes less adroitly; but it was all ad hoc. It neither understood the forces it was confronting nor how to handle them. And as political pressure mounted, the BBC never managed to convince the Conservative government that it was in control, not merely of money, but of almost everything.

Indeed, despite all of the reforms and the attention it had paid to Mrs Thatcher, the Corporation was still facing a real threat from the prime minister's economic liberalism. The BBC failed to win her over because, although it took her seriously as a person, it paid no real attention to the ideas she embodied. It neither sought to understand what the new kind of Conservatism meant nor to examine its own case in the light of the challenge. Gwyneth Williams, much later controller of Radio 4, said that she thought the Corporation had been 'bad at big ideas'. It was an odd organisation, apparently stuffily hierarchical, with myriads of arcane acronyms, and yet also deeply anti-hierarchical, with programme makers and the successes and failures of their ideas ultimately more important than any formal position. It was full of quick-witted, rather arrogant, competent, engaged people, by no means all of them left-wing, but there was a shared intellectual world view. Indeed, Mark Thompson, later a powerful director-general, said that when he joined the BBC in 1979 there were 'dominant, unchallenged views' in News and Current Affairs. At Lime Grove, Current Affairs producers saw themselves as the intellectual superiors of everyone: there was a kind of 'liberal consensus', he said.[127]

By 1987, Checkland had built a separate empire within the BBC, but although very close to programme makers it did not make programmes. It was a parallel universe, a more orderly, more humane place where decent efficiency ruled. He was on good terms with the governors, had his finger on the pulse of the Corporation, was capable of decisive action, backing things that worked and seeing things through. He was strategic and knew where he was going. But there was still chaos in the 'other' BBC world, and Checkland was not in a position to 'speak' for the BBC. He was as damaged by the confusion that developed around how the Corporation handled politics as everyone else. In the end the BBC could not be saved bit by bit. It needed to be saved by confronting head-on the growing challenge to the very idea of its existence.

Yet in the end, paradoxically it was the Conservative government itself which was to do that in 1985 when, apparently in attack mode, it set up the Peacock Committee to examine the case for replacing the licence fee with advertising revenue. Instead of destroying the economic basis of BBC independence, it produced a resounding and coherent defence of it.

3

NORTHERN IRELAND: 'THE RIGHT AMOUNT OF BLOOD'

'HAVE WE GOT TOO MUCH BLOOD on the screens, too little or about the right amount?'[1] Tony Hall, head of News, asked Denis Murray, when he was interviewed (or 'boarded' in BBC parlance) to be the BBC's political correspondent in Northern Ireland. It was a good question about balance and truth. Jonathan Powell, one of the negotiators who finally brought political resolution to the Troubles, said that Murray was a man of 'palpable decency' who 'created a better weather system', like many BBC reporters who came out of the conflict.[2] A universalist idea of truth was the rock on which BBC integrity was built, that it would say the same things everywhere, and not trim its words to particular audiences. But discovering how to put such a demanding principle into practice was a nerve-racking discipline during the Troubles. Reporting the cascading enmity on the ground and trying to handle the fissile relationship to governments tested the BBC more than any other event in its history. This was murder at home: it was the nation's first televised conflict, it was intractable and it formed a brutal national and international backdrop of Britain in a state of anarchy. The BBC suffered 'dog's abuse'[3] for 30 years: it was attacked with greater ferocity than any other medium because of its unique local and national role.[4] Yet, as well as 'instilling hard accuracy'[5] in a generation of reporters who worked in Northern Ireland, in the end the BBC played a part in transmuting violent opposition into politics. It built a common, trusted space where warring sides met as an audience – and came to accept some realities together.

Austin Hunter, BBC journalist, saw that he might not be able to bear reporting any more when he arrived at a house to do a story on yet another unexplained shooting. The dead man's brother, whom he had never met, greeted him familiarly, 'Och, Austin – do you want a cup of tea or do you and the boys want to do the interview first?' Hunter and the television report had become one of the familiar rituals of death in a place where dying horribly had become commonplace: 'That man knew I would come knocking on his door.'[6] At the end of the next weekend, when he had done stories on the murder of a contractor working for the security forces, when there had been the shooting of a member of the Ulster Defence Regiment, the deaths of three British soldiers in an explosion and the maiming of a woman caught accidentally in crossfire, he knew he had to get out. He was one of the small team of reporters who did 'the bad stories': 300 murders and their subsequent funerals in under a decade. In the small community each death and funeral was minutely scrutinised, felt intensely and part of a political theatre designed to mobilise opinion as much as memorialise the dead. Many of the victims had no political involvement, atrocities were frequent. It wore people out. The poet Tom Paulin spoke of the 'cadaver politic' of Northern Ireland.

The cameraman Peter Cooper looked back over the scene of a bomb blast in a pub full of Catholic fans watching Ireland playing in a World Cup match: in the eerie silence after the bustle of police and ambulances had left – 'blood, brains, teeth everywhere'. He took a shot of blood dribbling slowly down the side of a shattered beer glass which he knew could never be shown on television. He took it because he was a witness. Later a foolhardily brave Cooper remained on his feet filming as a Protestant gunman slaughtered mourners randomly at a funeral for IRA men. Picture editors were the 'real heroes',[7] the first to encounter the evidence of the orgy of violence being played out on the streets where they lived. Working under pressure to laboriously hand-cut a report for the Nine O'Clock News in the cramped hutch of the Belfast editing suite, one watched images of a young woman crashing out of a building, alive, but with her clothes blown away.[8] He 'lost' that bit of film.

John Reith had said that the BBC should bring to the public 'not the printable scheme of government but its living and doing'.[9] The problem for the Corporation in Northern Ireland was that the reality of political life was so disputed. The BBC began to reflect this painful veracity when Robin Walsh became the charismatic head of the BBC newsroom in Belfast in 1974, after working for UTV. It was an inspired appointment.[10] He pursued the truth with a terrier-like vocation. Walsh 'hammered' principles into journalists and was regarded with affection and terror in equal measure: the two most feared words in the BBC were 'Robin here' on the end of a phone. 'Newsrooms', he said, 'are not conducive to an even temper.'[11] A Northern Ireland Office official noted peevishly that 'he believes in the story rather than the consequences of putting it on'.[12] The misconception that angered Walsh most was 'that journalists revelled in the story of Northern Ireland – we didn't revel, we agonised, every day, every story, every word of every story, the timing of every story – we weighed everything, all the time'.[13] Walsh, a stylish, driven man, was the very model of a public service newsman, ruthlessly decent through indecent times. A generation of local reporters – Andrew Coleman, modest, clever; and Pat Loughrey, later the first ebullient Catholic controller of Northern Ireland; as well as trainees sent to Belfast from the centre, such as Tony Hall and Jeremy Paxman – began their BBC discipleship with Walsh in Belfast. But that was later.

*Robin Walsh in the 1970s – 'the two most feared words
in the BBC were "Robin here" on the phone'*

Seamus Heaney had identified the mood in 1966: 'Life goes on: something is rotten, but maybe if we wait it will fester to death.'[14] During this long prologue to conflict the BBC had faltered in reflecting the reality on the ground. The Corporation's apparent one-sidedness came from its constitutional obligation not to question the political settlement in the North. The Education department (in which Heaney worked) pioneered balanced exploration; Light Entertainment did its part; but there 'was a deafening silence from News' about discrimination against the Catholic minority in housing and jobs, and the gerrymandering that secured Unionist electoral advantage. The BBC was also culpable of not exploring the inner world of Protestant anxiety, as the dynamics of 'Protestant' political divisions were to be as much a part of the murderous chaos as Republican ones. It would have been useful too if the BBC had interrogated class more deeply as Belfast deindustrialised: the Troubles were largely a working-class phenomenon. The Corporation might have run into opposition with governments earlier, but neither this nor fear was the problem. Rather, it was a conspiracy of ignorance that stopped the BBC. Paul Fox, a forceful BBC broadcaster and administrator, a man of warm enthusiasm, said, 'The Corporation reported conflict in Rhodesia and apartheid in South Africa far better than it reported on injustice in part of the nation itself. It was a scandal.'[15]

'Flying into Belfast, the BBC aerial, its flashing ribbon of red lights just turned on for the evening against the black and green of the hill, was the first

Loyalist women occupy Broadcasting House in Ormeau Avenue in 1974;
the Protestant community felt betrayed by the BBC because they felt it was 'theirs'

thing you saw.'[16] The BBC had an existential problem: in Northern Ireland it was itself central to the story – because of its relationship to the entity of Britain, which the Catholic minority saw as the problem (not 'its' nation), while the Protestant majority had an intense and mythic image of its relationship to Britain. Resentment was a bony presence in both communities, and while the 'era of melancholy sanctity'[17] would shortly draw to a close in the Republic, no one knew this in the early 1970s. Both Republicans and Unionists murdered for fantasies of political arrangements that had never existed. Republican militants did not want better government – they wanted the British government to leave and for the North to become part of an ideal southern Irish state. Protestant militants did not want to cede any power to the Catholics. The 'vehemence, immobility and barely suppressed hysteria of extreme views on both sides'[18] made Northern Ireland painfully hard to report on: opinions were polarised on almost every event.

At the start, the BBC was unthinkingly on the side of order in Northern Ireland. Yet the legitimacy of this order was contested, and its exercise seen as unjust by the Catholic population. This was compounded by the situation the BBC faced in London. By 1976, Parliament and Labour and Conservative governments were more or less united in their approach to the crisis (although Labour was committed to a policy that Powell had to unpick eventually as a precondition of negotiations in the 1990s), while the 'nation', at least in Northern Ireland, spiralled into ever more monstrous division. The BBC was exposed because it could not report political disagreement in Westminster, yet was obliged to reflect the swelling disagreement on the ground in Northern Ireland. It appeared as if it was sponsoring opposition rather than reporting it. The Corporation is always in difficulty when an issue concerns the integrity of the British state, which the Troubles precisely did.

CRITICAL THREAT

Working out how to control such a febrile story in the public interest was a process inevitably littered with mistakes. These errors were magnified by the tense situation. The BBC faced the most severe threat to its independence in its history. Most Northern Ireland Secretaries and most prime ministers of either party threatened to use the licence fee as a means to bring the Corporation's reporting to heel. Constitutional niceties were abandoned wholesale by governments and officials wrestling with a desperate situation.[19] But the story of the BBC – with its own casualties, the dead, the fragile, the careers unjustly broken, the constant physical and mental tension, the buildings blown up, the everyday stoicism of getting the service out, intense struggles about what impartiality might mean in such a conflict, the threats to the licence fee and to the very existence of the Corporation that flowed from them – was about the application of the normal proprieties of public service broadcasting, some of which took very unusual forms in Northern Ireland.

At the beginning of the Troubles, between 1968 and 1974, 'no one had a clue what was going on, the police, the politicians, the paramilitaries, the media, the BBC. This thing blew up, they were all making policy on the hoof.'[20] Governments and ministers had short time frames in which to try to make a difference: 'One of the tragedies of the Province [Northern Ireland] was that of butterfly ministers: good ministers were promoted out of it and almost no one stayed in post long enough to actually understand the place', but 'the BBC was there all through.'[21] Disagreeing with government required hard nerves and steady judgement. Constant friction with government led occasionally to arrogance, especially perhaps in 'the People's Republic of Lime Grove', where the BBC's current affairs programmes were made. They suspected the government and the BBC hierarchy of collusive censorship and saw themselves as the shock troops of truth. Yet the BBC's persistent reporting of official use of physical force in interrogations, much disputed by government, was later shown to be accurate.[22] At the time there was a sense of careering headlong into crises that shook the very basis of the BBC. Conventions and proprieties toppled and governments intervened. With hindsight the mistakes were trivial in comparison to the courageous successes. The contribution the Corporation eventually made to reporting the conflict fairly, giving a voice to political communities, was a vital part of resolving it.

Much was 'lost in translation' between the realities on the ground in

Ludovic Kennedy presenting The Question of Ulster *in 1972. It provoked conflict because it had the temerity to bring those who had real power on the ground together in the studio.*

Ulster, the realities as seen from Whitehall, in the rest of the UK, and in the rest of the world, particularly the USA. All major confrontations between the BBC and its critics were in part because what was accepted as 'normal' in one world was seen as outrageous in another. The task of telling local stories in a divided community, of finding ways to gain the attention of the Catholic minority (who saw the BBC as the voice of 'the other side', and some of whom came to see not paying the licence fee as an expression of political opposition), and of telling those same stories in other parts of the UK – all in the end produced in Northern Ireland an extraordinary reporting force, and forged a powerful sense of responsibility at the heart of the BBC.

The BBC was well led. Charles Curran, director-general from 1969 to 1977, is often seen as 'conservative'. He could be stiff and was not urbane, yet he was a strong-minded man with a real grip on the Corporation. He said that 'when he had joined the BBC there had been three taboos: bullfighting, the Queen and Northern Ireland'.[23] His appointment had been a daring sign of taboo-breaking at the heart of the British establishment. Curran was the first Catholic and first grammar-school-educated director-general. Born in Dublin, he said he 'always felt Irish by sympathy'.[24] Asa Briggs, the great historian of the BBC, who knew him well, said, 'he was religious by real, genuine conviction, a man of principle'.[25] Curran was at first diminished by his chairman, Lord Hill, who believed he should lead the BBC. In 1973, Michael Swann, recommended by

Mrs Thatcher, was appointed chairman in place of Hill, when Edward Heath thought Hill caused too many problems. Swann, a distinguished scientist and vice-chancellor of Edinburgh University, with a wide intellectual grasp of the BBC's purposes, was a naturally robust but charming sorter of problems and leader of people. He was wise, secure, sensible and funny. He said that while 'Curran will be in the driving seat, the chairman will be the map reader'. They made the best team the BBC was to have at the top for the next fifteen years. But being right and able was not sufficient to protect the BBC against the mayhem Northern Ireland was to cause.

PICTURES

Television had changed the course of Irish history on 5 October 1968, when it showed the Royal Ulster Constabulary (RUC) beating civil rights marchers in Londonderry, who were protesting over institutional discrimination against Catholics, and the gerrymandering that secured Protestant political domination. Water cannon destroyed the BBC's camera, and in showing the surviving footage instead shot by RTE, the BBC crashed through a strong Northern Irish emotional prohibition against the Irish public broadcaster. Among those marching, not for Irish nationalism but for civil rights, were several sitting MPs, a patchwork of socialists trying to unite Protestant and Catholic workers on class lines, *sotto voce* Republicans and middle-class students. But to the Stormont government it looked like a traditional Republican parade, and was attacked as such. After winning the battle the RUC lied about the injuries it had inflicted, even though the assaults were plain to any viewer. The attacks on the protesters had been 'without justification or excuse', according to the later Cameron Commission.[26]

Yet the protesters got what they wanted: the attention of television. A few came from a strand of politics that believed in 'exposing state violence' by confrontation, but they all understood that a contested march guaranteed media coverage. The RUC had given them the images they needed. At Prime Minister's Questions, when a Unionist MP described the RUC as 'probably the finest police force in the world', Harold Wilson told him to watch the BBC: 'Up to now we have had to rely on the statements of him and others on these matters,' the prime minister said. 'Since then we have had British Television.'[27] Television had made corruption visible and had simultaneously become a battleground for the control of meaning. Usually the BBC saw itself as a 'responsible' and 'impartial' broadcaster, but these roles were set on a collision course.[28] The pictures marked the start of the Ulster crisis.

Immediately the problems that were going to define the BBC's conflicts with government emerged. Would broadcasting cause violence? How did you manage an 'exciting' story? Who had a right to speak to the British public and should the BBC or the government allocate that right? What do you 'balance' when power drains away from formal politics? How do you do impartiality when there are gross injustices all around? Did access to the screens confer authority as politicians and officials thought, or was it part of an interrogation that held real power to account, as broadcasters thought? The reality was a volatile mix of all these positions. The parade of contending views was a civic virtue in itself. At the start it looked like a nasty but 'normal' political crisis: something that would have a beginning, middle and end. Between 1968 and 1974, the BBC in Northern Ireland, under the firm hand of Waldo Maguire, the controller – dubbed 'The Viceroy' by the *Observer*[29] – went on firmly smothering issues that might raise temperatures. A powerful character with a 'harsh, rasping accent', Maguire commanded respect from those who worked for him. He was full of energy, always in the newsroom, 'skewed' with an Ulster Unionist approach. When he occasionally intervened 'to stop perfectly legitimate news programmes being broadcast', he did so because he was anxious that reporting should not 'make things happen'. Yet he gave the young John Simpson some good advice: 'Rank any story on a scale of 1–10 for importance.' If it comes below 5, 'don't push it'; if it comes out between 5 and 7, 'think very carefully'; above 7, 'just do it, don't even consider the consequences'.[30] Applying this rule of thumb was fraught. Maguire and his team were so swamped that news reports were often barely edited. Many thought ITN 'significantly better'.[31]

NAMING NAMES

When Harold Wilson sent in the British army, initially welcomed by the Catholic minority as protection against Protestant paramilitary attacks, the BBC saw their arrival as a return to some kind of 'normal' order. But the presence of soldiers trained to repel a Soviet invasion and just back from a bruising conflict in Yemen[32] was a factor in a rapid escalation in violence. The BBC was grateful when the army identified an early example of electronic warfare, as Loyalists jammed the BBC,[33] but soon came to distrust the army's news management. A recurrent army complaint was that the BBC was sympathetic to the rioters; a recurrent BBC problem was the army 'ringing up newsrooms and trying to give orders'.[34] Operation Banner, the army's name for its 38-year involvement in Northern Ireland, was 'a military campaign without a campaign plan'.[35] The army routinely misled the BBC about 'almost every significant episode for the first year'.[36] The BBC played a part in the emergence of a more sophisticated army communication strategy, one less inimical to public understanding in a domestic conflict. British forces were in a dreadfully exposed position, fighting a new kind of campaign in a community that appeared familiar, but was turning into a dystopian war zone. Over the next five years the army – often on bad intelligence – conducted 75,000 house

The BBC Belfast newsroom on a good day,
the shutters open and the sun streaming in

searches in a community of 400,000. It provoked hostility and attitudes in the army hardened under assault: by 1981 a regimental magazine talked of Republican women as 'Fenian whores, hard bitten gun-toting grannies'.[37]

Did reporting cause violence? If in some sense it did, was that a price that had to be paid for establishing a common territory of truth? The army seemed to think that news coverage 'would empty the nearby pubs of the side being abused, as men poured out to take part in the fight'.[38] A BBC official came from a sticky meeting with the most senior British officer in Northern Ireland, General Harry Tuzo, with the impression that Tuzo thought men in paramilitary groups like the Ulster Defence Association, who were 'peacefully sitting at home watching *Match of the Day*, would pick up their sten guns and go out hunting for revenge after hearing on the news that a Protestant had been assassinated, and perhaps he's right!'[39] The women who took the telephone calls in the BBC newsroom, logging an endless succession of corpses in allotments, kneecappings in factories and savage desecrations of bodies, would recognise the religion of the victim as they plotted it on the big orange and green colour-coded maps on the newsroom walls.

The government in Northern Ireland called for the BBC not to announce victims' names (because it led to retaliation), as did the Alliance Party, academics from Queen's University and researchers in Dublin who demonstrated that it made a difference and therefore ought not to happen. BBC governors returned to it repeatedly, the press demanded it, Whitehall called for it. Thwarted by the BBC, Stormont then demanded a 'one-hour delay' in identifying victims. By 1971 the RUC was refusing to give the BBC information about victims. The dilemma was acute, but the BBC realised that agreeing to any delay might well evolve into the selection and reporting of some events on a purely subjective basis, and the shelving of others: the first step to censorship.[40]

BALANCING ACT

At first the government in London attempted to cajole and bully the BBC story by story. Then it began to think through the problem more strategically. Frank Cooper, an immensely able civil servant in the Home Office, said that in Ulster the normal conventions of balanced broadcasting made things worse for the government. Normally balance was simple: 'Ministers describe their policy and the opposition spokesman has a reasonable right of reply; then political supporters of both government and opposition take part in debate often helped by experts.' But in Northern Ireland there were neither government supporters nor opposition in the usual sense: 'experts were all partial and it means that a fractious "opposition" has the virtual free run of the media'.[41] Government pressure shifted up a notch, questioning the principles of BBC reporting, then complaining to the governors.

Despite the BBC's Unionist bias in the beginning, the majority of physical threats to the Corporation came from Protestant organisations. To Ulster Protestants, the BBC's behaviour was another example of the duplicity of 'perfidious Albion' when it did not take their side. Protestant politicians were hostile to the BBC because they saw it as theirs by right. As they were 'loyal' to the British state, they perceived any time given to the opposition as false equivalence. The BBC was always the focus of anger in a way that the local commercial station, UTV, was not. A sulphurous new Protestant rhetoric was emerging which fused politics and religion. Ian Paisley's invective got him 'banned' from the BBC for a period.[42] Paisley represented a populist, Protestant working-class rejection of change. His wrath expressed a connection between 'no temporising in theology and no surrender in politics' that seemed nineteenth-century. When the BBC covered the Pope's visit to Britain (which it did with some care) he accused it of 'spiritual fornication and adultery with the anti-Christ'.[43] At meetings he would incite audiences against the BBC. Republican rhetoric, by contrast, 'travelled better'.

Brian Faulkner, the 'last hope of Unionism', who succeeded Chichester-Clark as the Unionist prime minister in 1971, saw himself as a 'moderate' and wanted to include the Catholic community better, but had a powerful appeal to grassroots Orange support.[44] Faulkner's policy of internment – detention without trial – was a catastrophe. Because the intelligence was so bad, the British army, which had opposed the policy, found itself breaking into homes almost exclusively in Catholic areas and dragging out mostly innocent civilians, not the 'leaders' of Faulkner's imagination. Harold Wilson thought it a 'recruiting weapon' for the IRA.[45] Three hundred and forty-two people were arrested, and seventeen people died in forty-eight hours of protests – ten of them Catholic civilians killed by the army, including a priest as he gave the last rites to a wounded man.

On the *World at One* the next day, William Hardcastle (who, with the editor, Andrew Boyle, was reshaping the Radio 4 programme into the best news machine on the BBC) spoke to the wounded man. He said he had been shot by soldiers as he ferried children away from the shooting, and that the priest had been killed as he was leaving to get help.[46] Other witnesses interviewed said that it had been in broad daylight, the soldiers knew what they were doing, and the priest's bishop backed up the wounded man's account.[47] Officials in Stormont complained that everyone interviewed had been 'from the same side of the politico/religious divide'. The BBC should adopt the 'controversial broadcasting' policy of presenting 'something from both sides in every programme' (as opposed to across the range of broadcasting, as was normal).[48] This was absurd – nearly everybody interned was Catholic, as was everyone killed or injured in the incident. The *World at One* team was contemptuous of the way the BBC in Northern Ireland 'was held in a vice-like grip by Unionists'.[49]

BBC staff in Northern Ireland were injured and threatened, and intimidation was a daily reality.[50] Colour television came late to Londonderry because BBC engineers from other parts of Britain refused to work on the local transmitters. The director-general said that he was not prepared to order them to do so, which caused local resentment.[51] The BBC governor for Northern Ireland wrote that there had been Protestant 'threats, obstructions and actual physical violence against cameramen and reporters'. The observation was repeated in 1974, 1978, 1980, 1983 and 1986. Cyril Cave, an intrepid cameraman, said he had been hit by just about everything, 'petrol bombs, paving stones, nail bombs' (known as 'Belfast confetti'). He had been clubbed over the head with concrete in a sock and hospitalised twice. Over the years BBC reporting teams developed tactics to protect each other. News crews needed a soundman 'who kept a wider watch on the volatile moods of crowds'. It was often women in crowds at incidents who led potentially dangerous changes in emotional temperature: suddenly becoming hostile, 'poking and hissing'. The BBC teams needed a driver who could get them out if things turned nasty, a reporter, and a cameraman, 'who was the eyes' of the unit. Sharing a dark humour with the emergency services whom they met at scenes of carnage, the BBC news teams learnt to operate like a military unit.[52]

Reporting in Bogside: BBC cameraman Cyril Cave and team, 1972

AFTER BLOODY SUNDAY: 1972–74

'Bloody Sunday' on 30 January 1972 was the decisive moment from which point a frenzy of murder rolled out: more people were killed in the following two years than in any others. The killing by British soldiers of fourteen people on a march hardened a new mood in BBC reporting. Keith Kyle, a reporter with a commitment to Irish history, was not allowed to describe the event as a 'massacre' by the BBC in Northern Ireland. He called it instead 'the military Londonderry Killings'. There was a fusillade of complaints from the army, from the Protestant audience in Northern Ireland, from the Northern Ireland Office, and from inside the BBC, but the head of News in London said 'no other word was accurate. If "massacre" was out of the question so then were "shootings" and "incidents". Even "deaths" fell short of what was required.'[53] Kyle managed to steer authoritatively through the conflagration. There was little that was showy in his journalism, just a steely professionalism.

Those closest to negotiations believed that 'all reporting, and perhaps especially BBC reporting with its authority, was a threat to negotiations that by definition had to be done in secret'.[54] By 1972 the Stormont government had lost control, and direct rule from London was imposed. The first new secretary of state for Northern Ireland was the wily conservative vizier William Whitelaw. He understood broadcasting impartiality, had a courageous war record and the 'magical ineffably graceful Whitelaw touch'.[55]

Later he thought that he should have stayed in the Northern Ireland job longer, but it 'physically quite exhausted me, I was mentally and emotionally affected'.[56] In 1972, he was constantly on the phone to Curran during negotiations over a Provisional IRA truce, anxious that a *Panorama* programme revealing his contacts with the Provisionals might derail his relationship with the Unionists (and his own backbenchers).[57] Curran responded that he agreed 'in the national interest' that he would make sure there was no rush of interviews with minor PIRA characters. He stood firm by the *Panorama* report, which did in fact reveal some degree of contact, because he thought suppressing it would be ineffective. Whitelaw 'expressed strong disappointment', but accepted the director-general's judgement.[58] Whitelaw quite often 'got things off his chest', but characteristically conversations tended to end in 'an atmosphere of marked cordiality and good humour'.[59]

Mark Bonham Carter, the BBC's deputy chairman, widely expected to be the next chairman, and the creator of the Race Relations Board, 'a paradox, establishment-born but risk-taker extraordinary',[60] visited Belfast to look into Protestant complaints. He concluded that the BBC must serve the Catholic population better. Curran's political adviser was taken to the roof of the iconic Broadcasting House in Ormeau Avenue, in Belfast city centre. Smouldering fires left over from the night's battles wreathed the city in smoke. He saw the 'terrible fascination' of guttering house fires, overturned buses littering the streets, and people picking their way to work around checkpoints. The effect was profound. Resources and new jobs flowed into the region. Catholic reporters were recruited, the newsroom upgraded, bomb-proof studios built. The mixed reporting community 'left their politics and cultural identity at the door as they came in'.[61]

Maguire bore numerous direct physical threats with a wry fortitude, but retired after a stroke, one of the many casualties of the strain. Curran upped the game in Northern Ireland and in the heart of the BBC in 1972 by appointing Dick Francis, a BBC programme aristocrat from the centre, to run Northern Ireland. Francis was part of the new broadcasting priesthood of self-consciously clever men: public school, Cambridge, sure of himself and sure of the importance of broadcasting. He brought cool command to the technical and human complexity of running vast live studio projects. He had run the first computer-enhanced election coverage of British and US presidential elections, and the massive global coverage of the first moon landing.[62]

The adrenalin in the BBC offices in Belfast could be overwhelming. Every news or current affairs programme led to 40–50 telephone calls of complaint. Abusive visitors came in off the street to shout at the BBC in person. Over the years there were 36 direct physical attacks on the building by rioters, three occupations by protesters, and a dozen car bombs parked directly outside (143 in the vicinity) set to detonate just in time to be reported on the evening bulletin.[63]

Dick Francis leaves the ruins of BBC Belfast after a bomb in 1974

Broadcasting House was first bombed in 1972. 'We were very lucky only to have lost sixty-five windows – and would like to congratulate the staff as no programme was interrupted as the glass shattered!' went a typical memo.[64] The newsroom was crowded and grubby, the iron bomb-proof shutters on the windows a political weathervane. When they were shut, the place was gloomy and beleaguered, filled with cigarette smoke, the floor littered with reams of contemptuously unread press releases from the Northern Ireland Information Office. There were scanners for the (illegal) monitoring of security communications. It was assumed that the compliment was reciprocated by the security forces. Mere bomb scares were not an excuse for not getting news programmes out, nor were they to be reported.

Local reporters began to imagine 'doomsday' fighting, street by street, house by house. 'Just as big nations live in terror of an atomic accident, so NI lives in dread of a stone age incident that might trigger a local holocaust.'[65] Gloria Hunniford recalled charred teddy bears, and seeing her first murder victim, 'a woman who'd been shot not far from Broadcasting House'. Chillingly, a UVF activist said on screen that a murder had been 'returning the serve'.[66] Between 1972 and 1973, 254 Catholic civilians, 125 Protestant civilians, 167 British soldiers, 26 members of the UDR and 24 policemen were killed.[67] By 1974 Ulster was convulsed by a frenzy of violence in which 1,144 died.[68]

Thirty thousand British troops streamed out of the docks into the town for the election on 28 February 1974, which was effectively a referendum on the Sunningdale agreement and 'power sharing', intended to bring the Catholic population into the political arrangements in a Council of Ireland. The Protestant community overwhelmingly opposed the agreement.[69] In London – in an extended programme which overran as it was going so vigorously – Jonathan Dimbleby launched an attack on the way the Corporation had ignored the history of Northern Ireland. In response, Robert Kee's great series, *The History of Ireland*, was commissioned. A five-part exploration of the roots of the conflict appeared later.

REPORTING THE STRIKE: MAY 1974

Curran's strategy was right. As BBC news became balanced, fast and reliable, it became necessary. Catholics and Protestants may have regarded the BBC with suspicion, but they came to share a dependence on its news in uncertain times. By 1974, there were at least six and often eight news broadcasts a day, and 98 per cent of the local audience listened. Yet the simple principle of telling the audience what was happening as fast as possible caused the next crisis for the BBC. The Corporation was trying to establish something close to a shared set of facts. But in May 1974, Protestant workers opposed to the Sunningdale power-sharing agreement started an unofficial general strike to stop it. Street barriers were erected, trapping the Catholic community. Harold Wilson's televised speech, calling the strikers 'persons who are spongers on Westminster and British Democracy', incensed the Unionists, but it articulated what many thought about 'their almost fascist display of unconstitutional muscle'.[70] Joe Haines, Wilson's press secretary, had struck the word 'spongers' out of the script. Wilson put it back in.[71] The speech, in a year with two general elections, against a background of union unrest and gathering inflation, was also directed at opinion in the rest of the UK.

Energy, transport, utilities and the docks were overwhelmingly staffed by Protestant workers, who ruthlessly shut down the businesses and services that made everyday life possible. British civil servants, reported *Panorama*, were planning for the Third World diseases which the failure of the sewage system would bring about. *The World at One* reported that the British army was planning to run the power stations, but the *Nine O'Clock News* said they did not have enough skilled officers. There were roadblocks throughout the city, a sinister paramilitary presence on the streets, the sky wreathed in smoke from fires, and the RUC unwilling to take on the strikers.

The BBC in Belfast, living in the everyday life of the region, pitched itself 'on the side' of citizens attempting to survive day by day. With newspapers closed down, the BBC told people the times of power cuts, where bread could be bought, where there were roadblocks and by whom they were manned, where marches were taking place, whether schools were shut, where doctors' surgeries were open, which maternity services were operating. This made it indispensable. Controversially, it also told the public where to obtain petrol vouchers from the strikers. This led to the accusation that the BBC was inciting Protestant action by publicising it, and enhancing its power by increasing a sense of the scale of the emergency. Francis said the public needed to see how the emerging groups were reacting, so that they could make a judgement.[72]

Stormont complained bitterly about the BBC but, replied the Corporation, Stormont 'seemed to be powerless and speechless' in the face of the strike.[73] It was the organisers of the strike, the Ulster Workers Council, who appeared to make the news. Francis was hauled into Stormont to see the Northern Ireland secretary, Merlyn Rees, who was desperately trying to get a hold of the deteriorating situation. Rees told him that the BBC had done incalculable damage by accentuating the drama with stories like 'day zero for farmers on animal feed' and the 'knife edge electricity', which enhanced the strikers' power. Francis replied that the BBC had been asking for a government spokesman for days and been refused, and that the strike was more effective than the government admitted.[74] Brian Faulkner, now the head of a failing power-sharing government at Stormont, said that the BBC's reporting had 'shifted power on the ground to the dissidents – the news had made a material difference'. What had started as an unofficial strike by Protestant workers ended with something that felt like a coup: the overturning of an elected government in Northern Ireland, and the collapse of the first power-sharing experiment. Direct rule from London was reintroduced in May 1974. Francis went on to argue, provocatively, that while the paramilitaries were interested in propaganda and often lied, sometimes they told the truth. He was also implying that the army and the police did not always tell the truth.

But who should judge between the value of the BBC trying to give an audience under real physical threat the information it needed, or the government wrestling with anarchy? The strike reporting, whatever the consequences, was an extraordinary improvement on what had happened before. The BBC had been a secure source of information, and that in itself was stabilising. After the strike, Francis wrote to the director-general, 'Right through the staff there was a tacit understanding that we would soldier on and that in 1974 the BBC would not be pushed around by anybody, self-appointed or elected.'[75] Curran defended the BBC: 'If ever there was public service, solid, reliable information, useful to those that were hearing it and yet objective to a degree that was almost incredible – this was it.'[76]

Language was combustible. Curran told editors that the word 'claims' was misleading. To say 'The Army "claims" and the IRA "states" was WRONG' – it all depended on context.[77] 'Murders' was the word when an organisation claimed to have been responsible for the death, 'killings' when the responsibility was only alleged.

The situation in which every meaning was examined minutely was the

*The intense scrutiny of meaning in Northern Ireland was fertile ground
for poets, several of whom, including Seamus Heaney (seen here in
1973), worked in the BBC's Education department in Belfast*

perfect breeding ground for poetry in the BBC Education department. Dark
violence, the feeling of being cut off from elsewhere, curfews that kept people
at home drinking and talking, produced a generation of poets. They found
audiences attentive to nuance: 'words were almost the only thing that still felt
very alive', said Margaret Heffernan. Seamus Heaney, Stuart Parker and Lesley
Bruce, poets working for the BBC Education department, helped transmute a
ghastly situation into a literary legacy of international value.

Some thought the BBC over-corrected for its previous Protestant bias
when it became more sympathetic to the nationalist side, both in Belfast
and London. 'It was partly a matter of who was oppressed and who was
in fashion, but it was partly compensation,'[78] said Paul Bew, the historian
who advised David Trimble from 1987. The BBC, he said, perhaps failed to
challenge what many saw as an almost unanimously pro-nationalist bias in
the rest of the media. This came partly from the image of an oppressed
minority, a kind of Marxist opportunism, and the idea that 'the racism and
conditions that the Irish community face today are deeply rooted in British

Colonial history'.[79] The nationalists were also simply better at propaganda than the unionists.

BOMBINGS AND NORMALITY

In London, putting what were then called 'terrorist' leaders on television was the most controversial issue. The BBC refused to use the word as it obscured politically difficult realities. Whitehall and politicians saw broadcasting as giving legitimacy to men of violence and many ordinary people objected to the dignity it afforded them. The BBC argued that as these men wielded observable power on the ground it was reporting on a reality that could not be wished away. An IRA spokesman issuing the threat 'let me warn them in Britain that they haven't seen anything yet compared to what they'll get in the not too distant future' was broadcast. The uneasy feeling that the IRA was 'winning' a propaganda battle was translated into fury at the BBC. When the IRA chief of staff, Daithi O'Connell, was interviewed he threatened that the gruesome bombing campaign would continue. Only four days later, the Birmingham pub bomb killed seventeen. MPs on all sides demanded that such broadcasts be banned. Lord Hailsham absurdly suggested that there had been a coded instruction hidden in the programme, and Enoch Powell demanded that the director of public prosecutions act. But the ITV *Weekend World* presenter Brian Walden, himself a Birmingham MP, said, 'Do not let us be so foolish as to deny ourselves an understanding of the mind of the enemy.'

The BBC was always under pressure to visit another place in Northern Ireland, 'normalcy'. The people of Northern Ireland agreed about so little, but did at times fiercely reject the image of their society as irredeemably dark and blighted. There was an anger that those who used violence gained access to broadcasting while 'the moderate majority's' voice was never heard. Perhaps they also instinctively understood that images of violence, portraying the place as beyond normal rules, would license enduring violence. The great Irish historian Leland Lyons, giving a lecture at Queen's University at the height of the Troubles, observed that it must be difficult for British TV viewers to grasp the idea of good coming out of Ulster, 'where the journalism of catastrophe has such hypnotic power'. It was almost inevitably seen as 'a place where bloodthirsty bigots of various obscure sects murdered each other incessantly for reasons no sane man could fathom'.[80] Lyons, whose own work explored the realities of the different communities rather than their myths about each other, was well aware of the normal decencies of the politically opposed cultures of Ireland.

While he admitted that 'the dominant image is that of the front page, pictures of destruction and ... ritual recital of overnight violence', Francis said that the perception that the BBC concentrated on the exceptional rather

The Multi-Coloured Swap Shop comes to Belfast with the young Keith Chegwin in 1979; the genius was consumerism and fun without money

than normal life was wrong. A far more nuanced picture of the conflict had been given, he said, by the 349 Current Affairs features on Northern Ireland, 24 documentary programmes, three major studio inquiries into the future, and ten in-depth documentary programmes that were broadcast between 1970 and 1977.[81] More significantly, there was everything else that the BBC was doing in Northern Ireland: orchestral work, children's programmes, and the conscious reflection of its life to the rest of the nation through visiting editions of *Gardeners' Question Time, Any Questions?, Brain of Britain* and the hugely successful *Multi-Coloured Swap Shop*, which attracted nearly five thousand excited children to a mammoth 'swap in' on a field outside Belfast, as well as drama and sport. So most programming was 'normal' and the everyday life of the moderate majority, said Francis, was well represented.

MASON AND NEAVE

Being secretary of state for Northern Ireland in 1976 was chilling. The police moved into your front garden and Security made it clear that in an ambush they would not be able to save your life, although they would kill or catch your assassins.[82] The routine plan of attack on the BBC rumbled on behind the scenes. Policy towards the Corporation, said an official, was: 'alternate love and affection with regular kicks in the guts'.[83]

Merlyn Rees, a cerebral politician, was succeeded in 1976 by a combative ex-miner, Roy Mason, who represented a more aggressive attempt to bring the situation under control. Mason wanted within his political time frame to actually change the conditions on the ground. He built an unlikely but close working relationship with Airey Neave, the Conservative shadow Northern Ireland minister, and hero and confidant of Mrs Thatcher (who 'had an almost mystical belief in Neave's ability to solve Northern Ireland').[84] It was an unprecedented situation for the BBC: a cross-party, premeditated attempt to control it, as part of a wider strategy in Northern Ireland. The BBC felt the effect of the shift in manoeuvre but did not understand its origins or the scale of the threat.

For Mason and Neave, the BBC was an instrument of state power they could harness in a bitter struggle to impose order in the public interest. After secret talks with the IRA had shown it unwilling to make any concessions, Mason had a new policy: criminalisation.[85] This policy stripped away the political status of prisoners and led to the hunger strikes of 1982. Denying legitimacy to paramilitaries, a policy pursued by Mason and the subsequent Conservative government, put BBC reporting in the firing line. Mason cracked down on the Provisional IRA so effectively that they were forced to reorganise. Sectarian murders declined, as a Peter Taylor programme pointed out. Meanwhile, broadcasting in the Republic came under severe government pressure. Section 31 was introduced banning interviews, and reports of interviews, with Sinn Fein: a 'broadcasting ban'. The BBC thought it unlikely that this would lead to the British government implementing such control, but it was a reminder of government powers. Curran said that in private Mason was 'more amenable' than his 'public robustness' might suggest, and he 'was not too worried by these early signs of zeal'.[86] He was wrong.

What came to be called the 'Second Battle of Culloden' was an unprecedented full-frontal assault on the BBC. In the autumn of 1976, after the opening of new studios in Belfast, the chairman, Michael Swann, and the Board of Governors gave a private dinner at which Mason launched into a 'thermonuclear explosion of rage and spleen'.[87] The BBC was behaving like 'a third rate tabloid newspaper' while he was 'trying to take the heat out of the situation'. Their reporting was making things difficult for the security services, the army and the government. (The BBC would have added the paramilitaries to this list.) He condemned a report about a pregnant woman who had been hit in the abdomen by an army rubber bullet. The BBC, he said, had given a propaganda platform to a collection of IRA and Provos 'all known to the Security Services'.

Mason's broadside licensed a storm of complaints from the great and the good eating the BBC's lunch. The head of the armed forces, Major General David Young, complained that the BBC glamorised the IRA and cast suspicion on army statements. Francis answered that it was because army information was so unreliable. The Lord Chief Justice said that the 'BBC would have given

Satan and Jesus Christ equal time', but also criticised the army, which had at first claimed that Majella O'Hare, a twelve-year-old girl, had been shot by the IRA, when in fact she was killed by 3 Para in crossfire. 'The army should put its house in order' but the BBC should consider 'what is good for the country, and what is impartiality', he said. Mason said that the BBC Charter should be rewritten to make it more responsive to security considerations, and he would get the licence fee cut. Bonham Carter told Mason, 'You must choose between managed news and freedom of speech' and pointed out provocatively that there was a Catholic case that was not being put forward. Roy Lilley, the editor of the *Belfast Telegraph*, said that the BBC was not on anyone's side, and that was the value of it. Mason thundered that the BBC was giving terrorists succour and swept out, leaving a reeling audience behind him. A Northern Ireland official, Kenneth Bloomfield, was shocked by Mason's 'extravagant' attack,[88] and said that he would have 'preferred to be in a steamy jungle or an icy waste' because his professional loyalty was to Mason, but his sympathy with the BBC. It was later dubbed Mason's 'Corsican performance' for its uninhibited bullying.[89] A rattled BBC Secretary asked hopefully whether it was just bluster. But the attack was calculated and part of a new strategy.[90]

Curran dealt with the crisis strategically. He told the Board of Management, 'For years the BBC in Northern Ireland had followed the wrong line. Now it was on the right line, and must stay on it!'[91] Swann reminded the governors that they must be discreet about the dinnertime confrontation,[92] but it was a vain hope. News of Mason giving the Corporation a bloody nose was immediately leaked, although several months passed before a full account appeared in the *Observer*.[93] Curran discussed Mason's threats with Robert Armstrong, the steady permanent secretary in the Home Office, sending him an account together with the BBC's defence, which no one had made at the time 'for the sake of diplomacy'. The Ministry of Defence and the Home Office thought the onslaught was 'regarded as a gaffe',[94] since the Home Office were seen as the keepers of the BBC. Curran said, 'Armstrong and I were of like mind on the matter.'[95] Swann said no real harm had been done[96] and Francis was told to find a public venue to make a speech explaining the BBC's dilemmas and methods in Northern Ireland in the near future.[97]

The BBC's response to Mason was a turning point. However serious the attack (and it would get worse), the BBC understood that it had to withstand pressure locally and nationally. Swann steadied the BBC and set a course. He escalated the response and sent a warning shot over Mason's bows and copied it to Neave: 'From the beginning we took the view that we had a duty to tell the truth – to every side in Northern Ireland, and to the rest of the United Kingdom where responsibility ultimately lies.' Mason was proposing 'managed news' but the BBC had chosen 'a free system of news' and they did not intend to deviate from that. Many Catholics still did not find the BBC credible. It was a shame that there had been no Catholics present at the dinner, 'but that of course is how it often is in Northern Ireland'. The BBC staff in Northern Ireland had the full confidence of the board. Mason's threat to the licence fee because he did not like editorial decisions was an attack on the constitutional position of the Corporation, and Swann asked for reassurance that 'it was not your intention to depart from the settled conventions that govern the handling of these matters by Government'.[98] Mason replied more emolliently, but he pointed out that the complaints had come from 'a wide spectrum of senior and responsible opinion'.[99]

When the BBC governors met early in 1977 to review the situation, in the eighth year of the Troubles, Francis contrasted high staff morale with the general mood in the Six Counties, which he said was 'perhaps bleaker than it ever has been'. The Battle of Culloden showed the director-general and the chairman swinging into operation together, but the carefully considered attack was a political turning point. The politicians would try to find other ways of dealing with the BBC: not by complaining about stories, but by changing constitutional conventions.[100]

Neave warned the BBC that backbenchers on all sides would be 'furious' about a programme on the IRA made by a young reporter, Jeremy Paxman.[101] Over coffee at a Privy Council meeting, Mrs Thatcher spoke at length and with 'great feeling' about the way the BBC enhanced Republican reputations and suggested that the prime minister, Mr Mason and Mr Rees, together with the Conservative opposition, 'should make a joint approach to the BBC governors to make it absolutely clear that no increase in the licence fees would be granted while these sort of programmes were tolerated by the governors'. Neave was unleashed formally on the BBC governors, the Corporation's central institutional bulwark.[102]

Swann went to see Neave and believed an upcoming speech 'would be a little more philosophical than he had originally intended'.[103] He was wrong. Neave addressed a full house in Parliament saying that the propaganda war was as deadly as any military campaign and it was being lost by the media. The BBC in particular 'pronounce on the security situation in Northern Ireland with studied grandiloquence and ignore the true dangers', and respond to criticism by 'blandly' referring to their guidelines and impartiality as a defence. It gave, he said, 'the impression they are not really on the side of the civil power in Northern Ireland. In elevating themselves above the struggles and duties of lesser mortals, they have lost sight of their responsibilities.'[104] He thought that media freedom needed reconsidering.

Neave believed that his legendary escape from the Nazi prison Colditz and his experience of running British agents in occupied Europe, together with his wife Diana's work on the joint SOE and BBC black propaganda operation during World War II, made him uniquely placed to 'win' in

Gillian Chambers and Jeremy Paxman in the Belfast programme Spotlight *in 1977*

Northern Ireland.[105] Unlike almost anyone else, he coveted the position of minister for Northern Ireland. 'The prisoner of war is not a criminal', Neave wrote in his dashing account of life behind the lines, 'yet he must employ all of the criminal's ingenuity and cunning.'[106] Neave believed in a mixture of sophisticated psychological operations (which is where his plans for the BBC came in) and a ruthless military approach (which is what Mason was beginning to implement).[107] 'Instead of the deadpan news item every day about death, injury, destruction and sorrow ... there ought to be a concerted attack on these barbarians.'[108] Neave's analysis was paradoxically similar to that of the IRA: this was all-out war. He thought that the BBC with its girlish delicacies about fairness acted as an absurd impediment to the national interest.

To put pressure on the BBC into perspective, at this time Mason also had his eyes on Thames TV over Northern Ireland. 'Some of their recent efforts have not been to our liking ...': programmes about the ill-treatment of suspects, visits to the Maze prison, and Peter Taylor the reporter were all mentioned. Commerce was the screw Mason proposed to turn on ITV. Before a meeting with Lord Barnetson, of Reuters and chairman of Thames,[109] Mason asked for the names and background of anyone in 'a senior position in any company which holds a lot of shares in Thames'. One firm was found to have considerable shareholdings in Rediffusion, which in turn owned a good deal of Thames: and its chairman and chief executive were 'unhappy about Thames TV's current exploits in Northern Ireland and have offered to use their influence to assist HMG's policies'.[110] Mason had several meetings and was 'satisfied' that Thames would behave better. Later, ITV and UTV, many felt, were cowed, but 'the BBC held on', said Pat Loughrey.

Dick Francis had suffered collateral damage and was promoted back to the BBC hub. The next controller of Northern Ireland, Jimmy Hawthorne, was a deceptively mild, canny Belfast Protestant who had been recruited by Curran after having run public information in Hong Kong. He was not a BBC metropolitan mandarin but passionately provincial. 'He was', said Stephen Claypole, who later took over from Walsh in London, a great defender of journalists and comfortable with security matters, 'sly and the man for the back channel'.[111] Hawthorne's tone was avuncular and pragmatic. If he could make a joke or a personal connection, he did. He had lost a close relative in a bomb attack, and later his wife was forced to take their children away because of threats to the family. Hawthorne worked well with Lucy Faulkner, the new Northern Ireland governor. She could be spectacularly difficult: one BBC memo was headed 'Defences prepared and answers ready for the Faulkner missiles'. Yet she was a forceful, intelligent woman who was quick and graceful in her appreciation and a real presence both locally and nationally.

At this point the BBC could still depend on the glorious imprecision of the unwritten British Constitution. Throughout the period, home secretaries, important ministers in cabinet, served by experienced and able civil servants, would – in the end – use their power to defend the BBC. So Rees, by now home secretary, brought his ministerial sights to bear on Mason and Neave. He said that he had been reviewing his powers and if there was evidence of collusion he could 'instruct' broadcasters 'not to broadcast specified matters or classes of matter'. These powers had never been used, and were drawn up in such a way as to protect the BBC's editorial independence – they could never be used 'to ban a particular programme or programmes relating to specific subjects'. Rees told Mason, 'I know that you are not advocating the introduction of any kind of censorship' (he was), but to issue directions of this kind, he warned, 'would be, and would be seen to be an act of censorship. There would be no way in which we could hide or obscure this fact.'[112] It would be a departure from all previous policy; there would be trouble in Parliament and the press. The home secretary was warning Mason off the turf, and described the settlement that was conventional. The BBC depended on it. But this convention was not as secure as it seemed – and a new radical prime minister might rewrite either parts of the equation.

In 1978, Ian Trethowan replaced Curran as director-general. He was not Curran's preferred candidate, and Curran had wanted to stay longer. Northern Ireland was one of the issues that was becoming so fraught that it needed 'a new approach'. Trethowan had worked as a political presenter for ITN and been a reporter since he was sixteen. The idea was that the BBC's problems could be eased by someone more eloquent in public. He was a very different, more socially assured character than Curran, less puritanical but an effective operator. 'He was of the school of sorting messes before they got larger.'[113] As a 'wet Tory' he was selected for his excellent Conservative connections, to try to put a clean 'face' to the Corporation.

Then, on 31 March 1979, at the beginning of the general election campaign, Neave was blown up as he left Parliament by a not-yet-proscribed Republican breakaway movement, the Irish National Liberation Army (INLA). It was a shocking assault on democracy and an incalculably damaging personal blow to Margaret Thatcher, who had been given her first job as a barrister by Neave. Three weeks later, she stormed into power with a Conservative majority. Three months later, the editor of *Tonight*, Roger Bolton, sent an experienced team to Northern Ireland. They managed to interview a member of the INLA claiming responsibility for Neave's death. It was 'referred up' through the BBC hierarchy in the approved way for dealing with delicate editorial decisions: Francis was consulted, and the interview was finally passed by Trethowan (who later regretted it) over the phone as he was putting on his dinner jacket in order to be presented with an award at the University of East Anglia. Meanwhile, government officials had got wind of the broadcast and told the new Northern Ireland secretary, Humphrey Atkins. At 7.45 p.m. Stormont officials phoned the BBC in Belfast objecting to the 'monstrous' broadcast.[114] Atkins phoned Faulkner (a widow like Diana Neave). No one from the BBC, she said ominously, was answering her calls.[115]

Bolton knew that Diana Neave ought not to stumble across an interview in which a man in a balaclava justified murdering her husband. But nor did he want it stopped before it went out. *Tonight* contacted No. 10, who in turn talked to Lady Neave's family. She was out to dinner, but had been alerted by a trailer and watched the interview. There was a horrible row. Humphrey Atkins called the interview a 'serious misjudgement', as the INLA had been guilty of 'foul crimes' in the recent past. 'As you must know, I instructed my officials to make plain to the BBC my own view that the interview should not be broadcast, but my protest had no effect on the BBC's decision. I very much hope the BBC will not make the same mistake again.' Trethowan replied, 'It is not clear from your letter whether you saw the programme, but I find it difficult to accept that it could have been regarded as "a platform" for the INLA. The man was revealed for what he was.' He finished with a quote from *The Economist*, which had written: 'To hear the enemy, in his own voice, justifying his acts, is not the same thing as accepting his justification. And it may help people to understand why the other side fights on.'[116]

Asked in a parliamentary question whether he would 'prevent traitors and other people who are at war with the United Kingdom from having access to the broadcasting media', Whitelaw, now home secretary in the new Conservative government, said it was not his business to condemn a particular programme, but terrorists who 'make war on society outlaw themselves from its privileges. The broadcasting authorities owe them no duty whatever gratuitously to provide them with the opportunities for the publicity they want.' A Northern Ireland minister, Giles Shaw, rallied Whitehall against the BBC. 'One of the reasons why the problem is "intractable" is that the BBC and other media have helped make it so ... We are sufficiently close to a war situation in Northern Ireland to warrant at least some closer understanding if not agreement between media and the government as to what are the acceptable parameters within which "freedom of the press" can be exercised.'[117] The last ever edition of *Tonight* had exited the screens with tremendous journalistic brio and a scoop. But there was something cruel in it as well. Yet in Northern Ireland the BBC felt that many widows had been forced to see terrible things during the Troubles.[118]

On Bank Holiday Monday, 27 August 1979, the IRA blew up a fishing boat killing Lord Mountbatten, one of his grandsons, his son-in-law's mother and a fifteen-year-old local boatman. Mountbatten's daughter, son-in-law and other twin grandson were seriously injured. That the fifty-pound bomb was detonated almost simultaneously with another that killed eighteen British paratroopers on the other side of the island, with a booby-trap that killed those who came to the assistance of the wounded, indicated that the decision to assassinate a distinguished old man and his family had been taken at the highest level. It was the largest number of military casualties from a single attack in the entire conflict. An IRA bulletin, part of which was reported on the *Six O'Clock News*, pronounced it 'a discriminate operation to bring to the attention of the British people the continuing occupation of our country. We will tear out their sentimental, imperialist heart.' The BBC created a 'magnificent and poignant'[119] event in the broadcast funeral. Mountbatten had laid down the ceremony he wanted in 1974 in 'a great letter', but the outside broadcasting team led by Mike Lumley captured the sombre mood of the crowd. The capacity of the BBC to enhance great national moments was taken for granted. The propriety of delicate decisions about how to capture grief but not intrude on a private dignity at the heart of a public event was part of public service broadcasting's role in collective national life.

'Many talk about a solution to Ulster's political problem,' wrote a political scientist, Richard Rose, in 1972, 'but few are prepared to say what the problem is. The reason is simple. *The problem is that there is no solution.*'[120] As early as 1975, General Tuzo had briefed the BBC that the army had concluded that they could not 'win' the conflict, although they could stop the paramilitaries winning it. The solution had to be political and involved 'talking with those who are seen as the enemy'.[121]

The BBC – accountable to the whole nation – was helping forge a public space that was the precondition for something better. The Corporation sought to vocalise power, giving an opportunity to speak to those groups and forces that were exercising power on the ground. It was speaking to the 'enemy', but it was also holding the 'enemy' up to scrutiny. Mrs Thatcher's government decided first to change the constitutional arrangements around the Corporation, and then to ensure that the next chairman was perhaps closer to its view, and that the governors were more sympathetic to it politically over Northern Ireland. The BBC argued that interrogating the motives and actions of the 'enemy' in public helped hold them to account. 'The public must have the evidence to make up its own mind,' said Swann. Northern Ireland would continue to test BBC principles and governments' attempts to bring resolution to the conflict. Yet Swann was surely right – an informed public is realistic, and such intelligent realism is the basis of democracy.

4

ARTS AND MUSIC:
CULTURE VULTURE

THE BBC UNDERSTOOD that it had to feed, as well as feed off, British culture in the interests of future audiences. The Cyclops eye of broadcasting could transform the fortunes of artists and players, movements and repertoires, stars and ideas by thrusting them into public attention. The BBC endowed with authority and popularity what it took up. In this way, broadcasting, with some of the same arrogance and sense of right as a great Renaissance patron, restlessly made and remade the canon. The BBC created communities of creators, communities of audiences, and informed both with critical balance. A good programme on the arts, said Gerard Mansell, 'looked spontaneous, but as if someone had thought very carefully about it, and had character and an idea behind it'. But by the 1970s the paternalistic, top-down making of taste, to which the BBC had aspired since the days of Reith, was increasingly under challenge from more pluralistic views.

MAKING MODERNISM

By 1970 William Glock's 'campaign of insurrection' as controller of Music had transformed 'the flat and pedestrian aura of musical life'[1] he found in the BBC, indeed the nation. If the BBC contributed to the arts generally, its role in music was more elemental. Since the 1930s it had made British musical culture. Glock had improved the quality of orchestral playing, re-engineered the repertoire and begun the transformation of the Proms from a London showcase of British musicians into a great international festival. He said, 'We get three thousand people every night at the Proms, and we don't know why they come, so we are going to change the programmes and see what happens.'[2] He tampered with the Last Night of the Proms, which had become a patriotic saturnalia under Malcolm Sargent, making it into something more musical. It was a disaster; he retreated.[3]

Inspired by a passionate dedication to modernism, Glock had brought the international avant-garde to Britain, catapulted the reputation of British music into an international arena, and fostered generations of young composers and musicians. Glock justified 'a creatively unbalanced' approach which gave more attention to neglected aspects of the musical repertoire, as a necessary aspect of building public taste. His modernism was not always appreciated: Frank Gillard said in 1982 that there 'was a parallel between what the left wing is doing to the Labour party and what advanced modernists are doing to BBC music ... trying to foist something on an unsuspecting British public'.[4] Robert Ponsonby, however, Glock's successor, stabilised this advance. In the space of two decades they elevated the quality of the nation's musical life and the sensibilities of the British public.

Glock's sense that music was 'a cause' was later even interpreted as part of a Cold War propagandist promotion of modernism. This was seen as the American riposte to the conservative Soviet culture of Russia and eastern Europe. In the pre-war era, both Soviet and Fascist authoritarianism rejected 'modernism' and so provided it with a progressive 'aura'. Modernism had been spread around the world by refugees from Nazi Germany and the Soviet empire. In the sixties the CIA had covertly sponsored *Encounter* magazine and other cultural projects. Culture was the territory of an intense Cold War conflict. For 45 years both sides occasionally arrested people from the other side, expelled them and shot down spy planes. By contrast, the best dancers and chess players, musicians and film-makers were sent out to the front line the whole time. The BBC was on the cultural battlefront of the Cold War.

But the accusations of cold warrior complicity confused political and creative judgements. When later critics said Glock 'ruthlessly propagated modernism – which left us with a gap between composers and audiences',[5] that said more about the bunkered conservatism of much listening than about Glock. It was also an understandable but misguided reproach from those composers who felt neglected by the turn to the Continent. When John Drummond took over as controller of Music in 1985, there was a new balance to be struck and work to be done putting a 'face' back on to BBC music and culture, generating publicity and excitement, which came so naturally to him.

The transformation of sound achieved in this period reached well beyond classical music, however. The BBC's Radiophonic Workshop brought experimental sound to an enthusiastic mass public (while in France it remained secluded in high culture). The early music movement re-imagined sound and the repertoire. Meanwhile, the emergence of independent popular music, which played ingeniously with electronic sound, found audiences because of the creative, open policy of BBC popular music programmes.[6] This was a remaking of music way beyond the policy of the controller of Music's remit – yet it showed the Corporation responding to popular taste, and resonated with a wide, cross-class, cross-age spectrum of the British public.

For all of Glock and Ponsonby's achievements in the public arena of the Proms and BBC concerts, it was not within their remit as controllers of Music to grapple with the central problem of how classical music programmes were put together within the Corporation. The broadcast output was the responsibility of the controller of Radio 3, who was rarely a musical expert, which was mad. BBC Radio 3 music programmes were made in a mildly deranged process, worthy of a Heath Robinson fantasy machine. Labyrinthine complexity and rigid demarcations were the product of habit, ossified into inviolable principle. When the young Nicholas Kenyon started work at the BBC in the mid-1970s, fresh from reading history at Balliol and working on the Bach festival, the system was rarely questioned by those who served it. He found it bewildering.

Listeners heard the product of three separate arms of the radio division, which dwelt far away from each other in different buildings. The music was selected and edited by music producers, an honourable tribe who guarded standards of sound quality and performance with uncompromising zeal. Christopher Hogwood, then an emerging young conductor, broadcaster and musical innovator, believed that producers' 'determined, exacting, patience' was an unsung gift bestowed on the nation's music.[7] Rehearsal time, the single most important commodity in improving the quality of musical performance, and indeed extending the repertoire, was spent intelligently by producers who were the BBC's 'musical ears'.

But for all of their omnivorous musical appetites the tribe had sub-ethnicities of warring musical tastes and rigorously separated professional practices. Live producers worked in Yalding House, Great Portland Street or Maida Vale. They related to concerts and orchestras, organised live events and scrupulously produced studio recordings. They went out a lot and mixed with the music profession. Gramophone producers lived in Egton House, an unlovely building near Broadcasting House. They were equally knowledgeable and understood the recorded repertoire 'with great sensitivity: some knew more about comparative performances than any one'. They depended on the record library, and barely went out at all. Never the twain did meet.

Once either kind of producer had made a programme – live or recorded – it was dispatched to the 'Music Information Unit', headed by the distinguished scholar Derek Cook. Here nested musicologists, historians and purveyors of interesting information, who wrote scripts to fit the fully formed programmes they had received. Then the music made in one place, accompanied by the script created somewhere else, was sent on its final journey to the Radio 3 Presentation department. Here, on air, famous presenters such as Cormack Rigby, Patricia Hughes and Peter Barker read the scripts that they had had no part in producing for programmes they had no role in creating, about music they sometimes had no knowledge of. 'People used to complain that R3 presenters were impersonal, detached and chilly,' Kenyon said; 'it was less a style and more a simple reality.'[8]

There were other walls in the bunker of music. In the late seventies the scars of the replacement of the mixed cultural broadcasting of the Third Programme with the more generic music station Radio 3 had not healed. The idea had been proposed by Gerard Mansell in his report 'Broadcasting in the Seventies' (1969). The leading opponent of generic broadcasting, the argumentative and respected music producer Hans Keller, wrote from within the BBC that a station focused primarily on music 'is unethical. Inevitably it turns music … into a drug.'[9] The tension, letters to *The Times* and vigilant suspicion of cultural treason engendered by the new service were still vivid.

There were not just different kinds of producer, live and recorded, there was also a theory that recorded music could on no account be mixed with live in the same programme. The rule had grown out of copyright restrictions and 'needle-time agreements' negotiated by the Musicians' Union to protect the livelihood of musicians and the survival of live performance. But it had got out of hand: frequently a commercial recording of a performance made by a BBC orchestra could not be broadcast. The players had to be shipped into the BBC's Maida Vale studio to reproduce the piece 'live' simply for broadcasting purposes. By the seventies the divide, which Christopher Hogwood observed 'was very severe', had sclerosed into a theological justification. It was argued that the difference between live and recorded sound was such that audiences would rebel in agony if they were mixed in one programme.

The rule was ridiculous when dealing with an emerging repertoire for which only some recordings as yet existed. It took Hogwood two years to make a groundbreaking series on the *Trio Sonata* about music much of which had not been heard properly for many years. Because he had made the series for the (live) Music department, he was not allowed to use what pre-existing recordings there were from the Gramophone department. He had to record everything from scratch. Later, when he replicated the series for Flemish radio, it took a quarter of the time, and cost half as much. This was BBC 'theology' wasting money.

Then the Music Information Unit's mighty files were, in pre-computer days, a marvel. Arranged by date, every script of every programme was kept in Yalding House. In Egton House, the Gramophone department had an entirely separate card index system of great fascination. Every time an item was broadcast, the composer, date, history of the piece and of its performance, and (critically for broadcasting) its exact duration were noted. But it was the backs of the cards, which might cross-reference music about witches, with bells, oboe performances or by Finns, which were an accumulating 'Aladdin's cave of musical knowledge'. Hogwood said that they helped create programmes, and prompted ideas, 'like a musical thesaurus'. Just going in and sitting with some cards was stimulating. A plan to make money by selling the index required much investment and came to nothing: it was brought to a halt at the letter 's'.

More broadly, music was part of the BBC's unstated duty to sustain a 'common culture'. From Radio 1 to the Proms, to the expensive television arts series, the challenge was, perhaps surprisingly, the same. There was a Reithian obligation to the quality of the work in itself, focused through a distinctive BBC vision of its audiences. Glock said that the BBC should give audiences 'what they will like tomorrow'.[10] Ponsonby, who succeeded him, said that by 1977 his programming policy was 'to balance the best of what is familiar with what we believed to be the best of what is not, whether it be new or old'.[11]

What elements did the BBC have to balance to give the best service to music and audiences? How did it keep audiences moving and learning? Certainly by supporting live performance in both the metropolitan centre and in the regions. There were difficult questions about the quality of the orchestras: how much did you need to pay to attract the best players? What conductors did you need to bring in, and what could you offer them? The market in musical stars, from Karajan to Callas, was internationalised long before that of football players. Any controller of BBC Music, responsible for the Proms and the BBC Symphony Orchestra, was an impresario identifying and enticing the right conductors and the right performers. You inherited some obligation to play the repertoire of 'British' music: from the classics of Elgar, Delius, Vaughan Williams and Walton to the living British tradition of Britten, Tippett and their contemporaries. The BBC had played a key role in exploring Bach and baroque music in the 1950s. Basil Lam had mounted a huge Radio 3 series, *Plainsong and the Rise of European Music*, in the 1970s. Imogen Holst had unearthed Monteverdi's music. Glock had re-established Mahler in the sixties. Television too had brought classical composers to a newly popular audience, especially through brilliant films like Ken Russell's on Elgar.

There was always a consensus that work from new composers had to be commissioned, so that 'British' music should not become a heritage trinket. Glock, Ponsonby and notably Stephen Plaistow developed this policy. Was this music to be played perhaps even when no one much listened? It was certainly the case that the composers the BBC espoused – Maxwell-Davies, Goehr, Maw, Birtwistle – became accepted into the repertory. But was this for the circular reason that the BBC promoted them? It was important not to let British performing standards get out of touch with the world, so the best foreign performers and conductors came, continually relaunching great classic and romantic music at the audiences. Meanwhile, there was an obligation to nurture young British performers and musical life in schools.

AFTER MODERNISM

Hovering over all music and arts programming in the seventies and eighties was a hard-to-crystallise query: what was to come 'after' modernism? If Glock

Pierre Boulez, the most original musical mind of the period,
rehearsing the BBC Symphony Orchestra in 1972

had revitalised musical life with a praetorian guard of experts, he did so out of a deep aesthetic empathy, but also in the belief that modernism was a kind of progress. Glock had reservations about Benjamin Britten as perhaps too mainstream, but he encouraged British composers. He was an ardent European, who had brought Bartok and Mahler into the repertoire, but also the avant-garde: Berio, Stockhausen, Nono, Henze. He brought in Anatole Dorati to retrain the BBC Symphony Orchestra, Colin Davis to bring a youthful approach to it and, in 1971, Pierre Boulez, 'the supreme musical thinker of the day', a great, charismatic conductor and composer who 'cleansed the cloth ears of the British public'.[12] Glock was shaping the BBC Symphony Orchestra into a professional and musically accomplished tool for performing the classical and romantic repertoire – but also making them capable of playing technically demanding modern music.

Boulez said 'anyone who has not felt ... the necessity of the dodecaphonic (twelve-tone) language is OF NO USE'. He added that the best solution to the problem of opera would be to blow up the opera houses, and startled the august worthies on the BBC Musical Advisory Board by saying that some contemporary composition amounted to 'frenetic arithmetical masturbation'.[13] Boulez's vision of musical life was the opposite of narrow dogmatism: it was a modernism that evangelically put music in touch with contemporary technologies and sensibilities.

John Berger's BBC series *Ways of Seeing* (1972) had already moved beyond modernism in the visual arts. A subtle set of television essays, it identified

Splintering modernism: Robert Hughes in The Shock of the New, *1980*

women's role as subjects of art and queried the nature of the spectating eye and the role of ownership. Robert Hughes's 1980 series *The Shock of the New* was seen as a riposte to Kenneth Clark's 1969 *Civilisation*. To go from Clark (the director of the National Gallery at a precocious age, an architect of ITV as a public service) to Hughes (one of the Australian generation, including Clive James and Germaine Greer, then taking British culture by storm) was 'rather like following a TV old claret with a foaming Fosters lager'.[14] They shared a passionately informed personal eye and used television to advance arguments. Hughes's identification of the role of 'shock' in art was more prescient than he understood. 'Shock' would be commodified during the eighties and become an exhausted cliché, as some artists pushed at the boundaries of taste in order 'to make an impression rather than as an artistic imperative'.[15] Shock, too, was an answer to the 'after modernism' puzzle.

In the 1970s, the canon was being ripped apart by young radicals. On the one hand, the 'Leavisite' notion of necessary 'authentic and great' works, which dominated British literary thinking, was being extended in ways that would have appalled the Cambridge literary critic, who had been so hostile to the enervating impact of the mass media on culture. Judgements of 'quality' were rolled out onto films, pop music, television, advertising. The BBC was comfortable with this: it usually acted as if it were possible to make discriminating choices between the best of almost any kind of culture. This process itself had produced a new kind of 'television' intellectual (identified by Joan Bakewell and Nicholas Garnham in *The New Priesthood*).[16] Melvyn Bragg was one: having worked for Wheldon's *Monitor*, and edited *The Lively Arts*, he said that television had made it the age of the 'mass-intellectual'. Bragg, an assured cultural judge with a gift for communicating, was the *bête noire* of the BBC governor and poet Roy Fuller: 'They made comparisons between Bragg and Harty and Parkinson. Mr Fuller brought up Johnson on the futility of comparing a louse and a flea.'[17]

Arena, the BBC arts magazine programme, 'a kind of *Panorama* for the arts', was creatively pushed by Alan Yentob, when he arrived 'in a rush of fresh energy and enthusiasm'[18] from a BBC trainee course. With Yentob's agile, aesthetic omnivorousness behind it, *Arena* meant that the Beatles, the Beat Poets, the Ford Cortina and James Bond movies were seen as 'good in themselves', alongside T. S. Eliot, W. B. Yeats and Francis Bacon. There was an energetic sense of extending the range of public understanding (and perhaps in doing so remaking culture as well).

At the same time 'art and culture' were moving away from the 'marginal' place Richard Hoggart had identified for them in a 1974 BBC Radio 4 programme: 'People may enjoy the arts, but at the back of their minds they know it is not "real": real life goes on elsewhere.' By the eighties the arts were becoming a major industry and a large part of everyday life, through the saturation of advertising with high-art images and music.

Government policy created a backcloth to BBC arts coverage. The Wilson government regarded the arts as something to be harnessed in 'purposeful' reform of the national character. This was aligned with a positive approach to modernism. The Labour government launched the Open University of the Air in collaboration with the BBC, whose art history courses on feminism and protest brought the reconceptualisation of the role of the arts into the mainstream. The Conservative government found a new way to conceive funding the arts by unfortunately calling them 'Heritage' and introduced museum charges. It took John Myerscough's seminal report *The Economic Importance of the Arts in Britain*[19] to relegitimise state investment in the arts, by recasting them as a successful industry. Meanwhile, the visual arts became an area of speculative investment which transformed art markets in a destabilising way. 'In the 80s the scale of cultural feeling has become gross, and its aliment coarse,' said Hughes. 'It is the driven consumption and regurgitation of images and reputations as a kind of bulimia: the neurotic cycle of binge and puke.'[20]

In music the issue of who had power in the BBC mattered more than in other areas of arts programming. In 1976, Humphrey Burton was brought back to the BBC to be television head of Arts by Yentob, after a stint at London Weekend Television, where he had edited and presented *Aquarius*, a glamorous and successful arts magazine programme. The idea was to revitalise *Omnibus* as 'an advanced guard for the new'. Burton ranged over the arts, but he was expert musically and thought that television could be a creative vehicle for classical music. He helped produce enthusiasm at all levels, 'from producers up to management',[21] and an increase in the number of music performances and programmes about music on BBC1 and 2. Burton surrounded himself with stimulating people and let them develop their own ideas, leading to a renaissance of innovative programmes.[22] He started the regular Saturday evening performance slot on BBC2, *The Lively Arts – in Performance*.

The BBC masterminded a decade-long battle with manufacturers to improve the quality of sound on television sets, with the Engineering department leading, cajoling and jump-starting the improvement. BBC bureaucrats 'endured and chivvied away at long meetings' to get the improvement that would make televisions fit for music. Colour television was taking over from black and white, cameras were becoming more sophisticated, and producers experimented with what Roy Tipping called the 'creative choreography' of music programmes. International prizes flowed for *All Clouds Are Clocks* (1976), about the composer György Ligeti; *Julian Bream: A Life in the Country*, a profile of the guitarist Julian Bream; David Bedford's *The Song of the White Horse* (1978), commissioned for BBC1; and Barrie Gavin's film about Peter Maxwell Davies in Orkney, *One Foot in Eden* (1979).

The worry was that such visual experiments distracted from the music. When Messiaen's *Turangalia*, conducted by André Previn and shown on BBC2, was discussed by the BBC's musical advisory body Lord Harewood 'adored' the 'wild' visual treatment of the movement 'Joy of the blood of the stars', but Lord Norwich found it got in the way, 'like a buzzing'. John Drummond said it was an experiment which might encourage new viewers but alienate Messiaen enthusiasts.[23] It was a conflict between television as a form in itself and as a medium of reporting. One vocal group was often unhappy: Promenaders complained about television cameras 'getting in the way – prancing about like preying mantis's'[24] in the Albert Hall. Yet the demotic eye of television, by making the Promenaders visible, enhanced the uniquely democratic nature of the Proms.

Audiences all over the world could see that the authority in the concerts lay, not with grand people paying more, but with a generous, cantankerous, opinionated populace, on the floor of the Albert Hall. It was a uniquely British, uniquely brilliant piece of BBC magic. Promenaders were concert-hall equal citizens.

Yet music was not well served in the BBC hierarchy then. A non-news

*Colin Davis conducting the Last Night of the Proms, 1971;
television globalised the Promenaders' unique role*

person would never have been put in charge of news, but music could be used as a route to managerial power. Ian McIntyre had a brilliant, acerbic mind, but in 1978 he was put in charge of Radio 3, which mostly broadcast music, about which he knew little, and remained there until 1987. His real passion lay in managing news and current affairs, and his relations with Ponsonby remained strained. In 1979, Aubrey Singer was made managing director of Radio, but did not love music. By contrast, Brian Wenham, in charge of BBC2, had an amateur but deep love of opera. After a 'state visit' to the Music department in Kensington House, he said, 'What can we put into the topper? Let's have an Opera month.' They did. Wenham summed up a discussion, 'Let's have some lovely upstairs downstairs in Valhalla,' and commissioned the Ring.[25] Alan Yentob knew that music was not his forte, but he immediately brought Burton back into the BBC, and this recognition was 'typical of Yentob at his enabling best'.

THE BATTLE FOR AUDIENCE TASTE

How was the BBC to build audience tastes? Glock's strategy had been to mix modern and earlier music. It did not always work: in 1985 Tony Burton produced the series *Mozart and ...* devoted to the six Mozart piano trios, alongside music by six twentieth-century composers. The Listening Panel complained that the contrast made the twentieth-century composers 'sound worse than usual',[26]

Alan Yentob with Arthur Miller for Arena, *the programme that made cultural icons popular and popular things cultural icons*

later observing that Harrison Birtwistle's *The Mask of Orpheus* 'makes Schoenberg sound civilised'.[27] But then they were not taken very seriously, as they were wrong.

Ponsonby said that he believed he had been appointed to be controller of Music partly as a 'corrective' to Glock, but he was to prove something as important: a consolidator.[28] He had had no broadcasting experience, but had run both the Edinburgh Festival and the Scottish National Orchestra, and had learnt to put concert programmes together there. Kenyon said 'Glock's programmes are recognised as iconic. Ponsonby's worthy – but duller.' The BBC tried to diversify audience growth: free 'College Concerts' in London music schools introduced twentieth-century music to new audiences (and tested new pieces). The BBC Symphony Orchestra and the London Sinfonietta played twentieth-century classics such as *Pierrot Lunaire*, as well as entirely new works, all presented 'very sensitively for young people' by the musicologist Arnold Whittall.[29] Hans Keller declared that 'radio's responsibility towards the living composer is the top priority of music broadcasting',[30] but only *Music in Our Time* (which Keller hated for putting modern music in a ghetto) was devoted entirely to contemporary music.

In 1984, Radio 3 devoted 10 per cent of its time to music by living composers, half of them British.[31] A 1980 edition of *Music in Our Time*, 'More stirrings of the sleeping giant', was devoted to computer music, and several concerts used the BBC's Radiophonic Workshop. This was, said Hogwood, 'a hotbed of things and ideas' developing cross-disciplinary experiments 'quite naturally'. David Cain worked with the workshop on the prize-winning scores for *The Hobbit*, which was serialised on Radio 4. The overall commitment to new music was vital: while the BBC Symphony Orchestra regularly played new British orchestral music, it was almost never performed by non-BBC orchestras because it was difficult to play, needed more rehearsal time and consequently was too expensive. This helped to justify the BBC's continued expenditure on its orchestras.

Ponsonby, Keller and later Stephen Plaistow, who became chief producer of Contemporary Music in 1979, were committed to performing works by British composers. In 1975, thirteen editions of *Music in Our Time* were devoted exclusively to British works, while in *The Voices of Today* British choral music was introduced by the composers, including John McCabe and Peter Dickinson. Plaistow felt it was important to reflect what was being written, even if it meant broadcasting works that were 'undistinguished, ephemeral, or even boring' – a somewhat radical interpretation of public service responsibility.[32] But he also had the rather more populist idea that the series should be retitled *Tomorrow's World of Music* (after the geeky and very popular television programme on inventions). Wisely, this was rejected.[33]

'No Bartok before breakfast' was an old Radio 3 saw. Nevertheless, what now looks like an impressive achievement in developing contemporary music was under continuous attack: Glock and then Ponsonby were both called to give evidence to Parliament, where MPs worried that they were ignoring musical heritage (code for being too modern). Aubrey Singer, ever waspishly goading on the inside, said that contemporary music should not be played during the day, and then defined it as widely as he could as music written in the previous fifteen years.[34] When Christine Hardwick, newly created head of the Music department, reported in 1984 that *This Week's Composer* was featuring a broader range of contemporary composers, such as Hans Werner Henze and Lutosławski, McIntyre said they might risk losing 'every last listener' if they played too much contemporary music.[35] Later, Hardwick seemed to have capitulated to the BBC philistines: 'We strive to keep the daytime free of contemporary music, so that it can provide a stream of pleasant listening for those who use it all day or dip in for a spot of classical music.'[36]

Throughout the period there was also the threat of commercial classical music. Between 1973 and the late 1980s, independent local radio stations had to make public service programmes in order to secure their licences to broadcast in a regulated system. When commercial local radio was set up in the early 1970s, the Musicians' Union had negotiated an obligation on the new advertising-funded stations to spend 3 per cent of their revenue on live music. So several had started their own classical orchestras, including Capital Radio's distinguished Wren Orchestra in London. Regulation worked. It improved

competition for programmes and quality. Just as their news offer on Independent Radio News challenged the BBC in a serious attempt to get the best news,
so the commercial network of local stations broadcast classical music (and
original drama and arts) that was an *extension* of BBC arts and music policy. By
1979, Capital Radio was attracting over 350,000 listeners a week to its well-made
classical music programmes. A BBC report in January 1981 identified a growing
cohort of listeners to serious music radio programmes other than Radio 3.
Nevertheless, commercial local radio was suspicious of the idea of a national
commercial network. (Classic FM emerged only later in the 1990s from Independent Local Radio.) Singer, concerned about how the commercial regulator,
the IBA, was thinking, employed its head of Radio Programming, Michael
Starks, to work with him.

The idea of a commercial station, committed to playing the bits of
music people already liked, posed a continual threat. Singer thought the new
commercial stations would attract audiences three times the size of Radio
3's market share of 2 per cent, challenging the continued existence of Radio
3. The BBC station needed to shake off its 'academic' image to reach new
and younger listeners.[37] 'An immense amount of time is spent in explaining,
expounding and preaching musicology every day.'[38] Walter Goehr urged that
listening should be enjoyable: 'if listeners get enjoyment and pleasure from
Radio 3 ... Then the audience will naturally increase'.[39]

Singer proposed that it should broadcast 'an easier' stream of classical
music on the lines of the American classical music stations.[40] Ponsonby, already
in constant guerrilla battles with Singer, replied that the BBC should strengthen
the 'innate' character of its own programmes rather than aping commercial
radio,[41] and he (wrongly) resisted simultaneous radio and television broadcasts. Later, in a 1986 paper 'The accessibility of Radio 3', McIntyre reported
that Radio 3 had 'lightened the musical mix', including Duke Ellington as 'This
week's composer'. But when John Drummond and Alan Yentob reported on
music and arts to the Board of Governors in 1987, they said that although the
output of serious music on Radio 3 continued to be large – over five thousand
hours of music – audiences remained too small.[42]

YOUNG MUSIC

The experience of television showed that ingenious programming combined
with adventurous scheduling could reap large audiences for classical music.
The Corporation's unique purposes and obligations to musical life were
embodied in the *Young Musician of the Year* competition. Audiences liked
competitions.[43] The BBC regularly broadcast the Leeds International Piano
Competition, showing the final live on BBC2. In 1975, Humphrey Burton had
been worried by the lack of any British players good enough to get into the

Humphrey Burton with Emma Johnson, winner of
Young Musician of the Year *in 1984*

final. He decided to try to use the focusing excitement of television to improve the performing basis in the country as well as to make a hit programme. The aim was to show viewers the pleasure serious music can give to performers, demonstrate the high standards of young musicians in the UK, and add a kind of thrill and lustre to playing for young people. The BBC sailed out to enthuse new young players, but during the 1980s the government removed support for music lessons in schools, destroyed the financial basis for them acquiring instruments, and demoted music in the curriculum. Classical music was ghettoised.

Ponsonby was dismissive: 'A Young Musician of the Year Competition sounds ill-focused and unlikely to produce results of the quality we spend most of our time trying to achieve ... Your competition seems to me to be viable in television terms, but dubious in radio terms.'[44] Humphrey Burton,

Roy Tipping and Walter Todds adventurously took the idea straight to Bryan Cowgill, controller of BBC1, who called it the most exciting idea put forward that year. It started as a seventeen-programme series with Burton presenting in a prime-time slot – after children's programmes and before the *Six O'Clock News*. From the start it attracted large audiences. The concerto final had an audience of over 6 million, while the *Last Night of the Proms* reached 12 million.[45] In 1982, it attracted larger audiences than *Nationwide*, which preceded it. It involved a different generation in classical music – although it was a television phenomenon as much as a musical one. Unlike open-access shows a generation later, the winners were chosen not because they were freakishly young or appealing but entirely on 'musicality and technical mastery'.

Young Musician of the Year had its critics.[46] In the 1980s, sections of the musical teaching establishment (ideologically at odds with the government) warned that competitions had a bad effect on young performers. The European String Teachers Association (ESTA) produced a report in 1984 criticising the programme for making performance into a 'gladiatorial sport'. It complained that the BBC was more concerned with its ratings: 'it is tragic that such a degrading musical equivalent of the "Miss World" contest should be the brain-child of the BBC'. The governors fretted, but the BBC's own body of the musical great and good, the Central Musical Committee, supported the programme and praised the care with which the BBC mounted the event.[47] Held every two years, with regional heats and the semi-finals and finals televised in Manchester, it filled seventeen early evening slots for the two weeks preceding the finals. Some objected to the fact that the competitors were 'amateurs', even though many of them went on to professional careers. In 1986, Yentob suggested greater radio involvement in the heats. Finally, when Michael Grade, director of programmes, Television, moved the competition to BBC2 in 1986, the audience shrank. Janet Street-Porter, perhaps revealing more about herself than the music, when she was made head of Youth Entertainment in 1987, said that it 'did not connect with *real* young people'.[48]

DANCE AND EARLY MUSIC

Dance programmes also attracted large audiences, but were expensive. The ballet budget had been cut in the late sixties, ending studio-made ballet programmes. Burton's desire to bring ballet back to television failed for lack of money,[49] and there were only two studio ballet performances in the late 1970s: a production of *Les Noces* with the Royal Ballet in 1978, *Pierrot Lunaire* with Ballet Rambert in 1979. Other dance programmes included the Stuttgart Ballet's *Eugene Onegin* in 1976, and an evening with the Kirov Ballet in 1979. 'Remarkable' ratings were won by *The Magic of the Dance*, a series on the history of dance presented by Margot Fonteyn, an iconic post-war British ballet star. 'Dance Month' on BBC2 in 1978 and 1980 was successful; and *Leda and the Swan*, a film made and choreographed by the dancer Lynn Seymour, commissioned for BBC2 and directed by Bob Lockyer, became a classic.

When Burton retired as television's head of Music and Arts in 1981 for personal reasons he wrote a few 'Thoughts for Chairman Wenham'. He said that, while the BBC hosted the best opera and dance in the world, it did little to create works for television, and needed to commission new work.[50] When Yentob took over, one of his first successes was Geoffrey Burgon's *A Mass for Man*, the first major dance commission for ten years, choreographed by Robert Cohan and shown on BBC2 in 1986.[51]

Another important response to what would happen *after* modernism was, perhaps surprisingly, early music. 'Leaner, crisper sounds were sweeping musical taste … there was a roundhead, puritanical mood about,'[52] said Kenyon. Players concerned with experimenting with the new found overlaps with the experimental investigations of the old. The BBC Third Programme had stimulated interest in early music in the 1950s. Denis Stevens, Anthony Lewis and Basil Lam had introduced listeners to composers like Dufay, Machaut and Tallis. By 1974 the chief producer of music programmes, Leo Black, worried that there had been a decline in programmes of pre-classical music just when the new ensembles founded by Hogwood, Trevor Pinnock and others were taking off.[53] Ponsonby replied, 'I am rather concerned that we are not adequately reflecting the public's rapidly growing interest in early music', observing that 'popular' composers were now earlier than Monteverdi: 'we can now count upon Byrd, Palestrina, Lassus, Josquin, and even Dufay … For all I know, Guillaume de Machaut is already popular.' The decision was made to substantially increase the playing of music from 1400 to 1600.[54] In 1976, *The Play of Daniel*, a twelfth-century musical drama, was performed at the Proms, while in 1979 Radio 3 broadcast the *Florentine Intermedii for a Medici Wedding*, in collaboration with the European Broadcasting Union.

The repertoire was one thing. But the really revolutionary innovation of the 1970s was the focus on authentic performance and period instruments. Britain had not led the 'early' music revolution, but one component, the countertenor voice, had survived in British cathedral choral music rather better than in Europe. Alfred Deller revived it as a vehicle for accurate performances of medieval, Renaissance and Baroque music. His 1946 BBC broadcast of Purcell's *Come, Ye Sons of Art Away* was an instant success and brought the voice to a wider audience. In 1960, he sang the role of Oberon in the premiere of Britten's *A Midsummer Night's Dream*, the first countertenor role in opera of the twentieth century, which was broadcast on the BBC shortly afterwards. Another British advantage was that viol playing 'was alive and kicking',[55] especially among women and amateur groups.

The definition of 'authenticity' led to many semantic and musical arguments, with a fierce undertow of righteous superiority. The musicologist Joseph Kerman said in 1985 that 'authentic' had as a term acquired 'the same cult value when applied to music as "natural" or "organic" when applied to food'.[56] Roger Donington argued that the hunt for the 'pure' approximation of the past was impossible. 'No music other than electronic can be performed without a blend of personalities between the composer and the performer.'[57] Michael Tippett said, 'There can be no absolute historical authenticity ... only a continuum from inadvertent modernisms to more scrupulous.'[58]

Early music presented a challenge because, as it had not been performed for centuries, there was no living tradition to learn from. Nor were the instruments easy to tune. Initially, the venerable tribe of BBC producers were an impediment to the movement: they regarded audibility and perfection of sound as a 'sacrosanct aspect of public service'. A BBC memo complained that 'one sometimes gets the idea that the instruments are more important than the players or indeed the music: in any case in what sense is a "reproduction" instrument any more "authentic" than another, also new, but traditional one?'[59] The 'amateurish sound and lack of reliable pitch' meant that there was institutional resistance to new performances of 'old' music. There was a 'traditional professional idea of accuracy, sonority and balance', Kenyon argued, that was challenged by the novel sounds of period instruments.

But Hugh Keyte, a BBC producer and early music enthusiast, persevered and put period instrument performances on the BBC. The liveliest and most influential of the early music presenters was David Munrow,[60] who energetically wrote and presented the *Pied Piper* series for children. In 1974, his Early Music Consort, performing works by Dufay, shared a Prom with the contemporary music ensemble, The Fires of London, and his series *Music of the Courts of Europe* came out 'full of gems'. Hogwood presented his own programme, *The Young Idea*. Radio 3 started *The Early Music Forum*, the first weekly programme devoted to early music, presented by Kenyon and others, which helped audiences to acquire a taste for pre-classical music. Just as CDs emerged, 'authentic musical performances' offered the record companies new ways of repackaging the entire repertoire for the new format. But audiences needed to see musicians enjoying themselves playing the music and the Proms performances of Handel's *Water Music* and *Messiah* in 1979 and 1980 'transformed' early music, said Hogwood, from an austere idea into 'something everybody could see was tremendous fun'.

The vigilant pursuit of high performance standards by high-minded BBC producers helped to make the early music movement 'a long term success'. BBC sound engineers were 'absolutely vital', making sensitive adjustments to equipment for recording and in performance to cater for the novel range of sound. The BBC also provided – just as it had with modern music – the vital ingredient of skilled musicality: rehearsal time.[61]

ORCHESTRAS

There was another, more intractable problem looming for the Corporation. By 1980 the problem of what 'to do' about the BBC's own orchestras had a long and embarrassing history. How many orchestras could the BBC support in a period of financial stringency? There was one view that some orchestras were playing the 'wrong' kind of 'light' music that was increasingly obsolete, another that so-called 'regional' orchestras were a sham. 'We did a survey,' said Aubrey Singer. 'Half of the players in Scotland just bussed in to play. They didn't create local musical culture as everybody said; they were Scottish on Tuesdays but Midlands on Wednesdays!'[62] But perhaps he would say that: Singer already had difficult relations with the Music department and was about to embark on a bloody confrontation with musicians.

Gerard Mansell's report 'Broadcasting in the seventies' (1969) had suggested reducing the number of orchestras from eleven to five, transferring the funding of Scottish and Welsh orchestras to the local arts council, increasing the use of recorded music (needle time) in place of live performances, and reducing the complex arrangements for paying fees.[63] In 1970, a well-judged Musicians' Union campaign, directed at a music-loving prime minister, led the Heath government to promise that the BBC would keep all its orchestras, supported by an increase in the licence fee. But the orchestras cost far more than the increase brought in.

In 1976, Howard Newby, managing director of Radio, prodded at the problem again. That year the Arts Council had a budget of £27 million, but the BBC spent £35 million on the arts (including Light Entertainment). For the BBC this was not 'patronage'. It was not done for 'art' or for the 'glory of the BBC', nor was it 'academic or narrowly professional'. It was always focused on what the 'public will want tomorrow'. Free of the tyranny of the box office, the BBC sought to produce 'a kind of energy field connecting audiences and creators in a two way system'. But by 1976 the BBC's eleven orchestras cost two-thirds of the radio music budget, and together with dance bands and light orchestras employed 1,500 players, more than 30 per cent of all the professional musicians in the country. Although the BBC operated as a necessary 'stabilising influence from the weather in which orchestral musicians live', Newby said that the number of players was far larger than broadcasting required. The 1977 Annan Report on the 'Future of Broadcasting' recommended cuts in the BBC's funding of music, and suggested the disbanding of the light orchestras.[64] Nothing much happened.

When Singer was appointed managing director of Radio in 1979, he decided to do something about the orchestras and needle time.[65] For Giles Oakley, a junior employee, Singer exemplified something 'terribly wrong' with the Corporation at the time, as he 'stuffed cigars after a BBC event into his pocket'.[66] John Drummond, a large, flamboyant character who was later a colourful head of BBC Arts, described Singer as a 'Bunterish figure, almost circular in shape, much given to whistling and jingling coins in his pockets'.[67] But Singer set about reinvigorating radio and wanted to end the restrictive agreements around musical performance: 'It was as if an actor, having done *Henry IV Part 2* at Stratford, wasn't allowed to perform that part at another theatre for another company.' Singer went about the task in a typically aggressive way, with 'a lot of sabre rattling'.[68]

On a trip to China, he got Trethowan and Checkland's agreement to a coup: and in March 1980 he announced dramatic orchestral cuts.[69] 'I carefully arranged to spring it on Hardwicke and Warburton,' he said gleefully of the two directors of Live and Gramophone music, and did not tell Ponsonby, the man in overall charge of the orchestras, until the day before the announcement. One hundred and seventy-two musicians were to lose their jobs outright and five orchestras, including the BBC Light Music Orchestra, would be disbanded.

John Morton, leader of the Musicians' Union, was a shrewd, funny man. He got on well with many BBC people, although there was real animosity between him and Singer. He believed he could win the political and public opinion battle. The BBC faced a more adroit campaign than they had anticipated. Singer would later call it 'the most traumatic time of my life'.[70] The BBC rightly worried that the emerging conflict 'looked like a personal duel'.[71] Just as the Conservative government stockpiled coal before confronting the miners, Singer had stockpiled music programmes: 'We had 4–500 hours in the can ... they saved us.'

Morton pointed out that it was hard to portray musicians 'as thuggish trade unionists when the pickets might be old ladies with violins'.[72] He thought the Union could win despite having no money to pay strikers. The union outwitted the BBC at every turn. Strikers held concerts, gave talks and 'play ins'. They picketed the Corporation, and Broadcasting House ran out of central heating oil when carriers refused to cross the picket line. At a mass meeting, the guitarist John Williams gave a charismatic speech saying they were defending musical life in the country. Conductors lined up behind the strike, a *Times* leader lambasted the Corporation for 'cultural vandalism'.[73] Malcolm Williamson, Master of the Queen's Music, wrote a letter accusing the BBC of abandoning the nation's heritage.[74]

In order to make the cuts look philistine, the BBC in Scotland cunningly offered up their Symphony Orchestra instead of the Light Orchestra that Singer had wanted to cut. 'It was all bloody politics,' said Singer, 'they were fooling.' Supporters of the strike sported badges saying 'Keep Music Live'. Singer's retaliatory badges were in a somewhat different register: 'Fuck Mother Hibbert [a leader of the Musicians' Union], Keep Music Recorded'.[75] The BBC was called into a special meeting with MPs, who, in an extraordinary off-the-record session, suggested that the Corporation pay for the orchestras by either ditching local radio or by taking advertising on Radio 1.[76] Ian Trethowan was hauled into one of the then new Select Committees to explain why the BBC was destroying the nation's musical life. It made a change, he said, from being 'beaten up' for wasting the nation's money.

Ponsonby found the strike anguishing: 'It was a terrible time, many of my friends were on the picket line,' and he joined them. He was dissuaded from resigning only by Glock, who said that he had to stay to preserve music, and Colin Davis, the conductor, who told him, 'your quiet professionalism will save the BBC'.[77] Ponsonby thought Singer was 'a bully to his juniors and toady to seniors'. Singer thought Ponsonby was a 'fuddy duddy'.

As the strike ground on, it dawned on everyone that the Proms were under threat. Morton said, with some satisfaction, that the BBC were blamed for this, not the unions. 'The way to the Albert Hall was past the negotiating table. The BBC was sitting at that table and the Musicians' Union was not,' Trethowan said at a Board of Management meeting. The BBC knew that the political case was slipping away. Twenty Proms concerts were lost as the union put on an alternative Proms season, including a First Night. Colin Davis phoned Singer and said he wanted nothing to do with the politics of the events. 'So why the hell are you conducting an alternative Prom then?' exploded Singer.

Then the BBC chairman's wife, Tess Swann, a professional viola player and prize-winning organist, intervened (as wives must) behind the scenes. Mrs Swann was a musical insider, sat on musical committees, and had shrewd political judgement. She had calmed Swann down when he was vice-chancellor in Edinburgh and riotous students led by the future prime minister, Gordon Brown, had 'caused perpetual confrontation'. Again she steadied a difficult situation. The BBC, she said, had 'mishandled' the whole affair. Making enemies of the musical establishment was ridiculous. Propelled by his wife, Swann swooped in and proposed that the situation be settled by outside negotiation.[78] Lord Goodman the 'fixer' was appointed, which caused BBC 'faces to drop', according to Morton, because 'The Blessed Goodman' was sympathetic to the orchestras.

Ponsonby said that Singer got things wrong because he had excluded everyone from the Music department from the negotiating team. The BBC Light Orchestra in Scotland was disbanded. By now the Symphony Orchestra had lost nearly 40 per cent of its players, as they thought it was to be axed, and 'the wrong players had left'. The academy training young musicians in Bristol was closed. The BBC was left with five symphony orchestras, employing a third of the salaried orchestral players in the country. The arts councils in Wales and Scotland and Northern Ireland were persuaded to increase their subvention and the BBC got a better deal on needle time and some movement on playing the music it had recorded.

PONSONBY, DRUMMOND AND THE PROMS

The brilliant young conductor Simon Rattle was appointed to the Scottish Orchestra and brought them triumphantly to the following year's Proms with *The Rite of Spring* – a piece that required a huge orchestra. So, said Morton, everybody who had lost their job got it back for a night. Checkland said afterwards that Singer had done what people had known had to be done for a decade, 'but only Aubrey had the guts to do it'.[79] Many thought he took revenge as well, when he amalgamated live and recorded music, leaving Ponsonby with the Proms but not Radio 3. The reorganisation would have made more sense if the positions of controller of Radio 3 and controller of Music had been amalgamated under a musician, as music made up most of the output of Radio 3. But this was not to happen until later. John Drummond, in his 1985 report 'Music and the BBC', said a new creative leap was needed in radio music and that the role of controller of Music had been reduced to little more than that of a concert promoter: Singer's 'last stab in the back to radio music before he left for television'.[80]

Ponsonby's greatest achievement was to secure audiences and prestige for the Proms, which he steadied after the terrible wound of the strike. They had become exciting under Glock. But Ponsonby, who understood live concerts, included more popular composers and raised the budget for Proms commissions sixfold. Those commissioned were often British, and a good mix of established and young composers. The works ranged from the avant-garde to the conventional, from Oliver Knussen's Third Symphony (1979) to Giles Swayne's *Cry* (1980).[81] Ponsonby approached composers sensitively to discover what they wanted to write.[82] He crafted a 'loose' theme for each year while keeping a 'beady eye on including what the public needs as well'. The 1976 American Bicentennial year was marked with works by American composers and in 1979 the theme was northern Europe. In 1985 there was a memorable late night electro-acoustic concert. Ponsonby began to include world music with a gamelan orchestra from Java and an all-night programme of Indian music. This was taking the Proms out to the world in a careful, intelligent and popular way. New audiences met new kinds of music. Ponsonby secured the Proms as a national institution, a civic festival and a front-ranking international event with 'distinctive programming and world class playing',[83] commanding world audiences and respect. The Proms became part of the BBC's sense of its own identity.

John Drummond was appointed controller of Music in 1984. He claimed that he accepted the director-general's offer only on condition that he also take over Radio 3, but he had to struggle for this.[84] Drummond said Radio 3 must become a lively network rather than the 'expensive, exclusive invalid' it had become.[85] Drummond had a deep musical education and was an object of suspicion to music producers. But what he did have was an eye for publicity and a persona that built on Ponsonby's quieter professionalism. Soon the whole of the *Last Night of the Proms* was televised, with the first half on BBC2 watched by over 2 million in 1985, and the second half on BBC1, with an audience of nearly 8 million.

BBC arts had faced a challenge from Channel 4 in 1982. Michael Kustow, the commissioning editor at Channel 4, funded productions with the aim of art television, not just the arts *on television*.[86] Talented producers, such as Barrie Gavin and Herbert Chappell, left the BBC to make programmes for independent television companies, while Brian Large went to the Metropolitan Opera in New York. Drummond and Yentob increased the simultaneous broadcasts on BBC2 and Radio 3, such as *The Music Room*, a new series of Sunday afternoon chamber music concerts. In 1987, Yentob assured the Board of Governors that with the help of Humphrey Burton and Dennis Marks he had aimed 'both to reflect and to participate in the broad range of musical life'.

The larger idea of what would follow modernism was never directly addressed. The BBC as an institution was British in intellectual temperament – empirical, and driven by the proper compulsion to lucidity, simplicity, clarity in the name of audiences. But it consequently often failed to confront large ideas. If there was to be reform and movement, what idea would it follow? The major challenge of the next decade was to be the struggle against a commercially enhanced populism, the apparently irresistible rise of audience measurement as the only (and consequently ruinous) way of assessing achievement, followed by managerial puritanism. What came 'after' modernism was the victory of market-led ideas. So the BBC's vision of cultural citizenship – in the Proms, BBC music and the arts more widely – became even more precious.

5

ATTENBOROUGH: THE PUBLIC SERVICE ANIMAL

VOLCANOES RUMBLE, LAVA SPEWS, lakes of molten rock heave and belch, clouds of smoke and steam billow satanically – and then cinders crunching under an approaching foot herald an arrival. Precariously high on the edge of a rim of a sinisterly busy crater – but also at the very beginning of life itself, because it all started from just such eruptions – someone is coming. David Attenborough appears: in slacks. Part a blond god, part a smut-covered witness, hair plastered with sweat, with a hole in the elbow of his jumper in an especially British tradition of masculine carelessness, part modern scientist with explanation at his fingertips. But most of all a Prospero, whose magic will permit us to gasp in wonder and apprehend the hidden order in the origins of everything. Focused on the huge phenomenon that seethes behind him, the story of *Life on Earth* begins.

In the first episode of the series, Attenborough sets a proportionate human measure – something like that of Michelangelo's golden mean – against which the almost incomprehensible vastness of evolutionary time is put into perspective. Mankind is simultaneously dwarfed – merely what Steve Jones the geneticist called 'froth on the top of the life of bacteria' – and the seeing eye of the camera and reflecting author of the narrative that begins to drive the programme. Attenborough created in the public mind an understanding of the fabulous elegance of the most humble and insentient beings, and the interconnectedness of everything in the great chain of being: yet he did it through a direct relationship with his own physical and mental attributes. In programme after programme, Attenborough will be used to provide audiences with a measure to judge size by: set against the infinitesimally tiny life of protozoa and single-celled creatures perceptible only through microscopes; used in close-up to give an intimate understanding of the size of crabs; to show how a playful troupe of young gorillas respond to a human; but also used to demonstrate the insignificantly small scale of the human person – and perhaps metaphorically the enterprise of humanity – as he strides alone across a distant valley against a background of mountain peaks, filmed from a great height from a wheeling plane.

Life on Earth was a more revolutionary set of television programmes than anyone had dreamt when they began years of work on it. Except Attenborough. The originality of the revolution was simple: that television could be used to make a coherent intellectual argument over the thirteen hours of a series. The coherence remade everything in the production. This grand idea was embodied in sentences 'that no one had ever written before in wildlife television'.[1] The writing was driven by the needs of the argument and its supporting evidence determined by logic, not by what anybody thought was practical. The sentences swooped all over the world to explain, for example, the jigsaw of findings that put in place the history of single-celled life. Attenborough's first script was thus revolutionary in its idealism: it simply described what Attenborough would like to see; he wrote as if nothing was impossible. No one had yet filmed 'the platypus with an egg in a burrow' or the 'yucca moth pollinating a yucca', let alone the 'coelacanth swimming'; indeed, very few of these recently discovered 'living fossils' had been found, and by the time scientists had got their hands on them they were not merely dead but pickled as well. The script sent the production team off after these revelations, and as the project developed they added 'more daydreams' of their own.[2]

Some in the BBC said that the idea was too academic for the public to grasp, others that the pan-continental shots would fail to make visual sense. Richard Brock, a director of the series who had worked with Attenborough often before, observed, 'People said you can't do it, you can't walk out of a savannah in Africa and into a savannah in North America, audiences will be confused.' Yet the audience followed Attenborough's argument, 'because it was so clearly written'.[3]

Life on Earth was Attenborough's essay on Darwin. Just as reading Darwin had transformed the narrative imagination of nineteenth-century writers and the public, so Attenborough instinctively thought that television providing a way of 'seeing' Darwin's ideas in action would create a leap in public understanding. Despite the difficulty Darwin had in finding words to express the startling ideas of evolutionary theory, scientists in the nineteenth century still shared a common language and literary references with the rest of the educated public – what they wrote could be understood without any specialized knowledge. This was no longer the case by the 1970s. Scientists were far more specialised, and the 'public' a larger, less coherent, more democratic group. Yet, conceivably, the 'ordinarily educated reader' that Darwin had in mind to communicate with could be replaced by the late twentieth century by that of the 'ordinary educated viewer'. 'Seeing' was what the public was developing new skills at – reading the visual grammar of programmes.

Wildlife films had previously either said 'these are interesting animals or this is an interesting place'.[4] *Life on Earth* did something novel: relentlessly unpacking both the history of evolution over time, so that starting at the beginning it moves through the development of life, but also illustrating the science that explains evolutionary processes. In 1973, as people began to assemble the ideas that would eventually turn into *Life on Earth*, the importance of studying animal behaviour was in the air. That year a Nobel prize had gone to Karl von Frisch for discovering the dance language of bees, to Konrad Lorenz for his work on geese and imprinting (which helped overcome the stigma of his association with National Socialism) and to Nikolas Tinbergen (who had spent several years in a Nazi work camp) for his work on gulls' adaptations to their habitats. The journal *Nature* told the scientific community that these awards marked the recognition of the emergence of 'animal behaviour from one of the less respectable corners of natural history to the forefront of the biological sciences'.[5] Indeed, *Nature* asserted that a new discipline – ethology, the biological study of behaviour – had finally been recognised. Filming animal behaviour accurately was a vital contribution to this new science.

The radical initial idea produced a whirlwind of innovation. It cost more, impelled a new form of organisation to get made, forced technological and aesthetic breakthroughs, was screened for longer, became a great landmark of the maturity of television, and was the highest form of public service broadcasting ideal: it did inform, entertain and educate. It became a phenomenon that broke all the expectations and rules of wildlife films. All of the subsequent great series from *Planet Earth* right through the Attenborough blockbusters of the 1990s and into the new millennium were in many ways developed aspects of arguments from the original programme. Mike Salisbury, who worked with Attenborough as a junior researcher on the series, observed, 'It was the whole sweep of the thing that changed everything. It was transformative working on it. David imagined it but I don't think even he realised how big a thing it would be.'[6] It led the world; it made the BBC Wildlife Unit in Bristol; people loved it; it made Attenborough a hero to the British public at home and an icon of Britishness all over the world.

It was successful because the story was so compelling and the mastery of television as a story-bearing medium so complete. Attenborough was working from a perfectly constructed narrative. Darwin recalled in his autobiography how, as a child, he had been 'a very great story teller – I scarcely ever went out without saying I had seen pheasant or a strange bird; these lies', he observed, 'gave a pleasure like tragedy'.[7] His capacity to put together the great plot of evolution was informed by his profound grasp of what a story might be, as well as his passionate empiricism. Attenborough was versed in every skill needed to use the capacities of television to enhance a narrative. Just as Darwin's theory of evolution was in the end a powerful overarching explanation, Attenborough, for the first time in broadcasting, would unpack the theory steadily over the series so that each programme built on those before it and there was a dramatic arc to the series as a whole.

Yet there is a puzzle. Why, in 1979, did the British public find such an alarming story of destruction of the weakest and the inexorable survival of the fittest so enthralling? The relentless cost of failures to adapt, as species after species become extinct, was displayed to an audience experiencing a dismaying sense of decline in their national lives. Britain had become 'the sick man of Europe'. During 1979, as the nation seemed to spin farther towards the improprieties of the Winter of Discontent, and a sense of ungovernable chaos threatening, the nation sat down with thrilled anticipation to watch the great, orderly, brutal story of the survival of the fittest. At a time when decline into the condition of a Third World state was commonly discussed, Attenborough inadvertently and yet boldly addressed a dread that was gripping Britain.

Thus on the BBC, a true television intellectual with a lifelong dedication to wildlife offered the British public a magnificent and moral education. The British interest in animals and wildlife has often been a sentimental and self-serving one. Yet throughout the twentieth century the world's first industri-alised society defined itself through its countryside and interest in wildlife. Attenborough wrote in an introduction to a book by Chris Parsons, 'The British are famous – perhaps even notorious – for their devotion to wildlife … The passion for the natural world, which can so easily become an obsession, is still widespread through British society. It leads the richest and the poorest, the humblest and the noblest, to stand for hours up to their waists in chill salt marshes watching wildfowl …'[8] *Life on Earth* was an attempt to direct this romantic engagement into a better-informed responsibility for the natural world. No one ever wrote it down quite like that, but it gave the making of the series urgency.

Part of the charm was the way Attenborough physically engaged with the subjects. Attenborough would clamber, be lowered, march through bat guano, happily throw himself flat on his face with little regard for mud or discomfort. But the public service ethic is what makes this selfless – and it is this which paradoxically makes the presenter so grand. While he took any physical risk necessary, 'he only did it for the story to get the pictures to make the point – it was never to show his endurance or his daring – it was only if it made the story better', a director on the series, Mike Salisbury commented.[9] Clive James, in a sprightly appreciation of the series, enquired, 'Where was Attenborough when I was a lad?' and replied, 'being a lad too … the difference between us is that he still is. Fresh faced and paunchless, Attenborough looks groovy in a wetsuit.'

THE NATURAL HISTORY OF ATTENBOROUGH

Life on Earth made Attenborough into more than a household name – it made him an embodiment of national character, a model of reliable virtue, and thirty years later the British public trusted him implicitly. It changed how people conceived of themselves in the natural world. It could not have happened without the exploration of deeply held public service ideals, and a fierce eye for opportunity. It is also a product of the personality that he brought to the programmes. His disarming modesty (a quality of great power, and especially valued in Britain) is combined with professional command and a ruthless creativity. Patrick Bateson, the distinguished Cambridge biologist and Master of King's College, said, 'He is just an extraordinarily brilliant intelligence with a very distinct vision of purpose.'[10] Aubrey Singer, another BBC baron who had developed science programmes such as *Horizon*, said, 'Under the boyish exterior there's a mind of steel that never stops calculating. I liked David but I was always in a way frightened of him. He hoped he'd get his way with charm, but by God if he didn't get it that way, he'd get it the other way.'[11] All of this smelted through a life of doing, showing, leading and thinking in the BBC. Attenborough was the product of the deeper history of public service ethics in the BBC, his programmes always the product of team intelligence, and it all came from a passionate dedication to nature. How did David Attenborough happen?

He was born the middle son of three boys, into a socially liberal and politically progressive home. It was a unique and distinct habitat – a mid-twentieth-century combination of high-octane principle, earnestness and evangelical belief in the absolute primacy of public service. Less usual in the public service classes was the desire to be centre stage and the gift to communicate – which he shared with his brother Richard, the actor, film director and producer. Warm and demanding, his immediate home life was securely middle-middle-class. But it was a self-made family whose remarkable journey of social mobility provided its offspring with a vision that saw no impediment ahead. An energising sense of limitless possibility and the lofty compulsion of duty produced vaulting ambition.

Had Frederick Levi Attenborough, David's father, been born a generation earlier he might have remained where he started – indeed, he had been born only miles away from the village from which the family took their name. Frederick's luck was that after the 1887 Education Act had made education compulsory, he had been able to progress, first at a school which offered free secondary places, then as 'pupil teacher', then at local teacher training college. After teaching in Wales and Liverpool, he won a rare scholarship as a mature student to Emmanuel College, Cambridge. He then became first a university lecturer and then the principal of Leicester College of Higher Education. He spent the rest of his life steering it towards full university status, eventually becoming the vice-chancellor. Attenborough's mother Mary was a witty, generous woman. Richard wrote, 'if "The Governor" was the studious visionary, beavering away behind the closed doors of the study, my mother was the doer'.[12] She was, he said, 'the most tactile, energetic and outspoken woman I have ever encountered'. As with David, no one ever saw her idle. Mary Attenborough had been a crusading suffragette, an opponent of Franco, a founding member of the Marriage Guidance Council, an early member of the Labour Party, a JP and a chair of local arts organisations.

The sons grew up in a puritanical household, but not a grim one – there was a lot of laughter, and Frederick would endearingly swot up on their interests. When Richard said that he wanted to be an actor, a tottering pile of books about the theatre appeared on the hall table. One germ of the idea for *Life on Earth* came directly from David's childhood. He recalled how as a small boy he looked forward with keen anticipation to the arrival in the post of his weekly part of H. G. Wells's *History of the World*. It gave him the double sense that 'you could know everything and more than that you *ought* to know everything'.[13] *The History of the World* was one of the great publishing successes of the 1920s, combining authority and popularity in numerous editions. It placed the geological and fossil origins of the world as a background to the social and political history of different civilisations, focusing, at the end of the empire, on British history. If Darwin's theory of evolution put man in his place, Wells's history put Britain in a final, ending place. History had, it turned out, been toiling away to produce the British. Wells's work was delivered (as *Life on Earth* was to be) in digestible weekly portions. It was this tradition of improving authority which Attenborough emulated.

Attenboroughs were expected to make a difference. Practical moral activism was a taken-for-granted part of the mix in the Fabian, socially involved home: Frederick chaired the local committee devoted to bringing Jewish refugees out of Germany, and the family took in two Jewish *Kindertransport* girls, Irene and Helge, while they were in transit to relatives in America, who then stayed with them for the rest of the war. In such families, competitive success is taken for granted, but the wholesome intellectual food comes with an additional requirement: to do good.

Attenborough personally was compelled by a passion to educate: a friend observed him on a beach on holiday 'leaping into full explanation mode' when he found the happy conjunction of an audience and an animal. It was as if 'he was doing a programme which normally would be for 15 million people, but there were these two slightly startled little children who were getting fifteen minutes on the sea cucumber, whether they liked it or not'. In a broader way, BBC public service broadcasting was the inheritor and developer of a historic strand of British educational reform. 'Societies for the Improvement of Public Education' had led to school reform, but the intention was a wider, less institutional, ambition to 'inform' and entertain the public. The BBC had been set up in a race to make the newly enfranchised electorate in the 1920s more responsible voters. By the 1970s, Attenborough's programmes, possible only within the public service structures of the Corporation, were part of an increasingly urgent challenge to make the public more responsible custodians of nature. Attenborough personally, and the BBC institutionally, was in a direct bloodline to a radical and reforming strand of British thought not tied to any political party, but committed to improvement.

Attenborough read natural sciences at Cambridge. *Life on Earth*, he said later, 'was just a standard first year university biology course – put on television, nothing grand'.[14] More accurately it was his Cambridge natural sciences course from the 1950s, where the discipline was 'alive and thriving', exploring the modern synthesis of Darwin's thought on evolution and Mendel's work on heredity. The task was to place animals in their correct place in the great evolutionary 'tree' of relationships. The university was a growing centre for the classic study of animal behaviour, and had also just set up an ornithological field station in Madingley, where W. H. Thorpe was doing pioneering work on bird calls, soon to cross-fertilise with broadcasting. Carl Pantin organised enthralling practical demonstrations of live invertebrates, water creatures in tanks, unexpected animals in different habitats. It was 'very very vivid, profoundly exciting just watching them – it was a brilliant moment each week', said Patrick Bateson. Meticulous observation was the most prized skill. Attenborough and his team used television to give to the many this weekly thrill for the privileged few.[15]

After National Service in the Royal Navy, Attenborough chose not to do a PhD, because it would be laboratory-bound, 'and that wasn't the way I wanted to study animals'. He married Jane Oriel, who was to be the mainstay of his career and private felicity. After a brief tedious spell as a publisher, watching in stifled horror as the hands of St Paul's clock moved slowly forward through the wasted day just outside his office window, he became a neophyte broadcaster. It was at the very start of television (which was at that point very much the junior relative of mighty radio). If Auntie existed, he said, she lived in Broadcasting House and 'tended to regard the fashions and moral attitudes of yesterday as being eternal. She was dignified in language and manners and certainly knew what was best for people. She regarded her young offspring in television as feckless, irresponsible and inclined to naughtiness.'[16]

One of the things Attenborough brought to *Life on Earth* was an unrivalled understanding of the possibilities of television – because he had invented many of the forms and run so much of it. When he started, the evening's viewing was introduced by women in evening gowns. The schedule was planned 'as a good hostess might arrange an evening meal. It started with something light – an hors d'oeuvre as it were, progressed via a main course of something weightier and was rounded off by an epilogue and a picture of Big Ben (a model, as it turned out, not the real thing, to give every one a time check).'[17]

At first Attenborough worked on a news magazine programme for the redoubtable Mary Adams. Adams decreed that a 'more natural' style of broadcast interview must be attempted. On the never-ending BBC hunt for the authentic demotic voice, 'natural gems' of unrehearsed ordinary people must appear. Attenborough found a spirited East End rat catcher and brought him back to display his craft – which he did with alarming enthusiasm. Anxiously, Attenborough had to explain that dispatching rats live on screen by bisecting them with a stroke of a cavalry officer's sword, or throttling them with bare hands, might unsettle the delicate stomachs of the animal-loving British audience. Live on air, the 'natural gem' thrust his hands into a cage filled with a 'maelstrom' of rats and, pulling out an enormous sewer rat, proceeded to swing it by its tail wildly around his head. Heedful of Attenborough's caution and concerned not to unsettle his public, he leered confidentially at the camera (while continuing to whirl the rat around like a Catherine wheel): 'now I don't want you to think that I am in any way *maltreating* this rat, but unless I get 'im slightly dizzy the bugger will bite me'.[18] Natural gems were not seen again on British screens for a generation – but the anarchy of the unrehearsable remained one of the slightly improper pleasures of wildlife programmes.

Before *Life on Earth*, the Bristol Natural History Unit powerhouse had made a number of programmes with Gerald Durrell, a genuine animal campaigner and conservationist. His comic masterpiece, *My Family and Other Animals*, had been a publishing phenomenon. While treating his family as specimens, Durrell gave his animals idiosyncratic foibles too. The anthropomorphic humour that distinguishes Durrell could, nevertheless, get out of hand, leaving animals as little more than an excuse for jokes. Such treatment was much disapproved of by scientists but very popular with the British public.

In Attenborough's hands, the humour is both directly controlled in his writing and part of the televisual appeal. The fun comes from the encounter between the unregulated indecencies of animals and David: the jokes are never *made*, they occur. Of course, filming animals produces a good deal of slapstick in any case: in one sequence on bats Attenborough finished the piece to camera by explaining that because of their phenomenal radar capacities the millions of swirling beasts flying above his head never bump into each other or anything else: at which point a bat flew straight into his face. Part, then, of a positively British tradition, for such stories always demonstrate the hapless insufficiency of the hero – that is part of their charm.

By the mid-1950s, he was in his element, out of the studio, off adventuring in the wilderness. At first, making a wildlife programme was, like a nineteenth-century expedition, a rather unplanned foray. In *Zoo Quest*, Attenborough accompanied a London Zoo curator on what were essentially animal-capturing expeditions. *Zoo Quests* mutated, perhaps because of uneasiness with the purpose of the expeditions: 'Filming animals in the wild, rather than capturing them, became our first priority,'[19] he wrote later. New camera

David Attenborough learning and charming in the cutting room, 1959

technology had also opened up the possibility of close-ups of animals in the field, making elaborate studio lighting less necessary.

Attenborough had risen inexorably through the BBC, moving from producing and presenting to organising and managing. In 1965, he became controller of BBC2. He was in charge of introducing colour to television – a series of technological and aesthetic challenges that made his eye and his understanding of the medium unrivalled. He had made BBC2 work, both in audience and in programming terms. He was a tremendous creative leader, but became restless as a BBC executive. In a sharp essay on 'Some observations of seating rituals in BBC committees and steering groups' he brought his anthropologist's experience to bear on the Corporation's ruling tribe, observing the way in which power and influence determined where people sat, how they entered rooms and how they behaved as power was brokered.

But the farther away Attenborough got from programmes, the more uneasy he became: running BBC2 had meant inventing programmes and managing the schedules, which was 'one of the big everyday things you took really seriously: it was the proper job'.[20] His next promotion, to director of Programmes, meant that: 'programme issues only landed on my desk when things were going wrong – when vast overspends loomed on a production, when judgements had to be given on questions of taste and language, when there were accusations of distortion, threats of libel ... otherwise my time was taken up with changes in management methods'.

Attenborough turned his attention to understanding humans in Tribal Eye; *at a wedding in Iran in 1975, the camera captures the exuberance of being David*

Desmond Morris was another pioneer in the field of televising animal behaviour. In the early stages of *Life on Earth* it had been suggested that he might co-present it. They were close friends as well as colleagues. Attenborough and his family went on holiday with the Morrises in Malta – a tax haven Morris had moved to on the proceeds of the worldwide success of his book *The Human Animal*. Morris recalled, 'I could see [David] becoming more and more agitated about not being able to make programmes'; the problem was not that he was not a good administrator, 'but rather that he was a tremendous one, and when he suggested that he was dissatisfied to the BBC they promoted him'. Attenborough would arrive all 'buttoned up and twitchy and "Where's the next committee meeting?" and then, after 48 hours, he'd get his binoculars out, put his walking boots on and relax: "I'm off looking at phosphatic nodule layers," he would beam, and off we'd go.'

Attenborough was routinely talked of as a future director-general of the Corporation – indeed, his jobs led remorselessly in that direction. But one observer said that when he looked at what a DG had to do, 'deal with the unions, deal with the government, deal with bureaucratic fuss', it was not appealing.[21] He made a momentous and unconventional decision. He gave up administering. Even Huw Wheldon, the great, humane BBC administrator and gifted presenter, disapproved: 'if you're the captain of the ship and you decide you'd rather be up in the rigging, then there's something wrong with being the captain of that ship'.[22] Will Wyatt, a young producer, asked for an

*BBC top dog: the newly appointed controller of
BBC2 outside Television Centre in 1967*

interview as Attenborough left, observing that 'here was as near a broad-casting saint as we were likely to get'.[23] It was partly a sense of adventure but also a profound preference for communicating and edifying. Most of all it was love of nature, and a sense that he might be able to change the way in which it was treated – before it was too late. Later he said that it was the best decision he ever made.

Attenborough was dissatisfied with the way in which wildlife programmes had settled into a rut – and bored by his own part in them. While on holiday he had the idea to make a big series that would explain evolution over time. This first sketch, which he sent to Aubrey Singer (head of Science), Chris Parsons (of Bristol) and Alasdair Milne (head of Television), had the basic Darwinian structure: a sketch of the taxonomy of related forms of life. By the final script the examples had become subsumed more clearly to the argument.[24] Yet the first sentence of the first draft has the whole scope of the final series within it: 'An intricate maze of connections links all living creatures inhabiting any one environment ...'[25]

Attenborough comments that the proposal could have been called the story of evolution – 'but that sounds as if it was about the past'. The ingenious solution was to use contemporary living animals, rather than historic specimens, to illustrate the argument. 'The quintessence of, for example, a lizard is only fully understandable in the light of the particular possibilities and limitations dictated by its reptilian nature and that, in turn, only becomes comprehensible in the light of the past.' Attenborough explained that previous programmes had 'seldom examined the basic character of the anatomy'. 'To a surprising degree', Attenborough pointed out, 'nearly all the events in this history can be told using living animals to represent the ancestral creatures which were the protagonists. The lungfish today shows how lungs have developed.'[26] The use of living animals transformed the proposal from a lesson or a lecture into the stuff of great television.

BRISTOL

Life on Earth was in part a response to a wider discontent shared among the highly committed team that had gathered in the Bristol Wildlife Unit. What messages were programmes communicating to audiences? What was the purpose of wildlife filming? 'Scientifically respectable' versus 'popular' was one tension in the team – resolved in a way by Attenborough's command of one at the service of the other. Close observation of and immersion in the natural world had re-engineered many programme makers into anxious campaigners. They were aware that the genre had transformed public attitudes towards animals. Even Elsa the Lioness, a series criticised for its cloying anthropomorphism, had nevertheless altered public perceptions of lions as fierce and dangerous animals: lionesses became hard-working 'modern mothers'.

How should public attitudes be altered and in what direction? No one sat around having arguments about 'whither public service wildlife?' in those terms, but there was an underlying seriousness to the puzzle. The intention of the unit in Bristol as far as wildlife was concerned was broadly similar to that in any other production specialism of the Corporation – to be successful, to produce quality work that changed the public by informing them. One aspect of this restless ambition to improve involved a sharp refocusing of attention: from privileging animals to focusing on the environments that supported them. Previously 'wildlife' on television had been concerned with things 'with legs and structures'. But understanding that the system of dependency and the ecology of habitats were the sensitive preconditions for survival was becoming an increasingly pressing concern. Life on Earth, by articulating the links in the chain of the development of life, was an extended essay on interdependence. Attenborough observed later in 1984: 'The initial concern of many conservation organizations was to protect rare animals. Maybe it was the very mobility of birds and animals that first attracted our attention to them ... the main problem seemed to be with preserving the butterfly, not the nettle it lives on, the panda, not the bamboo.'[27] Barry Paine, who worked on the series, recalled the frustration with zoos at the time which claimed to 'do' education but which concentrated overwhelmingly on big animals. Television, they all believed, had to replace the misleading campaigns of the existing wildlife organisations, which, hidebound by convention, were inadequate to the challenge. *Life on Earth* was in this way more radical politically than it appeared.

The series was made in Bristol, moulded, and pitched to perfection there. It could not have happened, let alone been so revolutionary, without the accumulated experience and ambition of the BBC Wildlife Unit. In turn, this was the progeny of the BBC Western Region, which through a succession of gifted controllers had maintained its independence and in doing so enhanced the nation's fabric. The Wildlife Unit was just one part of the Western Region's intelligent battles for local voice and authority within the Corporation. The unit had been exploring the technical, intellectual and organisational constraints of wildlife programming in a very BBC way, with one eye on the audience, and another on the integrity of programmes. All the while it had been successfully implementing imperial organisational ambitions in the Corporation, for Attenborough had been making wildlife programmes from London, but he had maintained close and friendly relationships with people in Bristol. What could have been a conflict of interest never developed. Instead, Bristol became – as it had always intended – a world leader. This regional prowess and the specialised division of labour were almost unique in the Corporation, although perhaps mirrored by the rise of Northern Ireland as a centre of world-class news skills or the Midlands for drama. But while Northern Ireland's prowess was thrust upon them, Bristol had chosen it. Bristol 'did' the region and it 'did' nature across the Corporation.

Frank Gillard was the first post-war regional controller. He had been a fine war reporter, the architect of the transformation of radio, and later the authoritative interviewer and holder of the secrets of the oral history of the Corporation's big beasts.[28] He came from the West Country and encouraged nature programmes because he loved the region's glorious countryside. Nature programming had been popular after World War II, perhaps buoyed by and in turn encouraging a turn back to countryside as a compensation for the ravages of the conflict. Desmond Hawkins, Gillard's successor, reflected that there was 'a great wish to get back to England, to have a look at it and see what could be done to restore it and make it the country we wanted it to be'.[29] When Gillard started to build up the natural history programmes in the region, his main problem was one of supply. People loved to watch animal programmes, but there was not enough raw material and, as much of it was amateur, it was unpredictable and often badly filmed.

The BBC Wildlife Unit's ambition was to become a British and world leader in the field but also a world resource. People wanted to see animals from distant places, and film-makers from distant places needed encouraging. Wildlife was becoming as oriented towards 'abroad' as news was. A series of bursaries for overseas film-makers was established. The BBC needed their films and knowledge – 'they learnt BBC standards and principles'. To strengthen the

*Frank Gillard, a public service broadcasting aristocrat; he developed
the Bristol Wildlife Unit as part of his beloved Western Region*

unit internationally, Gillard wrote, 'it needs some kind of working association
with individuals in other countries: the cameramen, producers, sound recordists, whose gifts could beneficially influence our output'.

Material also came from institutions such as the Royal Society for the
Protection of Birds: the BBC had little control over their product and was
consequently reserved about it. Most such 'little units' were 'a parlous sort of
enterprise', with often vague and conflicting policies. The third source was the
'specialist amateurs', who were, at least at that point, 'in some ways our most
valuable source of film'. Because of their 'exact and thorough knowledge' of
some aspect of animal behaviour, based on close methodical (and at times
obsessive) observations, they sometimes used the camera with genuine
originality. The amateurs had another advantage: they did not price their time
like the professionals. Indeed, Gillard and then Hawkins encouraged amateurs
to make more usable film, with continuity shots and longer sequences, not
least by establishing a wildlife film prize. Amateur obsessives remained an
important resource. Many of the early films shown on television had been
of ducks, observed Tony Soper, a founding cameraman in the unit, which are

'made for television because they're the right aspect ratio, four by three'. There was a lot of nesting too: nests stay still.

Attenborough observed that when you started to think of a programme on a particular creature, the first thing you did was find the expert. 'Somewhere out there is a man (and it was usually a man) who has a lifetime's interest in the behaviour of the spider you are interested in.' As Richard Brock put it, 'once you had found the Stick Insect Association or whatever then you were away'. Then Brock would visit the expert: 'I'd knock on the door and it was usually a very tall spindly person who'd got these stick insects in a room upstairs which his wife wasn't allowed to go in.' When BBC teams first went to Australia in the 1950s there were almost no amateur naturalists – and it used the wildlife film prize to encourage new interests. By the seventies, they had sprung up all over the continent.

The remit of the unit was to be more than a television programme generator: it would need authority. 'Looking further into the future', Gillard had written after the first five years of the unit's close association with Bristol Zoo and Bristol University, the collaboration 'might result in a small Institute of animal behaviour'. The ambition to use television to make a scientific contribution and not just to harvest science remained an important part of Bristol and indeed of Attenborough. Gillard argued, 'the same film can be pretty pictures to one and an important scientific document to another'.[30] But he suggested that 'the spirit of scientific enquiry must have pride of place. In handling this subject we expose ourselves to the critical scrutiny of scientists, and their approval is an important endorsement.' Beyond the prestige of being taken seriously there was necessary self-interest: 'We look to them as contributors, as source material and as elite opinion on our efforts. In short, we need their goodwill.'[31]

The introduction of colour meant a larger licence fee and a challenge for wildlife film-makers. Apparently colourful topics, such as volcanoes or scarlet ibises, looked too dark for the majority of the audience, who were still watching in black and white. Colour film at first set wildlife filming back as it needed better lighting and could be shot only in the day. New skills had to be developed before the lush colour of *Life on Earth* really worked. It took time to develop the scientifically literate teams that the series needed. There was an accumulated television intelligence that *Life on Earth* benefited from: competition with ITV helped build capacity, as Richard Brock recalled: 'There was a studio show which Desmond Morris introduced called *Life* … It was fairly scientific. So that was another slot which needed a team. So teams lead to more teams and more assistants, and so the thing starts to grow.'[32]

The first large animal series that had been broadcast had been 'bought in' from Gillard's 'professionals', who by the seventies often ran cross-national franchises selling programmes into many different television systems. These series were hugely popular and presented by a (nesting or mating) couple. The screens heaved with large Aryans and their blonde wives: Armand and Michaela Denis roamed the savannah in matching safari suits, and Hans and Lotte Hass explored the deeps in matching wetsuits. Hawkins in imperial mode wanted them for Bristol: both were far more expensive than any other material. The Hasses were genuine scientists and edited film carefully for Britain. But Armand and Michaela Denis were already a commercial brand whose films were increasingly contrived. By the late seventies, the Denises rarely made the programmes in the field; their appearances were just 'pasted in' later. The Michaela 'caring female tames orphaned animals act' was regarded as especially awful. The Bristol aim was to be as commercially successful as such a series could be, but decent, truthful, scientific and public-service. The appointment of Mick Rhodes as head of the Wildlife Unit from *Panorama* (made in London) brought fresh air and a set of better links back to the centre. *Life on Earth* was a breakthrough that stood on many shoulders.

BRONOWSKI AND CLARK

Big series were in the television firmament. They cost a lot, but they made television into a mature medium that told factual stories which were as engaging as movies but distinct in content and style. Attenborough had been responsible for several of these series and had reportedly arrived home after being made controller of BBC2 jubilantly asking his children what he should spend several million pounds making. Kenneth Clark had just made *Civilisation*, a magisterial series which ranged over artistic and cultural achievement, and an outstanding intellectual and television success. Bronowski, perhaps less entirely successfully, had made *The Ascent of Man* and shown that science could be made serious and popular. *Life on Earth* was almost a riposte to it. Such series required a presenter who was in charge of the knowledge they imparted. They cost a lot of money, but produced gratifyingly huge audience figures. The Natural History Unit eyed them enviously. Everyone in Bristol knew that 'sooner or later' they would have to make a great 'part work' on the world of nature. 'Unfortunately,' Christopher Parsons wryly observed, 'this was not so blindingly obvious to the Television Management in London.'

Bristol had one priceless currency to work with: wildlife television was very popular with audiences. People did not go out as much in the seventies and eighties, so Saturday night was the plum night. By then, the secure big hitters of the BBC1 schedule on Saturday night were *The Black and White Minstrel Show* and *The World About Us*. Wildlife, well presented, had a proven capacity to attract British audiences. There was also a growing world market that the BBC had its eye on. The idea made television sense. Attenborough brought another gift: by 1975, audience research showed he was among the ten most popular presenters on television. When they invented the 'Audience Appreciation Index' in 1982, he had a personal score of 85. He bestowed this munificence on any programme he appeared on. In addition Attenborough understood scheduling. Placing television programmes in the right places on the right nights at the right times was an art. On BBC2 Attenborough had himself invented what he called 'Sledgehammers' (the word Darwin used to describe the impact of evolution on natural life). This was a weekly series of thirteen episodes that filled three months of the year (which was how schedules were planned). Longer and 'it would lose its routine place in the week's viewing', while any fewer episodes 'would leave a problem of filling a few odd weeks'. He knew that each programme had to be fifty minutes long, so that it could be sold to America, where they needed ten minutes for advertising. So as Attenborough surveyed the vastness of historical evolution, 'Happily the schedules of creation seemed conveniently divided into thirteen parts.'

INCUBATION OF THE IDEA

'I became so full of it,' Attenborough said of Life on Earth in a frank and confiding letter to Milne, 'I am still very excited about it – it seems to me to provide a chance of doing new things in natural history programming.' The idea, 'which as you know has been around in a vague way for a couple of years', had really started to preoccupy him. He set about pulling the levers of power to turn the idea into a reality. Robin Scott, controller of BBC2 in succession to Attenborough, was shown a draft and was 'somewhat daunted' by its size, but saw its potential. Attenborough talked to Milne, who thought that creating great television was what his job was all about. However, because of a row with the Indian government over the reporting on Indira Gandhi, a series that the BBC had been preparing to make there had been cancelled. Milne wanted to use Attenborough to make a fast wildlife series to replace it. Attenborough replied carefully that he did not want to do anything that would get in the way of developing the new idea: 'jungle-jaunt programmes are something that I have done for a very long time. I am finding it increasingly difficult to tackle them with any degree of freshness (and indeed, to be candid, only <u>too</u> easy to do so with visibly fading enthusiasm).' He wanted to devote himself to Life on Earth: 'But if I were to have to put on my shorts and plod off to the jungle then they couldn't start till 1977' and the thought of putting it off that long 'saddens me very much'.[33]

Working on the series was 'an extraordinary formative experience'.[34] The stakes were high and it transformed careers. Had it failed they would have been altered for the worse. The quality, as is invariably the case in television, was the product of the team that worked on it. In the end the pooling of talents and the multiplication of creativity that it generated produced a focused idea of what the series was to be. Everyone fought for it even if they disagreed about how to get to it. The initial work was appointing producers, Chris Parsons, Richard Brock and John Sparks, who, Attenborough later claimed, 'were indefatigable in criticising the conventional assumptions of natural history and continually searched for new, un-photographed examples to illustrate our points'.[35] The producers then turned to assembling the whole team from a programme organiser (in itself an innovation pushed by Singer, who could see that the proposal needed someone to concentrate on the organisation and sort out problems full-time) through cameramen, sound experts, film editors and researchers, and commissioning an original and experimental musical score.

Attenborough himself was – everyone attests – a very good leader. He was especially sensitive to the most junior members of teams, taking time to know secretaries, preferring to deal with people directly. He was considerate: one cameraman's father died while he was making the series and his mother received a letter of condolence and a carefully inscribed copy of the book of the series when it was published. Chris Parsons said that he was 'the kind of person you could relax with whatever the level of the post he held'.[36] Someone who had worked with him for many years said that Attenborough understood 'the importance in a film team of pacing, of time off to recharge'.[37] He knew how to dispel tension, was sensitive to mood, 'furrowed brows in the office, money, schedules, BBC niggling'. In the field, when it was cold and the animals shy and deadlines close, Attenborough 'would do a little show – mimic somebody', ease the tension. Hilarious good company is what Attenborough liked. 'He would breeze in and make everything possible.'[38] It was a good way to drive people hard.

Attenborough was a gentleman: his code of values and behaviour one of decency, modesty, ambition, simple clarity of purpose and a passion for observation and wildlife. Modesty is an intriguing virtue. At its best it is associated with a single-minded concern with accuracy. It is also endearing and based on a respect for, and cherishing of, others' capacity. Everyone who worked with Attenborough testified to his modesty; great scientists observed it in his dealings with them; and it is in the record of his interviews, when he unfailingly places his own contribution within the context of the work and achievements of others. 'The real hero was Desmond Hawkins'; 'You should consider the contribution of Joanna Spicer'; 'I depended utterly on the cameramen'; 'the people who make it work are the directors'; '*Life on Earth* was absolutely made by the brilliance of the producers'; 'It is the scientists that really know what is happening'.[39] Always putting his own contribution in the context of other people was both genuinely kind and an example of a ruthless concern with accuracy.

Executive producer Chris Parsons was very different from Attenborough: quiet, rather more academic in manner, with a grasp of detail and an acute business sense. He was a key part of the team because he had worked so well with Attenborough before, and they brought a mutual respect and friendship to the task. By the early seventies, Parsons had been thinking of a large natural history series. His model at first had been 'the television equivalent of the glossy Time-Life nature books and other noted coffee-table volumes'.[40] Yet Parsons had also already identified a sense of limitation with 'the middle-class tone' of much wildlife programming, sensing that the programmes could have higher production standards and reach an even wider national and international audience. Parsons's idea was a written proposal for a 36-programme series in which the first section was on evolution, the next on behaviour, and the final parts on habitat. It was, however, also very different in manner from the eventual series: 'the story will be told largely through the work of scientists who are currently making discoveries whether they are ethologists, palaeontologists or whatever', he wrote.[41] Although nothing came of this audacious project directly, the idea behind it 'lay fermenting for a long time'. Parsons, while digging out old files, had searched around for a snappy title: 'I wrote down one phrase that at least seemed to include everything – Life on Earth.'[42] When the producers began to thrash out the detail of the project, 'things got a bit sticky', and Parsons thought Sparks was 'going out on a limb' and trying to make a series that was more like *Horizon*, too cerebral and dry. Richard Brock, meanwhile, was thinking of something glitzy and popular. In a piece of *post hoc* diplomacy, Parsons claimed to be 'in the middle' between Sparks's principles and Brock's hunger for success. He was actually closest to Attenborough's vision, despite significantly altering it. There was in this a shift in the balance of power. Early on, Attenborough had been thought of as 'a presenter', but now he became something far more authoritative. He had a compulsive vision: no talking heads, his own narrative driving the entire series, no confusions, no scientific disagreements on air, the clearest story told in the simplest way, and above all focusing visually on the wildlife. But the rows were intense.

Life on Earth was not immune from the more mundane tribulations of the times. As usual, what the unions might do was a preoccupation. The long filming planned over several years needed a team organised in a different kind of way. It needed to avoid the disruptions and restrictive working practices that were normal in a highly unionised workforce – not that anyone put it quite like that. Part of getting the programme planned was making sure that people working on it would be prepared to commit to it. In practice the issue was the craft unions, and especially the all-important cameramen. There was a cadre of specialist freelance wildlife cameramen emerging, and these would be hired when their expertise was needed. But the unit would need several full-time teams as well. The 'standard' BBC cameraman worked on a rota and went and shot football, mayors' opening galas and animals as required. This was seen as the most efficient use of resources. But Parsons and Attenborough knew that they needed to attract dedicated cameramen to the project, and develop their skills.

Martin Saunders, for example, was identified by Attenborough as a Bristol cameraman with a gift for filming wildlife. Saunders was frustrated by the rigid union demarcation rules, which had paradoxically resulted in outside free-lancers, who were more flexible, being commissioned for all of the specialist animal filming. He petitioned John Sparks, who reluctantly and experimentally sent him to film howler monkeys in Venezuela on his own. The Corporation, 'in order to save a bit of money', sent him on one plane and his equipment on another, so by the time the cameras and the cameraman were reunited he had lost four days out of a ten-day trip. He came back with arresting footage (although as Sparks had been so cautious about the enterprise he had been sent without a sound recordist, so later 'a sound recordist went down there to get howler monkeys howling to go with my footage of howler monkeys'). Attenborough typically charmingly sent him a congratulatory telegram, and Saunders went on to develop a larger role in the series.

Despite his all-encompassing enthusiasm for the project, Attenborough started writing the script four months too late. They had hoped to work in an orderly progression, research and scripting followed by shooting and editing. In practice it was frantic: they had to 'run the remaining script and research work in parallel with shooting to a far greater extent than originally planned'. Getting the ideas right was an even larger challenge in a long authoritative series: 'One of the problems is that palaeontological research is widespread and scientific papers come out each day which propose or challenge those recently published. Almost no one agrees on anything,' Parsons explained. It was one thing to make a single programme about some proposition or the latest theory, but it required far more work to 'put such a theory in perspective within our series'. In addition, with a series that was going to take so long to make, the work of synthesis and reflection would have to go on right until the end. The team's research capacity became formidable: 'The number of botanists, biologists, palaeontologists, geologists, biochemists etc we have already inter-viewed, telephoned, corresponded with, is far too long to list.'[43] One hundred and eighty-three institutions on every continent had been personally visited by researchers. The sheer intellectual synthesising effort was unprecedented, and it was this more than anything which in the end provided the series with its tone: one of informed and clear authority. Of course the public 'trusted' it. It was based on scrupulousness and knowledge stretched to the utmost.

MONEY MATTERS

Life on Earth was original and so successful because it cost so much. It was the most expensive thing any of those involved had made, and required a different kind of budget and better control. Traditionally budgets had been very loose, as filming in far-distant places with haphazard communications was unpredictable. Parsons explained, 'If I wanted to do a film on dolphins in India, if they agreed they would say, oh yes, okay, well here's £10,000, off you go, good luck.' To come up with a budget for *Life on Earth*, the only comparable series was *Civilisation*. But as Parsons observed, 'If you were going to film in a museum, you know where it is, and you know it's not going to move.'[44] Animals were less obliging. Filming them was full of happenstance and accident. How to come up with a budget for something no one had tried before?

Parsons and Salisbury arrived at a similar figure, 'about £1 million above the line'. It was to cost five times as much as anything else the unit had filmed and nearly twice as much as *Civilisation*. Drama aside, it was one of the most expensive things the BBC had done. Singer phoned up and asked, 'Do these chaps know what they are doing?', which made Parsons 'see red'. It was proposed that the production of the series would take about three years, that it would have three directors, two full-time film crews (as well as freelance specialists as necessary), two assistants and – an innovation, as previously mentioned – a full-time organiser, Derek Anderson, who was to keep the circumnavigating circus of production under control.[45]

The BBC could not finance it on its own. In 1975, approaches were made in America for co-production money. Universal 'winced' at the cost; discussions with Time-Life meandered inconclusively. Then they approached Warner Brothers, where the managing director of Television was Michael Peacock, an Englishman who had started at the BBC on the same day as Attenborough, a friend. Aubrey Singer was sent off to have lunch with him.[46] Peacock persuaded his masters at Warner to put in £300,000. Then the 1976 IMF crisis, devaluation of the pound and rocketing inflation put real pressure on the budget. Mick Rhodes anxiously pointed out that the project had in effect lost £12,000 in two days in 1976 with devaluation. The solution was to keep the cash in America in dollars.[47] By 1977, Rhodes reported that they had a reserve of £40,000: 'What this means is that at the moment all is fine, and with only a reasonable share of bad luck, we shall finish on budget ... but a couple of really bad trips could throw things out of balance.'[48] Attenborough single-mindedly refused any American contract that proposed (as was normal) to insert another presenter into the footage, or to replace his voice. The aim was strategic, long-term, to become a recognised international figure: even if the production lost initial investment.

Faced with a script bursting with pan-global explanatory sentences for which there was no precedent, years of filming to plan, and more hours of programmes to be made than ever before, the organisational challenge was daunting. So *Life on Earth* invented a revolutionary way of managing production that would become standard. Later the Corporation was accused of financial laxity, of managerial sloppiness and of inefficiency in this period. Yet *Life on Earth*, pushed by the power of the idea it was unpacking, produced a model of prudent organisation, solving the problems it faced with systems conceived and executed by those who understood the issues – not by any imported 'management consultant'. It came in more or less on budget.

FILMING

Parsons brought a fine organisational brain to the task. He moved everybody working on the project into interconnected offices: it meant that 'a lot of talking and sorting happened naturally'. The first breakthrough was that material would be shot not programme by programme, as it had been traditionally, but location by location and season by season, so that material for many programmes from one location could be scooped up in one five- to six-week trip. Once the filming started, film crews giddily circumnavigated the world, while patient teams of animal film specialists sat it out waiting for the behaviour they needed on location. Meanwhile other teams filmed behaviour in special studios, and others hunted down likely scientists and animals. Attenborough and his own team swooped down on stories that they had set going, harvested and then summed up for camera. All of this had to be planned around the diary of the animal world. Parsons produced a magnificent multicoloured chart of teams flying hither and thither. Anderson, in one progress report in 1977, captured the breathless whirlwind of production between August and October:

> Chris Parsons and Maurice Fisher [a cameraman] left again for Canada, Alaska and Malaysia and Australia. Weather fouled us up slightly but planned material with David Attenborough shot satisfactorily. Chris returned via New Zealand, New Caledonia and Fiji, David returned via Malagasy where he filmed a sequence with Mike Salisbury. In September John Sparks and David left for Australia and Japan, and Richard Brock and Martin Saunders spent three weeks in Venezuela.

> Meanwhile Maurice Tibbles, a specialist wildlife cameraman, had been in the USA and Canada 'filming some fine footage on garter snakes', had progressed to Switzerland and Germany filming birds, Austria to film storks, and had wasted 'two fruitless weeks in Gibraltar trying to film the autumn migration'. In the same month, David Parer recced 'in Papua New Guinea for the bird programme and is off to Australia for the Marsupial one'.[49]

Inevitably not everything went to order; although they were very excited and relieved to film a live coelacanth (for the first time ever), its performance was somewhat wan. Having been fished up from its home in the depths of the ocean, it expired rather promptly. 'The filming expedition to Panama in 1976', Parsons reported, 'was less productive than we could have hoped for. This was due to the non-occurrence of the rainy season which comes every November – and triggers mating of frogs etc – except in 1976.' Indeed, the weather and frogs in general were uncooperative: the non-appearance of the rains in Asia meant the non-appearance of flying frogs on that continent. Even the frogs carefully set up in the controlled environment of studios and laboratories were uncooperative. One cameraman in a studio in Devon spent 180 hours waiting to capture the moment froglets were spat out of the incubating mouths of their parent 'and then he went across the road to collect something, came back, and he had missed it'.[50]

Indeed, in organising the wildly globetrotting teams the unit had to keep a careful eye on the opportunities to film spectacular moments which only occurred infrequently. Take the horseshoe crabs sequence. Getting this required Attenborough, a film crew, producer, director and locally hired electrician with a battery of lights to converge on the eastern shores of Delaware Bay south of Philadelphia. An entire six-week filming sequence had been organised around one specific night – because an American biologist, Carl Shuster (who was also with them), had predicted a year before that thousands of horseshoe crabs (not actually crabs, but living examples of a stage in evolution dating back to the fossil record, 400–500 million years ago) would emerge from the sea in eerie determined silence to mate. They did it once a year when the tide and moon conditions were right, the whole process never lasting more than four nights and occasionally only two. Shuster's prediction was accurate and a beach full of creatures lumbered out of the sea wearing their rather Germanic-military-helmet shells. Attenborough picked up one of the unwieldy animals and, bringing it close to his face, explained its evolutionary place. To complete the sequence the team also scooped up sand and eggs from the spawning beach to dispatch to Oxford Scientific Films. There Peter Parks would simulate the conditions on the beach to show the eggs hatching.

As the deadline approached, managing Attenborough became challenging: 'There are times when David is required in two widely spaced locations at the same time, i.e. bird migration in the Bosporus and salmon spawning in Alaska both in the last week of August,'[51] Parsons reported, 'this is a bit of a problem.' The series could not have been made without an enormous increase in the number and reliability of international flights. One key reel of film of Attenborough in Venezuela went missing for a week, but was found just before the crisis 'went fissile'. Viewing and logging sequences, then cutting and editing them, were fraught.

One of the battles the series won was the advocacy of the very tiny over the large. It was important to be true to the fact that, over the expanse of evolutionary time, microscopic forms of life had taken aeons to evolve. Showcasing

Filming Life on Earth *in front of an anthill in 1979; dress code: flared*

the tiny was also about the importance of the ecology of habitats. Unlike most wildlife films, which had shown animals that people already understood, *Life on Earth* was to show how dependent larger forms were on the minuscule, as part of the more comprehensive story of evolution. The series was going to lock viewers into the drama of evolution and develop if not exactly sympathy then understanding of the importance of the microscopic: in evolution but also in the contemporary life of the world. The team took issue with the distorting concern of zoos with the large and the mammalian. Paine argued that 'people should just be more aware of the true extent of biodiversity and how the planet was being worked by animals: run by wildlife, by nature'. For Attenborough, the challenge was to make the interconnectedness clear. Wildlife broadcasting had previously been concerned with the exotic, the dramatic and violent, and large animals – or, if smaller, ones that the public appreciated. More specialised 'scientific' films, particularly on *Horizon*, had been made about less developed forms of life, but this big, expensive series devoted a great deal of time and attention to the microscopic – and in a way endeared it to the public.

Wanting to film tiny things was the easy part. Doing it depended on technology. 'At some point we had crossed a Rubicon,' Attenborough said; 'the cameras could see what the human eye could not – smaller than we can see, under water, in the dark.'[52] There was the question of lenses and lighting. The caterpillars in a famous Disney film, *Nature's Half Acre*,[53] were writhing – but that was because 'they were being fried alive by the lights'. Microscopic film magnified every vibration and in most previous films the subjects darted on and off screen disconcertingly. Attenborough had fought the technological battle from his earliest days in television and was keenly interested in what the latest bit of kit could do. *Life on Earth* benefited from developments in cameras and a new fast film developed by Kodak, which meant that pictures could be captured at much lower light levels. In addition, the BBC became the main patron of Oxford Scientific Films, which was used extensively in the series and which was by the late seventies a pioneer in technical wildlife filming.

The company had been started in 1967 by an Oxford lecturer in forestry, Gerald Thompson (together with his departmental technician, Eric Skinner). The entire unit worked out of a cupboard under the stairs in the Oxford Natural History Museum, where Barry Paine from the Bristol Wildlife Unit came across them when they were commissioned to film the Nobel scientist Miriam Rothschild's work on fleas. No one else had been able to capture the behaviour of fleas (and the fleas, as it turned out, of fleas).[54] Thompson, based in an Oxford college, consulted the physics and engineering departments and developed new water coolers for lenses and lights, a new camera bench which solved the problems of vibration, and novel ways of dealing with the problems of focus at very great magnification. A visiting delegation of Russian microscopic film-makers, accustomed to the huge resources of a state institute, was incredulous and dismissive of the ramshackle unit – until they saw the films it made.

The *Life on Earth* team worked in intimate collaboration with Oxford Scientific Films (OSF). Some of the most transfixing sequences in the film, especially using OSF pioneering backlighting of tiny magically transparent sea creatures, gave a new grace and weird alien beauty to the series. Edward Williams, who composed the brilliant and pioneering score, using very early electronic equipment, said 'what an opportunity these sequences provided, they were so mysterious'.

EVOLUTIONARY LEAP

Life on Earth defied all the empirically tested laws of programme ratings. These decreed that audience numbers always floated down over the life of a series and that even successful series did not develop loyal audiences of hooked repeat viewers but called on new audiences for each episode. *Life on Earth* started with a large audience which steadily increased. By the seventh week, more or less the entire nation sat down to watch it, and they had become addicted, returning week after week for more serious reflection on evolution: a concept that BBC research had shown the majority had only a very weak grasp of. It became a phenomenon. The critics were ecstatic.

Although the whole series is driven by a relentless argument and has a very distinct public service tone, within this coherence there is a great deal of variety. It is not symphonic and schmaltzy. It has grand magisterial moments, but much of it is far smaller-scale. The series delicately touches on the whole panoply of film genres: this is wildlife filming as adventure and romance, science fiction and domestic intimacy, grand argument, humour and genuinely moving encounter, all done with wit, élan and serious intent. The visual splendour is awe-inspiring: from the lush Gauguin greens of forests, to futuristic landscapes of mountains and deserts, like jagged wastelands in an abstract picture, or the territory of a Ballard dystopia reinforced by a science fiction adventure score, to the trembling ethereal transparency of sea creatures, cilia waving in underwater currents, to the wonderful images of lemurs' jaunty striped tails aloft as a means of communication with each other, but looking like punctuation in the scrub. Every picture counted, and was enhanced by argument and beauty.

The series gathered audiences because there was such unexpected drama in the palaeontological evidence, which hammered home the hugeness of evolutionary time, and by implication the fleetingness of human time. Yet Attenborough made clear there was more work to be done. The history of ammonites 'is full of puzzles: why for example did some ammonites uncurl and then curl up again?' Attenborough holds the whole together as our trusted and versatile guide. There is the power of the 'Attenborough whisper', used, for example, with the giant tortoises in the Galapagos, which conveys the audience in a hushed intimacy to the side of the animals. Those sitting on sofas in front of their televisions conspire with Attenborough not to disturb the beasts. It is a device that came quite naturally to him, but which added drama and lifted the sense of an encounter we are part of. Elsewhere, and in another mode, Attenborough describes with breathless excitement the huge leap of cells 'reorganising themselves into a new body – a sponge!', as he holds a blob of jelly close to his face in frank delight. Were audiences watching Attenborough, or taking a cue from his response, or falling for the object of his attention? Surely all three.

The series gave due attention to the tiniest forms of life revealed by the new cameras, from the hoverfly – 'a marvel of microscopic machinery' – to liverworts and mosses revealed in microscopic detail; images of tiny insects levering themselves over blossoms; orchids which have tricked wasps; lilies that stamp pollen on to the back of visiting bees with intricate systems of triggers and levers and sticky pits. Fertilisation has a score of perfect aptness and delightful wit of bells chiming. One of Attenborough's great advantages was that he understood what he was describing – and could explain it to audiences in a single, often unrehearsed account. He would turn away, clear his mind and 'just do it to camera', and this direct engagement with the moment made riveting viewing. On the Great Barrier Reef, as Attenborough closed in on a clam, 'it opened its shell a discreet millimetre and cut loose with a muffled social noise, visually detectable as a small cloud of pulverised algae … Some of us are not as good as Attenborough at waxing enthusiastic when vouchsafed a close up view of a giant clam farting,' observed Clive James in the *Observer*; 'Attenborough was as radiant as Her Majesty at the races.' For James the total effect is of gorgeous variety; it is life-affirming stuff.

One of the most memorable sequences in *Life on Earth* was shot accidentally, and the team had a row about it. In it, Attenborough is treated by a group of young gorillas as a plaything, or even as a being they might play with. Attenborough's wonder as they fiddle with his shoes and explore his face is palpable. Then, when they are bored, they move on. Attenborough wrote that gorillas are movingly similar to humans. Their perceptions are similar and 'their life expectancy is about the same as ours and they move from childhood to maturity and from maturity to senility at very similar ages … A stare is rude, or to put it in a less anthropomorphic way, threatening.'[55]

The unit had set out to do a serious piece about the evolutionary advantage of opposable thumbs. When the gorillas appeared and started to play, no one thought that was what they were there to film. Saunders captured the 'tiny sequence by accident' while getting on with the routine work of being a cameraman, dealing with the unpredictability of wildlife:

> you could be approaching an animal and all of a sudden it panics and it's gone, and you might never see it again. So there's this theory about taking a shot and then cutting the distance down by half and taking another shot, and cutting the distance down by half and taking another shot. So at least by the time you get in to get the real close-ups at least you've got a sequence.

When Saunders saw what was happening he took his own initiative and closed in on a profoundly moving encounter. The director was dismissive of it as 'Johnny Morris stuff', the rows went on into editing, several people wanted to cut it out. Yet it is a moral moment: providing an Elysian metaphor of the meeting of the world of animals and the world of man with no destruction or interference. It is a little glimpse of paradise that is at the heart of the series. It is also absolutely heart-stopping television.

SCIENCE

Was *Life on Earth* an original contribution to science or was it 'just television'? Biology departments came to a halt on the evenings it was on and the series and its progeny 'have recruited more people to biology than any other source: it was immensely influential – it showed us things we were desperate to see', said Steve Jones.[56] Attenborough himself had been a 'vast influence on the public and

*Attenborough with young mountain gorillas in 1978; the sequence
was filmed accidentally, and there was a row about using it*

on scientists', said Professor Patrick Bateson. 'He is a towering presence.' The
ambition to be seriously scientific was strong in the BBC wildlife programme-
making gestalt: not least because they related so intimately to scientific findings.
Some of the behaviour captured on film significantly altered scientific consensus.

As the film-makers set off it was well known that male antelopes aggressively rounded up females and herded them into their own special grounds to
mate: the he-man version of antelope behaviour. For several weeks, Salisbury
and the cameraman dutifully tried to film this scientifically authenticated
behaviour. The antelopes refused to oblige. Perhaps, Salisbury and his team
wondered, they were the wrong antelopes? Or it was the wrong time in the
breeding season? Or perhaps it was just exceptional behaviour? The evidence
of their eyes disrupted the findings of the scientists. Whatever the explanation, the antelopes did not seem to have read the script. The team in Bristol
began asking antelope specialists all over the world what was happening. The
arrival of a young female researcher from Harvard (herself an evolutionary
leap forward, a 'feminist' with a different set of expectations) confirmed, when

they showed her what was happening, what their eyes had already told them. Misled by inadequate science, they had been looking for the wrong behaviour. Lady antelopes – it appeared – did the choosing, delicately judging between the terrains held open invitingly by hopeful gentleman antelopes. Macho chaps were replaced, at a stroke, by choosing girls – and duly recorded.

Scientists (and academics in general) have long had deep reservations about the pollutions of popularity. Even Darwin had to be careful not to damage his scientific credentials by appearing too accessible. *On the Origin of Species* was 'just readable enough to sell, but unreadable enough not to be bracketed with journalism'.[57] Popular is usually seen as the opposite of rigorous, especially by academics. Nevertheless, the intense and creative milieu in Bristol produced a place in which 'something remarkable'[58] happened. The close proximity of the team meant that technical resources were exploited by the same people who were ranging so seriously across the science. 'You might think that a scientist might be reluctant to reveal to a television producer behaviour that he has taken years of sitting in some rain-drenched, insect-ridden jungle to observe and understand,' commented one member of the unit, 'but once they were convinced that their discoveries would not be distorted but presented as truthfully as we could manage, they welcomed us enthusiastically.'[59] This was particularly true of scientists whose findings were sensitive.

Thus the ethnologist Christophe Boesch had spent a decade patiently observing chimpanzees, concluding that they were omnivores who hunted and killed other animals. Such a potentially controversial finding, if handled sensationally, could have changed public attitudes towards them and added to the mounting threats to their survival.[60] But he trusted the Attenborough team to explain it properly. The tone of the unit and Attenborough was scientific and theirs was a scientific contribution, if not exactly a scientific finding. Scientists often feel isolated from the public, yet Attenborough and *Life on Earth* have for 40 years remained an avenue of understanding that scientists have not often been able to build for themselves.

Most academic studies of animal behaviour in the seventies ought to have been retitled, Salisbury remarked, 'Animal behaviour in August on a grant', because that was the month academics went into the field. By contrast, the wildlife film people observed behaviour over a far wider spread of time as they waited for the film opportunity they needed. They had another advantage too: while scientists use observations to provide evidence for theories, unbiased wildlife film-makers are sometimes more open to the evidence of their eyes. Cameramen in particular brought skills to the tasks: 'Cameramen have to be able to predict behaviour in order to get their film,' said Attenborough. Just as in war zones cameramen are good at reading the meaning of changing scenarios in a conflict, so in wildlife filming cameramen were 'almost instinctively sensitive' to changes in animal moods and behaviour: 'They have differently wired early-warning systems.'[61] Recently wildlife filming has become more commercial and highly competitive, in part because of the market for grand wildlife extravaganzas created by programmes like *Life on Earth*, but in the seventies many of the cameramen were 'just passionate and dedicated their lives to preserving animal behaviour on film'.

Life on Earth made a unique contribution to public service television, difficult for scientists to assess and yet surely part of scientific endeavour. Scientific discovery has nearly always been a product of a wide community of inquiry. The team grown by the BBC in Bristol represented, for the late twentieth century, something like the 'gentlemen scientists' that surrounded Darwin. Like the nineteenth-century pioneers, the BBC's team was rigorous, and it had similarly 'independent means' provided by the licence fee – not financed by the narrower protocols of the research councils as most scientists were. The team had a unique and voracious capacity to synthesise and assess research. They were nomadic, roaming over academic communities across the world (before the internet made these things easier), not bounded as scientists were by disciplinary divisions. They did so critically: judging, discarding and integrating new findings into their thinking. Yet television was rapacious. Research that had taken a whole lifetime of thinking and observation would be consumed and displayed in a few seconds of elegant film. Attenborough 'made it all look too easy', said Bateson. Being 'very sympathetic to criticism', Attenborough responded in later work by showing the work of the scientists as well as the team.

Attenborough was showered with the most prestigious scientific honours because, having insisted on writing the texts for the programmes, he ensured (and the team helped him fulfil this ambition) that everything he said was tightly accurate. Scientists appreciated that he never sensationalised, every word was anchored in evidence; 'he was very acutely fastidious about what he could and couldn't say', said Bateson. It was Attenborough's power to 'pluck out the central problems of any topic with an absolutely unerring eye',[62] however, which was so distinctive. Bateson observed that these programmes presented recognisably authoritative narratives back to scientists. Wrestling to the heart of complex situations and then giving an elegantly simple account of them is a broadcasting skill: in Attenborough's case refined to a very fine level. It is also the most revered quality in scientific research.

THE EFFECT

Attenborough placed mankind in perspective. 'Man's passion to communicate and to receive communication seems as central to his success as the fin was to the fish or the feather to the bird,' he said in the last programme. He says communication is so necessary to being human that we do it with the past when we decipher history, while mathematicians attempt to communicate truths through all of eternity. It has been a unique way of 'accumulating and transferring experience across generations'. The last part of *Life on Earth* turns to mankind, and 'this may have given the impression that somehow man is the ultimate triumph of evolution'. There is, Attenborough warns, 'no scientific evidence whatsoever to support such a view and no reason to suppose that our stay here will be more permanent than that of the dinosaur'. Were mankind to be extinguished, then 'a modest, unobtrusive' creature would move into a new niche – like the mammals that took the place of the dinosaurs. Evolution, he points out, is a process of survival. He goes on to his most important message, however: 'Although denying we have a special position in the natural world might seem becomingly modest in the eye of eternity, it might also be used as an excuse for evading our responsibilities ... The fact is that no species has ever had such wholesale control over everything on earth, living or dead, as we now have.' That lays upon us, he ends, 'an awesome responsibility. In our hands lies not only our own future, but that of all other living creatures with whom we share the earth.'[63]

While Darwin's theories provided the spectacle of the extinction of individual species and the fossil record offered evidence of cataclysmic events, evolution remained a narrative without interruptions (the mechanisms go on working even after the extinctions) and without conclusion. Attenborough offers the horrifying implicit message that human intervention may interfere with the enduring time of evolution. Mankind may be evolving but he is also driving his fellow species to extinction faster than species can adapt. This is the truth that haunts the series. Humans are 'the determining absence'.[64] They alone are stewards.

The key Darwinian moral message of *Life on Earth* was that 'mankind is not apart from the natural world. We don't have dominion over it.' There was indeed a single creator of everything: natural selection. Sexual reproduction produced variety, and the wasteful profusion of excess – millions of tiny pollen dusts floating out, hundreds of thousands of fish eggs sailing off into the deeps – and the baroque adaptations of life all evidence of its processes. But there were other lessons too: the probability of extinction and the fleeting insignificance of any individual lifespan. Milton had been Darwin's constant reading companion on the *Beagle*. *Life on Earth* brought its great popular audiences to Milton's appreciation of the fecundity of nature in *Comus*, in a kind of demotic modern poetry. Television stretched it to its scientific and aesthetic limits:

> Wherefore did Nature pour her bounties forth,
> With such a full and unwithdrawing hand,
> Covering the earth with odours, fruits and flocks,
> Thronging the seas with spawn innumerable,
> But all to please, and sate the curious taste?[65]

In the middle of gathering social and political unrest and economic decline, the British public was entranced by *Life on Earth*. It was so British, or indeed English, precise, clear, uninflected with grandeur of tone yet momentous. Beyond the elegance of the argument, the technical innovation, the cultured eye that cut films of such beauty, the driving urgency of inspiring awe for nature in the public, the privilege of displaying such wonders, is a simplicity. Attenborough 'just makes television'. Does that make him an original thinker? *Life on Earth* was the achievement of a team and the product of ways of mind and action that the BBC made possible. Attenborough was himself a public service animal who helped shape the value of the Corporation's public service, but who had worked within it and been formed by it.

Maynard Keynes identified a distinct national cast of mind in an essay on Malthus (but also, of course, on himself), which had been marked 'by an extraordinary continuity of *feeling*, if I may so express it, the tradition which is suggested by the names of Locke, Hume, Adam Smith, Paley, Bentham, Darwin, and John Stuart Mill, a tradition marked by the love of truth and a most noble lucidity, by a prosaic sanity, free from sentiment or metaphysic, and by an immense disinterestedness and public spirit. There is continuity in these writings not only of feeling but of actual matter.'[66] Attenborough would blanch at being placed in such a tradition. Yet he and his team used television in the tradition of disinterestedness and public value that Keynes describes. At a time when the British doubted themselves, he was a master of 'noble lucidity', a contemporary model of the unshowy, focused on the job in hand, effortlessly in command of the story of all of creation for everyone – on television. It made the battered British public more comfortable, more knowledgeable and in a way less frightened, watching something that took them out of themselves and yet told them truths about themselves.

THE ROYAL WEDDING: BRITISH SHINTOISM AT WORK

THE RULES OF ENGAGEMENT

The summer of 1981 was the summer of riots, as the poor and excluded from the urban ghettos of Toxteth, London and Bristol exploded with frustration and anger at the sharp rise in unemployment. Meanwhile, the Queen displayed 'guts, pluck and bottle'[1] when, shot at during the Trooping of the Colour, she was broadcast live by the BBC, coolly in command of her rearing horse. Then the nation cheered up with news of a wedding: Prince Charles was going to marry Lady Diana Spencer. The BBC was delighted. The marriage of the heir to the throne was an opportunity to produce a spectacle that the public and vast international audiences would revel in: it would tell a different British story after years of bleak economic misery. Together the BBC and the Palace knew how to make world-entrancing ceremonial theatre. BBC coverage of royal events had contributed to the monarchy cult, but the traffic was two-way. The public interest stimulated by successful royal events boosted television and the BBC. Up and down the Corporation, people began to plot how to build anticipatory excitement, capture the largest audiences, involve the regions, explain it to children and generally make the most of it. All of this was in competition with ITV, which was muscling in on the BBC's special relationship with royalty by setting up a Ceremonial unit.

The previous autumn, press speculation about who Prince Charles would marry had gathered momentum: a story driven by a developing media rapaciousness that the Palace would find increasingly difficult to manage, and that would expose the BBC to some difficult choices in the decade following the wedding. Royal reporting had been one of the tools used by the *Sun* in its emergence as an accomplished shaper and stoker of public mood. From 1975 the *Sun*'s James Whitaker and the photographer Arthur Evans tracked Prince Charles like wolves. In September 1980, they had a scoop – a distant picture of the Prince fishing in the grounds of Balmoral with a young woman. Meanwhile the *Mail*, transforming itself under brilliant new editor David English into the most powerful newspaper in the country, pushed the story ruthlessly. Its waspish gossip columnist Nigel Dempster boasted of having dispatched all previous contenders for the royal hand by revealing that they had slept with other people – or indeed that they had slept with the Prince.[2]

In November, ITN's *News at Ten* quite exceptionally devoted a whole bulletin to Lady Diana, while BBC news continued to ignore tabloid tittle-tattle. The head of BBC news, Peter Woon, did, however, dispatch Brian Hanrahan to prepare a profile of Lady Diana, just in case. As he believed the BBC Royal Liaison unit and the Palace would have refused his requests for interviews, Hanrahan just phoned up Diana's mother, Frances Shand Kydd. She inflated the number of O-levels her daughter had got and was confident that the inexperienced teenager would have no trouble handling the media because she had grown up so close to royal life. 'We are part of it,' she assured Hanrahan. He got the impression that the deal was done if not signed and sealed.[3]

Lady Diana was offered up as a 'suitable' bride partly because journalists like Nigel Dempster hypocritically policed a value system of exemplary royal sexual virtue in order to sell newsapapers. It was a system increasingly at odds with the common British experience. The *Guardian* had observed that the Prince seemed to need to find 'a virgin protestant aristocrat' to marry.[4] This was not BBC territory but *Woman's Hour* performed nobly, with items on young women's need for father figures, and the difficulties of marriages between people of different generations. Prince Charles had finally proposed to Lady Diana on 6 February 1981. According to Andrew Morton's account, she rushed home to tell her flatmates, 'flopped down on the bed and announced, "Guess what?" Her flatmates cried out in unison, "He asked you!" and she replied, "He did and I said 'Yes, please.'"'[5] The royal couple made their 'betrothal' public on 25 February and Hanrahan had a BBC scoop. He had hoarded the private telephone number of Diana's father, and consequently Earl Spencer gave his first public response to the news to the BBC. Later that same day, the engaged couple gave an interview to the BBC's Angela Rippon and Keith Graves (who had wisely arrived at work in a suit with a silk handkerchief in his pocket, and was dispatched by Woon in preference to the more dishevelled Hanrahan). During it, the Prince famously replied to the question of whether he was in love that he was – 'whatever love means'.

The republican MP William Hamilton called the engagement a deliberate attempt to distract attention from the latest unemployment figures: 'The winter of discontent is now being replaced by the winter of phony romance with the active connivance of the government.'[6] Yet republicanism was largely an eccentricity in 1981, not a swell of opinion. In an opinion poll four months before the wedding, only one man – a road sweeper in Bloomsbury – was ignorant of the event: 'Feel?' he said. 'What should I feel? I don't care, it doesn't affect me.' The seventies had seen a revival of interest in the monarchy, which the BBC had helped reflect, and the wedding was the beginning of a new frenzy of royalty worship, which perturbed shrewder courtiers and a more reflective section of the public. The Corporation, the broadcaster most in charge of the final collaborative monarchy-fest, the wedding itself, did not impose feelings on a duped audience.

On 3 March, the *Guardian* wrote that 'the BBC has taken a hand in the arrangements for the royal wedding', reporting that Will Wyatt had written to the Palace: 'Yr Highness ... you will know that the British summer is full of events,' the coverage for which was already planned. He helpfully added, 'This is to let you know we have outside broadcast facilities available on the following dates ...'[7] The chosen day, 29 July, was indeed one that the BBC had mentioned.

Public feelings of loyalty and affection for the royal family swelled. The Corporation crafted the long, pleasurable build-up of expectation: *Woman's Hour* discussed royal wedding dresses and their impact on bridal fashion, 'wedding nerves' and Diana's 'blow-dry bob' haircut, 'easy to maintain and contemporary, a modern girl's no-nonsense style' (unlike Her Majesty's disciplined coiffure was the implicit message). *Blue Peter* held a 'design your own' royal wedding commemoration plate competition, which more than fifty thousand children entered, and a cook your own Royal Wedding Flan demonstration: kipper and egg were, somewhat surprisingly, seen as appropriate celebratory fare. There were regular updates on 'The Royal Wedding in Your Street', and a special on all the ways in which the wedding would break records: the longest street party, the most watchers, the biggest cake.[8] *Top Gear* tested the new 'wedding' Ford Capri. Radio 3 explored the royal wedding music and ran a series on previous royal patrons. Everywhere else there were items discussing the mystery of the dress, the tiara, the lunch, the house, the bridesmaids and plans for the day.

BBC News continued to believe that the fuss about the wedding was sentimental bunkum, and ran a cheeky little item saying that although the wedding was good news for business, it was bad news for bears: six hundred had been slaughtered for new Guards bearskins for the big day. The BBC did show Lady Diana getting out of a car wearing a low-cut dress, but they did not draw attention to what Stuart Purvis at ITN had cheerfully directed his watching audience's eyes to: an exposed nipple. Purvis put a black line round it in case it was hard to identify. Diana Spencer's rather shaky home life was described but not questioned. It seemed modern of the royal bride to 'come from a broken home', like an increasing number of Britons. The BBC's coverage was one element in a great storm, as other TV networks, newspapers and magazines learnt the commercial value of a picture of 'Lady Di' on the front page. Interest in the monarchy was about to become an obsession: psychoanalysts talked of 'projection', the process by which personal problems are externalised on to another person or institution. In Diana, it was as if the nation and the world had found the perfect vehicle for a swarm of issues. The spectacle of her figure put her eating habits on the front pages where they would stay, punitively, till she died. People had often reported dreaming about the Queen; now the Princess entered the nation's sleep. Few understood the miserable mayhem the combination of this particular princess, her dependence on attention, a shift in mores, the pressures on the Prince who had chosen her, and developments in media were to wreak on the monarchy and, indeed, on Diana herself.

On *Nationwide* Diana was refashioned into 'a normal, fun-loving, contemporary girl'. 'Lady Diana Spencer has worked as a nanny and a nursery assistant,' enthused the *Six O'Clock News* on the day of her engagement. The BBC profile of her, broadcast two days later, said that she liked 'ordinary country things' and that 'like many young women in their first job in London', she had shared a flat with friends. It did not mention that her father had bought it for her for hundreds of thousands of pounds. Everybody colluded in the same myth: fresh and wholesome, contemporary and unspoilt. Yet although her cord trousers and jolly jumpers were just what any girl wanted to wear, and every woman's ambition to get thinner was admirably realised in her, her life was in fact far removed from most people's experience. She was an aristocrat from an older English Whig family than the parvenu Windsors. Few dared to point out that by contemporary standards she was almost a child herself and barely educated. She might have worked as a nursery assistant, but no one expected her to turn into a career teacher. The nursery was a holding pen, from which she was being launched on to the marriage market. Yet the media interpreted this exceptional experience as an 'ordinary' life and the BBC colluded.

The Corporation was an actor as well as a spectator in the changing basis of royal power. The BBC had 'produced' monarchy intimately from the start of broadcasting. John Reith, anxious to associate himself with the Establishment but also creatively making up new forms, busied himself around royal opportunities. The first royal broadcast had been at the 1924 Empire Exhibition at Wembley, and the BBC had persuaded monarchs to speak directly to their subjects, starting with the Christmas message in 1932. Reith had vigilantly overseen Edward VIII as he made his abdication speech, ostensibly as an assistant, but also to ensure that the unreliable monarch did not depart from the agreed script and make a last-minute appeal to the British public. The BBC was at this point protecting the constitution, in contrast to the Martin Bashir interview with Princess Diana later, which permitted her to challenge the monarchy without the usual rules of balance or questioning. The political nuances of the abdication would not be made widely public until a 1978 BBC Drama series on Edward and Mrs Simpson.

In 1865, Walter Bagehot, the constitutional theorist, had identified the significance of a royal wedding: 'A princely marriage ... rivets mankind.' The idea of a family on the throne 'brings down the pride of sovereignty to the level of petty life'.[9] The late-twentieth-century monarchy actively pursued the

Supper: The Royal Family, *1969*

'model family' as a justification of its role (along with philanthropy) and the Corporation had been a vital co-writer of this story. In 1969, the BBC had assisted in the wildly successful series *The Royal Family*. The idea came from a new royal press secretary, the Australian William Heseltine, arising from his feeling that the 'Royal family was almost too dull, and that one ought to lift the curtain of obscurity'.[10] The producer Richard Cawston managed to relax his subjects with 'a good team that faded into the wallpaper'.[11] The series was ostensibly concerned with the 'duties that go on behind the scenes'[12] and it did show the Queen and the royal family at work. But perhaps more rivetingly, it revealed a family drama.

The royal family emerge from these extraordinary films with clear personalities – the Queen as someone with a sense of comic timing as well as sturdy, impenetrable dedication to duty. She is shown meeting her prime minister, Harold Wilson, for the weekly appointment. Wilson bows, low and obsequiously. 'When do you actually set orf?' Her Majesty enquires. 'Tuesday morning, crack of dawn,' Wilson replies in Yorkshire. The 'family' have supper and discuss how difficult it is to keep a straight face on occasions: Prince Charles contributes a joke and seems to be ignored.

The film was a tremendous success for the monarchy – or so it seemed at the time. It was shown to vast fascinated audiences at home and abroad. It was a coup for the Corporation. Yet having declared war on those who exposed royal secrets, the monarchy had itself 'disclosed more homely facts than servants could ever tell'. The series was a landmark but also a problem: David Attenborough shrewdly observed that once the tribespeople had seen inside the headman's hut, the mystery would go. After withdrawing it from public view at the end of 1969, the Palace have never allowed the series to be repeated. By the 1980s, BBC producers were coming up with many other ideas for interviews with members of the royal family. Would Prince Charles like to talk about 'My Idea of Heaven', Princess Anne talk about her horses? Would Princess Michael of Kent, whose German origins had recently been much discussed in the press, like to give a regional news programme a tour around her house? Ideas flowed hither and thither, always seeking an interview with the royal 'Person' – and always rejected.

The formidable Jane Astell, head of the BBC's Royal Liaison unit, said, 'I was 101 per cent sure' that a whole set of proposals would be turned down as 'the invitations were too personal'.[13] Astell presided over an office at the top of Kensington House overflowing with paper. She had a fine collection of hats, a suitably Establishment tone of voice, and enjoyed tracking down horrible miscreant BBC programme makers who attempted to bypass her, 'as the Special Branch would a spy'.[14] She brokered the flow of requests from the BBC to the Palace, and tried to explain each side to the other. It was pointless, she exploded to one producer, asking the Queen Mother to donate a fishing rod to a charity she had little to do with. The Palace nearly always refused personal appearances, although Princess Margaret had done *The Archers* and *Desert Island Discs*. While *The Archers* was for an anniversary of the NSPCC, the Roy Plomley appearance was more calculated by the Palace at a point when Margaret's private life was controversial. The BBC accepted the deal. The Palace seemed to want to have its cake and eat it, letting personality out in public on its terms: a compact that would be shredded by the new cast member.

OUTSIDE BROADCASTING

When Mike Lumley, the Outside Broadcasts (OB) producer who master-minded coverage, first heard of the wedding, his immediate thought was to call the Abbey to get in with requests for camera positions before ITV. When the royal couple unexpectedly chose St Paul's, it proved a wasted effort. Two years before the wedding, Lumley had emerged as head of Outside Broadcasts after producing coverage of the funeral of Lord Mountbatten in 1979 with imagina-tion and respect. Plans always started with precedents. Outside broadcasting had an ethos, a method and a morality. At the very first outside broadcast in 1937, the televising of the Remembrance Day service, the producer had paid two small boys to run towards the Cenotaph, and had caught the headlines by showing them doing so. Yet it was soon recognised that such interference was destructive to the unique qualities of successful outside broadcasting. Peter

Dimmock, the thoughtful creator of the unit in the fifties, said in 1977 that the essence was 'to report real happenings, while they happen and from where they happen'. Finding a dozing spectator during a boring cricket match was the right way to comment on the proceedings, but 'tame actors and planted pretty girls in a crowd' were not. Dimmock's manifesto for outside broadcasting is an enduringly intelligent set of precepts. If a plane crashes during an OB broadcast then the commentator becomes a news reporter, but must still describe what is happening and not speculate on what they do not have evidence for. The failure of an event to behave properly might add to the drama of the experience, but the failure of OB to capture it seamlessly would be incompetent, and break trust with audiences. The broadcasts transformed distant citizens into intimate observers and were, potentially at least, democratising forces. The scrupulous veracity of what was seen on screen was part of the larger BBC value system.

By the 1970s, however, the tight core of expertise handed down from the beginning of broadcasting was under threat. Internal training had gone and experienced staff were leaving for ITV. Later in the decade, camera and satellite technology allowed news to move in on live events, and Outside Broadcasts as a specialism diminished. Toni Charlton recalled that, at music events, 'by the eighties I was producing people who didn't know a viola from a violin'. There was increasingly fierce commercial competition for important events. A televised Miss World competition or the Grand National attracted audiences of 20–30 million. But much outside broadcasting was the routine meat of the schedules – *Top of the Form, Multi-Coloured Swap Shop*, sport and church services. In 1979, nearly 20 per cent of the transmission time of both BBC channels was produced by Outside Broadcasts. In 1981 the OB units were still the masters of reality as it occurred. They thought of themselves as the 'SAS of broadcasting' because they were practical, physical, expeditionary and, as live events only happen once, very focused. They 'did not have silly things like actors, make believe and studios to deal with', said Will Wyatt.

Combining the drama of the unexpected with a steady visual and oral narrative could be fraught. Transmitting state events required a vast planning exercise, cash, creative ingenuity and a lot of adrenalin on the day. For the Palace, 'Planning', said Dickie Arbiter, an ex-BBC royal correspondent turned Palace press secretary, 'involves answering journalists' insistent questions: "Can we put a camera behind the altar?" "No." Answering foreign broadcasters' questions: "No, the route between the Palace and Westminster Abbey does not pass, nor can it be altered to pass, the American embassy in Grosvenor Square to make the route better for American audiences."'[15]

By the seventies, political and ceremonial routes in London were permanently cabled for outside broadcasting. There were discreet Tardis-like grey pillboxes hidden behind doors on College Green and along the Mall, containing broadcasting centres primed and waiting for events – secret manholes full of cables. Producers, engineers and the police 'walked the routes', reviewing the cable installations, considering the likely camera sites for different events, looking at changes in street furniture, applying the latest health and safety regulations. Later, under John Birt, these skills were outsourced and lost, but at this point they were firmly part of the BBC operation.

The BBC and the monarchy as two large symbolic and practical national institutions operated in a similar constitutional space. They both had an explicit commitment to abjure partisanship, yet were closely related to the political settlement: the Queen as the Head of State, the BBC as an 'impartial' broadcaster with a special duty towards the political process and the state. These roles were matched by another representative and listening responsibility to the 'nation'. The monarch, as 'head of the nation', is interested 'in the mood of the people, vigilant in taking its pulse', said Samantha Cohen, royal press secretary.[16] The BBC listens to and represents the nation to itself. The Corporation also established working and personal relationships with the Palace that helped shape the monarchy. People such as Godfrey Talbot moved from the BBC to press jobs in the Palace. The incomparable Frank Gillard had accompanied the royal family on their first foreign trip after World War II as the BBC producer: 'If I did anything to upset Their Majesties, or the royal entourage, my name would be forevermore mud in the BBC.'[17] Gillard helped draft the historic words with which Princess Elizabeth dedicated herself to the nation over the air on her 21st birthday: 'I declare before you all that my whole life, whether it be long or short, shall be devoted to your service ... But I shall not have the strength to carry out this resolution alone unless you join in it with me as I now invite you to do.' She repeated these words at her Silver Jubilee. If the monarchy was the 'decorative part of the constitution', then it was the BBC's Outside Broadcasts unit that by the late twentieth century brought this to the public. It produced the Crown in pageant mode, carefully dealing with organisers in the Palace, nudging them towards what it needed from the event to take it to the nation.

PRODUCING THE WEDDING

The Outside Broadcasts producer reduces complex, multiple things that happen simultaneously to a comprehensible narrative for viewers. Besieged by alternatives in a dynamically changing situation, he sits in his dark hut, and tries to produce coherence from chaos. He is a reporter with a front-row seat, yet conductor of the screened experience, ordering and shuffling images from camera crews (who keep alert to the mood of the crowd and the event around them), guiding and listening to commentators who might lead the pictures or depart from a prepared script. Things go wrong, soldiers faint, princesses are late, choristers start too soon, it rains. The producer creates a story for the viewing public, making sure that the emotional architecture finds the right place in the televised reality, but like a sculptor the stone is real. It took meticulous planning to bring off perfect shots, yet they had to be alert to the event as it happened. At Mountbatten's funeral, when Lumley heard the sound of the sombre footfall of marching soldiers, he recognised its emotional power and highlighted it.

Outside Broadcasts needed a commentator to bring the experience to life. At the Coronation in 1953, Richard Dimbleby had seen himself as 'an annotator – providing the background notes for the viewer and explaining each act in the ritual'. But he became something far larger, 'his voice, slow and reverential, [weaving] a pattern' around the event, and his words blended with the words of the ceremony 'so that it seemed to someone watching it on television as if the Coronation were being conducted not by the Archbishop, but by Richard Dimbleby'.[18] Peter Dimmock had written a set of terse instructions in 1952: '1, Watch your monitor; 2, Don't repeat the picture; 3, Don't be afraid of silence; 4, Don't talk over important events.' Although the commentator had to see the event as the public saw it, John Snagge said that at the Coronation he had to 'speak at a pace which was in accordance with the movement of people'.[19] The commentator also had to know everything the participants knew, and more than that, everything that an impartial expert could explain.

Every choice was dedicated to enhancing the emotional impact of the event as a whole. Before the wedding, a thoughtful letter in the in-house BBC magazine *Ariel* observed that the pressure to move into close-up shots too fast should be resisted: 'Considerable courage is needed to select long shots.' The producer needed to replicate the 'geography of feeling of an actual participant, from the distant glimpse of the procession to the excitement as it comes into sight'. The letter was preserved carefully – and Lumley was thoughtful about how best to modulate a long day's events.[20] He wanted to produce 'vibrant kaleidoscopes' and was proud of the sophisticated layering of images and sound, the insertion of pictures from Wales while the congregation sang 'I vow to thee my country', glimpses of royal gardens. A BBC stopwatch at the wedding rehearsal spotted a clash between the arrival of the choir and, one of the highlights, the arrival of the bridesmaids. The ceremony was altered to bring the choir in earlier.

Since the start of television, producers had made demands on the event itself. As early as the 1937 Coronation, the BBC had written to the Palace:

What I am going to ask you may seem impertinence! Please don't regard it as such. It is this: could you ask the King and Queen if they would be so kind as to look out of the Royal Coach window to the right as they approach and enter the main arch of Apsley Gate on their return drive to

Buckingham Palace on May 12th? ... There will be only a few seconds in which to televise them, and it would be a ghastly disappointment if they happened to be looking in the opposite direction, and not be seen at all.[21]

The King and Queen remembered and the royal family were thereafter always informed of camera positions. At a Palace consultation over the Coronation, Dimmock demonstrated the filming with a wide-angle lens. On the day itself he used a close-up. Nevertheless, as camera lenses became more powerful, tighter close-ups became more possible. The BBC complained of the way in which ITV were prepared to go in more closely. Yet Lumley thought that in 1981 'people still held back ... there was a feeling of significant respect' that influenced how close a camera would go in, with both the public and the broadcasters wanting to observe rather than intrude into the ceremony. Yet this was against the background, at least with Princess Diana, of an increasingly rapacious press, who were going to move in closer and closer.

PLANNING FOR THE WORST

The Palace, said a programme maker, 'is charming, sympathetic, understanding, courteous – and then says no'.[22] The first request for help in making programmes surrounding the event and for details of the plans for the day itself had been sent to the Palace in March. Michael O'Shea had replied that Palace planning for the wedding was not sufficiently advanced to make any decisions. By the beginning of April, Phil Lewis, head of Entertainment, was calling for 'Royal wedding tact ... one or two examples have come to light of the BBC appearing to run the wedding, which is in fact far from the truth ... please be careful.'[23] Cliff Morgan approached the Palace delicately, oozing respect, to ask whether the BBC could use a helicopter to take aerial pictures of the route to give 'a totally new dimension to television coverage of the wedding'. The reply came back: 'I am sorry to pour cold water on this lovely idea of yours,' but the Queen 'would not be happy' with the distracting noise. Morgan tried again: could they fly the route early in the morning before the wedding, or the day before the ceremony? A different kind of 'No' came back: many broadcasters had been asking for this. 'I am afraid that we cannot make any exception for the BBC.'[24] By the end of April, the BBC was getting frantic.

One reason for caution was a realistic anxiety about security: after the Mountbatten assassination, mayhem in Northern Ireland, the shots fired at the Queen, and disorder breaking out on inner-city streets, there might be trivial incidents or a large disaster. So many policeman were to be on the streets of the parade that there was a worry that crime would break out elsewhere – 'while the cats were away the mice would play', BBC planners reported. The security risk meant that the carriage processions were to move at a trot rather

If there were a security 'event', John Humphrys would handle it from
a new emergency communications unit; (left to right) Jenni Murray,
Humphrys and Brian Redhead in the Today *studio later in 1986*

than the usual slower pace. American broadcasters in the briefing before the event were, said the BBC commentator Tom Fleming, 'obsessed with how our cameras would deal with an assassination attempt, or how we would cover riots in The Mall'.

The shots fired in the Mall earlier in the year had exposed a communications failure between the police, who had not planned how to deal with such an event, and a confused BBC, which received no reliable information and which also had no plan in place. For an hour, millions of viewers were left in doubt about the meaning of what they had seen – with many phoning the BBC to find out. What might have been a serious assassination attempt had, it turned out, been blank shots fired by a disturbed young man. But the threats were real enough. A few weeks before the incident in the Mall, and four days after the death of the hunger striker Bobby Sands, a potentially devastating IRA plot caused an explosion as the Queen and the King of Norway opened the largest oil terminal in Europe, at Sullom Voe in the Shetlands. An undercover IRA unit had worked as engineers on the project for two years, but only one of the four bombs had exploded, and it was not on the platform the Queen was on. Instead of a vast, oil-fuelled explosion, there was minor damage barely mentioned on the BBC broadcast of the event. The Queen was characteristically unruffled.[25] The Corporation received a puzzled phone call from a man with an Irish accent asking whether it had been reported at all. The possibility

of an attack on the royal wedding ran like a dark undertow beneath preparations for the happy day.

For the first time, the BBC liaised closely with the police in advance, and
a news 'nerve centre' was set up to assess and analyse any disruption, with
access to the live feed from anywhere on the route. The BBC planned for
three possibilities – a 'modest disturbance with action on camera' (the main
commentator would refer to it, followed if necessary by a further, more
informed report), a 'considerable event that disturbs the ceremony but does
not require any further action', and 'a major event with aftermath disturbance
which stops the event'. In the latter case, Angela Rippon would handle the
immediate story, with John Humphrys on hand to take over commentary from
the more strategically informed newsroom. A reporter based at Scotland Yard
would be the first source of information. However large or small the incident,
'If anything happens it must be reflected by the commentator immediately …
In the event of a major incident then the story has to be covered.'[26] Directors
were instructed in the case of an incident not to editorialise, or even attempt
to explain, 'but to send it up to the BBC nerve centre for a decision on what
to show'. Cameramen were enjoined 'to keep watch' and not just to sit back
when their contribution was over.

PREPARED

Meanwhile, Helen Holmes, the BBC researcher on the wedding, began to
amass her mighty files, the background resource for everyone from commentators to electricians: every known fact on the route, the biography and
formal roles of the people involved, the origins and wording of the ceremony,
details of the flowers and the bell ringers at St Paul's (who were to include 'a
consultant gynaecologist, a pilot, a schoolteacher and an industrial chemist').
Anxiety was gathering, however, as the Palace had still not finally agreed to
any of the films the BBC needed to make in eight royal locations. Phil Lewis
said, 'In ten weeks we have to film, edit, write and dub. To achieve stories of
distinction and style we will need every minute of that time …' On top of this,
in 1981 even choristers had their shop stewards, and as usual the need was to
square the unions before the event. 'The St Paul's Choristers have already got
wind of the project and through Equity are demanding higher-than-minimum
fees which we are contesting.'[27]

By February, the BBC was worrying about how much the wedding
coverage might cost and considering sharing camera sites with ITV, but the
experience of the Jubilee made them wary of the idea.[28] By March, a little
competitive cunning was entering the BBC's collective mind: at the Board of
Management it was 'suggested that in trailing the Royal Wedding the BBC
should not overlook the opportunity to encourage the public to change

over from monochrome to colour'. Nearly 5 million households were still to make the change to colour and the higher licence fee it entailed. The Prince of Wales had suggested that the BBC might put on some kind of entertainment programme to commemorate the event. The delicate task of turning this down was passed right up to the director-general. Trethowan explained tactfully and carefully that 'sadly' there was not enough time to put together a show. 'As your Royal Highness said, the heart of it would be in good writing, and this above all needs time.'[29] By early July, the morning programme was at last taking shape. An interview opportunity with Lady Diana's younger brother Charles had been confirmed, to be filmed at Diana's family home, Althorp.[30]

BBC Radio London proposed an innovation: to broadcast throughout the night through PA speakers for the million people who were expected to camp out for a good position to see the wedding. To add to their joy as they tried to sleep, there would be phone-ins from families around the country and Tony Blackburn would be out and about all night in the radio car.[31] The idea grew into a single 'national' programme combining contributions from all the local radio stations. Birmingham thought it might contribute a story about the local Stourbridge firm that had made the royal bed; Manchester one about the sad plight of those who wanted to marry on the same day as the royal couple; Cleveland thought it might read out a couple of the winning entries to its royal wedding poetry competition. It was also 'a symbolic act of unity', according to the controller of Local Radio. This being the BBC, however, there were dark rumours of dangerous precedents, of long-term attempts to reduce local autonomy, and a plot to impose 'Broadcasting House, Fourth Floor' rule over the nation by producing a 'national' local radio programme. 'Lest you think there is some form of virulent anti-London fever in the manager's office,' protested Geoff Talbott, the manager of Radio Leeds, explaining his decision to opt out of the joint broadcast, 'here in the North there is not quite the universal salivation for the royal wedding that there appears to be elsewhere.'[32]

FIREWORKS

The broadcasters secured the public appearance they wanted. The BBC and ITN carried a joint interview on the eve of the wedding. The public reaction had been a great boost, said Lady Diana, fiddling with her earrings. Prince Charles said that he had enjoyed organising the music, and that he wanted 'everybody to come out having had a marvellous musical and emotional experience'. Asked about saying solemn vows in front of millions of people, Charles replied that he hoped it would be personal. 'I don't know about Diana, but I am more used to it, I think, knowing for years that there are cameras poking at you and recording every twitch you make.' Diana then said that she was beginning to get used to the attention, and that Prince Charles had been a tower of strength. 'Gracious,' said the Prince. 'I had to say that,' said Diana, ''cos you're sitting there.' Asked what interests they shared, Lady Diana came up with a list: 'Music, opera, outdoor sports, fishing, walking.' They sounded plausible. Except for pop, she soon loathed them all.

The picture of the busy man enchanted and tamed by a teasing and robust young woman seemed the very acme of modern sensibility. The not-so-discreet visit to a gynaecologist had also been reported: she was, it seemed, a fit brood mare. This fitted less well with contemporary views of romance, enhancing the image of the young woman as a sacrifice. At the wedding rehearsal she had wept. No one told the press. Toni Charlton made sure that instead of pictures from the rehearsal, only the 'bars' from the test card were transmitted, even to the BBC news (which Outside Broadcasts, rightly, did not trust to keep such a secret). OB had an ethic of personal responsibility. The BBC, having been given access to the rehearsal because they were utterly trusted, repaid it as a matter of honour – and human delicacy.

While everyone was having fun at the royal fireworks, Lady Diana spent the eve of her wedding alone. The BBC didn't have a great time either. The idea had been a magnificent London display, linked to celebratory bonfires ignited in sequence around the country. But it turned into a chaotic night with no one from the Palace seeming to 'produce' the event properly on the ground. Television showed groups of half-recognised foreign royals wandering aimlessly across the fireworks site, looking for their seats and familiar monarchs to greet. 'They had very little discipline all those royals.'[33] Things really got out of control when the first bank of fireworks accidentally set off the second bank. Field gunners waiting to fire a salute did not know what to do as fireworks ignited, and at one point a frenzied BBC cameraman was heard shouting, 'You've missed your cue!' in despair at the fireworks superintendent.

It got worse. The BBC's sound link did not work; the timings went wrong because of the fireworks debacle; the link to Scotland failed; the third wave of fireworks began to explode; and the commentator Raymond Baxter was so dire he was 'surely the only man who could turn Britain from a monarchy to a republic overnight'.[34] Baxter's reference to 'Princess Mark Phillips' did nothing to clarify the event as he ploughed on through his prepared script. 'And now the crescendo of Handel's great music will be accompanied by the best of the marvellous fire show ahead of us,' he intoned as the fireworks finally spluttered out.[35] Just as things began to settle down, a lone, late, rocket made everyone jump. Despite the pious devotion to the role of broadcasting as reflecting the real event, no one mentioned the anarchy. Afterwards Phil Lewis exploded: 'BBC Television went on air at a major royal occasion, with equipment and in conditions the like of which I have not seen in thirty years in television.'[36] While the dismayed Princess contemplated her fate, out in the

*Every picture was the result of Mike Lumley's planning
and the cooperation of the Palace*

park the BBC Outside Broadcast engineers had brought off a show 'by the skin of our teeth and nerves'.

THE BIG DAY

The wedding day itself, by contrast, was a wonderfully crafted piece of state and BBC drama. At 9.45 a.m. the BBC masterfully demarcated the end of the early morning build-up programme and the beginning of the ceremony itself with a sweeping panorama of the whole Mall. At the Cathedral, a frisson of shock was going around the waiting great and good. After the grand guests had settled in their seats, two scruffy men arrived to remove plastic covering from the aisle – 'designed to ensure a sort of pristine virtue for the carpet'. Having pulled the plastic off, the two workmen 'pranced' back down the Cathedral. It was rumoured, said Stuart Young, who was there and who had just become a BBC governor, that they might have been aping royalty. There was a great outcry and many letters of outrage. Roger Cary, in his inimitable BBC minute-taking style, called it the case of the *Two Gentlemen of St Paul's*. BBC crews at the event had been ordered to wear morning suits, and after a very thorough inquiry, the director-general and the heads of Entertainment, Events and Outside Broadcasts were able to report, on the very best evidence, that the unseemly men were certainly not BBC employees.

The Archbishop of Canterbury, Robert Runcie, gave the sermon at the wedding. When the couple visited him before the marriage, he found Prince Charles deeply depressed. He thought that it was an arranged marriage, but that 'They're a nice couple, and she'll grow into it.'[37] Runcie also observed that Lady Diana was 'very tender, very unformed. And yet had a sort of shrewdness.' The wise sermon, talking about how love had to be built, had been written in collaboration with the BBC's Religious Affairs correspondent, Gerald Priestland. The BBC camera positioned to film the vows was obscured by a bishop's mitre (not worn on the day of the rehearsal). To the sound of Elgar's 'Pomp and Circumstance' and Walton's 'Crown Imperial' the newly wed couple walked out into the sun to loud cheering. The Prince and Princess provided a new and final highlight with the first royal kiss on the balcony of the Palace. No one had expected it and it seemed to cap a fairy-tale romance. The nation and the world heaved a collective sigh of satisfaction. That evening, the royal family had a party at Claridge's, where they watched a video of the wedding, which the BBC had hurried to them, on large TV screens.

THE RECEPTION

After the wedding, the BBC took stock. The *Boston Globe* said, 'England pulls off ceremonies the way the army of Israel pulls off commando raids.' The *Sunday Times* said that it was 'the sort of thing that we over-do so well'.[38] The president of CBS and NBC in America and the head of Japanese Television all sent complimentary telegrams. The Kingdom of Thailand felt a particular affinity, with the director-general of Thai Television writing to say that 'the high level of competence and efficiency, the unswerving dedication to the project ... and the unstinted cooperation of the BBC' had produced a wonderful programme.[39] The later international obsession with the Princess of Wales was partly the product of this moment when the world had gathered together to watch the marriage.

The BBC won the ratings battle. By the time of the service, 24.6 million people were watching the BBC and 8.2 million ITV, a lead that was sustained. Altogether 85 per cent of the British population turned on to watch the wedding morning and, once they had chosen their station, very few flipped channels. Many others listened to the event on the radio, where Terry Wogan captured the largest audience.[40] But alongside those who felt that the BBC presenter Angela Rippon 'radiated wedding atmosphere', some found her 'too gushy' and a few thought the appearance of Dame Edna Everidge on the early morning show 'completely inappropriate'. The BBC's large audience had to do with Lumley's 'great sense of pictures, rhythmic direction and marvellous sound', but also with crafty scheduling, as many were captured by programming that started earlier than ever before.[41] In this sense, the wedding programme was a forerunner of breakfast television. The Prince and Princess were delighted, and later watched the BBC video of the event on the BBC wedding present to them – a new-fangled video machine.

The BBC Programme Review Board, however, was not uncritical. Lumley had captured and created a wholly satisfying emotional moment, producing 'wonderful pictures, a much better visual rhythm than ITV'. But the event had been treated as if it were a feature programme when in reality the faster, less reverential approach of News would have been better – ITV's version had been 'livelier'. Some BBC insiders thought that Alastair Burnet's 'capable and intelligent commentary'[42] on ITV had been sharper and more newsy than the BBC's. Unease was expressed at the way in which 'ITN was moving in on important public events', and using them to win the new-technology arms race against the Corporation. Because the *Today* radio team had done so much work on the wedding beforehand, they were 'soaked in the mood of the occasion', and some thought caught the atmosphere more acutely than television. There was also a review of relations with the Palace: would it be better to be devious or go through the proper channels? *Nationwide* complained that it had used the proper channels but had got no help. Chris Capron, the accomplished new head of news 'output', suspected that people who had agreed to be interviewed for *A Prince for Our Time*, the biopic that saw the Prince transformed by the proposal from royal romantic ditherer into modern action man, had withdrawn at the last minute under instruction from the Palace.[43] Lime Grove said that it had obtained an interview with Prince Charles 'by avoiding the official channels'.[44]

Afterwards *Blue Peter* asked children what their special memory had been. Ten-year-old Ranjit said, 'I was so happy because it was the Royal wedding, afterwards my eyes were hurting me with all the watching. Then we had lots of Indian food and cakes for the party.' A five-year-old liked the bit when they kissed: 'That made me feel sort of funny,' she said. The BBC had taken a public mood of solemnity and happiness, enhanced and stoked it, and fed it back to the people.

But the euphoria of the wedding turned out to be a kind of willed collective fantasy. A re-engineering of public values was under way. The BBC was in for a difficult time, as was the monarchy and the British public. Since World War II, whatever the failings of the British constitution and the British economy, the common sense and gumption of the people were taken for granted in the BBC. Now the BBC needed to navigate an uncertain new world where 'the right to self expression had become an article of faith'.[45] It was replacing British 'reserve'.

Even before the fragility of the relationship between Charles and Diana brought new dilemmas for the Corporation, the Palace thought the BBC difficult to deal with. A Palace press secretary and former broadcaster, Dickie Arbiter, said, 'If the BBC was nice about the monarchy in one programme it seemed as if it felt that it had to be a bit nasty somewhere else, there was a definite rhythm to it all ... the BBC was like a bovver boy with a steel toe cap.'[46] Yet the BBC's terms of trade were different from those of the paparazzi, who salaciously tracked Lady Diana into gyms and on to the beach even when she was pregnant. The BBC's 'special relationship' with the monarchy was also under competitive threat. Alastair Burnet, the presenter and one of the architects of the power of ITN, had developed a close personal relationship with the Prince and Princess. He was to conduct a notably 'gentle' interview with the couple at Highgrove, in which they presented themselves as a businesslike team. The interview was, it turned out, emollient propaganda. This was not what the BBC objected to at the time, however. Bill Cotton said that ITN broke the rules by winning their exclusive interview in exchange for a considerable donation to Operation Raleigh, an adventure charity.[47] It was reasonable to explore using royal exposure for charitable purposes. But the BBC was worried about a change in its ability to broadcast such events – free – to the nation. Milne returned from a special meeting with royal officials and reported to the governors that the interview had caused great displeasure at the Palace'.[48]

MONEY AND THINGS

The British public had an eager appetite for inspecting royal 'things'. Television could provide the frisson of peeping behind closed doors at how royalty lived, combined with inspecting spectacular national heritage: a hybrid of *House and Gardens* magazine, gossip and self-improving popular 'education'. Several proposals to make programmes about the houses and things the Queen owned were batted away by the Palace (including a folksy one with Arthur Negus, the presenter of *Antiques Roadshow*).

Then a better idea had emerged: to make a series exploring the history of the British monarchy through royal collections, for release in the year of the Queen's Silver Jubilee. Prince Philip suggested that the BBC invest in the production, have first rights to show it in the UK, but that any further income from international sales should go to a royal charitable trust for the preservation of the vulnerable collections. The Palace was also proposing that it control the making of the series,[49] and that a committee chaired by Prince Philip, on which the Palace was to outnumber the BBC by seven to two, run the project.[50] Richard Cawston, brought back by the BBC as someone who the Palace felt comfortable working with, said that the Palace's financial proposal was 'a monstrous suggestion',[51] since the BBC took all the risks without any guarantee of recouping the costs. In the end, Swann wrote a careful letter, a compromise was reached, the Corporation would get 40 per cent of the profits, and planning for the series began.

Michael Gill, who had made the great Kenneth Clark *Civilisation*, was producer, and the distinguished Cambridge historian J. H. Plumb was to write the scripts. Prince Philip's ideas for the series were enthusiastic and insightful. They record some of an intelligent man's observations on the role from inside the institution (some arrived via diplomatic bags from royal progresses abroad). He pointed out that what one monarch chose personally become part of the national collection of the next, and emphasised the transient role of a monarch and the ultimately mysterious essence of monarchy. The private life of a monarch and their public role had never been divisible, he observed, and there was a permanent and complete fusion of state and person in the monarch. It followed that royal taste, which found expression in the things they collected, evolved and responded to history because it was also personal. He contrasted this vigorous individuality with the stagnation of culture in communist, or 'comrade', regimes. Indeed, he argued for the superiority of the exercise of individual personal (and royal) tastes over any decisions made by councils or committees, let alone the carping of professional critics. Those collective cultural decisions, he argued, inhibited freedom of expression, and repressed the emergence of what was most needed, discriminating individual taste.[52]

Michael Gill was initially wary: 'Although the idea is highly attractive, I felt if not carefully handled it could appear a monstrous plug for royalty. At a time when the mood of the country seems to be taking a definite shift left, this could emerge as a reactionary series that could be harmful for the BBC.' One solution was to concentrate solely on the things, not the people. A better alternative was to reconsider the role of the real subject of the series, the monarchy. 'In a divisive time it would seem a Good Thing for the BBC to reinforce those elements that unite the country. I don't mean pap or by looking back with nostalgia. Of course it's possible to look at royalty through Willie Hamilton's eyes as one of the dividing elements, as a gang of bone-headed aristocrats who have made a lot of loot.' But he wanted to see them as historically shaped individuals who had also helped forge the nation. 'This process has been going on for over a thousand years and is still a living entity.' The tone should be neither 'admonitory nor adulatory'. It needed a presenter 'with a sympathy for beautiful things, with a sense of history, highly intelligent but with a human touch, able to move as easily with footmen as with royalty' and with a 'cool, ironic eye for human foibles'. Huw Wheldon had this 'protean range' and was chosen.[53]

Members of the royal family appeared: the Queen describing the weight of the state crown, Prince Charles rowing in a loch, the Queen Mother giving viewers a personal guided tour of the gardens of her own Scottish castle. There were conflicts with the Palace about scripts. Why, asked the Palace, were there so many references to Charles II's mistresses? Why was there so much emphasis on the Victorian period, when royal taste in art was unfortunate?

The discriminating taste of a great public service television creator:
Huw Wheldon introducing the taste of monarchs in Royal Heritage

In the middle of shooting the series, Wheldon needed cancer treatment and wrote from hospital that the series was 'a dog's dinner almost by definition, an uneasy meal between Royalty, Art, History, Guided tours and poshed up Open University Introductory series ... I hop skip and jump from Palace to cutting room, avoiding at all costs Royalty and (if possible) film editors.'[54] Finally, in the Jubilee year of 1977, an illuminating thirteen-part series entitled *Royal Heritage: The Story of Royal Builders and Collectors* was ready. It probed gently at the dividing line between national heritage and personal fortunes, and proposed the idea of public service monarchy. The Palace and the BBC were deeply distrustful of each other along the way, with some reason. The final triumph was as much a product of the tension as of the collaboration.

IT'S A ROYAL KNOCKOUT

Just as public attitudes towards the monarchy were shifting, there was also an alteration in the relationship with the monarchy of those who dealt with it within the BBC. Wheldon was one of the BBC generation with distinguished war records, men who related to the monarchy with a deep personal respect, because so many of them had 'fought and bled for the nation' in World War II.[55] Frank Gillard had reported from the bloodiest World War II battles; Jim Moir had been in a tank regiment; Paul Fox had fought through France. It meant that they had a deep, personal relationship with the monarchy. Some of them also organised the BBC as if it were a military enterprise. Peter Dimmock, the architect of Outside Broadcasts, had been in the Royal Air Force, and he lent the unit its expeditionary identity. Even Light Entertainment was run like a small regiment because the director Tom Sloan had come straight out of the army into the BBC. These men had a different relationship with national symbols than succeeding generations.

By the 1980s, few at the top of the BBC had attitudes of natural loyalty shaped by experiences of war. A more reserved, distanced view emerged that 'we have a relationship with the royal household, not the family exactly, but the platonic ideal that is the Palace', said Will Wyatt. It did not help that royal reporting was seen as a 'graveyard of news in the Corporation'.[56] The cynical newsroom judgement was that royal news was either establishment propaganda or tabloid frippery. From the late seventies on, royal correspondents were selected more for their popularity with audiences than their understanding of the institution. Kate Adie, Michael Cole and Jennie Bond represented the *Express* and the *Mail* of the BBC – without the *Mail*'s determination to go for the jugular.

When Godfrey Talbot had been appointed BBC royal correspondent, he had been summoned to the Palace to meet the King and Queen. By the late seventies, reporters barely met the royal family except by accident. They were more clearly 'outsiders' than before. Royal reporting, which had been solemn and reverential, had become an uneasy mixture of show business and politics. Royal correspondents seemed uncomfortable in either context. The most difficult problem was that 'news' was basically a gritty form about things that had gone wrong. So a 'news' story from a royal tour that could be pitched into newsrooms was not that it was a tremendous success, which is what the Palace hoped for, but that something unexpected and preferably embarrassing had occurred. A more constitutionally informed reporting would have avoided this. On Adie's first royal tour, to India, the usual round of formalities was enlivened by 'chirpy' demonstrations about immigration controls in Britain. The accompanying officials demonstrated 'years of Foreign Office training by standing next to a demonstration and ignoring it'. For Adie, this was the story. But since every royal visit is a political act, its political meaning implicit and vulnerable to damage if expressed, the concentration on the trivial was often frustrating for the Palace.

It was perhaps a sign of the BBC's changing views of the monarchy that royal correspondents now thought of themselves as sharp-minded sceptics. Bond and Adie reacted to the suspicion that they might have become Palace 'trusties', and perhaps the view that it was a 'female' job, by adopting a combative independence. The job of 'Court correspondent', said Kate Adie, one of the BBC's 'grander' titles, was 'unceremoniously dumped on me, because I failed to think up any quick excuses not to do it'.[57] Asked to do the job, Jennie Bond was excited, but 'above all I was determined not to deliver a flowery script. Gushing was *not* my style.'[58] To the Palace every Bond story came with 'a sting in the tail'.[59] Yet royal reporting made both of their careers.

These journalists were anxious about being seen to be deferential, and were frequently frustrated by the palace *omertà*, as the story about the collapsing royal marriages became more volatile. Changes in the ownership and politics of the press meant that previous deference was being replaced by a hunger for revelation, with proprietors more interested in circulation than anxious about offending royalty. By the time Adie was reporting, the tone of most BBC royal correspondents suggested they were doughty, cynical outsiders to the pointless pomp of the royal round of events, as the notion of the model royal family disintegrated very publicly in a series of collapsed marriages, vulgar behaviour and the deep unhappiness of Princess Diana. The BBC could have been more thoughtful, more enquiring, more intelligent.

But if deferential British royalty worship was on the wane, to be replaced for a decade by a destructively febrile royal story, if the monarchy like the BBC was under greater pressure than ever before in the twentieth century, when the happy emotional extravaganza of the royal wedding was replaced by a punishing hostility, in time and another turn of the wheel a new image of the monarch would emerge – as the stalwart, dependable, dutiful ruler: the 'People's Queen'.

7

THE FALKLANDS: 'OUR BOYS'
VERSUS 'THE BRITISH'

AT THE END OF MARCH 1982, a tip came into the BBC's Plymouth local newsroom that something was 'going on' at Royal Marine bases in the city. Narrow West Country lanes were jammed with convoys of service lorries, heading into Portsmouth and Plymouth, where the navy was mustering ships. BBC staff poured back into the station, unasked, to answer the flood of telephone calls from servicemen's families. One reporter from the region, Tony Byers, said that the real division in Britain was not between those 'for' or 'against' the Falklands but rather between those whose lives were touched by the conflict and those distant from it.[1] The tension around the programme *Good Morning Devon*, listened to by 60 per cent of the local population during the conflict, was intense, as staff worked through the nights putting out the news that came overnight from the South Atlantic. Frank Gillard, the legendary retired head of the region, a BBC aristocrat of impeccable judgement, phoned a local MP for an update on Westminster opinion. The MP's wife answered the phone and disagreed with his view that people in the West Country were more affected by the war than those in London. London dinner parties, she said, now routinely broke up to watch the news.

Only a few days earlier, Lord Carrington said he found his job as foreign secretary 'as exhilarating as ever', in a talk broadcast on Radio 4 to celebrate the bicentenary of the Foreign Office. He warned that it was a fallacy to think 'that there are little countries far away to which we need never pay attention', but his foresight did not save his job. He had already raised concerns about Argentinian threats to the Falklands, sensing that the policy of 'procrastinat[ing] the problem away'[2] would not work for much longer. Alarm bells had rung when some Argentinian 'scrap merchants' had landed on South Georgia. But it was not until BBC Monitoring reported on 31 March that an Argentinian fleet had set sail for the Falklands that the grim prospect of a foreign invasion of British territory became clear.

The Falklands campaign would turn Margaret Thatcher from unelectable to unassailable. Its success gave her the confidence and political capital to pursue radical domestic policies. It bestowed on her an image she relished

– the high dominatrix of British and international politics. Anthony Barnett, an opponent of the war, called it 'Churchillism'. The invasion hit Thatcher as a 'deadly' shock. 'She felt anger, shame and sympathy … deeply and instinctively.'[3] She was carrying the worst recorded opinion poll ratings for a prime minister, and she knew that without a decisive response her career would end in humiliation, the Conservative Party would be out of power for a generation, and Britain's much-discussed decline would become precipitous. At the beginning, it looked like an expensive bit of opportunism: 'a heroic folly, the sort of folly of which myths are made', according to her biographer, John Campbell. However, 'instead of finishing her; it was the making of her'.[4]

The BBC faced three wars. The first was reporting the campaign itself. The second was truthfully reflecting the variety of opinion in the country, keeping the public and the world reliably informed, and so sustaining its own (and consequently Britain's) reputation abroad. The third was the domestic battle for political authority conducted by No. 10 – during a period when the prime minister's fortunes were mutating fast and unpredictably. This sharp realignment of domestic power in Mrs Thatcher's favour, indissolubly linked to a national emergency, would make impartial and accurate reporting hard. For Mrs Thatcher, recapturing the islands was not only a matter of national honour and justice, her career depended on it. As a politician, she needed enemies, 'to fuel the aggression that drove her career she had to find new antagonists all the time'.[5] While attempting to resist, the BBC walked into the trap of becoming an enemy. It underestimated her radicalism.

The first the British public knew about the landing was when Harold Brierley, the World Service's dynamic Latin America correspondent (he had to be dynamic – he covered half of the continent), reported that Port Stanley had been taken. His report was based on Argentinian sources and a call that a stubbornly heroic telephone operator in Stanley, Eileen Vidal, had managed to make to HMS *Endurance*. This was the only Royal Navy ship in the area, then on its last patrol before being decommissioned. A BBC defence correspondent, Christopher Wain, had been dispatched to Argentina, originally planning to go on to the Falklands. He reported from the 'enemy' capital throughout, under pressure but never in danger. At an emergency cabinet meeting at 7.30 in the evening on Friday, 2 April, there was still no direct confirmation of the invasion – adding to the impression of the government's humiliating incompetence. 'We supplemented the wires and had a radio with the World Service brought into the outer office,' said Sir Frank Cooper, the permanent under-secretary in the Ministry of Defence.[6]

In January, the BBC Monitoring Service in Caversham, a magnificent piece of national sensitivity which listened to and evaluated the world's broadcasting and press, had produced a report suggesting that General Galtieri, the new brutal right-wing dictator who had taken power in 1981, was making 'louder nationalistic claims' than before about what they called 'Las Malvinas'. But nobody quite recognised it as a famous Monitoring Service 'first alert'. Tension had been predicted to rise, but not until the following year – a major anniversary of British control of the islands. Other issues, such as developments in Poland, seemed more pressing. Nor was anyone of any seniority listening: eyes, ears and effort were turned towards the Cold War Russian threat. 'Frankly,' said John Nott, the minister of defence, 'we had other more serious things to concentrate on.'[7] No one thought the activity was anything more than the usual Argentinian sabre-rattling.

THE UN/IMPORTANCE OF THE FALKLANDS

Margaret Thatcher was at her best during the war: fiercely focused, respectful of advice, but decisive, scrupulous of parliamentary and personal proprieties. Charles Moore, her biographer, said 'her natural, maternal, human sympathies and her ardour for British servicemen's welfare' made her more sensitive than any male politician would have been to the awesome responsibilities of sending young men to die. She called it 'The most totally concentrated period of my life.'[8] Behind the scenes, it was acutely difficult to maintain the vital American support. William Whitelaw said, 'No one who was not closely involved could possibly realise the diplomatic skill and determination with which Margaret Thatcher played this immensely difficult hand.'[9]

If Mrs Thatcher was resolute once the Argentinians landed, she had been careless beforehand. Argentina had concluded that she was unlikely to be sentimental about a far-flung piece of imperial confetti, and certainly would not want to waste money on it. 'What but a bleak and gloomy solitude,' Samuel Johnson had observed of the Falklands in 1771, on the eve of Britain's takeover, 'an island thrown aside from human use, stormy in winter, and barren in summer; an island which not even southern savages have dignified with habitation … where the expense will be perpetual and the use only occasional.' Denis Thatcher, on a triumphal progress around the islands with his wife after the war, observed, 'We sure as hell didn't go there for the real-estate; it's miles and miles of bugger all.'[10]

The Falkland Islanders' claim to protection was based on the newly minted and acclaimed right of self-determination. It was just that they rather exceptionally wanted to *belong* to an empire. Argentina had a vicious dictatorship that killed nuns and children, 'lost' members of the opposition by dropping them out of aircraft, suffered from crippling inflation, and launched a foreign adventure to distract its citizens. But both sides had half hoped, and half expected, that the will to stay among the islanders themselves might simply dwindle away. A British governor had proposed 'euthanasia by generous compensation'[11] as a solution. A 1980 census had put the population of the

Falklands at 1,813 and declining by 30 a year. But, as their families had done for 250 years, the islanders wished fervently to remain British. They had been in the Falklands far longer than most mainland Argentinians had been on the continent.

JOURNALISTS ABOARD

The first sea lord, Sir Henry Leach, splendid in full naval uniform, 'gold epaulettes, the lot', strode into the emergency cabinet meeting in Parliament, having had a colourful altercation with a policeman at the gates about his lack of a pass. He said that nothing could be done to prevent the occupation, but if Britain mustered its most powerful force then repossession was possible. The cabinet, led by Thatcher, decided to dispatch a task force to retake the islands. There were few other options: had Mrs Thatcher faced Parliament the next day with no plan in hand, her government would have fallen immediately to a 'No Confidence' motion. Cecil Parkinson, seen in the BBC as her 'personal roving media minister' and preferred successor, left cabinet 'deeply gloomy'. Responding to Argentina's invasion by sending troops equipped to fight the Russians to overcome a defended landing in the coves and bleak headlands of a remote set of windy islands was like doing a D-Day 8,000 miles away, with the wrong kit and without the planning.

During the emergency debate on the Saturday the right bayed for an aggressive response, but the idea of casually mislaying a bit of Britain to an unpleasant foreign dictatorship also infuriated the left. The debate did not shape policy, as the decision had already been taken to send the task force, but the announcement 'probably saved the prime minister and the government from falling', said the BBC's political editor, John Cole. The phrase that they would seek to 'restore British administration', he explained, was felt to be less provocative than the restoration of 'rule'.[12] Enoch Powell's warning in Parliament, reported on the Six O'Clock News, that the nation would now learn 'of what metal she was made', stayed with her. The Commons rounded on John Nott, who as a cost-cutting defence secretary was more responsible for the military unpreparedness than Lord Carrington, the foreign secretary, who had resigned (and who had been unhelpfully aggressively interviewed by Robert Kee on Panorama). Alan Clark recorded in his diary: 'Poor old Notters ...was a disaster. He stammered and stuttered and garbled. He faltered and fluttered and fumbled. He refused to give way; he gave way; he changed his mind; he stood up again, he sat down again. All of this against a constant roaring of disapproval and contempt.'[13] For the BBC (and the nation) the outcome of the enterprise seemed uncertain.

The decision of the Sun to 'back Maggie' and denounce as a traitor anyone who expressed reservations about the conflict helped bury the mistakes. The paper was being put together during a journalists' strike by a skeleton staff of thirteen, including the ebullient new editor, Kelvin Mackenzie. Powell's words were echoed in the *Sun*'s 'Show your Iron, Maggie'.[14] Unlike the unfathomable Irish beast, Argentina felt like a simple, old-fashioned kind of enemy. The paper pitched the war like a football match, or one of the then-new computer games, loudly reviling the enemy, labelling dissenters as quislings, and calling the 'establishment', the BBC, the FCO, the professions and the Church of England the 'enemies within'. In the past, the BBC had often been subject to fierce criticism, but rarely accused of disloyalty. During the Falklands, the *Sun* framed the BBC as 'against' the nation.

Another view held the war to be a bit of postmodern myth-making. James Cameron on Radio 4 summed up one kind of response to the conflict, as 'a sillier, dottier, insultingly fatuous episode' than he had ever seen before, 'a bit of post-imperial exhibitionism that shows we have reached our dotage as a nation'.[15] It prompted Oliver Whitley, a retired BBC mandarin, to reply tartly in a letter to the BBC's thoughtful weekly, *The Listener*: 'The Falkland Islanders do not need to have produced anything which appeals to Cameron's fastidiousness, in order to have a title not to be deserted or dispossessed. It is enough that they have lived in a wild place and free and have loved it.'[16]

The director-general, Ian Trethowan, chaired a sombre emergency meeting of the News and Current Affairs Board. He said that the BBC would find it hard to get its 'footwork right' in the twists and turns of the war: 'The problem was precisely how to define the national interest.' He added that 'balancing the public right to know' with the 'military need to win ... was not going to be easy'.[17] And while the BBC ought to be careful not to imperil military action or diplomatic negotiations, or appear to 'relish' the conflict for its newsworthiness, it must nevertheless represent British opinion as fully as possible. Trethowan said that scepticism about the 'ability of the military forces to achieve military objectives' was widespread, but the worry was that 'the mere reporting of doubt might seem calculated to undermine British military action'.[18] It was a prescient analysis of the dangers ahead.

One problem for the Corporation (and Mrs Thatcher) was how widespread doubt was at the beginning. Cole said that although even cabinet ministers had 'very grave' reservations about the likely outcome of the campaign,[19] many Conservatives would see any coverage of dissent as 'pure speculation because dissenting views were being kept so private'.[20] A BBC poll as the fleet sailed showed that although 72 per cent of the British public were in favour of the task force being sent, 80 per cent did not expect it to fight when it arrived in the South Atlantic. A later poll as it passed Ascension Island showed a steady 30 per cent opposed to the conflict. The BBC had a duty to represent this range of views. But the prime minister saw the reporting as a threat.

Alasdair Milne in 1982: there was great excitement at his appointment,
the first television programme maker to become director-general

CHANGE AT THE TOP

Alasdair Milne was prince-in-waiting, due to take over as director-general in July. Trethowan later believed that he should have given his successor the chance to start with a clean slate by staying on longer and taking the flak. The Falklands reminded Milne of Suez, when he had produced prime minister Eden's broadcast to the nation, and been deeply shocked by the intemperate and desperately ill premier's direction of a war and threat to take over the BBC. He concluded that his first job was to protect the BBC from irresponsible politicians. Thus he 'was in defensive posture from the start – and always thought himself right'.[21]

It was clear that a risky war with British lives and honour at stake, but not a total war of national survival, would cause tensions between the BBC and the government, especially one in such a beleaguered political position. The earlier Curran / Trethowan solution to the increasingly volatile relationship with government had been to bring back Dick Francis, with his experience of the political sensitivity of Northern Ireland, to head a new directorate with oversight of News and Current Affairs in 1977. Francis was supposed to alert, avert, command and control, but ended up, because he had none of the resources the task needed, just reacting to crises. Milne mistakenly thought that as 'editor in chief' he should control News (and that it was wrong to combine radio with television news services). So over Christmas 1981, Francis and Alan Protheroe, his deputy, painfully broke the directorate up, before Francis was sent off to be head of Radio, leaving Protheroe ruminating on his future. A newsman who had started life on the *Glamorgan Daily News* and headed BBC news in Wales, he thought he had run out of BBC jobs.

After a day of panicked consultation closeted with George Howard, Trethowan said 'working with Alasdair will be like a rollercoaster, fun sometimes but bloody awful in the troughs'. They created a new post – assistant director-general – with responsibility for the editorial standards of the BBC's News and Current Affairs. But the real job was watching Milne's back, and picking up the debris. Their first choice, Brian Wenham, turned it down as 'a bed of nails'. Francis was no good, he and Milne did not get on well enough. They didn't think Monica Sims could manage it – Milne was a man's man – and they needed someone immediately available.

At 4 p.m. on a bleak January day, Alan Protheroe was summoned to a meeting with Trethowan. After three urgent calls from the chairman's office, he finally went to Broadcasting House. When Howard put the advantages of the job to him, in full chairmanly pomp, Protheroe began to giggle 'like an ordinand'.[22] But the position of 'director-general's flak-carrier-general' – Protheroe's self-appointed title – was a flawed one. He had no direct position in the hierarchy and no money to make programmes. Worst of all, he was there to sort out problems, not stop them erupting. The Falklands was a baptism of fire. Protheroe had rows with Bernard Ingham, rows – tinged with hysteria – with the Ministry of Defence (MoD), and shouting matches with the army. A nice man who many journalists came to see as on their side, he did not have the capacity to settle issues and never developed an orderly way of identifying problems. There was 'no way of proceeding, nothing was written down, it was just a collection of individual interests', said Stephen Whittle, who later dealt with standards of journalism in the BBC. It was, he concluded, 'a condition of perpetual panic stations'.[23]

THE WAR ON THE GROUND AND THE WAR IN WHITEHALL

As with the case with many other 1980s problems, the reporters in the field and the BBC's news operation came out of the war with enhanced reputations, trusted by the British and foreign public. Brian Hanrahan's immortal phrase about Harriers leaving on sorties, 'I counted them all out and I counted them all back', was an invention of trustworthy propriety that secured the nation's affection and trust. The line was actually given to him by the cameramen, Bernard Hesketh and John Jockel, to get around an MoD prohibition on giving any figure after Argentina had claimed it had shot down some Harrier jets. Jockel said, 'I don't know what the fuss is about. I saw them all go out, and they all came back,' inspiring the only line by a BBC journalist to have made the *Oxford Dictionary of Quotations*. But another BBC – the 'corporate' centre – would end the war in an antagonistic relationship with the government. The problem for the BBC was the way in which the military campaign became not merely the basis for Mrs Thatcher's political survival but the cornerstone of her political ascendancy.

The prime minister was a more subtle and insecure politician than the bustling, indomitable image sculpted by Ingham: he wanted news that would cement her authority and keep morale buoyant. For their part, the military and the MoD were worried only about one thing: not giving anything away. Had the BBC distinguished these two different pressures, it might have trod more daintily through the minefield. It suspected, reasonably, that military reasons were on occasion used to disguise political purposes. Yet the military were dealing with terrifyingly tight campaign margins and a foreshortened time frame. Small additional factors could tip the outcome decisively against the British. The number of Exocet missiles the Argentinians held (was it five or nine?) and information about the mistakes in their ignition systems (which meant they twice failed to explode on landing) were proper matters of anxious censorship. According to Sir Frank Cooper, who led the MoD, delay in the announcement of the sinking of the *Sheffield* was another such matter. The loss of two Harriers in fog depleted British air support by one sixth. When the container supply ship the *Atlantic Conveyor* was sunk, the British army had, just before landing, lost nearly all the equipment it needed for land warfare. All of this was life or death to soldiers, and success or failure to the mission. It made misleading Argentina vital.

JOURNALISTS AT SEA

During the frantic preparations to embark an army and organise a flotilla to sail 8,000 miles and engage in an invasion that no one had prepared for, journalists were not prominent in the naval mind. No berths were allocated for them at all. The Ministry of Defence was besieged by 160 organisations demanding places, with the BBC submitting 30 separate requests across the spectrum – from the *Today* programme to a documentary unit working on a programme to be called *Sailor*. Everyone phoned Ingham. Reluctantly, space for six journalists was found. Rather cunningly, the Press Association, which chose the first tranche of journalists, did not include anyone from *The Times*, the *Sunday Times* or the BBC, so extra places had to be made for them. Ingham 'waved the prime minister's name' at the navy and the number of journalists sent with the task force was raised first to eleven and finally to 29, including the tabloid reporters Ingham knew had to be there. But despite repeated requests, journalists from the World Service, the internationally recognised BBC voice of authority, were deliberately, and shamefully, excluded.[24] But then why hadn't the BBC centralised its requests and prioritised them?

*Jenny Abramsky, a sympathetic news manager who made
her mark during the Falklands War, in 1986*

Jenny Abramsky, the BBC Radio news manager, recalls an atmosphere of
'shambles' in BBC newsrooms, where a call went up for 'Anyone with an Irish
passport?', which could be used to enter Argentina. John Simpson had one
and was dispatched. Brian Hanrahan had just returned from a sailing holiday
and was told to get to Portsmouth by eight o'clock that evening. He knew
nothing about defence, but said, 'the advantage of being innocent in those
circumstances is that you tend to ask the questions people back home would
ask. Why are they doing that? What effect will it have?'[25] It was a motley crew
of journalists who were startled to be told, at Sunday lunchtime, to make for
Portsmouth. John Shirley from the *Sunday Times* had broken up with a girl-
friend and wanted to get out of the office.[26] Michael Nicholson, the star ITN
reporter, was on a walking holiday and was put on a light aircraft to get him
to the dock.

Most of the journalists knew nothing of the army, few expected eventually to go to war and none was properly equipped. One was a gardening

correspondent who lived nearby. The MoD issued the journalists with accreditation documents in Arabic, left over from Suez. The alternative – eastern European and Russian documents – would have 'let another cat out of the bag altogether', said Sir Frank Cooper.[27] Journalists and sailors encountered each other as alien tribes. The navy 'thought we were the enemy', said Hanrahan. This first phase had many farcical elements, of the sort identified in Evelyn Waugh's media and war satire, *Scoop*. Robert Harris, the brilliant young political editor of *Newsnight*, in his first book, *Gotcha!*, wrote, 'the Navy fought Whitehall, Whitehall fought the Government, all three fought the media and the media fought each other'.

The BBC's Robert Fox did have some defence experience, and was dispatched on a later boat: 'I became aware I had more autonomy, more independence from the office than in any other conflict.' On board the *Canberra*, Fox shared a cockroach-infested berth in the depths with the Independent Radio News journalist Kim Sabido. 'Mind you, [the Captain] would have had us in the bilges if he could.' Hanrahan was told by an officer that anything he reported could damage the task force: 'any trouble from you and I'll put you in leg irons'. Little happened as the fleet sailed towards Ascension Island – the journalists filing stories filched from the World Service, to be censored by 'minders' from the MoD on board, and then again in London. Copy was picked up by news organisations from a hastily erected hut in the MoD courtyard. The censorship was inconsistent and frequently ridiculous. A report saying that everyone was fit, apart from one sailor who had broken an ankle, was censored. Reporters were banned from mentioning the sky, the sea, other ships, where they were, the food, what exercise the troops were doing on board, let alone how many troops there were, or which troops they were with. A report saying that it was censored had 'censored' cut out. Under the terms of a standing agreement, neither the BBC nor ITN ever revealed that their reports were censored.

The mood became darker after they left Ascension Island, and reporters began to suspect that the censorship was badly misleading. A report saying that only the weather would determine the next phase of the campaign had 'weather' deleted and 'politicians' inserted; a report that said (accurately) that the Port Stanley airstrip had not been damaged by a Vulcan raid was changed to 'it appears that attacks have been successful'. Broadcasters were particularly hard hit as opportunities to get film back were sabotaged. Hanrahan spent days being winched pointlessly from boat to boat. There were dark suspicions, reinforced after the landings, that the MoD discriminated between journalists, and that Max Hastings (seen as more 'in favour' of the war than many others) often seemed to get his stories through when others failed. However, the BBC journalists with the task force established intelligent and mutual trust with some of the naval and military commanders. 'Anyone on the fleet was better than anyone in London,' said Fox, 'and anyone directly involved in the operational

Brian Hanrahan aboard HMS Hermes *sailing to the Falklands – the BBC won the front-line reporting war*

side of affairs was better than a media handler.'[28] The trade between some of the journalists and some of the military was 'a trade between quite grown-up people', said Hanrahan.[29]

Despite mutual distrust between the political and military sides of government, both shared trepidation about the impact of images of conflict on public morale, based on the belief that Vietnam had been 'lost' because of the popular response to the reality of war seen on their screens. There was never a public ban, but in practice there was a clear policy to prohibit distressing pictures. Don McCullin, the pre-eminent war photographer of the time, was repeatedly refused permission to travel to the Falklands. 'They found room for a million Mars Bars, but not for me.' Television journalists believed that even when there were opportunities to return film they were obstructed. When the invasion took place, they were the last to be landed and were kept offshore for four days. Film was 'lost' in transit. The Falklands media policy may have seemed chaotic, but one policy was decisively delivered. There would be no battlefield images.

Meanwhile, naval commanders could not understand why precious space on communication signals had to be taken up by 3,000-word colour pieces on 'life on board', let alone the *Sun*'s delivery of pin-ups to the task force: 'The Page Three Girls are going to war'. Stories of Debbie Boyland 'all ship-shape and Bristol fashion in her nautical naughtys' hardly seemed to warrant jeopardising vital naval communication. The vulgar, jingoistic, warmongering tone of the

Robert Fox reporting from on board the Canberra *on the way to the Falklands*

popular press in the Falklands War had not been a feature of any previous combat – and was never repeated. The 'Johnny Gaucho' and 'Argie bargie' humour, as if they were World War II comic book enemies, was in fact very different to the tone of the popular press during that war. Fox reported to the BBC that men going to fight found the *Sun*'s headline 'Stick it up your Junta! The first missile to hit Galtieri's gauchos will come with love from the *Sun*' distasteful.

RADIO

Despite not having its own reporter with the task force, the World Service was a vital source of information and framed international thinking: 'The navy used it the whole time ... operational decisions were made on the basis of it.'[30] The Falkland Islanders found it a lifeline: 'We want to say a big thank you to everyone in the World Service,' said a letter after the war – and when World Service reporters went on a warm and celebratory tour after the conflict, 'they felt as if they were part of the family in the war'.[31] As international negotiations became the characteristic of the second phase of the war, the World Service and Monitoring were the only reliable sources 'for understanding how things were developing'. The Latin American service worked around the clock and Caversham went into emergency mode. People worked double and treble shifts, slept in the building, and produced a key report on the attitudes of over twenty Latin American nations to the war, showing their support for Argentina to be real 'but limited'.

News of the Charge of the Light Brigade had taken 20 days to get back from the Crimea; pictures from the Falklands took 23 and were 'like the dead sea scrolls by the time we had them'.[32] The lack of television material had some odd effects: stock clips (of Argentina's navy, of the task force, of missiles) began to wear out from overuse. Computers were in their infancy for TV graphics and still blocked by the unions, so *Newsnight* built its famous sandpit of plastic ships. 'Current affairs programmes came to resemble a strange hybrid,' wrote Harris, 'between children's television and sport,'[33] as a small army of watercolourists produced tasteful painted representations of ships at sea and landings.

It also became a radio war. Radio 4 was run by the most senior woman in the BBC, the creative, punctilious Monica Sims. A colleague at Programme Review Board described Sims as seeing and hearing everything – with an alarmingly well-based view of everything as well.[34] The station became adept at breaking schedules for parliamentary and ministerial broadcasts, and giving the conflict context.[35] The forceful young Jenny Abramsky came into her own – dealing with correspondents, No. 10 and the MoD over casualties and making sure that news was not announced until next of kin had been informed, 'all with a compassionate, astute, professionalism'. A good manager of people, Abramsky extended the practice of 'pooling' further than it had ever been considered and talked directly to her competitors in other media outlets – so that Mike Nicholson of ITN and Max Hastings, the *Telegraph* correspondent, were frequently heard on the BBC. She also dealt wisely with the impact of the war on young reporters with little experience of combat.[36] Milne wrote a much-appreciated note of congratulations to the radio operation at the end of the war.

'OUR TROOPS' OR 'THE BRITISH'

The Ministry of Defence's decision not to brief journalists off the record had the unintended consequence of creating a vacuum. *Newsnight*, an innovative new programme on BBC2, stepped into the breach with informed analysis. It was transformed into a formidable institution by the conflict, a finishing school for classy talent, pumping out broadcasting leaders – John Tusa, Caroline Thomson, Mark Thompson, Mark Damazar – and creating a platform for powerful independent voices such as Robert Harris, Jackie Ashley and Jeremy Paxman. It had been created as a content solution to a technological shift. Television pictures of events in distant places had previously come laboriously to Britain, arriving too late for daily news. Current affairs programmes were often the place where these pictures could be seen. But by the late seventies the speed of satellite broadcasting meant that what had been current affairs became news.

During 1978 and 1979, the idea emerged of a programme to cap the

The first line-up of Newsnight *presenters in 1980: Fran Morrison, Peter Snow, David Davies, the inimitable Charles Wheeler, the voice of reason and inquiry*

evening on BBC2 that would break down the wall that had been built between Current Affairs, which explored 'implied views and positions', and News, which doggedly held facts sacred. The *Newsnight* idea was to provide a deeper analysis of the 'story of the day': to interrogate, supply background and argue, 'not opinionate'. The first editor was George Carey, and the idea slogged its way around the BBC, getting marginal support from Wenham, 'who never committed to anything', and none at all from Milne, who told Tusa and Carey 'you're on your own boyos' in a lift. The next problem was to struggle through union opposition. News and Current Affairs had different conditions of service and it took Carey and the Personnel department nearly a year to deal with the 52 final conditions necessary to make the programme possible.

The idea was to sum up the day, but unlike *The World Tonight* on Radio 4, which settled and wrapped a day, *Newsnight* had a different mood of agenda-setting. 'We hated working to a formulaic news agenda.' While they respected and feared ITN's *News at Ten*, there was contempt for the BBC's *Nine O'Clock News* – 'stuffy, out of touch, pedestrian, with a brute view of the public', said Carey. The main competition was *Weekend World* on LWT with the implacable, and very clever, Brian Walden. *Newsnight* needed to be a programme with a personality, yet it was also intended to be authoritative and evidently a team production. Tusa and Peter Snow with Peter Hobday were the main presenters, whose role was 'to draft and redraft the introduction, a long considered piece that had to frame the issues of the day', Tusa said. 'It was terribly exciting.'

Newsnight came into its own during the Falklands because it filled a gap between the excellent but limited vision of the reporters with the task force and the vacuity of the MoD's announcements. It became a nightly seminar which called on a wide range of experts whose informed speculations rattled the MoD. Interviews, films and discussions made up for an absence of pictures. The programme was on at an unexpectedly good time, as by 10.30 p.m. more news was coming in from the South Atlantic. Teeming with talent, the programme worked night and day – and produced three extra editions over the Easter weekend as the task force sailed. The sheer heavy lifting of the technical problems was formidable. When film did arrive, it had been flown to Montevideo, edited there and then sent via satellite to the BBC. Staff were exhausted.

The biggest row was over how the BBC described British troops: a *Newsnight* report brought matters to a head. The accusation that the BBC used impartiality as a cloak for a presumed moral equivalence between Argentina and Britain lay behind the objection to the BBC's description of troops as 'British' rather than 'ours'. Denis Thatcher was on his way to the House of Commons when he heard a BBC broadcast about an unconfirmed loss. He said, 'I will never forget it. How could the bloody BBC question the integrity of the military or suggest that the incident could be made up? I was livid with rage and have hated them since that day.'[37] For Mrs Thatcher, it demonstrated that the BBC was not 'on our side'. Yet the prime minister blurred the line between the Argentinian cause and the Argentinian people, in contrast to British policy in World War II that had fiercely distinguished between Nazism – the ideology it was fighting – and the German people.

A report by Hanrahan was the origin of the problem. Reporting from the task force itself he had talked of 'our forces'. This was clear and proper in a report from the front line. But it raised alarm bells, because the convention from a distance in London was different. The editor of Radio News, Larry Hodgson, put up a memo on newsroom noticeboards. 'Please do not say "our forces" when you mean "British Forces",' it read. 'It is contrary to BBC style. And, to some ears, it can give the impression that we are taking verbal sides – which we don't do even against (to quote secretary of state Haig) "a bunch of thugs".'[38] It was followed up in a note that went to everyone in the BBC, headlined 'NOT OUR TROOPS'. It went on, 'We should try to avoid using "our" when we mean British. We are not Britain, we are the BBC ... No listener should be in any doubt that when we refer to "our man in Buenos Aires" we are talking about a BBC correspondent, not a British official.' The Corporation was preserving its integrity, and in doing so protecting its own foreign legitimacy, which was in the British national interest. It was not a matter of loyalty, but of efficiency.[39] But these notices were seen by guests without any explanatory context, and misunderstood. Outrage at BBC treachery flew around the

Conservative Party. Yet even the MoD spokesman Ian McDonald always talked of 'the British forces' and never used 'our'.

It came to a head in a *Newsnight* programme on 2 May. A piece on the Falklands began with the presenter, Peter Snow, saying to camera, 'There is a stage in the coverage of any conflict where you can begin to discern the level of the accuracy of the claims and counter-claims on either side. Well, tonight – after two days – it must be said that we cannot demonstrate that the British have lied to us so far, but the Argentines clearly HAVE.' The scripting of the piece had been intended to emphasise the credibility of the British. But the tone was unintentionally superior and seemed to imply equivalence in unreliability between what was a remarkably unpleasant regime and Britain. As it happened, BBC journalists were finding Argentinian sources frequently reliable, however, and the British government ones often misleading. Snow was an Olympian Wykehamist, a hugely popular broadcaster, and had never meant any such slur, but nuances in tone (even if unintended) altered the impact of words.

The BBC's policy of calling troops 'the British' rather than 'ours', however (even if no one in the BBC seemed to recall its origins), was government policy. It was long established, started at the request of the War Office in 1941, repeatedly negotiated, reinforced during the Cold War, and last reaffirmed between the MoD and the BBC in 1977, only five years before the Falklands War. The naming of troops had always been a political matter – and a flexible one. It was not a matter of 'BBC' style, as Hodgson said, but a matter of a carefully worked-out principle – an ingrained precept, not a stance for or against a war.

During World War II, a war of national survival, in which the BBC's patriotism was not an issue (despite furious arguments about the most effective way of broadcasting), naming troops was desperately important, and the overriding consideration had always been what would make best sense to listeners. But there was also a nervous sensitivity to audiences abroad – not alienating allies really mattered. An army made up of soldiers from the Dominions, India and all of the nations of the United Kingdom was fighting on 'our' side, but it would be politically damaging to say that they were 'ours'. The first solution was to call them 'Empire troops', but it was certainly never 'our' empire. Any 'implication of ownership is to be AVOIDED'. Correspondents were firmly instructed to use 'the ...' rather than 'our' Empire, and the government went out of its way to instruct the BBC not to use 'our' about any part of the British army or the Allies.[40] Then talking of British, or worse English, troops also caused hostility in Scotland, Wales and Northern Ireland, from 'shipyard director down to the rivet-boy', according to a War Office press officer.[41] Similarly it was agreed 'We don't say "our submarine" or "our destroyer", because the BBC does not have any such weapons'. The precision of the language embodied key democratic, or at least anti-propagandist, values.[42]

The day after Snow's report, John Page, a Conservative MP and former artillery officer, caused a press feeding frenzy by calling it 'almost treasonable'. The *Sun* jauntily headlined it 'Treason! MP lashes TV Man' and said, 'We are caught in a shooting war not a game of croquet ... A British citizen is either on his country's side – or he is its enemy.'[43] Mrs Thatcher agreed: 'The BBC had a responsibility to stand up for our Task Force, our boys, for our people and the cause of democracy.' Although Michael Foot hit out at the 'hysterical blood lust' of some of the press, Conservative backbenchers drowned him out in a mood of noisy outrage. The only political group in Parliament supporting the BBC were the newly formed Social Democrats, with Bill Rodgers saying that, in the current parliamentary atmosphere, there was 'real danger of political interference' in the BBC.

Yet by this point in the war the BBC's defence that it was being blamed as the harbinger of bad news was wearing thin. 'The BBC was not there to boost morale, but neither was it there to be superior,' said George Fischer, the Hungarian refugee who was a sharp corrective to common attitudes within the BBC. Chairman Howard took charge and went out to defuse the row: 'The BBC is not, and could not be, neutral as between our country and an aggressor ... one of the things that distinguishes our country from Argentina is that we have the good fortune to live in a parliamentary democracy ... one of the greatest virtues of living in a free land is that our people wish to be told the truth.' But the BBC 'always says things like that', said Mrs Thatcher; 'it is no defence for letting our boys down.' She urged people who were unhappy to write to the BBC: 1,816 people did. This represented fewer complaints than the BBC had received over World Cup coverage in 1978. The Corporation also received 342 letters of support. Many of the letters of complaint, however, were couched in reasonable terms and were a cause for alarm. The BBC was also attempting to shift the tone of reporting. 'The mood in the country is very anxious and sensitive – we should be especially careful of it,' said Milne. The war was a dreadful initiation for him, and David Holmes, the BBC Secretary from 1983 to 1985, and Colin Morris sent him supportive notes.

The press were after the BBC. In a speech to the International Press Institute in Madrid, Dick Francis explained that 'The BBC's contribution consisted in no more than providing the most reliable account possible of confusing and worrying events.' But the British press instead picked up the line that the 'widow of Portsmouth is no different from the widow of Buenos Aires ... To suppress pictures of Argentinian widows alongside British widows [as the *Sunday Times* had just done] for fear of appearing unpatriotic would be ignoble'.[44] The speech had a clear argument, and was directed at foreign opinion which the BBC – unlike the MoD – was acutely aware of. It was surely true, and a mark of humane British values. But the British press leapt on it gleefully as further evidence of the BBC's lack of patriotism.

The war darkened with the sinking of the *Belgrano* on 3 May, and the loss of 323 men. The mood of the *Sun's* infamous overnight headline, 'Gotcha!', which was replaced in later editions, contrasted starkly with the mood of the task force itself. Fox said that sailors gathered on deck in an intense quiet. Expecting retaliation, they were scanning the horizon for aircraft, but they were also looking for survivors. 'It was sombre, anxious – not triumphant at all.' The BBC reminded its newscasters that 'the tone of announcements ought to be steady'. The next day, Argentina hit back and sank the *Sheffield* with an Exocet missile, and the task force lost three Harriers. Mrs Thatcher sat stunned beside Nott as he made the announcement in Parliament. 'The bragging and self-confidence of the campaign evaporated,' according to Simon Jenkins and Max Hastings.[45] 'The uncertainty of the military gamble has become sharper,' wrote Hugo Young in the *Observer*. 'From airport to television studio, [the foreign secretary] Mr Francis Pym trails clouds of ambiguity.' The immense risks of the campaign were suddenly starkly apparent. The mood of the country changed.

PANORAMA AND CONSERVATIVES

The War Cabinet was panicked, and William Whitelaw said he dreamt about the Falklands every night. Conservative hostility to the BBC escalated to lynching level during this tense week. The *Panorama* of the following Monday unleashed a storm. It included an important but incendiary piece by Peter Taylor from the UN (where diplomatic negotiations were running into the sand) with an interview with the Argentinian representative in New York, so giving a member of the junta exposure on British TV. There was a report by Michael Cockerell about opposition to the war. A 'former member of the cabinet' was quoted as saying, 'the government had impaled itself onto many hooks of its own making' and Tam Dalyell, MP, early in his magnificent career of outspoken dissent, said that the chiefs of staff – especially in the air force – had always had reservations about the campaign.

There was a row within the programme team. On the eve of the controversial *Panorama*, the presenter, Robert Kee, watched the programme with the editor, George Carey, and Chris Capron, the head of Television Current Affairs. Kee disagreed with the tone of the interviews he saw. Capron argued that it was important that the objections to the war were seen to be expressed by Conservative and moderate MPs, rather than the usual left-wingers,[46] but Capron and Carey had reservations of their own and the film was re-edited. The following morning, Kee said that he would not be prepared to present it, but Carey brought him round again. At the same time, the War Cabinet met and anxiously noted that Argentina seemed to be winning the international battle for opinion. That evening, Kee presented the programme, but never saw the very final cut of the film, as he was talking to Cecil Parkinson ahead of a live interview in the studio. Mrs Thatcher, on her way out to dinner that evening, caught sight of the beginning of *Panorama* – and stayed watching 'transfixed', according to Ingham. She thought that the film magnified a 'few dissidents', implied that the chiefs of staff opposed the expedition, and let her, the army and the country down. She left, late for dinner, and seething.

The BBC switchboard was swamped with furious complaints about a defeatist and traitorous programme.[47] Sir Anthony Meyer, a Tory who had appeared on it, was stopped in the corridors of Parliament: 'I remember you at Eton and your mother at Datchet. You are a disgrace to your school, your regiment and my country!' Meyer was deselected at the 1983 election by his party. Nott wrote to Howard privately, saying that pictures of the Chief of the Air Staff had been used illegitimately to imply that he had reservations about the campaign. The Chief of the Air Staff complained in person, but in carefully moderate terms.[48]

Milne and Howard were summoned to appear before the backbench Tory MPs' Media Committee: Whitelaw wanted to 'let them get it off their chests'. Whitelaw was under immense pressure, however, to use the powers that governments possessed under the Corporation's Charter to take it over and to direct what it broadcast. These powers existed to cover the transition to war in a nuclear attack. Whitelaw saw the bloodletting as a last-ditch attempt to protect the BBC from something far worse: government control. The room was packed with more than a hundred MPs, including a rare sighting of Edward Heath.

It started with a moderate question from Tim Rathbone, asking whether the BBC had got the 'balance right'. Milne replied 'yes', and that opinion polls showed steady public backing for the BBC. This was met with a braying stampede of outraged Conservative MPs. 'I hope the BBC is keeping in touch with its lawyers, and you with yours,' said one. 'Because you are going to need them!' Winston S. Churchill demanded that Howard resign or sack the journalists who had made *Panorama*; another MP said that the BBC was 'obsequious' to Argentina. Howard (sweating in the heat – and furious as only a Whig grandee could be when confronted with a mob of vulgar Conservatives) said that Milne would answer all the detailed questions. The MPs barracked Milne: 'Speak up!', then 'Stand up!', then barked, 'Take your hands out of your pockets!' It was horrible.

'Splendid, splendid,' said Whitelaw, as they retreated to his room for a whisky. It bonded Milne and Howard in defensive horror at the Conservatives. Although Milne said that press reports of blood and entrails were exaggerated, one MP said that 'The Christians versus the lions looked tame by comparison.'

In Moscow, *Pravda* called the attack a cunning plan to boost 'the corporation's aura of objectivity'.[49] On the *Today* programme, Brian Redhead asked Howard whether the programme overexposed 'some maverick voices', and Howard replied, 'When you recollect that thirty per cent of the British public are not in favour of the government's policy, this ought from time to time to be looked at.'[50] On ITN Milne said, reasonably enough, that the BBC had made mistakes, but to call it a traitor was absurd: 'the nation was in an emotional state and we have to deal with that'.

Despite several backbench MPs phoning to apologise for the BBC's treatment at the committee, the braying onslaught shook Milne. It reinforced his belief that politicians had to be resisted. He and Howard had behaved well as a team, but they had been sent into a trap. To make matters worse Kee wrote a letter to *The Times*, thanking Milne and Howard for their support but disowning the programme that he had presented – 'in the interests of truth for which the BBC has always stood'.[51] He said that the film identified 'in a confusing way *Panorama*'s own view of the Falklands' crisis with the minority view it was claiming to look at objectively'. Howard said that Kee had 'ditched the BBC and the BBC ditched him'.[52] Milne suggested that he 'be put in cold storage'. The BBC could hardly be seen to sack him at that point. In the end, Aubrey Singer wrote him a 'stiff letter', and Kee resigned. When the deputy chair of governors asked, 'Was the programme actually fair?' Milne answered that the row about it was unfair – the answer to another question. Yet the public remained rather steady: many of them did not like everything the BBC had done, but 81 per cent believed that the BBC, not the government, 'should decide' what coverage to give, and 53 per cent thought that it had been right to show the film.

ACTION

When elements of the task force landed at San Carlos, thousands of soldiers had to stream unprotected across miles of beach in daylight. They were 'utterly vulnerable' to an air attack, which luckily did not occur. The assault out of the beachhead was delayed as a consequence of tragic and severe losses. Five ships went down in five days. The loss of the *Atlantic Conveyor* rendered the force very under-equipped for a land war, and the loss of helicopters and lack of adequate air cover left the troops exposed. The loss of the *Sir Galahad* and the fate of the dreadfully burnt Welsh Guards were to haunt the regiment for decades.

Fox had won the support of the Paras as the task force headed down to the South Atlantic, learning battlefield first aid and 'throwing his admittedly unfit frame into commando PE courses'. He broadcast as the landing happened: 'We're going down the ramp ... a British Parachute force is back on the

Falklands,' he said in 'a slightly staccato tone',[53] barely controlling his emotions as he landed at Carlos. When Hanrahan saw Fox for the first time since leaving England, wearing full combat gear and in a task force signal department, he said, 'Good grief, what a sight!' But he was thinking – 'what a stink'.[54] By now Hanrahan and Fox were trusted and familiar BBC faces and voices, and their reporting from the front line was followed eagerly.

In May, the MoD proposed starting a 'black' propaganda station, one purporting to be neutral but whose only purpose was to carry messages slanted in the British interest. It was to be called 'Radio Atlántico del Sur', broadcast on a frequency close to that of Argentinian radio. Its aim was to 'encourage occupying Argentinian troops to surrender with minimum resistance'. Then the MoD 'informed' the BBC that it was going to take over one of the BBC's four transmitters on Ascension Island to do so.[55] The Corporation was alarmed; if it simply acquiesced it would be acting like a branch of government. The Foreign Office weighed into the argument, and Francis Pym fought it in cabinet.[56] Bernard Ingham doubted whether 'downmarket propaganda tricks' broadcast through a requisitioned transmitter 'with the objective of sapping the morale of the Argentinians'[57] would be successful. He thought that it might be so bad that it would enhance the BBC's reputation. The War Cabinet decided to go ahead with it after the BBC and the Foreign Office pointed out that the transmitter could be 'requisitioned' under clause 19 of the BBC's Charter. The station was generally seen as a joke: the BBC Monitoring Service, perhaps not entirely impartially, said that it offered music and 'good sound advice to surrender'.[58] The presenters had Cuban accents,[59] the music was wrong and the government stance all too evident. It was commercial in sound and 'bordering on the vulgar'. But Ingham was right. The overtly propagandist station further enhanced the credibility of the World Service – especially among the many English-speaking Argentinian officers.

The next crisis involved the serious allegation that a BBC report had announced battle plans. Paratroopers at Goose Green heard on the World Service that they had taken the very Argentine garrison they were preparing to attack. It seemed likely that the Argentinians had been listening as well and a helicopter appeared – although later it emerged that they had believed the report was just intimidation.[60] The Paras' commanding officer, the dashing Colonel H. Jones, believed that the broadcast had removed the element of surprise, but bravely decided to continue with the operation. Max Hastings and John Shirley reported that a furious Jones had threatened to sue the BBC. Hastings said, 'when they heard the broadcast the troops' reaction was rage'. If a BBC correspondent had appeared, 'he would have been sent to a prisoner of war cage'. The reaction was completely understandable on the front, where they knew nothing of what the press were saying. 'How many enemies are we supposed to be fighting?' Jones had asked. Fox, however, who was with Jones, and who took the initial brunt of his fury, said that Jones threatened to sue not the BBC, but Nott and the government.[61] Jones, who had expected a smaller defending force than the one he was now confronting 'and whose position had just been broadcast, literally to the whole world',[62] was killed, leading from the front during the assault. He was a gallant man. Fox was in shock when he reported the battle on Radio 4, as Gordon Clough humanely took him through the story.

The report was not the BBC's fault, however. No. 10 had been anxious about the way in which the campaign seemed to have stalled and the impact of losses on public morale. It had been briefing for several days that 'significant action was to be taken'. Ingham had said that he expected 'Stanley to fall within a few days' and was the source of a story in the *Telegraph* and *The Times* that Mrs Thatcher had 'ordered' the assault force to move as fast as possible.[63] The World Service was only repeating the story that Goose Green had already been won – carried two days before in the *Telegraph*, and in the *Daily Express*, which carried a front-page banner headline: 'Goose Green is taken'. These stories were the product of a House of Commons Defence Committee briefing by Nott. Christopher Lee, a BBC defence correspondent, had checked the story and been briefed by a politician that the attack on Goose Green had started and that it was 'no secret'. He checked it with the MoD, and broadcast the news at 1 p.m. It was this that was repeated in the World Service report. At 3 p.m. the prime minister announced in Parliament that troops were on the move, and two hours later the MoD confirmed that troops were near Goose Green.[64] The press had (wrongly) announced that the attack had already happened, but this did not stop them suggesting that Jones's death was a direct consequence of the BBC story.

David Ramsbotham, the head of Army Communications, told the World Service, 'I will protect you to the hilt.' Goose Green had been better defended than the Paras had expected and, in the heat of the moment, the BBC had been blamed: 'It was the prime minister, No. 10 and the defence minister who were to blame.'[65] Later Ian McDonald, the MoD spokesman, phoned, 'in a personal capacity', to apologise for the government attack on the World Service.

The World Service played an immensely positive role in the war as the islanders' 'lifeline', trebling the hours broadcast to the Falklands, and keeping the scattered community in touch, along with their own local station, which kept broadcasting although under Argentinian control. Argentina tried to jam the World Service and brought a boatload of television sets 'to integrate the Malvinas into the media-cultural sphere'. (The islanders enthusiastically bought them on the very good hire-purchase terms offered by the invaders, knowing they would never have to keep up the payments.) With nearly thirty reporters now in place across South America, Fox reported that 'the British ground forces had received virtually all their information about the enemy from the World Service – and had been extremely grateful for it. Their own sources of information were patchy.' He knew that operational decisions had been made on the basis of BBC broadcasts.[66] Hanrahan said that from the South Atlantic end, problems seemed to be caused in London by 'rival attempts to "manage" the news on the part of the MoD and the Fleet'.[67] The World Service was reliable and intelligent, and 'far better than the military information service'.[68] It played a vital role in informing the forces. That was why Jones had been listening to it.

The Falklands War ended with the triumphant retaking of Stanley, 24 days after the Task Force had landed on San Carlos beach. It had been an extraordinary feat of military planning and delivery, backed by a fiercely focused prime minister. A complete news blackout ensured that Mrs Thatcher was the first to announce the victory in the House of Commons. For the BBC in the West Country, the return of the fleet was 'a hugely emotional, very exciting, desperately poignant event', said Tony Byers. Protheroe said, 'it was difficult to define the mood of the country', it seemed to have been 'Thank God for that, in the Reading/Tallow/Maidenhead axis', he said condescendingly of conservative England. He was wrong. Winning felt like a national, not a narrow political, event. Losing would have meant national humiliation.

VICTORY

Mrs Thatcher had had a very good war, which she was about to translate into a spectacular electoral triumph, but she did not have a magnanimous victory. The nation was relieved and restored by the campaign: it transformed the country's view of itself. Matthew Parris hoped she might emerge as 'a bigger person, she will acquire mercy, she will find grace'.[69] Yet there was a triumphalism in her, directed less at the Argentinians than at the cowards who had not backed her. The BBC, she felt, was one of them. Speaking to 5,000 supporters gathered on Cheltenham racecourse, she declared, 'Today, we meet in the aftermath of the Falklands Battle' (note the capital B). 'Our country has won a great victory and we are entitled to be proud.' But her conclusion was a domestic one. 'When we started out,' she claimed, there were waverers and faint hearts, 'the people who no longer thought that we could do great things – that we could never again be what we were. Well, they were wrong.'[70] The war cast a long shadow for the BBC. It mishandled Ingham's request that they 'pool' film of the highly secret trip Mrs Thatcher made to the Falklands after the war.[71]Although the government had no right to 'instruct' the BBC about the use of its own resources, it was a silly row to have. The BBC – even the really gifted and dedicated young producers – had perhaps failed to really appreciate the change in her (and perhaps the nation's) mood and stature.

Mrs Thatcher took the victory parade, which the Queen, whose son had fought in the campaign and whose entire family had served in the navy, would normally have done. After the televised Service of Thanksgiving, she was said by Denis to be 'spitting blood' over a sermon by the Archbishop of Canterbury, which argued for compassion for all victims of war. Runcie had been one of the first to enter Belsen, and had been awarded the Military Cross for gallantry. Whitelaw said, 'I felt he spoke exactly for me. His words in St Paul's were those of a soldier who understood war, and he expressed his admiration for those who fought and gave their lives. But bitterness and revenge are bad grounds for future action, and against the most basic religious beliefs.'[72]

In 1983, with a general election looming, No. 10 phoned the director-general and said that Mrs Thatcher would like Brian Hanrahan to report on her campaign. His quiet decency was warmly trusted by the nation. 'It would suit her very well,' said Ingham, 'so that's agreed?' The BBC, quite rightly, sent Nicholas Witchell instead and dispatched Hanrahan to follow Michael Foot, the leader of the opposition.[73] Accomplished broadcasting interviewers Brian Walden, Robin Day and Ludovic Kennedy found her increasingly hard to engage, but she was rattled and incandescent after an ordinary voter, a geography teacher named Diana Gould, challenged her about the sinking of the *Belgrano* in a way that no professional interviewer would have done.[74] The prime minister visibly bit back her anger, and thought (incorrectly) that the BBC had planned it. She stormed out of the building, saying to Sue Lawley, the presenter: 'Only the BBC could ask the prime minister why she took action to protect *our* ships against an enemy ship that was a danger to our boys.'

Was the BBC a target for government action during the campaign? Asa Briggs, working on the history of the BBC, encountered a harassed and darkly exhausted Milne, who told him that he was having to keep papers in his own office for safety.[75] The director-general's and chairman's offices were swept for bugs.[76] At the beginning of the campaign, Protheroe and Milne had spent days negotiating a slight shift in the orientation of the American communications satellite that would have made getting pictures from the Falklands possible. The last thing formality required was for the MoD to send a request to the USA. It was never sent.

At the end of the war, John Tusa said that the BBC 'suits' had protected the journalists from the rows. The 'task of the policy people was to keep the politicians at bay', he said, 'and to say we will take the crap, you just do the job.' The BBC was acting in the tradition that it had established during World War II, when telling even the unpalatable truth provided 'the BBC and the nation with a reputation for trustworthiness'. The chief of the air staff, Lord Trenchard, wrote Howard a thoughtful letter at the height of the crisis. He was complaining about a Corporation failure, but said that the overall reporting continued to be very fine. He ended, 'I am glad that I don't have your job.'[77]

The BBC had challenged and tested arguments about the reason for the war and its conduct. But standing up against government was no substitute for a more intelligent strategy for relating to it.

In September, after the end of the war, Mrs Thatcher came to have dinner with the BBC Board of Management. 'In full Boadicea form', she harangued Milne and the BBC chiefs (all men) about the ways in which they had failed the nation. In a brief respite, while people left the table for the lavatory, one BBC executive whispered to another, 'Thank God the director-general has gone to get the SAS – they're the only people who will get us out of this.' (It was after the siege of the Libyan embassy.) Mrs Thatcher had subdued her audience into a satisfactory, silent, cower. Then Bill Cotton, a man of character and humanity, pushed his chair back from the table. 'Prime minister,' he said, 'are you calling the BBC traitors?' She was halted in full flow – she knew that she had gone too far.

8

ETHIOPIA: BIBLICAL FAMINE, NEWS AND CHANGING AID

THE SIX O'CLOCK NEWS

In the autumn of 1984, as the days drew in, an Irish rock musician, restlessly aware that he was broke and that his career had stumbled,[1] sat down on an ordinary evening to watch the news. Then, vast national audiences watched the news at the same time, as families gathered around one television together at set times of day. News punctuated everyday experience, as did popular music, comedy, soap operas and sport. Television was a window into a wider world, a 'box of delights'. Meanwhile young people's involvement with popular music, partly shaped by BBC Radio 1's eclectic menu and television, had created a vast field of unfocused energy. Bob Geldof did not know it, but what he saw on the news would prompt him to unleash this simmering power for new purposes. Briefly, Africa became newsworthy, and the impact would unintentionally revolutionise aid organisations, change the direction of government policy and create a new model of charitable giving. A puzzled and sometimes fierce critical reaction to what Geldof started would kick off a long interrogation of the role of aid. The consequences of this for those in whose name it was given were not known at the beginning. The reaction, then, was a simple and widely shared feeling of shame and outrage. A BBC story prompted the feeling, and the BBC was to become the institutional vehicle for transforming it into a new kind of global action.

The BBC *Six O'Clock News* on 23 October led with a story about fearful hunger in Ethiopia. Ron Neil, the ambitious editor of the pioneering show, had bumped into the BBC's South Africa correspondent, Michael Buerk, at seven that morning in Television Centre. Their chance meeting would help to get the story on the air. Buerk had come straight from Heathrow, carrying an onion bag full of video cassettes. The flight had given him time to reflect and shape the piece: 'It took half a continent to get the opening right, working and reworking the sentences, with the shotlist in front of me, but the mind's eye back in Wollo and Tigray,' he said. 'I tried to recapture what it was like to be there.'[2] As Buerk helped cut the first version for the lunchtime news, hard-bitten editors wept. The public responded strongly to this short item and Neil was determined to put out the whole story at six. By the early evening, people in newsrooms across London and the wider public knew there was something significant to be seen.

The story opened in a momentous register, quite different from usual news pieces. A slow, wide shot panned across a great space filled to the distant horizon with incalculable numbers of people in great distress. The desperate victims moved in a landscape apparently without any of the structures of civilisation. Ripped out from life, they could only wait for help. Filmed by Mohamed Amin, one of the world's greatest news cameramen, a passionate, wily Kenyan, it combined panoramic shots that revealed the scale of the mass of people with unbearable tight shots. Individuals, tall, elegant and dignified, despite their abject condition, looked, unusually for news reports, directly at the camera. The scene in Ethiopia was unique: 'famine' can be a long, grinding and hidden process with people scattered across a region, but in Korem hundreds of thousands of people had congregated at a feeding station. As if to underscore its otherness the piece was nearly eight minutes long, three times the normal length of a news item. Buerk's perfectly crafted commentary – simple, awestruck – set it apart. He found a language that was biblical and a tone of disciplined, repressed anger:

> Dawn, and as the sun breaks through the piercing chill of night on the plain outside Korem, it lights up a biblical famine, now, in the 20th century. This place, say workers here, is the closest thing to hell on earth. Thousands of wasted people are coming here for help. Many find only death. They flood in every day from villages hundreds of miles away, felled by hunger, driven beyond the point of desperation. Death is all around. A child or an adult dies every 20 minutes. Korem, an insignificant town, has become a place of grief.[3]

Amin and Buerk, professional witnesses to other people's tragedy, were horrified by what they had seen in northern Ethiopia. 'You can't remain untouched when there are people dying as far as the eye can see,' said Amin. The story showed the effects of a chronic food crisis that had turned into a catastrophe, apparently because the rains had failed, food had not come in and no one knew about it. Neil said, 'we had all seen pictures of famine but these images were so haunting and powerful, we wanted to give the audience a greater sense of the scale of the story rather than swiping it past them in a few seconds'.[4] Later, critics argued that the story showed the plains of Korem as deathly quiet, that Buerk's story had failed to include the scream of Ethiopian jet fighters overhead flying northwards to bomb the rebels, or the pods of rocket launchers all around. The war between the Ethiopian government and

Michael Buerk reporting on the famine in Ethiopia

the rebels was in fact the context for the movement of people and the acute food shortages. Yet Buerk's story had concluded with shots of the attacks and his story the next day dealt with the conflict in greater length. But 'Most journalists and aid managers', according to Tony Vaux of Oxfam, 'continue to take the view that it was in the greater interest of humanity to keep the issues simple and elicit the largest possible response.'[5]

Television often shows *effects* – causes and structures are almost impossible to provide with convincing visual images. In 1981, Amartya Sen, the Nobel Prize-winning economist, had demonstrated that famines were the product not of a lack of food but of unequal rights to food and unequal resources:[6] 'famine' was a social and political phenomenon, never a natural disaster. He suggested that the media and free speech within a nation were 'the best protection against hunger'[7] as they held the political system to account. In Ethiopia, the international media were perhaps holding the world to account in an attempt to substitute for the missing local agitation. On this occasion, audiences felt as if they were in the shoes of the reporters – television had made them not bystanders but witnesses.

Geldof felt he had seen an international scandal. 'You could hear it in the tones of the reporter,' he said. 'It was not the usual dispassionate objectivity. It was the voice of a man registering despair, grief and absolute disgust at what he was seeing.' The crisis looked immediate and had broken on audiences as a revelation, with all of the sudden surprise of news. Geldof, who felt 'that I had to do something to rid myself of complicity in this evil', phoned his wife Paula Yates, who was about to present a popular ITV show, *The Tube*. She handed the phone over to Midge Ure from Ultravox, who had recently been top of the charts. Geldof and Ure began to think of using popular music, the making and selling of which they understood, to raise donations. The sense of responsibility was widespread. Eleven-year-old Karen Eley wrote to *Blue Peter* that she and her brother were so upset by the story (their mother had left the room to cook supper so they saw it on their own) that they made a guy and took it out on the streets to raise money (it was just before Bonfire Night). 'People prodded me and a dog nearly went to the toilet on my brother,' she wrote. They raised £87.81. Women in Belfast, members of an impoverished community suffering from conflict, organised to sell their wedding rings to raise money for Ethiopia.

Why did Geldof respond so powerfully? Born in Dublin, he was familiar with the iconography of hunger. The devastating Irish potato famine in the nineteenth century was 'caused' by both the destruction of staple crops and the monstrous failure to respond to the starvation. Meanwhile, starving yourself to death for principle was a peculiarly Irish vehicle of political protest. Just two years before, in 1982, eleven Republican prisoners in Belfast had killed themselves in this long, anguishing way. Geldof was no Republican, but hunger resonated with his sense of responsibility.

By the end of the day 7.4 million people had seen the story.[8] By the standards of the period that was a good, but not immense, audience. The BBC *Nine O'Clock News*, out of rivalry not with ITV but with the new *Six O'Clock* programme, and perhaps out of a symptomatic failure of news understanding, put it as its fourth item (beneath a legal wrangle about the end of the miners' strike and a proposed visit by President Mitterrand to Britain). Yet the story had broken through an invisible barrier. Many of those who had seen it were mortified – as Geldof had been. By the end of the next day it had been rebroadcast by other news organisations and two-thirds of the British public had seen it.[9] By midnight the BBC switchboard had received nearly three thousand calls and emergency staff had to be brought in to deal with them. Oxfam was overwhelmed by over one thousand calls, including three offers of planes.

After the broadcast, coverage of the famine by the quality press increased tenfold. 'British drawing rooms have been invaded by pictures of children dying of starvation in Ethiopia,' *The Times* reported, 'a disaster whose coming has been predicted by aid workers for years … [yet] the present shock is a tribute to the emotive power of television pictures.' The *Guardian* led with the story and the *Telegraph* had it on its front page. It was when it turned into a front-page story in the popular press, however, that it escalated into an event. On the day the story was broadcast, Chris Cramer, the effective 'output editor' on the *Six O'Clock News*, offered a set of stills to the *Sun*, which replied, 'We're actually not interested in famine.' Two days after the broadcast, the *Sun*'s front-page headline was 'Race to Save the Babies', and it sent its own reporters and photographers to Ethiopia.[10] Newspapers and other broadcasters scrambled to cover the story. As money flooded into charities, this also became a story in a media feeding-frenzy. That it seemed both urgent and soluble fitted news values.

Convinced that the story was important, Cramer worked furiously to sell it around the world. Simply seeing the piece mattered. The American broadcaster NBC – at the height of its power, size and authority – had turned down Cramer's offer of the piece before it was broadcast. The NBC editor who had seen it in London, however, was so moved she had sent it to New York anyway. Exceptionally, the piece was broadcast accompanied by the original Buerk commentary – 'it was a first and a last time that a BBC news item was transmitted untouched like that by a US network', said Cramer.[11] Then NBC took out a large advert in the *New York Times* extolling their own compassion. By the end of October 1984 the uncut news piece had been transmitted by 425 of the world's broadcasters and seen by an estimated audience of 470 million. Cramer said, 'Sadly, for decades we can look at people dying and think nothing of it, and just go off to the supermarket ... this was realising something was incredibly significant and making it interesting at the same time. It was a relationship between the camera lens and human beings made in a way that we rarely do. All of those things were perfect and that is unusual – mostly you just throw it on the air and move on.'[12]

But why had this one BBC story had such an impact? Like the career of many news stories it had an element of almost arbitrary success, but it was certainly not accidental. The natural assumption is that great news stories proportionately reflect events. Yet at any moment other momentous events may be being ignored: media attention is fitful, determined by resources, values, habits and audience attention. David Rieff points out 'most of the world's horrors never get any air time at all'.[13] An Ethiopian, Dawit Girogis, wrote in puzzlement, 'The magnitude of our tragedy was suddenly matched by an outpouring of sympathy from every corner of the world ... Was the world simply ready for another drama, another thrilling real-life tragedy?'[14]

The awesome story that Buerk and Amin produced was the last in a series of stories, none of which had taken off. Buerk himself had done an earlier Ethiopian story, driven by competition with ITN. Producing news for the whole commercial network, ITN was scrupulously independent from the rest of the commercial system. It was a well-funded and hard-hitting news machine, pushed, to the advantage of the journalists and the news values within it, by public service quality control. In early 1984, Charles Stewart, an expert development documentary maker, had been in Ethiopia making an ITV film on soil erosion and drought, one part of a longer series to be called *Seeds of Hope*, partly funded by the Television Trust for the Environment. What he found on the ground led him to make a one-off and urgent film renamed *Seeds of Despair*.[15] He persuaded ITV to bring the transmission forward to July 1984. The Disasters and Emergency Committee (DEC), which had been established by the BBC itself as a conduit for legitimising appeals that could crash through BBC and ITV schedules, coordinated an appeal across all the broadcasters.

The BBC news desk 'felt wrong-footed', as it would have to carry the DEC appeal, wanted to beat ITV and had no report in hand. Buerk 'got a rather alarmed phone call instructing me to find some starving Africans to use in the appeal, but also to run on the News'. Charles Stewart had made a brilliant documentary: 'all I was doing was a cheap and cheerful news piece, actually a cheap and cheerless news piece in this particular case'.[16] Buerk sent a legendary telex to Oxfam: 'Help. Have had request from BBC in London relating to an appeal to be televised next Thursday entitled "Famine in Africa" … need urgent advice on where I can leap in and out quickly with pictures of harrowing drought victims etc. to be edited and satellited … money no object, nor distance, only time.'[17] Paddy Coulter, the head of communications at Oxfam, suggested Wolayita, in Ethiopia, close to Addis.[18] Buerk's story did scoop Stewart's ITV documentary by a few hours and was used on the DEC famine appeal on 19 July, fronted on the BBC by the popular presenter Frank Bough and on ITV by Joanna Lumley.[19] By the start of October the British public had donated £9.5 million to 'Famine in Africa', a record total in the DEC's twenty-year history.[20] As the appeal closed on 19 October, agencies began to warn that the situation in the north of Ethiopia was catastrophic, and Buerk was sent again, accompanied by the incomparable Amin.

Earlier, Peter Gill, a development expert, had made a programme called *A Bitter Harvest*, due to be broadcast on 18 October. It compared the overflowing grain silos in Europe, shut merely to preserve the price, with empty granaries in Ethiopia. Gill said the film provided 'a measure of analysis to complement the news … Current Affairs can sustain a political thesis – ours was that here was this grotesque imbalance between the grain mountain of Europe and starvation in Africa.'[21] This would have 'scooped' Buerk's story, but then ITV editors went on strike. Alan Sapper, the general secretary of the Association of Cinematograph, Television and Allied Technicians, refused to make any exception for *Bitter Harvest*, despite the urgency of its subject matter. 'Volunteers' were allowed to edit the film, but only after Buerk's report had already been broadcast.[22] Cramer pointed out that 'There was fierce rivalry between ITN and BBC news – especially with a new BBC news management and a new editor of the *Six O'Clock News* – they must have choked on our exclusive.'[23]

Another structural factor helped the Ethiopian story: it fitted a novel news agenda. Bill Cotton, managing director of Television, and Michael Grade at

BBC1 had been battling to regain audiences lost to ITV for the early evening schedules. The previous year, the long-running early evening news magazine programme *Nationwide* had been axed (either because it had become too dangerous politically or because audiences were falling away). It had been replaced with *Sixty Minutes*, which was a folksy downmarket failure. Peter Woon, head of News and Current Affairs, created the *Six O'Clock News* as a hard news programme, not a magazine, prepared to give longer attention to stories that mattered.[24] Previously, broadcast 'news', whether on the BBC or ITV, was seen as a bulletin of record, dominated by home and foreign round-ups, rapid gallops through half a dozen stories in a minute. 'The idea of developing a story or explaining it at two or three minutes' length was hardly contemplated.'[25]

The new *Six*, however, was to be deeper: a 'current affairs-decorated news programme'.[26] The idea was that people needed to know the headlines in the morning, but as they came home from work they were more 'relaxed and open to a fuller appreciation of context'. In Cramer, the new programme had an exceptionally able output editor, and in Neil, an instinctive editor putting the show together. While other news programmes were still relying on the old cardboard illustrated images, only the *Six* had access to new computer graphics. The pilots invented the concept of BEXPO – the 'brief exposition' of a story which might take a minute or so to explain with imaginative graphics, longer than the standard ten-second in-vision introduction. The first big challenge facing the new programme had been the bomb explosion at Margaret Thatcher's hotel at the Tory party conference in Brighton, which had been covered well. Neil and Cramer recognised the Ethiopia story was just right for this longer, careful model.

Buerk had been a journalist since he left school, starting on the *Bromsgrove Weekly Messenger*. News, and he was a News man, despised Current Affairs as 'limp wristed, effete and engaged in what amounted to little more than late night mutual pleasuring with like-minded politicians'.[27] While Current Affairs thought newsmen 'were the benighted foot soldiers of broadcasting ... capable, like lowly invertebrates, only of responding to external stimuli.' He brought a lifetime of reporting to a wide, non-metropolitan public, tuning his tone perfectly to the sensibilities of British audiences. His stark and accomplished reporting – simple, factual and terrible – partly explains the impact of the piece. There was no hidden agenda. One of the puzzles (and no doubt frustrations) for many other journalists, Charles Stewart, Peter Gill, Jonathan Dimbleby and others, was that their stories had come out of a longer engagement with Ethiopia, yet for some reason had not captured the public imagination as this one story did.

Other factors made the British public susceptible to such a story. It broke in the approach to Christmas, when audiences are known to be more open to thinking of others and acting charitably. The miners' strike had ended in abject defeat earlier in the year. Whole British communities felt abandoned. The government, however dynamic, seemed to have defined compassion as an ideological irrelevancy. Perhaps the public reaction to the story was a counterpoint to the harsher mood of individual self-interest that characterised the period (both in Britain and America). According to Mike Appleton, who would later produce Live Aid, 'It was a knee-jerk reaction to starvation ... You're going home to have a meal that night but you see somebody who's not been fed and you assuage guilt by putting your hand in your pocket.'[28]

DERG

The public response sprang from the idea that a previously hidden scandal had been revealed, and that no one had done anything to relieve the abject misery. Yet famine was not new in Ethiopia, and there had been many accounts of the developing crisis. Jonathan Dimbleby had made an ITV film about the 1973/74 famine which had occurred under the regime of Emperor Haile Selassie.[29] The film contrasted the lavish preparations for the marriage of the Emperor's daughter with the desperate condition of the people. Shown in Addis, it helped bring Selassie's reign to a bloody end. He was replaced by a rabidly ideological government, the Derg, who, in a Pol Pot-like way, proceeded to murder such professional classes as existed in Ethiopia. The leader, Mengistu, strangled the elderly Emperor personally. By 1984 the Derg was conducting a pitiless campaign against rebels in the north, and was the main cause of the population movement and the famine. The Derg was keen to talk about 'drought' but never discussed 'famine'. There were repeated warnings, however, about a food crisis from 1982, including a few articles in the UK press.[30] In a 1983 BBC appeal, Esther Rantzen warned of several million people descending on Korem because of drought. Viewers were exhorted to donate to prevent a repetition of the seventies tragedy.[31] ITV broadcast a similar appeal, using Dimbleby.[32] It raised £1.9 million, but did not stir wider attention.[33]

The worsening of the food situation was well known – it was just that none of the stories took off. An earlier BBC report produced bleak images of the famine, but did not cause much reaction at the time.[34] By May 1984 Libby Grimshaw, a Save the Children Fund fieldworker in Tigray, was despairing at the inability to draw attention to the gathering horror she was personally dealing with.[35] Television was good at portraying extremes but far less able to communicate the build-up to famine which the agencies were trying to draw attention to.[36] Médecins Sans Frontières had tried but failed to persuade French TV to make a film about the crisis. CBS in America rejected a proposal on the grounds that it was 'not strong enough'.[37] Oxfam proposed chartering a ship to take supplies – merely as an eye-catching way to get public attention.

The BBC story had revealed what the Ethiopian government was attempting to keep secret.[38] You had to butter up 'some really grisly secret police' to get permission to travel, said Buerk. Amin was legendary for his devious success at getting stories. Shimelis Adugna, head of the Ethiopian emergency council, was sacked by the Derg for warning of a growing crisis.[39] Dawit Giorgis, who replaced Adunga, defected to the West in 1985 and wrote *Red Tears*,[40] an account of the famine from inside Ethiopia. He said that, by March 1984, 16,000 people were dying from starvation every week. 'Korem had become the death bed of thousands ... Meanwhile, in Addis, Marx and Lenin posters and flags decorated the roads.'[41] It did not help that the estimate of the amount of food required had been reduced – but that was because the international response was so low. Oxfam said that they had understated the urgency and scale of the problem. But they also highlighted the tension between the agencies' long-term development work and the distraction of being diverted by short-term emergency relief.[42]

Mrs Thatcher's attitude to foreign aid mirrored her suspicion of the welfare state at home.[43] Hugo Young said that she saw it as a 'bastion of complacency', ripe for 'the full Thatcher treatment'.[44] Britain's aid budget had fallen since the Conservatives had come into power. As a proportion of GDP, it had dropped from 0.52 per cent in 1979 to 0.31 per cent in 1983, when the international target was 0.7 per cent.[45] Timothy Raison, the aid minister, had survived in Mrs Thatcher's government despite being a quintessential wet. 'He was an effective minister in a place she did not care for,' said John Cole, and he fought a rearguard defence of aid.

The government certainly knew that an Ethiopian emergency was developing fast. In late 1982, the British embassy in Addis had reported 'continuing problems both of drought and excessive rain which will result in at least 4 million people needing help this year'.[46] Raison's aid ministry, the Office of Development Assistance (ODA), made an urgent request for assistance for Ethiopia to the special government emergency fund. The head of the Disaster Unit refused – it was not apparently a sufficiently serious crisis.[47] After the BBC story, however, 'Sir Humphrey' flew into action: it was the impact of the story on public opinion which led to a sharp change of tactics at the heart of government. The publicity enabled officials to act. The day after Buerk's first report the government pledged an extra £5 million towards drought-affected areas in Africa and 6,500 tonnes of food aid for people facing starvation in Ethiopia. Two days after the broadcast, the Foreign Office set up an Ethiopian Drought Group with direct links to No. 10 and the MoD. It dealt with policy and met daily.[48] Before the television report, the British ambassador in Addis had unsuccessfully pleaded with government to send an official to see the crisis on the ground. After it, the embassy was inundated with visiting officials. In a packed Commons debate on aid (a subject that had never filled the benches before) the Liberal Democrat MP Russell Johnston said, 'The entire aid world has been screaming from the rooftops for the last eighteen months that what has happened in Ethiopia was about to occur, yet it was only when we saw it in colour on the screens in our living rooms that the government acted.'[49]

But it was also that the media were pushing the government on a hard-to-manage, essentially political story. 'Compassion' was trumping and burying the more complex political reality. Meanwhile, the government was developing a policy to defend itself against domestic public opinion rather than strategically concentrating on Ethiopia. Tom Eggar, parliamentary secretary at the ODA, said, 'We knew of the famine problem obviously before it broke. I think it would be fair to say we had not quite realised the impact it would have on public opinion once the pictures came through. That of course influenced government policy. It would be silly to pretend that it didn't.' The broadcast and public and press response led to a summit meeting at No. 10, chaired by Mrs Thatcher, just six days afterwards. It led to a new cabinet committee that sat every morning. At a time when Robert Maxwell, the owner of the *Mirror*, was chartering a plane to triumphantly deliver cornflakes and babies' nappies to the starving of Ethiopia, Charles Powell, the prime minister's private secretary for foreign affairs, said, 'The prime minister has agreed to provide two RAF Hercules aircraft for three months in the first instance ...'[50]

The decision to use the RAF was a good way of showing the British public how much the government cared.[51] But it didn't help starving Ethiopians much. Aircraft brought supplies to airfields rather than to areas where people needed them. Raison observed that, despite Mrs Thatcher's reservations about the unpleasant Marxist regime in Ethiopia, she was particularly enthusiastic about the airlift.[52] Moreover, the ODA was forced to pay for it out of its aid budget. Just before the story broke the government had in fact announced a further 6 per cent reduction in its foreign aid budget, to be implemented in November.[53] The cut was abandoned after a Conservative backbench revolt on the issue. So the government slashed the BBC's World Service instead.

The story and its aftermath changed government behaviour all over the Western world. For the first time, there was an energetic public interest in poverty and starvation in the Horn of Africa.[54] Human Rights Watch said, 'the publicity given to the famine represented an earthquake in the relief world'. EEC donations went from $111 million in 1983 to $325 million in 1985. US donations rose from $11 million in 1983 to a staggering $350 million in 1985.[55] The American foreign policy adviser in the White House, Henry Kissinger, said, 'Disaster Relief is becoming increasingly a major instrument of our foreign policy.'[56] Alex de Waal, an acerbic critic of aid, put it more bluntly: 'For Western governments the political priority became to avoid embarrassment at the hands of figures like Bob Geldof. Aid became a strategic alibi.'[57] Both diplomat and analyst were attempting to identify the new media-enhanced authority of celebrity on policy. Indeed, the huge growth in funds was associated with a damaging shift of policy. Long-term developmental goals, slow to deliver, difficult to picture, were relegated in favour of funding disaster relief.

Mrs Thatcher's zero-sum view of the Cold War, suspicion of the Foreign Office and hostility towards overseas aid meant that the real driver of British government policy was not compassion but the determination not to be manipulated by a Marxist government. The cynicism was realistic. Ethiopia was a client Russian state, with a fundamentalist government shockingly indifferent to its people. It spent two-thirds of its budget on defence, and was attempting to repress a rebellion in the north. The British government was worried that any additional aid would be used to support an 'obnoxious, repressive and anti-western regime'.[58] The first long-term British policy objective was 'to supplant Soviet with Western influence in the Horn, especially Ethiopia'.[59] The British embassy in Moscow reported that the veteran Soviet foreign minister, Andrei Gromyko, blamed the 'current famine conditions on neo-colonialism', and said that 'so-called aid' was being used 'to preserve the conditions for the exploitation of manpower and natural resources'.[60]

In a bizarre repetition of the famine a decade earlier, in 1984 the Derg regime was preoccupied with 'celebrating' ten years in power. Festivities were orchestrated by specially imported North Koreans, with their unparalleled expertise in coordinating mass audiences in great theatrical events. The staff of the Ethiopian Relief and Rehabilitation Commission, whose job was to collect data on famine and to make requests for assistance, were ordered to spend weeks on banner-waving practice.[61] No one could get aid into the country as the key port of Assab had been commandeered for cement imports supplying lavish building projects around Addis for the anniversary jamboree, while the extra taxes raised to pay for these contributed to the famine. In March 1984, there was a meeting of the Ethiopian politburo to determine the next ten-year plan, and Colonel Mengistu dismissed any talk of the food shortage: it was just a passing, temporary setback.[62] Anyone who raised the subject of famine was accused of 'working for imperialism' or, even worse, being an agent of the CIA.[63]

Although British suspicion of the Ethiopian government was justified, the lack of any serious thinking about an effective policy for dealing with the famine and its causes was striking. Meanwhile, celebrity was gaining a media-enhanced authority. It was about to be unleashed in the restless form of Geldof, on policy-making itself. Later in the year, after the story had grown into an ongoing narrative, BBC news caught Geldof cornering Mrs Thatcher about using EU butter mountains for food aid.[64] Mrs Thatcher said, 'Mr Geldof, it is not as simple as that.' To which he replied, 'No, prime minister, nothing is really as simple as dying, is it?' Later, John Simpson interviewed the prime minister, who deftly scored points against both the European Union and the Soviet Union, demanding that the surplus grain from Europe be sent to Ethiopia and going on to talk about the arms that the Soviet Union were supplying to the country: 'You see we provide help in terms of food. You can never look to Russia for that kind of support ...'[65] The framing of the 'famine' by the tabloid press as an act of fate with no political dimensions ignored the complex reality, as indeed did the Geldof campaign.

BAND AID AND LIVE AID

It was the impact of the BBC story on a novel source of riches, fame and power, that of popular music and entertainment, however, which was most transformative. Popular music in its many forms and tribes was international, and the British music industry a world success that by 1984 had pumped out leaders for decades. Several days after the original story, Ure helped the demoralised Geldof draft a song, 'Do They Know It's Christmas?', in the back of a taxi. Then they commandeered every notable pop star – McCartney, Duran Duran, Spandau Ballet, Boy George, Elton John, David Bowie – to perform it to raise money for Ethiopia. Geldof, with a ruthless single-mindedness, shattered every commercial, legal and financial barrier to maximise revenue from the record. It was recorded, pressed, packaged, promoted for free, sold by retailers who took no profit, with rights cleared by lawyers who worked without a fee. Geldof shamed the Conservative government into waiving the VAT on its sale. (As a matter of principle they refused, but under public pressure agreed to make an equivalent donation.) Geldof unpacked the whole production process and re-engineered it for charity. It was the birth of a new economic model.

In 1984, the BBC's *Top of the Pops* was the most potent instrument in creating a hit record. It was guarded with scrupulous integrity in the face of an industry that would do anything to get a Number 1 launched. The BBC rule was that records could be played on the show only after they had entered the official chart listings (and record companies developed ingenious ploys to get over that first step). So Geldof appealed to Michael Grade, controller of BBC1, who, cunningly, cleared five minutes of the schedule before *Top of the Pops*[66] to launch the video of 'Do They Know It's Christmas?'[67] David Bowie asked everyone to buy the record: 'If you cannot afford the money, then club together with someone else to buy it.' A butcher in Plymouth phoned to ask whether there was any problem with him selling the record, and emptied his shop window of meat to fill it with the single. It sold more copies than any record that had ever been released in Britain.[68] It had been expected to make £70,000, but in the end it brought in £8 million – giving the Band Aid organisers a sense of independent power.

Celebrity involvement in charitable causes was completely new in 1984. The greater public in the 1980s was less knowing than now, and loved it. It

Live Aid is announced at Wembley, 1985: left to right, Bob Geldof, Janice Long, Adam Ant, Elton John, Gary Kemp, Tony Hadley and Midge Ure

generated publicity which kept the plight of Ethiopia in the headlines. Mark Duffield from Oxfam said, 'The TV pictures unleashed an unprecedented surge of humanitarian concern and popular mobilisation throughout Europe ... the response represented a populist form of anti-establishment politics ... Band Aid cut through red tape and chartered its own aircraft, rented its own trucks to distribute food ... and thereby shamed donor governments.'[69]

Roger Laughton was running 'Network Features', a remote department which was originally responsible for the TV transmission schedule. It had evolved into a maverick production centre (before there were independent producers) working out of huts near White City. Laughton said it was the 'West Bromwich Albion'[70] of the BBC, yet it was not at the bottom of a hierarchy. Laughton was a considerable figure who could range over the Corporation in a creative way. Mike Appleton had his own 'self-sustaining group' (the 'Rotherham of the BBC') within Laughton's which made the programmes that defined, promoted and showcased classy popular music: *The Old Grey Whistle Test* and *Riverside*. These programmes reflected the other end of popular taste from *Top of the Pops* – committed, serious about music and its impact, and generating large audiences for late night programmes, which was the nirvana for channel controllers. Entirely by chance, the other bit of the BBC that worked in the same office as Appleton was *Global Report*, which covered the developing world. By accident, the BBC had created the perfect environment for understanding what to do next. A mutual friend told Appleton that he and

Geldof were 'wandering around like a couple of old virgins – just phone him up'. In six weeks from their first conversation, the BBC, 'driven by the engine that is Bob', put on the biggest rock concert there had ever been.

Geldof had a simple idea of two fund raising concerts: one in Wembley and one in Philadelphia. The involvement of the BBC transformed this into an integrated, international, groundbreaking extravaganza, melding news and current affairs footage into a grand rock concert seen globally, an event of a kind that had never happened before. Appleton said, 'gradually the world moved in and the unification became bigger and bigger ... it was like a snowball you couldn't stop'. Laughton, however, had a pump-priming advantage: 'Ideas are wonderful and skill is wonderful but the thing that makes television work is a budget and I had a budget,' he said. When they took the proposal for a mammoth televised rock concert, which they called *Global Juke Box*,[71] to Graeme MacDonald, the controller of BBC2, Laughton said, 'Don't worry about the money. I've got your money locked up in my safe and I will divert it through this event.' Prudently, he also went to see Michael Checkland, who was never opposed to the manoeuvring of money for sensible purposes, but liked to keep an eye on it. Then Laughton began to get people to agree to clear schedules, an unprecedented request at such short notice. No one had broadcast through the night before. The sheer size and flexibility of the BBC began to work. Laughton said, 'The BBC had many faults, but one of its strengths was a very strong sense of collective purpose and the ability to get behind something that people believed in.'

As time was insanely short, Appleton could only phone up people to tell them what was wanted and then leave them to get on with it. Geldof was energetically crashing through systems to make things happen, and across the BBC people set about steering the organisation's resources to deliver the event. One producer worked night and day getting foreign broadcasters to integrate the schedule – only the Japanese were difficult at first, 'and they came round'. Another did nothing but sort out which organisation in each country could take donations from television. The deadline concentrated minds: 'there was no referring up and no quibbling – it made it easier really'. If it was global at one end, it was local at the other, as Appleton attempted to clear the rights so that thousands of showings in church halls and schools could raise more money. The enterprise was characterised by cooperative goodwill. 'It was an amazing feeling,' said Appleton, 'you were sort of driving a bus and everybody wanted to get on that bus ... it looked like a sort of bus going out of Karachi just covered with people.'[72] Michael Grade had initially been sceptical because it seemed a precarious risk to stage such an ambitious broadcast with so little preparation. As it began to take off, however, he agreed that the transmission could switch over to BBC1 when BBC2 shut down for the night, and that it could continue to relay the American event through the night.[73] Thus the two

Wembley during the Live Aid concert, 13 July 1985

concerts were united and offered to the whole world in any time zone. As the event ballooned, Appleton recalls looking around his tiny, shambolic office and thinking, 'We just can't do this show ... it feels like getting BBC Radio Cambridgeshire to cover the General Election.'[74]

It was also in a particular context. One of the unintended effects of Thatcherism had been to politicise popular music: many musicians came from communities under economic stress. *The Old Grey Whistle Test* was the classic venue for some of this hugely popular, politically inspired music – groups like the post-punk Joy Division, with their weird otherworldly sound created out of the apocalyptic dereliction of de-industrialising Manchester. UB40 was named after the unemployment form, the Jam and U2 made political singles that went to the top of the charts. There had been more organised movements too, such as 'Rock Against Racism' and 'Red Wedge'. (The latter had been spectacularly unsuccessful at assisting in the election of a Labour government the previous year.) Live Aid transformed this alternative sentiment into a mass and popular phenomenon. The message was that governments had failed Ethiopia and that in some way the massed hordes of fun-lovers were taking charge instead. Live Aid was the event that made protest mainstream.

On 13 July 1985, eighty thousand enthusiastic young people crammed into Wembley Stadium and waited patiently all day in the burning heat – from time to time cheerily pleading to be hosed down. The Prince of Wales and Princess Diana were there in (slightly uncomfortable) person, Diana sporting a prim silk dress when rock chic was called for. Simultaneously, vast crowds packed JFK Stadium in Philadelphia. Live audiences, however, were no more than the necessary atmospheric background for the many millions who watched the event on TV. Status Quo, Paul McCartney, Bob Dylan, Mick Jagger, Elton John, David Bowie all played, and Freddie Mercury of Queen gave what many thought was the performance of his life. Phil Collins performed on both continents, and tried (but failed) to broadcast from the Concorde that took him across the Atlantic. The Buerk and Amin story was reshown – showcased as the rationale for the action.

The most dismaying sequence cut moving images of a tiny, fragile young Ethiopian girl struggling to stand up, set to 'Drive' sung by The Cars. It was dangerously close to an exploitative taste barrier. Appleton was clear that the scene should not be shown again without great care, but that live, in the context of the event, it was legitimate. For many audiences, it was the most affecting part of the concert: the sense of her determination and need inspired a desperate race against time. It was repeated twice, and then David Bowie dropped his last number and said he wanted the audience to see the Cars sequence again. Donations reached their peak when it was on air.

Nobody had ever run a telethon before and very few people had credit cards. Geldof was worried that the audience would not know how to donate. Michael Grade, watching at home, had a dreadful moment when Geldof said 'fuck' on BBC2 at three on a Saturday afternoon, in the middle of sacrosanct family viewing time. But no one complained, not Mrs Whitehouse (Grade's perennial *bête noire* from the National Viewers' and Listeners' Association), nor the BBC governors.[75] BBC research showed that half of all TV sets in Britain tuned in at some point during the transmission – 30 million sets.[76] The BBC Radio 'Appreciation Index' reached an unprecedented peak of 92. Listeners had commented, 'It was fabulous and I'm no pop fan.' The television audience was equally excited.[77] People – the BBC research pointed out – wanted to be part of 'this historic event'.

The international response was groundbreaking: 120 countries watched the concert in the most complex international extended production that had ever been broadcast. A germ of an idea in the BBC's 'Rotherham' had evolved through the powerhouse of BBC news and its engineering capacity into a world phenomenon. It raised more than £100 million worldwide.[78] That it was run by the BBC, a public service broadcaster not taking profit, may have helped to minimise the cynicism at the sight of large numbers of international divas getting together for an event that made them look altruistic and put some of them back on the map.

Live Aid had metabolised a BBC news story into a mass experience that revolutionised giving. Poor people have historically given more generously than the better off,[79] but Live Aid and the BBC elicited 'an unprecedented surge of humanitarian concern and popular mobilisation'.[80] A BBC report said campaigns 'were reaching the pockets of people whom aid charities had previously failed to reach, most notably the youth and people in non-professional occupations'.[81] As traditional venues for assistance, such as the Labour movement and the churches, declined, it seemed as if another – secular, consuming, youthful and enjoying itself – had emerged.

THE LIVE AID EFFECT

The sheer volume of Live Aid giving overturned BBC processes and precedents. Philanthropy had been a creative and worthy part of the BBC's national mission since the first Charity Appeal in 1923, and the creation of a BBC Charity Appeals Committee in 1927. *Blue Peter* had ferociously protected the right of every child to give equally, irrespective of income, by organising creative campaigns that depended not on monetary value but the capacity to collect things, galvanise others, perform. Edward Barnes, head of Children's Programmes, said that the concern was 'to learn that giving is what everyone can do to be a citizen'.

The *Blue Peter* model was later to be rolled out for *Children in Need* and *Comic Relief*. Before Live Aid, however, the Corporation had maintained an iron grip over charitable access to precious broadcasting airspace – a form of 'free advertising' – through the adjudications of the Central Appeals Advisory Committee,[82] which the Corporation had set up in 1929. The Live Aid phenomenon had simply sidestepped that whole vetting process. In 1984, the annual income of the regular radio *Week's Good Cause* was £690,456, and television raised £597,682 for a range of carefully vetted appeals. During the Live Aid concert and over the next fortnight, £30 million pounds was given, mostly in quite modest amounts by ordinary people

The shift endured: *Comic Relief* raised £300 million over the next two decades; *Children in Need*, which the BBC had run since its earliest days, raised £70,000 a year in the late seventies and £4.4 million in 1985.[83] One effect was to transform charities into much larger organisations, ever more dependent on larger donations. Between 1983 and 1984, Oxfam's income doubled.[84] The income of Christian Aid and Save the Children leapt spectacularly. The DEC appeal launched the previous July had been due to close in the middle of October but remained open, eventually collecting a record total of almost £15 million.[85] And all this was separate from the money-spinning success of the Geldof enterprise, from Band Aid through Live Aid and the associated events, such as Sports Aid, which themselves raised remarkable amounts. It had effects all over the world. Thus in Japan the concert raised the largest amount ever, and for the first time the Japanese people gave generously to a foreign cause. Some argued that it changed how Japan saw itself in the world: less separate, more integrated, more responsible.

Blue Peter *fifteenth anniversary party in 1979; it had
already invented a new kind of charitable giving*

The BBC had always conferred credibility on any charity that it gave
airspace to – and it worked hard to ensure that this public trust was legitimate. Yet the revolution in giving raised practical problems for the Corporation, about how to process the immense sums of money that flooded in, and
problems of principle, over how to maintain public service impartiality while
being so intimately bound up in projecting and organising what were essentially campaigning events. Geoff Buck, one of Checkland's intelligent resource
managers, set up robust accountancy systems to deal with the flows of money.
'The new image of charities may produce huge discrepancies in income from
year to year,' his report said, 'encouraging a new breed of floating givers
with no stable allegiances and little understanding of the requirements and
achievements of the charities they have supported.'[86] The BBC was obliged to
provide audiences with 'authoritative information and guidance', to support
them in making informed choices about the organisations they might give to.
Live Aid had changed the manner of fund-raising from explanatory to exhor-
tatory, and the Board of Management worried that it 'took a large part of
the decision away from the donor'. In the new model, enticing programme
content attracted audiences who were encouraged to give to a broad cause –
hungry people in Africa or deserving children in the UK – and the umbrella
body distributed the money. Geldof wrote that he thought people were 'giving
money to me and Live Aid in preference to one of the established organisations'.[87] Meanwhile, Jimmy Savile's charitable work brought him honours,

public affection and helped make him such a cherished BBC performer, an important pillar of his respectability.

The most ticklish problem Live Aid posed for the BBC was whether it had inadvertently crossed the line from impartial reporter to campaigner.[88] Mark Ellen, one of the original presenters, said, 'Live Aid had begun as an event which the cameras covered, but it ultimately became an event staged by the BBC.'[89] It was the new shape of media events. Previously, the BBC had hosted legitimate appeals, or reported on charitable campaigns outside itself. Buck's report said, 'Charity has moved from being worthy, boring and patronising to being newsworthy and exciting.' But it concluded, 'We must not campaign, or allow ourselves to be used to campaign ... and we must ensure that our output does not embrace the agenda of any particular campaign group.'[90] One answer was to develop the 'information and understanding' aspect of appeals. *Comic Relief* (the germ for which came out of a moment's hilarity that broke tension in the rehearsals for Live Aid) and *Children in Need* were directed to develop longer, informative leads to the actual events. And the Corporation became more involved in assessing the legitimacy of the projects that were to be funded. Impartiality evolved as 'neutrality' had to be tempered by hard judgements.

The BBC in fact had a 'bias against politics' which was central to its obligations. It worried about the danger of charitable appeals drawing it into political controversy; it worried that it might inadvertently prompt donations for propagandist causes; and that the public would not support appeals that seemed political. The Corporation had founded the Disasters and Emergencies Committee in 1963 precisely to legitimise appeals and coordinate the distribution of funds to the appropriate charities. Rather than commanding the schedules, the DEC could only 'request' time, and appeals had to be a response to a calamity, not part of 'normal fundraising'. All of these principles helped reinforce the analysis of emergencies as natural disasters. The BBC was very cautious about permitting DEC appeals where the causes of the suffering were political. The Board of Governors believed that 'Man-made disasters with political implications ... fit uneasily into our rules'.[91] In the case of a DEC request for an appeal for war-torn El Salvador, the suffering was not in doubt, but it was caused by political conflict. After considerable discussion the El Salvador appeal was allowed to go ahead with the guarantee that aid could be distributed in areas of fighting, but the BBC's reservations were confirmed when the response to this appeal was disappointing.

At that point, the distinction between 'natural' disasters – floods, earthquakes, droughts – and 'man-made' or political crises – wars, rebellions, oppression – appeared clear and simple. The later understanding that the human impact of any natural disaster is the consequence of the political and social structures it encounters was only slowly emerging. The more professional mastering of what are now called 'complex emergencies' – the interaction of wars and hunger, population dispersal, health crises – took time to develop.

What were the consequences of all this activity, money and assistance for the Ethiopians whose plight had prompted the extraordinary cascade of change? The cynics in Mrs Thatcher's Conservative government had been at least partly right: sending aid had helped support a tyrannical Marxist regime. Alex de Waal argued that the 'famine' had been a weapon of war against those who supported the rebel troops. Ninety per cent of the aid went to the government, but only 22 per cent of those who were starving were under their jurisdiction. Over half of Ethiopia's national budget continued to be spent on defence and running the largest army in sub-Saharan Africa. Their Soviet-supported battles in the north against the Eritreans and Tigrayans were the biggest in Africa since El Alamein.[92] The Africa Watch report on the famine published in 1991 spoke of 'the systematic use and denial of food relief for military ends …'[93] De Waal was a scathing critic: 'it is no longer seriously disputed that the massive inflow of aid … contributed more to the survival of the Ethiopian government – whose army was the main reason for the famine – than the famine-stricken peasantry'.[94] Jason Clay and Bonnie Holcomb, working on the ground, said that 'the provision of "humanitarian assistance" with no questions asked, helped the Ethiopian government get away with murder'.[95] In 1986, Geldof wrote of the pragmatic decision he had made on the ground as he watched people being moved away: 'The issue was clear, do we help people in an area that is at best dubious or do we make a political judgment and refuse? But I myself being Irish knew that a diaspora was the natural consequence of famine.'[96] Many survived because of the aid that streamed in: the tiny girl who had struggled to her feet in the heart-stopping film became a tall and graceful young woman – although her family had been deported from the rebel area by the Derg government. Geldof maintained an eagle eye on the integrity of the aid that was delivered: he was a formidable learner.

According to De Waal and others, the unwillingness of the aid operation to engage with the realities of the war was a consequence of the 'de-politicisation of relief', which meant that a 'natural disaster' model of human suffering prevailed.[97] But all humanitarian disasters are the consequence of political structures and decisions. The BBC's quite proper anxiety about its involvement in 'political crises' inadvertently reinforced an image of disasters as unintended, uncontrollable calamities. The pressures on charities to minimise the political aspects of their work, and the public's resistance to donating without knowing which side represented innocence, got in the way of more realistic explanations of suffering. Amartya Sen, whose work explained famine not as a natural disaster but as the consequence of political rights, and indeed the freedom of the press, wrote to *The Times*:

The appalling famine in Ethiopia calls for international help on a massive scale. It also calls for clearer economic analysis of the causation of such famines, if tragedies of this kind are to be avoided in the future. In particular, it is important that we stop trying to explain famines exclusively in terms of food production per head ... Starvation must be seen as a general economic and political problem.[98]

But it was to take decades before such a sophisticated political explanation was to become acceptable.

The Ethiopian famine also set an impossibly high bar for famine stories. Most subsequent abject misery failed to look as appalling as the plains of Korem.[99] There was no simple resolution of the conundrum the story had posed. What Buerk and Amin had put on screen was a field of people dying for lack of food, and in absolute misery. Yet the answer to the critics of the BBC story that set the whole thing going was not that the news had got the story wrong, or that audiences had misunderstood – but that more and better reporting was necessary to educate a generous public in the complexity of difficult political realities, and, indeed, to assist those who suffer by informing compassion.

WOMEN IN THE BBC: THE TRIUMPH OF THE TROUSER SUIT

IN 1976, SUSANNAH SIMONS, a novice BBC studio manager trainee, got into a Broadcasting House lift, wearing her dashing new Biba trouser suit. The head of her training scheme, with her on their way up to the Olympian mysteries of management on the sixth floor, reproved her: 'Susannah, you know perfectly well that the BBC does not allow you to wear trousers.' So Simons took the trousers off there and then, in the lift. For the rest of the day she just wore the jacket. It was the age of the miniskirt, and while a hemline five inches above the knee was apparently decent, trousers were not. At her annual appraisal she was told, 'Susannah must learn to communicate more spontaneously.'

Jenny Abramsky – on the same course as Simons, where for the first time half the intake was women – said this gender balance represented a defining moment.[1] They were all so proud to have got into the BBC. They found the work so rewarding. But such an irrational rule jolted these young women into understanding something more difficult about their relationship with the Corporation. A new 'monstrous regiment of women' had arrived in the BBC. Overturning outmoded sartorial conventions was just the start of their work.

In 1974, Joan Bakewell wrote of Alan Whicker, then at the peak of a popular television career, 'He is a sexist and one of the most charming in Television (believe me the competition is keen).' She described a report of his on Rio as the television equivalent of a *Playboy* spread, full of scantily dressed girls, and descriptions of the carnival dripping with leering innuendo. Had a woman reporter talked of New York, she said, as 'all masculine – tough, erect, hard', they would have been told to keep their 'sexual neurosis off the screen'.[2]

Mores were different in the eighties. Yet, even making allowance for this, there was little the Corporation could do about some of the problems that were imposed on it, and that the wider political climate made it hard to deal with. In circumstances of this kind, the BBC was trapped. A new senior BBC administrator, appointed to a job with strategic reach across the organisation, surveyed with satisfaction the elegant wood-panelled office in Broadcasting House. It was evidence of having 'arrived'. A large 1930s safe with a wheeled handle seemed to signify the exciting scope of the new post. What might it contain? The BBC Charter? The Armageddon File, with instructions for what the BBC was to do in the aftermath of a nuclear attack? Ronnie Stoneham, the expert from Security, arrived with the combination. After clearing other staff out from the side office, he swung the safe open. It was empty except for a slim manila envelope. This contained a completed expense form, evidently for the use of a prostitute on the Orient Express by the chairman, George Howard. This unexpected and remarkable document had been left as a warning by the previous incumbent. No BBC manager would have condoned or even understood such behaviour – yet to whom could the BBC turn? The chairman had been imposed on it by the government, but as an insider he was also a defence against government hostility. A great landowner, a man with a fine war record, a widower: how and where could a complaint about him be made? Faced with this predicament, the new administrator set about grappling with his behaviour. Standards in public life were to alter.

By the early 1970s, the cadre of senior women who had joined the BBC in the unique circumstances of World War II had retired, and none had come up behind them. By the end of the seventies the clever university-educated women who were now flooding into the BBC found themselves in an organisation shaped by eddying tides of sexism. They were never victims, found ways to manage it, loved the BBC and their work, went right to the top, but felt that their fight had been for the more vulnerable women farther down the ladder, who had no political voice of their own.

The sixties had altered private lives with the pill (first discussed on *Woman's Hour* in 1963, in somewhat guarded terms) and with a wave of legislation that legalised abortion, rationalised divorce, and launched the steady march of equality legislation. Women were streaming into work: the proportion in the UK workforce doubled between 1970 and 1980, and although many of them were in part-time 'women's jobs' in light industry and the service sector, these were becoming dominant as heavy industry declined. This move into the workforce was a long-term change that would revolutionise family life (and in turn create a whole new service sector of work). The Women's Liberation Movement had been making news since the mid-sixties, formally founded in Britain at a vast conference in Oxford in 1970. Although often characterised by the media as rabid 'bra burners', it was the sound expression of a seismic shift in women's expectations. Women were more visible in public life: Harold Wilson had been notable for promoting a phalanx of powerful women ministers. Mrs Thatcher notably failed to do so.

In 1970, Germaine Greer had published *The Female Eunuch*, which provocatively argued that women had been made 'fat and lazy' by their dependence on men. Juliet Mitchell, a gifted young academic, began running consciousness-raising classes, published *Woman's Estate* in 1971, and launched a more psychoanalytically informed analysis of women's condition which was less about 'blame' and more about causes. Both argued the feminist case up and down the BBC's airwaves. The anthropologist Mary Douglas had explored the role of housework in a groundbreaking book, *Purity and Danger*. (Dirt, she demonstrated gratifyingly, was relative not absolute. It came in systems – *Woman's Hour* had much fun with this. Sociologists showed that putting the rubbish out was a male task, folding sheets a female one.) Since Doris Lessing in the *Golden Notebook*, dramatised on Radio 3 in 1969, had begun a movement of path-breaking feminist novels that pinpointed female consciousness, feminists had been arguing that the 'personal was political', and the implications of this were tumultuous. Talking about sex, bodies, gender and power became *de rigueur*. Indeed, for the young women entering the BBC in the mid-seventies much of this early feminism seemed old hat, unanswerable, settled. The world had changed except, they were to find, within institutions. Young professional women's expectations had become boundless. But they were going to have to remake the press, the universities, business, the law – and the BBC.

An influential 1970 report by the think tank Political and Economic Planning investigated the role of women (or lack of them) in management in industry, the civil service, the law and the BBC. *Women and Top Jobs* said that the Corporation 'ought not to assume it has equal opportunities for women and should examine what it means by equal opportunities'.[3] But it also identified what was special about the Corporation. The BBC cannot 'be tidy', said the report: 'It is among other things a film industry, a music industry, and one of the largest publishing organisations in the country … it gathers together under one umbrella a large number of self-contained specialisations';[4] one shape could not fit all. 'The most striking feature … is the difficulty of discerning any regular pattern of careers in the Civil Service model.' The very term 'career pattern' was disapproved of. The Corporation needed to be able to take any really clever person it wanted in: 'there are no recognised qualifications for senior staff – or even the most junior staff'. No set procedure for promotion, no pattern of time to be spent in different departments. It was because the BBC had been a flexible organisation that 'Empires have risen and fallen as public taste has altered and as demands have altered. This has meant the speedy rise of people who have found themselves in the right place at the right time.' The Corporation, it observed, needed very clever, very creative people. It needed to nurture talent.[5]

But although women were able to thrive in some areas within the BBC, on the whole they were very rarely promoted up the Corporation's hierarchy. This had consequences for the kind of organisation it was becoming and the kind of programmes it made. By 1969, of the 23,376 people employed in the BBC, 8,723 were women. But they made up less than 5 per cent of the top four grades of the Corporation.[6] The lack of women at the top was holding back women farther down. The BBC was missing out on half the pool of the gifted, creative people it needed.

EARLY BBC WOMAN

The history of women in the Corporation was not one of meritocratic, Whiggish progress. It was a more hesitant process. At the beginning, women had been very prominent in the Corporation. They had built BBC departments, held the highest jobs and created many of the enduring forms of public service broadcasting: those catering for women and children and the broad sweep of political and cultural life of the nation in Talks, Drama and Current Affairs. In 1926, John Reith instructed all new directors: 'I think we have been wrong in our attitude to the women on our staff, not taking sufficient interest in or a broad enough view of their responsibilities ... they should be as eligible as men for promotion. There is no reason why a woman should not be a station director.' (He added, 'Of course, I realise that it would be extraordinarily difficult to find one suitable.')[7] Hilda Matheson, already director of Talks, set up the first news service in 1926 for the General Strike, and women worked on the early bulletins. The first BBC political series, *The Week in Parliament* (later renamed *The Week in Westminster* and still broadcast), was invented and edited by Margery Wace in 1929 to help newly enfranchised women make sense of politics. Mary Somerville became head of the Education Department and Isa Benzie had been head of the Foreign Department. Mary Adams was the first television producer in 1937. In general, these were well-connected women who made use of their contacts. The BBC set a progressive example: 'Women are not compelled to resign at marriage, equal pay for equal work is on the whole respected, while married women are not debarred from applying for more senior posts.'[8] This was groundbreaking at the time. There had always been women governors, and women audiences were taken seriously. Women appeared on air – Sheila Borrett was the first female announcer in 1937, Olive Shapley made groundbreaking documentaries, women's voices were heard. But as the BBC trebled in size during World War II, a new generation of able women took charge of programmes and moved up the Corporation.

But by 1959, Mary Hamilton, a radical and political governor, was writing to *The Times* complaining of the lack of women in commanding positions, in a BBC with 'no Evelyn Sharp and no Mary Smieton' (pioneering women civil servants). And in 1970, *Women and Top Jobs* warned that 'The number of really senior women will fall sharply', as those 'remarkable' women first employed during the war retired. Women were often in jobs without departmental responsibility, and those who succeeded remained single, treating the job as a vocation – 'they had paid a high price for a career'.[9]

Something had gone wrong, ability was not rewarded rationally. Women's opportunities were boxed in. The formidable Grace Wyndham Goldie had retired in 1965, after inventing many of the forms of political television and forging a generation of television administrators and programme makers – men like Milne and Baverstock.[10] The most important woman in the BBC later was Joanna Spicer, who had come into the Corporation accidentally during the war. 'If she had been born in another period she'd have been Disraeli.' Operating through diplomacy, with 'a mind that cut like a knife',[11] she helped create BBC2, oversaw the introduction of colour television, and led the international negotiating that made the BBC the dominant player in the European Broadcasting Union and a counterweight to the vast American interests. David Attenborough said, 'she was the most important overlooked person in the history of the BBC'; she was not given a title, but 'just got on with running the place'.[12] Charles Curran, the director-general, at his narrow-minded worst, had told her, 'No woman will ever be appointed above the level of assistant controller.' The job of 'Programme Planning' was invented for her, at an angle to the BBC management hierarchy, because she correctly believed men could not bear formally working beneath her.

Claire Lawson-Dick had served Radio 4 for nearly thirty years when she applied to be head of the network. Instead Tony Whitby – a funny, gifted man, seen as a potential director-general – was appointed. When she went to congratulate him, 'He flew across the room, kissed me and still holding my hand, said "You will be asking yourself why him? ... Why not me? And I really don't know what to say".' It was done, said Lawson-Dick, 'with such high spirits that I really loved him for it and we worked together in complete accord'. Whitby was an inspired choice, but Lawson-Dick's generous creative talent was merely taken for granted.[13] Later, Monica Sims applied to be controller of BBC1, but the governors' discussion of the appointment was blinkered. They never considered the pioneering shape of her work at the BBC and appointed a candidate who had little of her steely professionalism and persuasive charm. Verity Lambert, the creative first producer of *Doctor Who*, had to leave the BBC to make a career large enough for her ambitions.

There was a disjunction between the programmes the BBC broadcast and its lack of self-reflection on what they meant. BBC programmes did not ignore the winds of change in women's lives, but held them at a distance as if they were in another world. In 1973, Anne Sloman and Professor Anthony King, in a far-seeing series for Radio 4, *Westminster and Beyond*, interviewed leading women politicians. King asked Margaret Thatcher whether there could be a woman prime minister. 'Well,' said Thatcher, cautiously but hungrily, 'it's possible ... I don't think it will happen in my life time.'[14]

Women like Sloman were closer to the ground than the organisation they worked in. In *Yes Minister*, Sir Humphrey Appleby explained why none of the forty-one Permanent Secretaries was female: 'If women were able to be good

The 1979 intake to the BBC's General Trainee Programme: the first ever with a majority of women; back row (left to right): Teresa Hunt, Charles Miller, Leila Green, Wesley Kerr, Mark Thompson, Olga Edrick; front row: Belinda Giles, Suzanne Franks, Fran O'Brien, Cathy Collis, Max Whitby

Permanent Secretaries there would be more of them wouldn't there? Stands to reason. Don't want that do we?'[15] Nor apparently did the BBC. Between 1954 and 1970 the General Trainee Scheme (the key way for potential high flyers to enter the Corporation) had selected eight women and 102 men. In 1975, it went wild and doubled its annual intake – to two women.

In 1970, when the Equal Pay Act was passed, the BBC was already complying with the quite weak standard imposed. In 1975, the Sex Discrimination Act, and the Employment Protection Act, made it unlawful to dismiss a woman because she was pregnant. The formidable vice-chair of the new Equal Opportunities Commission, Elspeth Howe, had her eye on the BBC: 'it had a duty to take a lead when half its audience was women ... I really lost my patience'. It was a place 'where really able women worked and where they should have been recognized better'.[16] She had lunched members of the Board of Management and governors and wanted the BBC to set an example in allowing more part-time working, wider advertisement of jobs, crèche facilities.[17] But the BBC hierarchy saw her as embodying yet another external government pressure, rather than as raising a fundamental issue of principle, that of how the BBC should represent the audience it served.

The media became a focus of feminist research and campaigning. Seen as powerful socialising forces, films, television and the press were the source of stereotypes that created and reinforced damaging images of women as passive, domestic, incapable. These images influenced how women saw themselves and how men saw women. The sexual revolution of the sixties altered the moral geography as radical feminists and traditionally right-wing conservative movements coalesced around opposition to pornography. One explanation advanced for the spread of damaging media images was the lack of women in media industries.

Women in the Media was a highly professional campaigning group, including the veteran *Guardian* journalist Mary Stott. It persuaded the Advertising Standards Authority to alter its regulations to protect women and children better, helped form the remit for Channel 4 as a broadcaster with special obligations to women's interests, and agitated about the dearth of women in senior positions in all the public service broadcasters. In the Lords it said, 'Women appear to be entirely excluded from senior jobs in the Corporation: and if not the result of deliberate policy the effect is just the same, in every level women are discriminated against.' Then the Women's Monitoring Network identified media stereotypes in reporting, finding that 'violence against women is treated as commonplace and exploited for its news and entertainment value and marketability'[18] in the press, while broadcasting was responsible for showing women as incompetents across a range of programmes from comedy to news. Another feminist organisation, Women in Focus, produced a code of conduct saying that women should not be defined by relationships as 'miner's wives' or 'mums', nor black women as victims, social misfits, seductively sexy or demure pawns. It found that 'discrimination against women in the content of the media is related to discrimination against women in media occupations'.[19] The Corporation later became a model place for women to work: yet the wider media problem of how women were represented was – unexpectedly – to deteriorate, not improve.

THE LIMITATIONS REPORT

By 1973 some of this had filtered through to the Board of Management, which began to fret. Of the 1,434 managers in the BBC, 81 were women. There were more women governors (three) than there were women in top jobs in the BBC itself; the pool of women at the top of the organisation had actually declined and there were no women at all at controller or board level. The head of Personnel was dispatched to report on 'Limitations to the Recruitment and Advancement of Women in the BBC'.[20] His report included a priceless litany of the uninhibited expression of prejudice. The 'problem' was found to be the volatility and weakness of women, and another, unconscious theme was the unreliability of men, who could not be trusted in the presence of women. It is an eloquent document from a pre-modern world. Women (or 'girls', as they were mostly called in 1973) were apparently seen as quite unsuitable for any advancement or indeed employment in the Corporation for a florid set of reasons.

While the head of Radio News thought, according to the 1973 report, that employing more women would be a good idea because more than half of his audience were female, he had six women in a backroom staff of 120 and no female reporters, explaining that women were 'no good' at hard news. Women, he assured the investigator, would be overcome with feeling if they had to announce, read, let alone cover any upsetting story. Those women who became dedicated were 'not really women with valuable instincts but become like men'. And men did not like taking instructions from these unsexed women. Women newsreaders were unacceptable as they sounded 'as if they came from Cheltenham Ladies college'. Mary Goldring on Radio 4 was – it was acknowledged – 'unusually competent and knowledgeable about economics', but sounded 'lah-di-dah'.

The editor of Radio Current Affairs thought he might employ a woman as long as she didn't giggle, and thought that women might do better on radio than television (where audiences would be distracted by what they looked like). The head of Television News thought that more women would be a good idea (in theory) but audiences wouldn't like to see women in dangerous places, as they would feel protective towards them, nor could he send them to the Middle East or Northern Ireland because it would impose too much of a burden on other members of the team. (This was especially bizarre, because two notable women BBC reporters were in the thick of the Northern Ireland conflict.) Women could not operate cameras because they could not lift heavy weights. Women were no use announcing because if they did not smile audiences would not like it and if they did smile they were not taken seriously: 'announcing represents the supreme authority of the Corporation', so needed 'a man's voice which is suited to all occasions'. In Light Entertainment, the controller 'considers his artistes uptight and his comedians neurotic'. Consequently, the production assistant in the studio 'has to be a chopping block on whom the artiste can vent his spleen, although both can share a beer in the bar afterwards'. For good measure, 'the pitch of the female voice' was objectionable, variety stars needed 'stern handling', and women could not deal with 'camp Kings Road humour', as well as the necessary 'barracks room fun', and were not 'natural dealers in humour'.

You could not have women in the Sports department because of the 'changing room problem'. Meanwhile, women engineers would let loose steamy jezebels on the settled marriages of unsuspecting and uxorious engineers. At this, the welfare officer (a woman) remarked tartly that people already had affairs with their secretaries and that 'if adults are going to be tempted they are going to be tempted' – but it was a lone voice. Meanwhile, women could not work in pop because they were too weak to move equipment, could not drive lorries because 'of the wind and rain', could not climb ladders, were not tall enough to paint scenery, and the 'down to earth nature' of pop groups needed 'handling firmly', which sensitive females were not suited to.

When interviewees were asked to consider more general explanations for the failure of the BBC to promote women, there was a litany of reasons. Women were not aggressive enough, didn't like competition, needed encouragement, had to look after other people, children and parents, found the scrutiny if they did make it to a top job difficult, and did not get promoted because they did not do well enough earlier on. Of course, there were also 'menopausal tensions', 'emotions' and the firm view that it was bad for children for their mothers to leave them – even if they wanted to work. To cap it all, if women were professionally competent and dedicated to their work they then rendered themselves useless (unlike men presumably) because they became too narrow and 'unaware of whole life skills'.[21]

One anonymous progressive soul on the Board of Management annotated the report (and another outraged soul carefully preserved the outrage in the archive) with *'rubbish'* at a particularly lurid diatribe about women's lack of reporting capacity; *'not good enough'* at the argument 'The BBC's job is to broadcast not to provide equal career opportunities for women'; a pensive *'true'* at reports that female audiences reacted strongly against women on screen; *'Absurd. What about ambulances and the Queen during the War?'* at the suggestion that women could not do 'heavy driving'; and finally, at the comment that 'There is often male resentment to accepting orders from a woman', the liberal annotator had had enough, adding, *'NUTS'.*[22] The 1973 report had flushed out the prejudices, exposing their absurdity (it certainly does not endorse them) was its purpose.

Over the next decade, whatever the institutional problems for women, the working relationships between men and women had been moved into a different public frame. By the time of Monica Sims's 1984 report on a similar theme – written by a woman and talking with women rather than about them – the tone and sensibility are utterly different.

Indeed, most of the arguments in the 1973 report were exposed as specious in the 'other' world of the Overseas Services (the World Service) in Bush House. There, women were presenting, editing, being journalists, and in charge, and it was all part of the natural order. The controller (a Russian) said that, with his background and being used to women doing bricklaying and clearing the snow, he found British attitudes very odd: 'It is almost as if men and women are racially different.'

1973–83

The report launched a regular 'Analysis of Female Staff' so that the BBC began to count where its women employees were, and led to all jobs in the BBC being formally open to women. In 1974, in 'Women in the BBC – One Year Later', the director of personnel noted that there had been little progress and that there were still an 'unduly small percentage of women in senior posts'.[23] It was as if it were all just a natural force and that the BBC had nothing to do with what happened within it: 'The war-time wave of women is all but spent,' concluded the report, 'and the succeeding new wave is still, it seems, gathering energy.'

The young women trooping into the BBC became aware that they 'came from a world that had changed, but the BBC hadn't'.[24] It was no accident, however, that a clever, principled set of young women were attracted to the Corporation; they wanted to be close to what they saw as a transformative power in people's lives. Television, broadcasting, the media, all seemed such influential, interesting and contemporary places. Whatever they found when they arrived in the BBC, they had been stirred and inspired by what it had offered audiences. Margaret Drabble, the novelist of the moment, who always included a television producer or director in her stories, described Clara – her aspirant heroine in *Jerusalem the Golden* – much as these young women were, in a state of 'rapt and ferocious ambition and desire'.[25]

They were collectively formed by parents who, having survived World War II, were hopeful and bold about their children's futures. The 1944 Education Act had educated them in grammar schools (although a significant proportion of the women had also been to private schools); the NHS had kept them healthy; and radio and TV had opened their eyes to wider horizons of culture. Harold Wilson's expanded universities had taken them to higher education. Personally, they believed that they could do anything and have it all. Later, Fran O'Brien, a Current Affairs producer, said, 'We were the golden generation.'[26] They wanted interesting jobs, intended to excel at them, and for the first time nearly all of them intended to have children. Work was going to have to adapt.

What problems did they face? Simple administrative injustices; barriers of expectation and habit; social prejudice and a demoralising barrage of everyday demeaning attitudes; a working environment that was shaped around the needs of men; an institution with a tendency to relegate, dismiss, ghettoise women's capacities. Yet, beyond their intelligence and ambition, they were armed with a BBC principle: the BBC had to represent and serve its audiences if it was to survive meaningfully, so obviously it had to respect women's experience and abilities.

Unfair regulations that discriminated against women had to be identified and patiently fought one by one. In the early seventies, Thena Heshel, a pioneer of disability programming, found it too demanding to return to work

Joan Bakewell interviews Henry Moore; Bakewell had
to 'reinvent' her own career three times

with tiny children, and wanted to go part-time. She was finally allowed to do so, but on condition that she was demoted and excluded from the BBC pension scheme.[27] Together with the head of Personnel, a male 'hero', George Tree, she spent four years battling to get women the right to pass their pensions on to their husbands, as men could pass them to their wives.

Sue MacGregor and Joan Bakewell, for many years the only women presenters on the *Today* programme[28] and *Late Night Line Up*, discovered that they were paid less than the male presenters. Later, when Bakewell told the director of Programmes, David Attenborough, that she was worried about what she might do next, he said, 'Don't worry, Joan, you only do it for the pin money ...'[29] When Patricia Hodgson became Secretary she asked why she was not allocated a car (as every previous Secretary had been) and was told she was a woman and did 'not need one'.

Then there were lavatories. Significantly, there were no female lavatories on the sixth floor, where the senior management offices were. When Sims and later Abramsky attended meetings, a temporary sign was ostentatiously put outside one of the men's lavatories. For about three months it read coyly: 'Temporary Women's Facility'. In Kensington House, there was a Gents on every floor, but a solitary Ladies, with an external door, in the basement by the rubbish bins. One group of women working in a distant Lime Grove wing had to go down several floors and through a long corridor for a Ladies, but worked next door to a Gents. Having commissioned a 'Ladies' sign from a graphic designer, they just stuck it on the door. The impact was immediate: men stopped using the lavatory. It was, said one, 'The most effective takeover I have ever been involved in.'[30]

Then there was the daily grind of casual discrimination, sexist attitudes, the clash with male culture. Frances Donnelly, a radio producer, was instructed to take down her women's lib posters from her office walls by Stephen Bonarjee, the head of News. MacGregor made five programmes on Militant Women which were relegated to the witching hour. What was new was that there was a 'critical mass'[31] to share jokes about it, and a new common collective rejection of it. One aspect of this was the hilarity with which women metabolised, shared and in the end rendered sexism harmless. Yet although these successful young women on their way managed it all, they understood that younger, less powerful women were potentially vulnerable.

This daily power game did not even have a name until the mid-1970s, when the term 'sexual harassment' was coined by a group of American academics and caught on.[32] In many organisations, some men just took it for granted as an expression of power. The sexism at the very top of the BBC, and the *omertà* was a factor, but different from the abuse of vulnerable young women. Jimmy Savile and Stuart Hall – and others – were parasitical intermediaries to the glamorous power of popular culture. The aspirant, educated young women working in the Corporation were affected by sexism, but largely they managed it. They were gathering the authority to name it.

Some men had never encountered working women before and were threatened by the influx. The closed male culture of joking innuendo, suddenly exposed to women, became less private and more threatening. One union report in the seventies talked about production assistants as a 'wife at work', others said that the role was to keep the (all-male) camera crew happy by supplying them with sweets.[33] Camera crews could be generous and helpful to young journalists, telling them how the BBC did things and with an eye for a story. They could also be appalling: undermining reporters with a constant undercurrent of sexist banter, cheerily clocking up overtime and unnecessarily protracting shoots on foreign stories when women reporters needed to get back to little children. Women who wanted to work in camera crews had 'a very tough time'. Even in the late 1980s, a news cameraman at a union meeting said that women could not work in news crews because they were 'tarts'. There was, he told a packed union meeting, 'only one use for a woman on the road'.[34]

When Abramsky became an editor of *PM* in the late seventies, one man left in protest. Sandra Chalmers became the first woman manager of a local radio station in Stoke, where there was only one other woman in the newsroom. A male colleague continually undermined her in an environment of 'management by piss-up', leading a guerrilla insurrection against her from the BBC

Monica Sims: the first woman head of Radio, and author of the Sims Report

drinking club. When the first woman was appointed Secretary, a male junior burst into tears,[35] and said he could not work for a women superior. When Abramsky was promoted to be head of Radio News she was persistently treated with conspicuous discourtesy. Finally faced with aggressive rudeness at a news meeting, she walked out. She said that she did not expect people to agree with her, but did need 'the simple human decency of respect'.

George Howard, when chairman, had treated the BBC rather like a private fiefdom. He had entertained extravagantly at the BBC's expense. But the other problem was that '"droit de seigneur" was his motto'. When travelling around the country for regional meetings he would demand 'a pretty young journalist or producer' to sit next to at the dinner. At a publicity party on a boat down the Thames, an increasingly frantic BBC mandarin spent most of the time trying to stop Howard being photographed with arms around young BBC employees. He was 'always touching up women', said Ros Sloboda, who, as secretary to Trethowan and then Milne in succession, watched him closely.

A canny and efficient woman, Sloboda knew Howard had to be managed. At a large dinner for musicians, he sat next to an up-and-coming female composer. The next morning the BBC Secretary, a decent man in a peculiar place, phoned asking for the personal telephone number of the young woman for the chairman. Sloboda went home and consulted her flatmates. Then she phoned the composer's parents and the young woman herself answered. She said, 'Can I speak to you absolutely frankly as one girl to another? He's a dirty old man. Leave this to me.' Sloboda gave the chairman's embarrassed messenger the number of the young woman's agent: 'all *professional* queries have to go through the agent'. It saw him off.

There were other powerful men who abused their position. New workplace mores were being forged. Men on the *Today* programme were 'misogynist, courteous and patronising'.[36] The great Huw Wheldon and the apparently saintly Malcolm Muggeridge both groped incontinently. Robin Day, probably the greatest political interviewer of the period, was presenting *World at One* when Bakewell was in the neighbouring *PM* office, and said, 'Tell me, Joan, when you interview men on your programme do they stare at your breasts?' Sexual harassment was routine: one journalist would feel the thighs of the programme's researcher, Ellie Updale, every morning to see whether she was wearing tights or stockings; another producer would drop paper clips on the floor to get a Light Entertainment director to lean down to pick them up; popular presenters on the main news programmes would back new members of staff into corners. Sarah Nathan, a young news planner, after coming back from America on a Harkness scholarship, found the newsroom 'gloomy, old fashioned and overmanned', not improved when an editor of Radio News pinched her bottom while he was on the phone to his wife. The 'fearsome banter' and the male joshing of the 'girls', who were starting to make their way as more senior figures on programmes like the *Today* programme, were 'just normal'. Much later, when women, including Caroline Millington who started as a journalist and became a manager, compiled a list of chaps who they had had 'trouble' with – presenters, journalists, directors, administrators – gales of laughter greeted each name.[37] But these women told Monica Sims, investigating for her 1984 report, that they could 'cope' with sexual harassment.

One case threatened to become a public scandal, and it changed women's attitudes. A man in a position of authority was known to proposition younger women, especially secretaries, for spanking sessions. For years women had negotiated their way around him. But a new and more senior group of women in Kensington House sent a formal complaint to the BBC head of Personnel and the story began to leak into *Private Eye*. At first, Brian Wenham dismissed the allegations as harmless. Eventually, when the Kensington group prepared papers to take to the governors, a compromise was found and the man was posted to a BBC job – abroad – with an expensive apartment in New York.

Women often saw it all as funny – classic examples of men's ridiculousness. On the 1974 general election programme, a posse of women – secretaries, researchers, producers – was working all night for the editor, Anne Sloman. A hapless male press secretary produced a set of pink T-shirts emblazoned with 'We can keep it up all night' for a publicity stunt, for the 'girls' to wear jogging around Hyde Park. He was told what to do with his T-shirts. A presenter on the *Today* programme had found the story of the first test tube baby, Louise Brown, too technical and 'female'. The women in the office held a sweepstake. The winner would get a bottle of Burgundy for coming up with a story that forced him to say 'uterus' on air. If they could get him to say 'fallopian tubes', the prize was champagne. While working as news planners, Sarah Nathan and Anna Brennan were nearly sacked for adamantly refusing to schedule a Miss World beauty pageant. They struck a deal: Miss World was covered, but a hapless male reporter believed to be in need of 're-education' was sent to report on a 'Reclaim the Night' feminist march (against prostitution).

Prejudice had effects. By 1980, Olivia Seligman, a news reporter, was working on *Today* when there was an assassination attempt on the Pope. Sent to Rome at no notice with Robert Fox and an Italian-speaking secretary, Seligman managed to get the story back – at one point cutting tape with her teeth – but instead of compliments on a great story, she was told that 'a young slip of a girl should not have been sent'. Angela Neuberger's boss in Current Affairs apologised to her for not promoting her, but he thought she would not mind because she was about to get married. When women were promoted, they were repeatedly told 'it's only because you're a woman'. *Newsnight* had been launched with four male presenters, and when Ellie Updale became day editor they were 'proud they had been so progressive, not ashamed they had taken so long!' *Panorama*, 'horrendously male', had 'a really very odd atmosphere', said Jane Doganis, who worked on the influential programme. 'Everything went on behind closed doors.' She felt 'extra second class' because she was a woman with children. Richard Lindley, in a brilliant account of *Panorama*, later argued that the stories the women produced had a narrower focus than those of the men: 'life isn't all about gynaecology or sex-related issues either'.[38] The women producers 'contributed to a growing tendency on *Panorama* to focus on the interesting and entertaining surroundings to a story rather than the story itself' – seen by some as 'Vanity Fair' journalism. *Panorama* was packed with clever, opinionated men who saw themselves as the praetorian guard of public service current affairs. They were from the same universities as the women, but exercised another kind of attraction and control over them. Prejudice was composed of customs, attitudes, behaviours and expectations that were implicit expressions, not of a natural order, but of a particular disposition of power.

Radio was always more enlightened than television. It was free from the tyranny of the visual and had an intimate relationship with its women audiences, while television provided more for the 'general audience'. Each time a woman crashed through one of the barriers, others followed. Some male hostility to women was more about class than gender. 'The real tension' in BBC newsrooms, said Olivia Seligman, a news editor, was between the 'school of life old lags', journalists and administrators who had worked their way up through local journalism, and the new breed of university-educated women and men coming into the BBC. Within this, there were subtler class divides: women reporters came from provincial universities, while women producers and potential managers came from Oxbridge. Yet, for a brief window, the class system was unstable as people flooded into new universities: York and Sussex, Essex and Kent produced BBC women as well. Anna Carragher, a studio manager, was from a working-class Northern Irish family. Her father's shop had been burnt out in the Troubles and she was sending money home. Her Catholic background meant that she was far more suspicious of the British army and was seen as a dangerous radical, 'though others felt that I wasn't radical enough, because coming from Northern Ireland I was so hostile to the paramilitaries!'[39] She felt at a loss at first in an organisation full of middle-class girls.

Drinking, in the BBC clubs of every building, in offices and meetings, was part of the macho culture. Indeed, the Corporation was awash with alcohol. Even though *Woman's Hour* went out at 2 p.m., a drinks trolley was available (although MacGregor said 'staff and presenters never drank'). On *World at One*, as soon as the programme was off air at 1.30 p.m., the drinks trolley appeared – ostensibly for the editor and guests, although some reporters joined in. One of Updale's jobs on the programme was to collect a bottle of gin and a bottle of whisky from the club, and as you got new bottles only if you handed in the empties they would be finished each day. Her other regular task was to collect the money for the two bottles of wine that the team needed as well. Monica Sims recalls confronting the 'liquid lunch' when she joined the BBC in 1953. She was told that she would be expected to go to the BBC club and drink beer every lunchtime and remembers asking, 'But when do we eat?' Hodgson, a small woman, discovered a taste for organic real ale (small bottles, low alcohol) when confronted with competitive spirits consumption on the Board of Management. Drinking fuelled attitudes and was incidentally a way of excluding women.

But the new generation of energetic young women were not ground down, and relished the challenge of *Rough Justice* and *24 Hours*, *Newsnight* and the *Today* programme, *Panorama* and *Woman's Hour*, framing the intelligent discussion of the nation. Making programmes was intense and exciting. The dash to broadcast deadlines by teams of young people, working long hours and feeling urgently important at the heart of the national conversation, buzzed with flirtation. Relationships melted and formed in the heat of the moment.

They worked long hours; the 'spirit of programme making was seductive'.[40] Having in a variety of ways sorted out Mr Right from within the BBC or outside it, these young women started having babies. Colleagues reacted with horror, and they quickly learnt to lie, delaying telling anybody until the last possible moment. 'I remember standing sideways and hoping no one would notice,' said Francesca Kirby-Green, working in Current Affairs editorial. When Abramsky went to see the personnel officer in charge of her senior grade, he knew nothing about maternity legislation as he had never dealt with a senior pregnant member of staff before. Originally designed to protect pregnant women working in heavy industry, maternity leave obliged women to take ten weeks off before the child was born and seven afterwards. These busy young women did not do physical work and wanted to spend time with the child when it was born. So Abramsky, who had worried that she might lose her job over her first child, lied about the due date of the second (so that she could have more time after the birth with the baby). Carragher was working on *Newsbeat* when she got an 'attachment' (temporary, career-boosting work in another department) to *World at One*. Dutifully, she told the editor she was pregnant, and he promptly took her off the attachment list. Routine hospital pregnancy check-ups were more acceptable disguised as 'taking a car in for a service'; rushing home to a sick child was disguised as a plumbing emergency to 'save face'.

When Ros Sloboda first applied for the job with Trethowan, he turned her down, worried that she 'might be thinking of having babies'.[41] She wasn't married and wasn't thinking of babies at all. 'All the senior PAs were clucking that it would never work,' she was 'the wrong age'. When the job came up again no one applied, because Trethowan had a 'terrible, unjustified reputation for not getting on with people'. She applied again. Married (by then), and being frank, she told him, 'I am thinking of having a baby, I'm not having much luck, but if I manage it, I will come back afterwards.' Desperate, because nobody else had applied, he took her. The head of Office Training (wonderful BBC title – 'HOTS') found a replacement when she did have a baby and she returned after maternity leave. Yet attitudes towards maternity leave were changing fast. By the late seventies it was 'if' you came back after. In the early eighties Angela Neuberger said, when she had her third child, 'it was automatically assumed that I would be back at my desk after a few months along with dozens of other working mothers'.[42]

After maternity leave, the first months of a new baby's life were often punishing. Frances Hill, the solitary female engineer, was sent off on transmitter repair trips in distant parts of the country, five nights a week. Hodgson was put straight back on the night shift at the Open University. Reporters would be sent on foreign trips. Family life was different – not yet reforged by these women and their partners – so that half-terms and school holidays were never mentioned, just guiltily snatched. Women who took time away from the BBC in the very early years of their children's lives found that when they returned they had been demoted and had lost all of their pension and employment rights. Gwyneth Williams, later controller of Radio 4, returning after five years out with her children, was working in a more junior capacity than the one she had left and on a temporary contract. She applied for a different BBC job to get back to a permanent contract. None of the people who should have interviewed her turned up, and Williams returned to edit a programme (next to the man who had been her junior but who was now her superior) in floods of tears, 'sobbing, heaving, weeping my heart out'. He just carried on editing.[43] The BBC was falling behind Channel 4, where Naomi Sargant, the first head of Education commissioning, fought to have women presenters, if they were experts, rather than the grand old men who dominated programmes. She put heavily pregnant presenters on screen for the first time. Liz Forgan, recruited by Jeremy Isaacs from the *Guardian* woman's section, with a brief for women's programming, fought for women. Caroline Thomson, later at *Newsnight* and a public-spirited administrator, had started out in the 'freer, outsider, liberating air of Channel 4'. By the late eighties nearly half of the management board of Channel 4 was female. The effect on screen may occasionally have got out of hand – Sargent admitted that for months 'Greenham Common women dominated the channel's output. Even the pensioners' show discussed the "older women and protest"' – nevertheless broadcasting was being put in touch with half its audience properly.[44]

Commercial television was also ahead in childcare, setting up a nursery while women had to battle for years for one at the BBC. The Groundswell Campaign for a BBC crèche, started in 1978, was as much a battle for the heart of the BBC as it was about its ostensible purpose: to unite men and women in an argument for childcare facilities. Steered by Christina Driver, a 'quiet, effective' ABS union organiser, it produced a magazine, which Giles Oakley, an editor of *Open Door*, and a passionate believer in equal opportunities, helped edit. 'It wasn't really a single-issue campaign. It mattered because it won the argument for equality.' He thought it made it 'impossible to say the very reactionary things people had said before', and if the first generation of women with children had had to be very hard-headed, the campaign made it easier for women lower down the BBC system to be heard. The campaign maintained a tone of reason, and was in the end helped because Vincent Hanna, a larger-than-life NUJ Father of Chapel, supported it.

Men who were patrons of women made all the difference. Andrew Boyle employed Sue MacGregor on the new *World at One*, which became one of the most important radio news programmes. The main presenter was William Hardcastle, an ex-editor of the *Daily Mail*, and the show became hard-hitting and investigative, with a dedicated team – separate from the almost entirely male newsroom – of three men and three women. MacGregor said, 'I don't think those of us working for *World at One* realised just how pioneering it was to have gender equality, we just took it for granted.' Women's appearance on screen and on air was important because they reflected back to society a more accurate image of women's role. As late as 1977, Curran replied to a complaint by Women in the Media about the lack of women on screen – just one to every three men – by saying they 'represent the participation of women in public life'. Gillian Reynolds, the most influential and thoughtful of radio critics, pointed out that while a male presenter was expected to be a 'surrogate lover, all bold flirtation and innuendo', women were supposed to be demure – both locked into implicit, unacknowledged stereotypes.[45]

Margaret Jay's easy authority on *Panorama* brought an assured clarity to programmes about women and children and early identified AIDS as a key issue. She was a clever empress, comfortable with high politics as prime minister James Callaghan's daughter, and married into the intellectual aristocracy of the Labour Party. Yet a brilliant, argumentative history of *Panorama* said that she reported 'just occasionally with too much authority'[46] – women were in a double bind. The presence on screen and radio of Julia Somerville, Joan Bakewell, Moira Stuart, Mary Goldring, Sue MacGregor, Libby Purves and Annie Nightingale 'reflected a change in the BBC's attitude towards women as well as changes in society'.[47]

Finally, after ITV, and after a concerted campaign by Women in the Media, Radio 4 led the way with permanent newsreader Sheila Tracy in 1974, and BBC1 followed in 1975 with Angela Rippon, the first woman to read the main evening bulletin at nine o'clock. The director of Television said, 'Barriers crashed, taboos lay shattered and Lord Reith probably stirred and muttered in his private Valhalla.' Rippon said, 'I knew if I made a hash of it no woman would be allowed another chance for at least five years.'[48] Sue Lawley, who had worked alongside Michael Buerk as a Thomson trainee on the *Echo* in Cardiff, had a sharp intelligence, expressing an aspect of middle England's commonsense tartness back to the nation. The usual TV 'duo' for news was an older, more authoritative man and a younger, prettier, woman. Lawley broke this mould. At the start of the *Six O'Clock News* on BBC1 in 1984, Lawley was the elder and more experienced presenter – 'the older woman and the toy boy', as one producer put it later.[49] Yet women were still treated differently from men. Bakewell was left languishing three times at the end of a contract – it was as if no one in the BBC had any idea of cherishing a female communicator whose career the Corporation had formed. It was a waste of resources and value. Robin Day, Ludovic Kennedy, David and Jonathan Dimbleby – all were constantly reused, reinvented. But women were seen as disposable.

There was another task: including women in the national conversation. *Any Questions* on Radio 4 and *Question Time* on BBC1 brought together panellists for programmes that, at their best, shone a light on British affairs in an uncomfortably direct way. The mood in the room was unpredictable, although both programmes maintained a highly disciplined courtesy, quite different from the emerging culture of phone-ins. The 'experts' had to have interesting views. Carole Stone ran *Any Questions* with an ongoing web of contacts, as if it were a dinner party, always composing the combinations that sparked. Pioneeringly, she used MacGregor as a guest chair for the programme. But the common pattern was for three men and a woman. Robin Day would query the calibre of any woman suggested for *Question Time*. One of the problems was that, while likely women speakers would turn the offer down, saying they could talk only about things they knew about, 'few men ever worried about whether their opinions were well based or not'. The production team thought that *Question Time* should be an engine of change. They were proud of finding speakers, such as Edwina Currie – before she entered Parliament. 'We thought we had won the battle,' said one producer, once a pool of women had been identified and included, but 'you just have to win it every week.'

The resistance to widening the net and including women was far worse in other parts of programming. A BBC Light Entertainment producer, asked to comment for a book on women in comedy, responded, 'That will be a very short book.'[50] When Sheila Hancock, at the height of her career, wanted to do a sketch about prejudice against women, the BBC's response was 'it will break your image'. She said, 'They thought I was good at doing funny ladies and little tizzy things.' Maureen Lipman and Eleanor Bron pointed out that in, for example, *Last of the Summer Wine*, women were 'grotesque or flirty … either harridans or sex objects', while the men were 'characters'. In *Steptoe and Son*, women had always been presented as a threat to male relationships – 'the outside elements that have to be ejected to preserve the stability of a recurring situation'.[51] On the other hand, legions of new young directors were moving through drama: Antonia Bird came straight from the Royal Court, some of the most important writers were women and they found directors and producers who fostered talent. The production team for Fay Weldon's wonderfully malignant fantasy *Life and Loves of a She-Devil* was largely female.

Women found a splendid escalator to deal with the obstacles built into the BBC system – 'attachments', temporary moves from one department to another. The Corporation at its best was a creatively unexpected place, and attachments were a cunning mechanism honed to its fluid needs. As an institution it needed those within it to assimilate its values, to feel duty towards fairness and public service in as broad a way as possible, and it needed people who could throw themselves flexibly into the minds of audiences in their different moods and needs. Attachments gave people a sense of the intellectual architecture of the Corporation, and they were funded centrally, so that receiving departments were highly motivated to take on a free pair of hands. They could be terminated at the end of the period – so the department did not have to commit itself unless the new person proved useful. Apart from the new skills, the chance to find an unexpected niche and the invaluable sense of the internal spaces and the sheer reach of the Corporation, attachments allowed women to move sideways, and remake themselves, trumping inbuilt prejudices.

Attachments were not for the faint-hearted, however. Dropped into a new department with new priorities and new ways of working, people sank or swam. They learnt new things about audiences – the Westminster-obsessed view from Current Affairs put into perspective by the view from Music and the Arts, the view from Manchester quite different from the view from Glasgow. Francesca Kirby-Green was working in the technical world of film editing in the *Panorama* cutting rooms, and got a transformative attachment to the editorial staff of *24 Hours*.[52] It made her into a pioneering woman producer, when there were only a handful of them across the Corporation. She went back to produce *Panorama*, which had been a bastion of clever machismo.

Abramsky had an attachment from Studio Production to News, where her sure instincts for managing people and steady eye for news principle launched an important career. Updale's attachment took her out of cutting rooms to research and journalism in *24 Hours*.[53] Angela Holdsworth used 'the bridges and ladders' of attachment so that by the early eighties she had become a distinguished documentary producer of programmes, including a landmark series about women, *Out of the Doll's House*. Hill joined the Corporation as a trainee engineer when she was sixteen – the only woman among 500 men. ('My friends remarked how lucky you are – but I said not if you saw the men.')[54] Attachments across departments gave her an overview of the skills she needed and a wide training: she eventually became one of the most senior engineers in the Corporation. Carragher started in 1970 as a studio manager and made her first move up through an attachment as a producer to *Newsbeat*. She moved steadily through News and Current Affairs and, having had three children, became the first woman controller of Northern Ireland. She took on an acutely exposed and politically delicate role of tremendous responsibility with steely principle.

Hodgson knew she was a competent, but not natural, Open University producer – and for a couple of years, when she was trying to have a baby, did not apply for jobs that came up. With a sense of duty and responsibility, it did not feel 'right' when she hoped to be on maternity leave. After the birth of her son, Hodgson returned to work to find herself at two in the morning driving through the snowy winter of 1981 to edit on the night shift of the OU, which had recently moved out to Milton Keynes. It was unbearable with a tiny baby. Then her boss, an executive producer at the OU, showed her the job description for the role of deputy secretary of the BBC, which he had just applied for. She saw in an instant that it was the kind of thing she could do. Six months later she got an attachment to the Secretaries Office, and then a permanent

Women and politics: the all-women production team of Question
Time, *1982 – front row: Liz Elton, the redoubtable Barbara Maxwell,
Patricia McLernon; back row: Melita Phillips, Robin Day, Ann Morley*

job as a deputy secretary under David Holmes, who said admiringly that she 'very, very, very efficiently dealt with the paper', letting him 'get out and about' in the corridors and offices of the BBC. The 'papers' included satellite negotiations and the Peacock Report. She became the first woman Secretary and one of 'the best strategic minds in the BBC'. Attachments kept the BBC blood flowing and transformed opportunities.

Mentors or sponsors mattered for careers too, and there were men who were sympathetically appreciative of the capacities of younger women. Johnny Wilkinson, BBC Secretary – a very decent, nice man, and efficient 'sorter' of things – was 'tremendous'. Martin Esslin in Drama was warm, inspiring and helped young women producers and writers. Tony Smith, the editor of *24 Hours*, 'liked working with women – he valued them'.[55] Three good ideas were mandatory at scary morning meetings, and he surrounded himself with clever young people. Abramsky owed the first jump in her career to Aubrey Singer, who was no feminist but did think that the BBC under Curran, Trethowan and Milne had 'failed to nurture middle management' and had been 'eviscerated' by ITV and then Channel 4. Singer had an eye for talent. Having been moved sideways to head Radio, he set about lifting morale to 'give them a sense that they were an important service in their own right'. He thought, 'There were a lot of able women about the place, mostly in the wrong jobs,' and that women would breathe new life into radio. He made Monica Sims the head of Radio 4, the most senior woman in the organisation; made Abramsky head of Radio News; and took Christine Hardwicke out of the ghetto of the Gramophone Library. It was not, however, all progress. Since 1948 there had been only one female Reith Lecturer. Lists of suitable women thinkers were compiled – but it took until 1994 to find another woman.[56]

Women in power, such as Sims and Abramsky, promoted other women. This group already had a greater collective sense of themselves as a generation, and began to shape work and programmes to their needs. The informal 'women's group' in Kensington House lasted as a source of encouragement and shared experience for decades. The ratio of women to men in jobs there was higher. Current Affairs had more regular hours, which women with children needed. Sally Feldman and Claire Selarie battled through to become the first official BBC 'job share' when they both had small children and became *Woman's Hour* editors. The programme was transformed when Jenni Murray, with a wonderful voice and a demanding tough-mindedness, also joined. They 'saw themselves as an empire where the rules were different but the job was to see everyday life for women clearly'.[57]

Question Time, a powerhouse of BBC politics, was put together by a largely female team. Barbara Maxwell, the legendary producer, rose from being a 'young and impatient secretary'. When Roger Bolton first met her, 'she wore a mini-skirt that was little wider than a belt, and her flame-coloured hair poured down over her extravagant bosom'. She introduced him to the wilder aspects of BBC gossip. ('Derek Amoore, the editor of *24 Hours*, shot at pictures with an air pistol in his office, was wiry, eccentric and found women hard to work with. A *Panorama* producer was having an affair with an African princess ...'[58]) Maxwell developed the *Question Time* Book, a ledger made for each programme of the composition of the audience – carefully balanced for politics, gender and ethnicity – the answer to outraged politicians who stormed out saying that the audience had been rigged against them. *Question Time* was no backwater, but, unlike daily news journalism or the *Today* programme or *Newsnight*, its intense weekly rhythms could accommodate a family life. 'A weekly crisis was just fine – a daily crisis too wearing', said Carragher. These women were at the heart of one kind of BBC significance, moulding the nation's political argument, but they were also 'creating working conditions that suited us just like men had done before'.

TOP WOMEN

In 1984, things came to a head. Stuart Young, chairman of the governors, was an old-fashioned entrepreneur who had almost never encountered working women at a high level until he came to the BBC. But he was a decent, right-thinking man. When he was about to appoint the first woman Secretary, he phoned her up and discussed how they would manage business – should he open the door for her? She said that if they met socially outside the BBC it would be lovely, but when about BBC business he should go through doors first as the chairman. He had dinner with Geoffrey Howe, the Conservative politician and his wife Elspeth, who had worked both as deputy chair of the Equal Opportunities Commission and on the Broadcasting Complaints Commission. They reinforced what people in the BBC were telling him – the Corporation was still failing to promote enough senior able women. The Board of Governors commissioned another report, 'Women in BBC management', to be written by Monica Sims, newly retired, and with a mission to improve things for the women who came after her.

'It was just such a relief to get the problem named,' said Abramsky. The Sims Report was clear, persuasive and moving, putting the case for women not just as an issue of justice, but more forcibly as an issue of the BBC's fundamental democratic role: 'An organisation which serves the whole population needs the contribution of men and women at all levels.' The case was not for 'discrimination' in favour of women, but for better management to improve the experience of both men and women. The BBC needed to be staffed by the most able at every level, and it was losing real female ability. Decision-making could not be separated from programmes.

Instead of children being a 'problem', she put them on the first page of the report. The reason that the BBC had so few women in top management positions could not have been put more starkly, or expressed more poignantly. The Corporation ought to recognise 'the distinctive talent of women and encourage them to undertake managerial responsibilities'. The main impediment was that

> many women take a carefully considered decision to leave the BBC in order to have children and look after them. It is so difficult for those who wish to come back ... many BBC mothers feel that they must keep on working even when the children are very young in order to preserve their career prospects. This puts a great strain on them and often on their husbands. The effect on children is unquantifiable.

She said she had not encountered any 'male-chauvinist' reactions to her inquiry and was careful throughout to argue that any improvements for women were likely to improve men's experience at work as well. But it was an organisation 'in which women are seen as stereotypes and often assumed to be secretaries, wives or mistresses'.[59]

The Sims Report was a milestone but it was not a magic wand. It needed men on the Board of Management to take it more seriously, but they were preoccupied with another kind of politics. In 1987, Clare Brigstocke made a programme dealing with women's experience in the BBC. In it, Michael Grade apologised for what he said was a failure to promote women, and recognised that a BBC principle was at stake. At Programme Review Board the programme was attacked, by a woman, saying that Grade had made a dreadful error by apologising when the Corporation was under intense political attack. Brigstocke was 'hopping-mad'.

Yet by the early eighties, for the first time, the number of women on BBC training courses began to equal that of men, maternity leave was normal, family life had begun a long evolution. Sims's argument that caring for ability *and* equality was a matter of BBC principle was vital. It was a view of the Corporation's role that went to the very heart of its purpose. Ensuring that there were women at all levels of the Corporation, and making sure that the men and women who served the public shared the lives of the society they reflected, adding to it value and insight, 'was not just a matter of legal equality but a belief that women can bring different qualities of style, thought and feeling to the benefit of the Corporation as a whole and to the image it presents to the public'. The Corporation had to extend these lessons to other areas of discrimination and yet balance the relationship between equality and ability, between representativeness and the creatively unexpected. The BBC had always existed to improve. It needed the most able people to do it. The new generation, that 'monstrous regiment', was inspired, with a good deal of wry amusement, by a sense that the Corporation could be remade, and that in doing so they would have fun and serve the nation better.

10

LIGHT ENTERTAINMENT: PUBLIC SERVICE POPULAR

COULD THE BBC COMMIT to the vulgar vitality that the times called for? The television-addicted British public broke the law if they did not pay their licence fee, so the BBC had to give all of them something they relished. Particularly in the seventies and eighties, the BBC had to justify millions of pounds of public intervention in a media industry that, unlike the rest of the harsh economic landscape, was dynamic and growing.

The most compelling intellectual and political case that emerged in the eighties against the BBC was that public service broadcasting ought only to make the 'quality' programmes that the market did not support, those that commercial broadcasting organisations had to be dragooned by regulation into giving the public. Leon Brittan, when he was home secretary, wondered whether the BBC ought to make broadcasting across the whole range, 'including perhaps not very elevated programmes?'[1] Limiting the BBC to the lofty, and reducing its capacity to entertain everyone, would have left the ITV companies cheerily to do what they did best, providing great swathes of fun to the largest possible audiences. It would have been the end of the BBC, as the universality of the licence fee would have become hard to defend. Equally destructively, it would have ripped out the duty to relate to the whole British public in all of their moods. It would have shattered the Corporation's accountability – never only a matter of constitutional arrangements, always more vigorously alive in its relationship to audiences. That is why the industrial and political opponents of the BBC pursued this line – usually in a spirit of high-minded regret for the Corporation's failure to be 'more ambitious and inspiring',[2] as the *Mail* put it.

Being 'popular' mattered viscerally to the Corporation. The BBC's whole moral purpose depended on how it connected with the British public through a period of personal and national anxiety. As deindustrialisation made traditions of employment and ways of life extinct, the uncertainty of the seventies was succeeded by a more punishing mood in the eighties. The BBC had to find the right place in people's lives. It needed to put the public 'on its side', said Bill Cotton, the head of Light Entertainment, a remarkable maestro of the

Bill Cotton Jr, head of Light Entertainment: 'a joyous man', said Michael Grade

popular. He meant programmes like the Christmas Day schedules, pure enter-tainment and sporting events that steadily captured and kept audiences of 10, 12, 25 million British people. 'Occasionally you have to bomb them', and make the largest impression on the largest audiences, said Bryan Cowgill, when he was in charge of BBC1. Gross popularity was one of the BBC's purposes.

COMEDY

Frank Muir said that a comedy show was like an aspirin, 'you take it for half an hour and it obscures your symptoms of worry, depression and stress'.[3] Producing sublime television comedy, of the calibre of Eric Morecambe and Ernie Wise, was a demanding art. Clive James described the duo as 'somewhere in the middle of a class system, but the classes are not social they are showbiz'.[4] Their mastery of footwork, timing and language was peerless. Their mild innocence and silly brilliance expressed a benign 'Britishness', encapsulated in the sketch about the extremely light 'Accrington *rosé*', where 'the Brothers Beamish kept budgerigars ... the budgies tread the grapes. It takes four budgies six hours to tread one grape ... you can taste the millet. Half a bottle of that and you'll fall asleep with your head under one arm.'[5]

Much comedy – *Fawlty Towers, Not So Much a Programme More a Way of Life, Yes Minister, Blackadder, Not the Nine O'Clock News, Dad's Army* – was self-evidently of public service value. But comedy was the easy part of delivering public service and popular programmes. Not at all easy to make, but easy to defend. Comedy works when it identifies something that audiences recognise as true, so its relationship to the way people live is acute. Great comedy was always recognised as 'quality' broadcasting. As such it was legitimate BBC territory. But the very popular and less witty broadcasting that the BBC also needed was more awkward. Ideally, BBC1 had to find programmes that were classy but not prissy, fun but not brash, red-blooded but not loutish, playing with the borderline of vulgarity but not in bad taste, and all the time in some discernible way true to other BBC values. The trouble for the BBC in the seventies was learning how to be more competitive at entertainment. In the seventies, the BBC was taking fun seriously but had got too close to aping ITV. By the early eighties, the BBC was perilously close to losing to the opposition. In 1982, ITV had ten programmes with regular audiences of over 14 million. BBC1 had only one (*Last of the Summer Wine*),[6] and although BBC1 and BBC2's combined audiences just beat that of ITV, by 1983 it was on the verge of being overtaken by the commercial companies. It made the Corporation more vulnerable to the attacks that were swirling in the political firmament.

'Popular entertainment' was where the Corporation met ITV head-on in ferocious competition. To win, the BBC needed brio, identity and leadership. It was finally saved by getting the right bosses in place, sorting out the programmes and the schedules, and 'cheering the programme people up, telling them when things were good, making it work'.[7] It was saved by Bill Cotton, as head of Light Entertainment: his decency, values, common sense, sheer exuberant individuality and delight in life. But it was also Michael Grade (who said that Cotton was his 'father and mentor', guarding his back from the BBC at the centre, 'the W1 Branch matey'),[8] who changed the 'popular' weather. Both Grade and Cotton understood that creative programme ideas came up from the very bottom of the organisation.

Grade, attracted back from America in 1984, was a buccaneering controller of BBC1. In a period of rank suspicion between the governors and BBC managers, the governors thought Grade 'could do no wrong'. He racked his brains for things to tell them, and charmed them. But the Corporation could not win an ideological battle with the press. Grade said, 'If we put out programmes popular enough to send the ratings soaring, we were accused of offering moving wall-paper, and "no more informative than the penny dreadfuls" as *The Times* put it. But if ratings fell, the same newspapers attacked us for taking licence fee money under false pretences.'[9] Grade was good for ratings, and he had another star touch, said Cotton – he got the BBC talked about.

There were other kinds of popularity that mattered. *Yes Minister*, a rapier-sharp exposé of the mores of government (and of all life in institutions), was

Yes Minister: *Paul Eddington, Nigel Hawthorne, Derek Fowlds, 1986;*
Mrs Thatcher's favourite programme, watched over tenderly by Alasdair Milne

hilariously successful. It told an unending story of wily mandarins running rings around politicians. Whitehall would empty as those who ran the nation dashed home to see each week's deliciously titillating account of the reality of low life behind the affairs of state. The BBC solicitously sent Mrs Thatcher copies. 'It was one of the only things she really watched out for,' said Bernard Ingham, who never missed an episode.[10] The BBC cared for *Yes Minister* tenderly. Anthony Jay and Jonathan Lynn, the writers, were paid 'the top rate' (of an unheard of £10,000 per episode).[11] Milne loved keeping an attentive eye on the storylines: 'always sensitive to political balance'.[12] It was so forensically well informed that it was a kind of news.

But as John Howard Davies, the head of Comedy, said, the repeats of *Terry and June* (a pedestrian comedy about marriage) got bigger audiences. If success meant audience size, then *Yes Minister* failed, 'but if you qualify it as a programme the governors loved, and the great and the good thought was great, then it was a huge success'.[13] Prizes mattered, as an outward and visible acknowledgement of 'quality'. National BAFTAs and international Golden Roses flooded in.

A BBC head of Light Entertainment, on a trip to America, was greeted by a market-savvy network broadcaster saying, 'Gee. Does that mean you have Heavy Entertainment over there as well?'[14] It was a good question. Was there anything distinctive about the Corporation's popular offer? The Corporation had to produce material that relaxed people, distracted them, made them laugh, which affirmed and if possible informed them. 'The absurdities and frivolities of the human condition as well as its more serious aspects are worth celebrating. A good belly laugh can also be life-enhancing,' said Colin Morris, a BBC Secretary, supporting the new popularism.

'Entertainment' was code for 'mass' audiences and, while very large audiences were composites of smaller audiences, it also meant 'working-class' – at a period when this class was about to be radically re-engineered by economics and politics. 'Popular' meant Radios 1 and 2 as well (but they had particular demographics in sight: youth, and lower-middle-class respectively). It meant sport (which had men in mind) and dramas (which attracted women). And it meant things for 'families to watch together'. BBC1 'popular' meant cross-class, cross-age-group, cross-gender, composite audiences. It meant scheduled for the bits of the evening (early to late-middle), the bits of the week (Friday–Sunday, and above all Saturday night) and the bits of the year (autumn to Christmas and public holidays) when the largest audiences were available. Paul Fox, a television entrepreneur with perfect popular pitch, said that in running BBC1 a controller had to 'keep one eye on the audience figures, one eye on the quality of the programmes and … have eyes in the back of your head to avoid staleness, mediocrity – the greatest enemy – and above all, not to under-estimate the good sense of the viewing public'.[15]

The BBC was traditionally queasy about 'the popular'. As Roy Fuller, the poet and a considerable BBC governor in the seventies, put it, the BBC needed to show that 'it was bent on avoiding what Dr Leavis called the "cretinisation" of the masses by the media'.[16] ITV believed that it understood 'popular' better than the BBC, was comfortable with blatant copies of American programmes, and by 1982 spent twice as much as the BBC. ITV 'did' popular because the bigger the audiences the larger the advertising revenue.

The BBC had had to be pushed into 'pop' radio by the pirate stations and the emergence of commercial local radio in 1972. By the late seventies these new popular forms were taken seriously. But television was different. As Colin Morris said in 1986: 'There are managers who would have gone to the stake cheerfully for Real Lives but would be boiled in oil rather than have to defend Bob's Full House … better, if the cause is just, to be gaoled for breaching the Official Secrets Act than be sneered at for transmitting Blankety Blank.'[17]

PROGRAMME REVIEW BOARD: THE HEART OF THE BBC

On Wednesday mornings at Programme Review Board, heads of Light Enter-tainment 'nestled for comfort'[18] as close as they could to the chair, who was usually the managing director of Television. They knew their programmes were likely to come in for some savage criticism, despite being 'the heavy artillery in the war for ratings'.[19] Often at the generous end of BBC salaries,[20] they also knew they were easy meat within the collective BBC culture as 'the barbarians inside the gate', said Will Wyatt.

Programme Review Board was a magnificent weekly mechanism of self-reflection – a free-ranging discussion of what discriminating senior programme connoisseurs felt about the delivery, style, purpose and effect of every programme, informed by stark viewing figures. It was attended by heads of all the London production departments and resource units (outside broad-casting, film editing and publicity), by visiting regional bosses, and by invited programme makers (who prepared for it assiduously). Gains and losses in the set-piece battles for audiences were tactically and strategically assessed. Bill Cotton called it 'the heart of the BBC'.

Discussion started with the BBC share of the overall audience: in October 1977, BBC1 had 44 per cent of all viewers, ITV had 50 per cent and BBC2 had 7 per cent; the mood 'pursed lips, tight-ish'. It then proceeded on to the weekly pattern of audience attention, the ratings of individual programmes, and trends in audience figures. There was a lot of gossip, and wit was at a premium. It was a face-to-face trading floor of programme and personal repu-tations. Programmes were marked by the collective BBC intelligence: 'should prosper', 'steady', 'rock steady', 'building' and 'dying slowly', 'drawing peace-fully to its close'.[21] Jokes and cynical worldliness were much relished.[22] Once, when the meeting got heated as the Corporation and ITV were locked in battle over audiences for the new breakfast shows, Cotton brought the acrimony to a sudden halt by shouting, 'Remember the battleship Potemkin!' Puzzled executives stared. 'They put too much faith in the ratings,' said Cotton. Having restored good humour and sense, he gathered his papers and left to do something on the shop floor of programme-making – which he relished.[23]

Michael Grade's angriest moment at the BBC was when two of Milne's special advisers attended and one of them declared, 'I have been brought into the Corporation to think.' Grade exploded, 'What do you think we do all day? Stick bits of film together!' Grade said that intellectual snobbery ran through the BBC 'like a fault line'. The implication was that 'the mechanics' (the non-Oxbridge programme makers) 'fiddled about and occasionally came up with a brilliant programme by accident'.[24]

The success of Light Entertainment, perhaps even more than the other baronetcies, was a matter of personalities, because of the volatile qualities and personal connections – of writers, performers, directors, producers – that made for successful pleasure. 'The world I live in,' said Tom Sloan (an earlier head of Light Entertainment), 'is full of temperament and tantrum, it's shoddy, and can be despicably cruel and as kind as Christendom.' Managers were inevitably 'feeling vibrations in the air and making subjective judgements all the time', said John Howard Davies, head of Comedy. Previous heads of Light Entertainment had been 'kept behind a cordon sanitaire' – in case popularity 'got out of hand'.[25] They were seen as a breed apart in the Corporation's rigid class structure. In 1974, Bryan 'Ginger' Cowgill became controller of BBC1. He came from a decade in charge of Sports, where he had transformed the Corporation's reporting and changed the presentation of football in particular into a mainstream event.

Sport played a very large part in attracting very large audiences. It was live, unpredictable, unscripted and awash with emotion, 'the true theatre of television'[26] – tribal for audiences and teams, yet focused on individual skill, luck and character. In 1974, the BBC had an almost unchallenged role in televised sport. ITV had always treated it more gingerly. Although there was an argument about whether television attracted audiences away from live events or drove interest towards them, the BBC outside broadcasting units' *Grandstand* and *Match of the Day* were almost uncontested. Earlier, Cowgill had made the technological innovation, introduced the new way of reviewing a game, and coined the term 'action replays'. Audiences were initially perplexed, but action replays would go on to alter the very conduct of sport.

Between 1974 and 1987, a revolution transformed sport and television. The amount of sport shown rose from 739 hours in 1979 to 1,769 hours in 1982. More significantly, the BBC did not see itself as a commodifier of sport, and this unrealised commercial value was seized upon by others. Enhancing sporting coverage was one element of the plan of one of the greatest media entrepreneurs of the twentieth century. 'Sport', said Rupert Murdoch, was 'the battering ram of pay TV.' He invested in football and changed every aspect of the game. The BBC, which had created audiences for sports like snooker (Wenham's idea, and it fitted the shape of screens perfectly), saw its share of the nation-gripping football and cricket begin to plummet as it was priced out of a new market.

BILL COTTON

The appointment of Bill Cotton as controller of BBC1 in 1977 – the first head of Light Entertainment to become so senior in the BBC – was a sign of what a remarkable man he was, but also of how vital to the Corporation popular television had become. Cotton was a 'joyous man' with a throaty chuckle, shrewd, 'ebullient and convivial … of impeccable taste and judgement',[27] said Michael

Grade. He was an endearingly avuncular presence, though also a man of his generation, as his language revealed. A woman who was a nuisance would be 'old bugalug', a woman he respected 'madam', one he didn't like 'Old Mrs Clutter Britches'. He would innocently throw arms around women, and called Will Wyatt 'petal'. Colin Morris, a young clergyman fresh from pastoral work in Africa, had just been appointed head of Religious Broadcasting when he pitched up to meet Cotton. He was given 'the once over' by Cotton's devoted PA Queenie, and greeted by a boom: 'Hallo, my darling!' Morris was shocked, 'even though I had been in the Marines'.

Cotton went on ascending: first to deputy managing director of Television in 1981. 'There were cheers when it was announced that the Board of Governors had appointed Bill Cotton.'[28] Milne had promised him the job of managing director of Television when it came up in 1982, presiding over the entire television offer. Cotton was the right man for the task, having an exceptional talent for human juxtaposition, for nurturing creative teams,[29] and for 'picking talent when they can do it' at the right moment and 'stretching' them at the right speed. He waited, he said, until Cliff Richard 'had something in his diddy-bag he could do'. He had, he said, a very basic rule of thumb: 'if nobody else turned up could this person actually entertain anybody for half an hour?'[30]

Milne, however, was too weak to get what he needed. Snobbery played a role. Howard, the chairman of the governors, preferred the more urbane Aubrey Singer (with whom he had travelled in China), who was also made deputy director-general. A sense that Cotton had been betrayed swirled toxically in the atmosphere, further weakening Milne. Singer had many virtues. He had played a key part in inventing popular scientific television work – originating *Horizon* and *Tomorrow's World*, and backing the great scientific series by Bronowski and Attenborough. He was full of ideas, a controversialist, technologically literate (not to say geeky – his office was always crammed with the latest equipment). He had preached that the BBC was losing its social purpose, however, and that 'entertainment' had displaced education and information. Howard had preferred Singer precisely because he was not a 'popular' or 'entertainment' sort of person. He was not, however, the right man for seeing off the opposition, or describing a proper BBC populism.

It was the lowest point of Cotton's career. Wretchedly unhappy at being torn away from his beloved Television Centre, where the corridors and studios were alive with programmes being made, he might easily have left the Corporation. But when Howard was replaced by Stuart Young, 'who took selling lots of things seriously', Milne persuaded him to replace Singer (who was given a CBE to sweeten the pill). By then audiences were being eroded, and ITV looked as if it was moving into BBC 'quality' territory. But Cotton turned the BBC figures around and gave the BBC popular purpose again.

Cotton said that entertainment depended on 'the upward thrust of ideas', and always preferred the shop floor of programme creation to the sixth-floor business of management. He understood how to translate performances into the particular rules of successful television. He knew that the screen needed intimacy, relationships, not rhetoric and projection, and that writers, performers and production teams could easily be squandered, but needed to be fostered if they were to satisfy the voracious maw of broadcasting. BBC Entertainment saw itself as different from the opposition because it nurtured talent. Cotton found the right writer for *Morecambe & Wise* (Eddie Braben) and saw that the sweet irony of their own relationship made them perfect for television. He paired Ronnie Barker and Ronnie Corbett, leaving script teams space to play with ideas. He set Michael Parkinson up as a talk show host. After seeing a show in the Netherlands, he persuaded a reluctant Bruce Forsyth to be compere for a BBC version of it, called *The Generation Game.* He engineered the right vehicles for Dave Allen, Cilla Black, Val Doonican and Dick Emery. He oversaw the creation of iconic comedy from *Dad's Army* through *Blackadder* to *Not the Nine O'Clock News*.

'Entertainment' came in dynasties with ties to the world of older show-manship. It had different rules from the rest of broadcasting. Identifying and managing the elusive stuff of a charismatic performance was a matter of hunch and personal taste. Cotton comforted fragile show-business egos as he held court over long lunches at a favourite Chinese restaurant in Kensington. It was an area governed by codes of personal honour: Cotton was as 'straight as a die'. At a Christmas party, Eric Morecambe agreed a deal with Cotton and 'shook his hand on it'. When he later reneged on the agreement, Cotton was deeply shocked, 'and ashamed for him'. But he pointed out to the governors that 'We have "lost" Morecambe & Wise to ITV for a reputed £62,500 per show against the £10,000 paid to them by us.'

One answer to the question of whether the BBC produced a popular entertainment with an identity of its own lay in Bill Cotton's career. He was repeatedly offered far larger salaries with more money to spend on shows in commercial television, yet he stayed with the Corporation. His unshakeable loyalty was a personal quality – but also an expression of the distinction and discrimination he felt he could exercise within the BBC. He was, said Attenborough, 'the very personification of public service broadcasting'.

What made BBC Light Entertainment different from its commercial competition? Huw Wheldon, the great BBC intellectual of a slightly earlier generation, had argued that it was the elusive 'quality' of the programmes which mattered, that programmes 'are not good because they are popular. They are popular because they are good ... in themselves.'[31] He was arguing that external pressures to deliver audiences had to be balanced with the internal momentum to produce programmes that seemed proper, intelligent and part of the BBC's purpose.[32] But he was also putting the case against the traditional intellectual hierarchy: 'Popular programmes can undoubtedly be bad,' he said. 'So can unpopular programmes. It is also possible, and this is very important, for good programmes to be popular, and for popular programmes to be good.'[33] Wheldon was articulating a shift in values that saw 'popular culture' and even 'mass culture' as worthy of serious attention. This view had been developing since the 1950s, and was to become almost dominant by the late eighties.[34]

AMERICA

BBC Entertainment tended to define itself negatively 'against' American television, even though it bought the great hits like *Dallas*. There was an uneasy relationship between 'take-away', bought-in programmes and the more wholesome 'home-made' ones, the constant worry that the 'sugary', lowest common denominator of American entertainment would prove addictive to audiences.[35] At a Prix Italia Festival in Capri, Singer gave a tempestuous warning of the imminent 'Americanisation' of European broadcasting. An American television executive described him as a Jeremiah. Singer replied, 'You may be right, sir, but Jeremiah was generally on the ball.'[36] It was a BBC 'rule of faith' that ITV filled its schedules right up to the regulated limit with American repeats. Yet American shows provided immediate schedule fillers and it was cheaper to buy them than make your own. The 'public service' ideal was to buy 'discriminatingly'. Anna Home, who was the head of Children's programming and a formidable defender of standards, said that 'quality American programmes are just the very best of their kind: you wouldn't want audiences to miss them'.[37]

As money became tighter in 1977, the BBC commissioned an internal report on foreign programming, which waxed eloquent on what the BBC was missing out on. The report reiterated the encomium that 'it is not BBC policy to pursue mass appeal audiences by buying programmes ...',[38] but its purpose was to persuade the BBC to do just that. It cited *M.A.S.H.*, a comedy based on the Vietnam War, as an example of what the BBC was lacking. This darkly funny show was hardly typical of the material on offer, but it was an example likely to persuade the high-minded BBC bosses of the American route.[39] The other Holy Grail was selling BBC programmes into America.

David Webster (on legendary expenses, it was said, flying on Concorde and living in an 'opulent' apartment)[40] was sent to America as a permanent front for the BBC commercial buying and selling there.[41] Consequently, the BBC did buy more from America and the audiences loved much of it. Bryan Cowgill 'prided himself on American purchases like *Kojak* and *Starsky & Hutch*'. Cotton had a different view: 'Given the choice, we ought to use our

Morecambe & Wise *(here with Cliff Richard, centre), 1973: sublime silliness*

rubbish, rather than their rubbish.'[42] Selling programmes abroad was all well and good but 'our job is to produce good shows for the British public', not make them with one eye on the American market. Commercial television was different, he said: 'I don't blame other companies for producing shows for America. Part of their duty is to make money. As a public service, the BBC's duty is to make good programmes,'[43] and indeed some programmes (such as *Morecambe & Wise*) which were hugely popular in the UK and defined a shared British sensibility failed in America.[44] Cotton said, 'I am not interested in the 17 million if it means abandoning what the BBC has been providing for 60 years: quality *and* popularity.'

BLANKETY BLANK

Could the Corporation lead in entertainment or would it follow the commercial rival: 'At what distance? And with our nose in the air?'[45] Occasionally, a 'pall of embarrassment' seemed to hang over Television Centre whenever anything 'very' popular was on. In 1979, the Corporation shyly put its foot in the water of commercialised pleasures with *Blankety Blank*, a modest game show based on an American model with a quiz and celebrities.[46]

The BBC had competitive formats, but they were about prowess and the prizes were honorific not material. Later, Jon Plowman said that there were things 'that you just didn't do, giving away cars, and winning huge amounts of money ... the business of prizes and quizzes was always tricky'.[47] *Blankety*

Blank, however, was carefully pruned for BBC sensibilities and hosted with ironic panache by Terry Wogan. A BBC manager said that he expected the show to start giving copies of Reith's autobiography as prizes, there was such an air of fastidious disdain around the whole thing. *Blankety Blank* revelled in a tacky set and managed to hover on a line between a game show and a send-up of the game-show enterprise.

Not that the cerebral bit of the BBC noticed. After the first two or three weeks, Milne asked for a vote at Programme Review Board on whether or not it was a 'suitable' programme, making his own disapproval clear. Jimmy Gilbert, in classic Light Entertainment department defensive posture, asked that the programme be allowed to survive until it was clearer what audiences made of it. They loved it and turned it on in their millions. The controller of BBC1 said 'that he had taken the controller of BBC2 to his first experience of this programme – and he had survived!' Desmond Wilcox said that he hoped it had been a form of vaccination.[48] If it were possible to broadcast 'rubbish and give pleasure to millions … in an output of 530 shows from Light Entertainment in any year, there was certainly room for 16 editions of *Blankety Blank*'.[49] By 1979, armed with high audiences and high audience appreciation figures, the programme had become 'respectable'.[50] By 1980 it was declared an 'important' part of the Corporation's output.[51]

RATINGS AND ADVERTISING

In the seventies, British television was making better comedy than the American networks. The *Sunday Times* said, 'The joke is to the British what the philosophical concept, let's say, is to the French, and we thus take our comedians a lot more seriously than our philosophers.'[52] American production was locked into 22-show runs that squeezed the last drops out of successful series with little pause for refreshment.[53] The British scheduling block was 13 programmes, which allowed each series to be hand-crafted. Then, said an American producer, 'Television is berserk with the ratings, the crawling around like crazed insects scrambling to climb this tree to be number one. There is no room for creativity … the view is how do we get to be ahead of the other two networks … rather than how do we do a terrific show.'[54] Public service values could operate as a mask for inefficiency but they also provided a shop floor for creative talent.

When to 'kill' a format, or how to revitalise one that was still delivering but in decline, was a perennial problem. But the BBC saw itself as developing rather than 'exploiting' content. Many of the iconic shows had tiny runs.[55] To 20-year-old Californian students in 1979, the 'initials BBC spelt *Monty Python*',[56] despite the fear of television buyers that the show would be incomprehensible to American audiences.[57] Yet there were only 45 episodes of it. In 1988, the new president of CBS in America wrote to Paul Fox, by then managing director of Television, anxious 'to foster a productive comedy relationship' between the Corporation and CBS, because the BBC was the source of comedy that was sweeping America.[58]

In light entertainment, the BBC had one vital advantage over ITV and American productions: no advertising breaks meant that the rhythm of comedy and drama programmes was far better. Commercial television had shorter (22.5 minutes) slots compared with the BBC's (29.5 minutes).[59] While BBC programmes could have a beginning, a middle and an end, ITV had to have 'a beginning, a middle and a *crescendo*, have the break and then do a beginning, a middle, and end again'.[60] Commercial television programmes had to have 'hooks' to bring audiences back – this broke the story in drama, and wrecked the momentum in comedy.

THE VALUE OF FAILURE

Staying with programmes or performers could be very effective; a less aggressive relationship to ratings paid off; and investing in talent rather than buying it in was a key public service strategy. A sitcom could expect audiences of nearly 18 million. Yet the first series of *Last of the Summer Wine* and *The Good Life* started with low audiences of 5 million. Usually, the second series would start on the large inherited audience and build on that again, but the audiences for both of these programmes plummeted back down to the beginning again. In ITV, this 'would be ringing warning bells',[61] and the shows would have been dropped. *Last of the Summer Wine* went on to run for 35 years. *The Good Life* is seen as emblematically important with brilliant performances and is still on BBC screens today.

Fawlty Towers looked like a problem from the start. The first script report for John Cleese and Connie Booth's situation comedy in 1974 was not promising:[62] 'I'm afraid I thought this one as dire as its title.'[63] The reaction of audiences was puzzled and the press reviews bad: 'Long John Thin on Jokes'.[64] Fawlty's cringe-making contempt for anyone with less power than him, and grovelling sycophancy towards those apparently more important – against a background of petty incompetence – was brilliantly original and yet recognisable. It was a savage indictment of Britain and its pretensions. The 'habitually rude' Basil substitutes lower-middle-class condescension for the working-class racism in *Till Death Us Do Part*.[65] But it was not until it was repeated that audiences got the hang of it, and it became a legend. There were only ever twelve episodes yet it was a milestone in television. Plowman said the BBC thought 'writers of comedy, they're special, they know how to make people laugh, *don't let them go for a second*, if it doesn't work now it'll work later'.[66]

Fawlty Towers, 1975: *class was the enduring topic of British comedy*

NEW COMEDY

Light Entertainment was certainly late to feminism. Neither the department nor Weekly Programme Review showed any signs of being inhibited by political correctness. Light Entertainment was resistant to women producers, directors and writers. It was a sign of a dangerous 'old-fashionedness' that some found frustrating. Programme Review Board blithely commented that Marti Caine's 'rather metallic costume' had been peculiar and 'had given her an emaciated look which had led to rib-counting'.[67] It had a loud disagreement about whether Shirley Bassey had got fatter or thinner (and what difference it made),[68] and cheerily minuted that 'Tracey Ullman was a star, the many parts of whom were well worth hanging on to'.[69]

Radio was often still the place where new comedy writing bubbled up. One strand was black humour made very close to human misery, often by performers with an intense relationship to their parts. As Peter Black wrote, much British comedy 'lay not in neat resolutions, as in American comedies, but in eternally, comically unresolved conflicts'.[70] British comedy was often about class, which continued to produce a magnificent selection of taboos and demarcation lines that audiences greeted with enthusiasm. *Fawlty Towers*, *The Two Ronnies*, *Porridge*, *The Young Ones* – all these most successful comedy formats reflected on the British class system's baroque variety as an eternal *vérité*.

TASTE AND DECENCY

News and Current Affairs were in the front line of battles over BBC political bias; Drama over violence and political values; and Entertainment and Comedy over taste and decency. This last was a more mobile frontier because public mores – which were also the topic of comedy – changed with bewildering speed. There was also British hypocrisy – what people enjoyed was not what they admitted to liking. The tabloid press simultaneously fed off the BBC's popular programmes and thrived on denouncing the BBC's undermining of the nation's morals. Indeed, the Corporation did have a duty towards public and collective life. Frankie Howerd, in an interview with Gloria Hunniford, said, 'to be vulgar is not the same as being filthy, tasteless or offensive ... Comedy is like walking through a minefield.'[71] The Corporation believed that it distinguished itself from ITV by being less 'smutty', with ITV's *Benny Hill Show* as the benchmark of what to avoid. Innuendo and scantily dressed women had to be handled carefully (because the public both loved and might be offended by them).

Production teams saw 'complaints' as a hostile force to be dodged if possible, because they led to 'management' interfering in good programmes. BBC producers' guidelines laid down rules and provided an outward and visible index of changing British mores. Thus the Corporation's 1950s regulations prohibiting the representation of homosexuality were themselves deeply offensive by the seventies. The danger was as much that the Corporation would become 'stuffy' and out of touch as that it would broadcast something shocking. Indeed, since the sixties 'shocking' had become a word of praise rather than blame. 'Offensiveness' was about where and when the item was placed in the schedules as much as any intrinsic quality. Frequently, a live audience reacted differently to a later broadcast one – a risqué comment on *Quote, Unquote* got uproarious laughs during recording and a wave of complaints when it was broadcast.[72] The departmental attitude was often 'phew we got away with it once, but it won't pass the repeat test'. This particularly affected shows that depended on topical allusions, which were often honed and adapted up until five minutes before transmission, making 'upward referral' or any other bureaucratic process impossible. Taste could not be pinned down completely. Its exercise was not a formal procedure but a careful, perhaps inevitably fallible, exercise in balancing judgements. A Cotton or a Grade usually walked the line between decent and offensive nimbly.

Not the Nine O'Clock News opened one show with a sketch based on the recent Channel 4 programme *The Death of a Princess*, which had become a cause célèbre. The documentary had shown the public beheading of a young Saudi princess accused of adultery, and the Saudi government had objected vociferously. The hapless junior Foreign Office minister, Douglas Hurd, was sent to Saudi Arabia to apologise in person. Saudi Arabia was not only the main source of oil but also the most important Western ally in the region. The British public were, on the whole, scandalised by the apology – though keen on the petrol.

The sketch opened with an earnest young man looking into the camera and saying, 'I'd just like to say a word to you Saudis, we're most dreadfully sorry about all that fuss about it. If you want to cut the head off your Princesses, go ahead, it's not a problem, we'll let you have one of ours, no, no, come to think about it we'll let you have two of ours.' Cotton, head of Light Entertainment, phoned Brian Wenham: 'Did you see what went out on your network?' Cotton thought that the Saudis had not objected because 'somebody said to them "look, you can complain about a drama, a documentary, but if you start complaining about comedy, you know, you'll get nowhere! You're best not to have seen it!"'[73]

Then, at the end of the year, extracts were being compiled for a Christmas show. Cotton saw that a clip from *Not the Nine O'Clock News* was to be included. On his way home, he suddenly realised that no one had told him which sketch they were going to use, and that 'I know what the fuckers are going to do, they'll put that Saudi bit in'. So he stopped the car, found a telephone box, discovered he was right and got it cut out. It was a very funny piece, but repeating it so long after the event would 'rub it in, it's a long time since then, now it becomes an insulting thing'. On the whole (as against the Whitehouse attack), the Corporation produced a range of brilliantly managed programmes that permitted the creative, scourging effect of humour to work properly.

While rows about the BBC being 'ahead' of popular taste might be worrying, they were not embarrassing. When the Corporation was 'behind' taste it was different. Somewhere in the sixties, Reithian conservatism had mutated into something more like Reithian liberalism. The BBC 'establishment' thought of itself as culturally 'liberal' and abhorred racism – though not enough to appoint any black general trainees until Wesley Kerr in 1979, and then he found it stifling. BBC Children's programming was far more sensitively in touch with changing social reality: *Play School* and *Blue Peter* had black presenters and in Floella Benjamin the BBC found an iconic talent. Yet by the seventies, what was identified as 'racist' was a febrile category. The Corporation went on broadcasting *The Black and White Minstrel Show*, and its 'blacked-up' white performers, in an important family slot, long after many people thought it ought to have been put down. It had a classic variety format, with singing, dancing and comedy, and had been 'one of the pillars of Saturday night' since the sixties.[74] The trouble was that it had a big audience and sold abroad. It was a vital ingredient of a 'big export business for the BBC in Swaziland',[75] said one defender.

There was a kind of decision to wean the public off it by making it less good. 'Asked if there had been fewer minstrels in the cast than usual', Bill Cotton said there were fewer 'for reasons of cost'.[76] More positively (and always arguing that 'blacking up' was just a convention and not offensive in itself), it launched the careers of black performers such as Lenny Henry. When Jimmy Gilbert took over as head of the Light Entertainment Group, he asked, 'Could the show stand major exposure?'[77] It had begun to seem like a pariah.[78]

ITV appeared to be more in touch with the way in which attitudes around race were moving. *Love Thy Neighbour* was a successful ITV sitcom, in which the BBC officials noted 'viewers were encouraged to laugh *with* coloured people, not *at* them'.[79] *Rising Damp* contained 'a character played by a black actor who had been so evidently part of the team, and intellectually a leading member of it, that jokes about race had caused no offence'.[80] By the time the Minstrels were finally axed, the programme had become such an embarrassment that nobody officially notified the cast.[81] It was written out of BBC history. In 1986, when the 50th anniversary of television was celebrated, *The Black and White Minstrel Show* was not even mentioned.

By 1982, BBC1 and BBC 'popular' was in a tailspin that Singer could not reverse. When Cotton took over he 'personally' booked Terry Wogan to host *Wogan*, a new chat show early in the evening, three nights a week. Ironically, it was precisely the kinds of show that the BBC had been anxious about – chat shows, soap operas – which altered the game.[82] Pushed by competition with the new, edgy Channel 4, James Moir, head of Variety from 1982 to 1987, began hunting for classy young talent. A new wave of 'alternative comedians' was emerging, and female performers and writers like Dawn French and Jennifer Saunders were recruited. Alexei Sayle was given his first television opportunity by Sidney Lotterby and Moir.[83] A distinct entertainment philosophy was developed for BBC2: less familial, with contemporary taboos in its sights.

THAT'S LIFE

That's Life was started in 1973. It was a hybrid show with a star, Esther Rantzen, and it lasted for 30 years. The idea was to combine 'good-hearted' entertainment with campaigning consumer journalism, in a 'light and shade' magazine rhythm of jokes and serious reports. It took consumerism out from the discriminating middle classes into a mass audience. Public service values lay in the spirited public interaction with the programme and its campaigns.[84] Letters flooded in, containing individual 'funny or serious' accounts (marked

'Good story – if true' or 'fun and true-ish' in the office) and filled with unexpected themes. At the time, there were other consumer programmes, such as *You and Yours* and *Money Box* on Radio 4, but the tone of *That's Life* was more indignant, though 'never cross or scolding'.[85] The broad humour and tone created a sense of a shared (and indeed commonsense) view of the wrongs that needed righting.

Determined to 'beat ITV', Cowgill rescheduled *That's Life* from a 'classy' slot late on a Saturday night to the great popular slot immediately after the nine o'clock watershed on Sunday evening. The audiences leapt and it became a family show, regularly reaching audiences of 9–14 million. It once had 22 million viewers, following a programme in which ten dogs roamed free over the set – combining the staples of sex, animals and live spectacle. One small bitch had 'unexpectedly' come on heat and in the ensuing mayhem, as the beasts chased her over the studio, an Airedale cocked his leg over a plant: 'there was pee everywhere'.[86] Rantzen argued that the audience trusted and identified the programme closely with the 'presenter', so she needed the authority of being the producer too. Milne, whose 'sharp manners disguise a kind heart',[87] agreed. It was an original formula that for years was one of the most popular shows on British television.

That's Life had a cavalier relationship to budgets: 'In view of the prodigious overspend resulting from the zoo film,' went one memo, 'wonderful though it was, the Still Birth project must be held over to next Spring.'[88] In 1984, the programme's editor said that in order to keep the 'like-all-other-programmes-we've-got-to-save-some-money' lecture to a minimum, it had to spend more thoughtfully and deal delicately with the unions so that time off was taken rather than overtime payment. Finally, he added: 'We are making a reduction in the number of bottles of wine available on Sunday evenings.'[89]

Rantzen was the 'star', a pioneering female broadcaster who developed a completely new style of television campaigning. After she became producer, 'she began to run a little wild – because there was no natural way of controlling her left'.[90] She had had a long affair with the head of the General Features department, Desmond Wilcox, complicated by the fact that his popular wife also worked in the same BBC building, Kensington House. He was 'noisy, talented, and high profile', and had continued (unusually) to appear on screen as well as manage production. When they married in 1980, there was tabloid frenzy – and a rebellion. Eventually, all ten of the senior producers complained that it was impossible to launch anything new in the department when competing with their flamboyant boss and his wife.[91] There was a BBC rule that spouses should not work together. So Rantzen and the production team were moved out of Kensington House and down to the winding corridors of the Lime Grove swamps.[92] Esther had to carry the programme alone.

Rantzen was feisty, funny, popular (especially with women), and a

Esther Rantzen and the That's Life *team*

forerunner of the contemporary celebrity. She used her private life and interests to fuel the programme productively, but always in a public service mould. Personally descended from a long line of socially and politically engaged women, she moved TV into domestic philanthropy and activism. The production team was largely female. It became 'like a family', with children running around 'in a kind of hippy way', and husbands drinking together. *That's Life* was popular not least because of the tone: loud, brash, brimming with lightly worn righteous indignation. With its strangely shaped vegetables and animal jokes it was peculiarly British, out of the same tradition identified by George Orwell's essay on the comic postcard.

But its real achievement was to be alerted to genuine public anxieties by relating intimately to its audiences. In 1981, one in 70 of all the women in Britain expecting a baby responded to a *That's Life* request for their experiences of pregnancy and childbirth. The astute Rantzen, who was in the middle of her own childbearing years, sent a questionnaire (sponsored by the Spastics Society, and put in envelopes by Girl Guide volunteers) to every woman who had written in, and produced the largest-ever survey of newly pregnant mothers. It was a magnificent piece of television activism. The survey helped sensitise hospital staff to mothers' needs, got ministers to take the experience of maternity services seriously, and changed army practice – introducing a commitment to get soldiers back home for the birth of their children.[93]

The success of the programme was measured in captured scalps. In 1985, the editor said that they had alerted the nation to the dangers of cosmetic surgery; 'changed the nation's equestrian habits' by highlighting dangerous riding hats; made children's bedclothes safer from fire risks; persuaded Parliament to introduce a cooling-off period for hire purchase agreements; and exposed puppy farms and the iniquities of veal crating. They questioned the Conservative MP Neil Hamilton's use of parliamentary time to try to get chewable tobacco licensed in Britain. They returned again and again to mental health issues and the problems of the new proposals for 'care in the community' that were emptying mental hospitals with little consideration of the long-term needs of a vulnerable group. Rantzen said that the programme had three typical targets: con men who exploited 'ordinary little old people', incompetence in government departments and private firms, and the absurdities that arise because of the rigid application of rules and regulations – a target that she thought went 'deep to the heart of the British psyche'.

It was evidently providing a 'public service', audiences loved it, and it was one of the first British formats to be sold abroad. Many commercial TV entrepreneurs like Peter Bazalgette and Simon Cowell started their careers on it. The show was politically adroit, on the one hand exposing healthcare failure and malpractice, on the other running campaigns that depended on a cooperative relationship with the Health Service, to establish the liver donors' register, for example. The programme's ethic of personal responsibility helped it avoid political rows. It talked a lot to ministers, but largely as people who needed to know about problems rather than as people who had failed to solve them. It was small 'p' political and probably rather conservative. Rantzen said that the idea was to ask 'Wouldn't it be more sensible if?'[94] rather than make any kind of direct complaint.

In 1986, *That's Life* ran a professionally researched survey asking for viewers' experiences of childhood. The team expected to elicit complaints about physical abuse, but was overwhelmed and unprepared for 50,000 callers on the night, adults and children, desperate to confide stories of sexual abuse. It was harrowing, unexpected and shaming – but Rantzen swung into action. She and her team did not ignore the dark evidence – they did something about it and made it public. The response was a charity that provided an expert telephone service for children in difficulties to call for help. The Corporation (led by the dedicated John Cain) had pioneered 'help lines' which provided advice and information at the end of programmes, so there were practical precedents. ChildLine was an elegant idea that sprang from a public service purpose and Rantzen's irrepressible eye for a campaign. It was copied all over the world. Mrs Thatcher spoke warmly in its support at a reception at No. 10, but omitted to mention that it had been started by the BBC.

In 1969, the sexual abuse of children had been removed from the Department of Health register of offences. It was seen as a consequence of 'unhealthy' repression: modernity and sexual freedom, it was assumed, were withering the problem away. In 1972, the word 'paedophilia' was not included in the *Oxford English Dictionary*. But a new perception of children as sentient witnesses with rights of their own, combined with feminism and its analysis of male power, and empirical sociological and medical research, was about to overturn what experts saw when they looked at children. 'It was as if a shutter had shot up,' said one social worker and child analyst; 'we suddenly saw things with new eyes.' [95] It took a conceptual revolution to help concerned, humane, dedicated professionals understand what they were observing.

In 1972, first in America and then in Britain, the 'battered baby syndrome' was identified.[96] This toppled previous perceptions of accidental injuries to children and revealed that within some families extreme physical cruelty to some children was deliberate and habitual. *Nationwide* considered the problem and *Woman's Hour* discussed the government report on it. Then, in 1974, Arnon Bentovim and his research group at Great Ormond Street Hospital for Children went further and identified systematic sexual abuse.[97] Recognising that families could be such dangerous places for children required a disorienting change of perspective and broke such profound taboos that it took doctors and social workers years to adjust. 'Incest' had come to be seen as a rare problem, but this was something apparently widespread. Nor was every identification secure, and it took several court cases and an overhauled assessment system to begin to settle reliable diagnoses.

Rantzen's survey in 1986 and the foundation of ChildLine in 1987 produced another shift in perceptions – taking recognition beyond professionals (after a period of intense expert and legal argument) to a wider public apprehension of the dark reality of some children's lives. The crisis provided a glimpse of previously unimagined social disorder, in which children sometimes in outwardly respectable families were raped and abused. Not by strangers, but by fathers, stepfathers, grandfathers, uncles and family friends. It showed that many 'normal' heterosexual men sexually used dependent children. It was hard to understand, and social work journals reverberated with disagreements. Some of the pressure from the media and social workers produced panicked responses. In Cleveland, 137 families were identified as abusive; many of them were innocent. The cases led to the Butler-Sloss report on child abuse, and ultimately to the Children's Act of 1989, which for the first time put the interests of children rather than of families at the centre of proceedings. Later, several prosecutions for 'satanic' abuse rings (peculiarly attractive for the media) were shown to be wrong. Rantzen had helped stimulate this wider, public understanding. But it was to take another shift in perceptions for abuse within institutions to be recognised.

JIMMY SAVILE

The BBC was harbouring its own horror. Most Corporation crises took the form of a clash between it and governments. This was far more uncomfortable – a betrayal of audiences, who had enjoyed a performer whose appearance on the BBC seemed to guarantee a propriety beneath the lurid exterior. Jimmy Savile exploited the music-hall aspect of entertainment in Britain, the culture of cheeky innuendo. But in his case, he did exactly what he said.

The BBC failed to understand the motivations and vulnerabilities of young women who flooded into programmes like *Top of the Pops*. Sexual mores were in a muddle, and the BBC was not alone in its confusion. Too often, the BBC saw these girls as 'fans' exercising new sexual freedoms (which some of them were), rather than vulnerable. When the mother of a 16-year-old girl, Claire McAlpine, who had killed herself and left a diary that detailed abuse, complained to the BBC about *Top of the Pops,* her complaint was not treated properly – and when she was referred to the police, they did not pursue the case either. An inquest cleared the BBC of blame: it found that McAlpine lived in a world of fantasy and took her life while the balance of her mind was disturbed. She was a troubled young woman, with a difficult personal history, who had fantasies of celebrity and fame. An eminent lawyer, Brian Neill, had already been commissioned to investigate allegations that records were plugged on programmes including *Top of the Pops* in exchange for sexual and financial favours. Bill Cotton knew about the report, and the accusations about payola, and it led to the introduction of a minimum age for audience dancers (which girls tried to get around), and later a system of chaperones and parental permissions for the programme. Because of ongoing criminal investigations, the report was not made public at the time. Savile was only one of several DJs investigated.

Savile shamelessly abused victims in hospitals and secure institutions as well as the BBC. As the playwright David Hare wrote, 'in a life roiling with sinister self-knowledge, nothing is more chilling than his declaration: "There is no end of uses to a motor caravan." ' Savile himself claimed that he had 'more front than Blackpool'. Yet although the *Sun*, the *Mail* and *Private Eye* ran stories on him, Hare argues that 'The popular press, always loudly boastful of its fearlessness, was effectively scared off.'[98]

Savile's power to abuse derived from his popularity, constructed by the BBC and enhanced by his proximity to the energy of popular music and wider publicity. It was given legitimacy in the first instance by his charitable and NHS work. It was secured by the way in which politicians, monarchy and church all made use of his popularity, and gave him the image of a *protector* of the nation by using him as a on the 'Clunk-Click' seatbelt campaign, as a patriotic evangelist on the 'I'm Backing Britain' movement, as an adviser on prisons, in

Broadmoor, and horrifyingly on adolescent sexual mores. As a Metropolitan Police inspector said: 'Savile groomed the nation.'

He first reached the BBC's attention (and employment) as a DJ. Canvassing for more work, he sent the BBC a press cutting of his appearance on *Juke Box Jury*, which, he said, had brought 'life, zip and zest' to the programme. Soon he was appearing on a range of Manchester programmes. He became a regular DJ for *Top of the Pops* and had a string of programmes on Radio 1, such as *Savile's Travels*.

These shows were light entertainment based, but he was used more widely. The public service veneer of serious social concern that the Corporation elicited and provided made him even more authoritative. He was painted on to programmes about children and young people as if he were an expert, despite having no family and no training. He was used on *The Teen Scene*, a 'discussion programme about young people', dealing with teenage 'problems', growing up and morality; and a series called *Other People's Children*,[99] which discussed 'parenting – in a magazine format', was based around him. *Look North* built a programme around him on 'outside activities for teenagers who are unmanageable at home'.[100] Meanwhile, vicars queued up to have him on *Songs of Praise* and *Speaking Personally*, a 'personal approach to ethics', and on *Speakeasy*, a 'popular approach to contemporary problems'. BBC1 used him for *In My Opinion*, a children's version of *Question Time*. He was especially useful around Christmas – *Nationwide* used him as Father Christmas in 1979. There were 'Savile's Santa specials'. New Year's Eve programmes were broadcast from Stoke Mandeville Hospital and Leeds General Infirmary (ironically, in the late seventies, a centre for pioneering work on child sexual abuse).

Two BBC programmes[101] – *The World of Jimmy Savile OBE* on BBC1 in 1972, and *In the Psychiatrist's Chair* with Anthony Clare on Radio 4 in 1991 – were retrospectively perturbing. Both were intelligent programmes that asked Savile probing questions about his lack of a private life and the demons that drove him, but presented him as peculiar and perhaps sad – not a predatory paedophile. In not looking over the precipice, however inadvertently, they reassured the public that he was no kind of threat.

The problem of understanding Savile was one of perceptions. Savile delivered audiences. The times were more innocent. The mores of young women were rapidly altering, but there was a confused response to this. Intelligent, careful, responsible people working alongside him did not notice anything wrong with how he behaved because they had no conception of his secret world. Savile, said Helen Pennant-Rea, an idealistic producer and a warm, sensible woman who worked closely with him on *Speakeasy*, appeared to be acting very professionally, albeit in his own eccentric way. At the time, she believed 'that he was driven to redress the balance' by 'helping young, not very articulate people to put their views to important, powerful people'.[102] It was a valuable skill, one she believed to be part of a BBC mission, and it never occurred to her at the time, because the idea was not part of the repertoire of thinking, that he might exploit the young women who were thought of as 'fans'. It was only with the benefit of hindsight that she saw his 'apparently affable and tactile behaviour' utterly differently.

The novelist Andrew O'Hagan later pointed out that Jimmy Savile 'never liked children, never had any, never wanted any, and on the whole couldn't bear them, except on occasion to fuck ... He managed all this quite brilliantly, hiding in plain sight as a youth presenter full of good sport.'[103] He was one of those names which the Corporation made. It was the programme format of *Jim'll Fix It* that entranced a generation. Why was it given to him? The BBC mistook the 'star' performance that endowed the value (and attracted the audiences) for the successful programme formats that it had created.

Emerging in the seventies, 'celebrity' culture became a media staple. The new form of fame required a commoditisable 'private' life. The story that Savile wove, and that the Corporation was – along with charities, the NHS and Mrs Thatcher, all unwittingly – the agent of projecting, was that his 'private' life was one of endless, selfless money-raising for charity. He fitted a BBC need very well: 'wacky' but doing good. His popularity was real, and a protection. Chillingly, children's programmes and *Look North* in 1969 discussed and visited his travelling 'bus'.

What did the BBC know or understand about Savile? Light Entertainment was a department which wrote very little down: most thinking was done face to face. There is no trace in files of the period of any anxiety about (or referral up or sideways or discussion of) any of Savile's behaviour. An early commercial scandal over an endorsement of Green Shield stamps (in which he flashed not only his BBC programmes but also his recently awarded CBE, so it seems likely that the Palace would have rapped his knuckles) is represented by a cutting in the files, but if there was any rebuke it has left no trace. Bill Cotton, Jimmy Moir and Bryan Cowgill were close to the world of entertainers, but were as blinded by Savile's persona as the public was. Those working every day beside him in hospitals, in the police, in politics and in the BBC failed to understand what they were seeing. Savile was uncouth in public, uncouth on the sanctified territory of hospital wards and in places of refuge and safety; he looked uncouth and said uncouth things. This all operated as a kind of cloak, and the risks he took were his thrill. He left a stain on everything he touched.

Many popular performers in entertainment in the seventies were odd: their performances came from extreme personalities. Indeed, the audience's enjoyment of Frankie Howerd, Kenneth Williams, Kenny Everett, even Hancock – all gifted comedians – was nevertheless less puritanical than in many other areas – entertainers were permitted licence. Savile had none of these gifts but he did have fame.

Rantzen had exposed child abuse and, in ChildLine, done something about it. The power she used was generated by the rapt attention of good-hearted audiences enjoying BBC entertainment. But it was a power Savile used as well. It was based on the trust of audiences, given because they enjoyed him, given because the BBC and his other institutional work appeared to guarantee virtue, which gave Savile the power to intimidate and abuse the vulnerable.

A series of inquiries – into the BBC (led by Dame Janet Smith), into the NHS and into the police – found uncomfortable stories of abuse within institutions in the past. Just as children had been abused by people known to them within family circles, an infernal machine of exploitation had established itself in public places as well. Young women had complained and had not been heard, with their charges not properly acted upon, investigated or backed up with proof. The problem posed for the BBC by these findings was not principally one of recognising how it had failed to understand or act in the past, nor even of securing children's safety in the present. In many ways those were painful yet relatively straightforward tasks. The BBC's real challenge is to uncover the corruptions of power and the exploitation of the weak that are still being overlooked, dismissed or ignored now.

DRAMA: THE
DOMESTIC HOMER

IN 1985 AND 1987, the BBC televised two serials, *Edge of Darkness* by Troy Kennedy Martin, a tender and alarming thriller; and *The Singing Detective* by Dennis Potter, autobiographical, influenced by 1940s movies and musicals, yet singular. These were innovative masterpieces of television – unexpected, beautiful, passionate, telling terrible and awesome human tales – and huge audiences were utterly gripped by them. Because they confidently crashed conventions of naturalistic television, and clichéd morality, they had critics, and caused rows. But this was public service originality at its highest – adventurous and rewarding for audiences. How could an organisation that made such iconic and enduring new culture – popular, radical, intelligent and affecting – be under any kind of threat? Why weren't politicians crowing at a national triumph?

BBC drama was the public's domestic Homer: a place where people gathered together enthralled by stories and the comforting repetition of narratives. Despite Britain's theatrical energy and the slicker international world of movies, television's storytelling place in everyday life wove it into the nation's sensibilities in a novel way. 'The beloved box', said Dennis Potter, 'is tabloid newspaper, picture book, sports stadium, concert hall theatre and cinema, peculiarly crabbed ... but overwhelmingly in the present tense'.[1] He said he was more concerned with 'interior drama' than external realities, because although television viewing was full of distractions (tea and talk), nevertheless people watched it 'in a peculiar way, with all of their barriers down ... it sits right in the middle of all the mundaneness.'[2]

It was this demotic space which made such innovators of television dramatists. For Potter, Ken Loach, Ken Trodd, Tony Garnett, Michael Wearing, Troy Kennedy Martin, David Mercer, Alan Bleasdale, Simon Gray, Caryl Churchill and Fay Weldon, 'the hospitable small screen offered democratic opportunities of reaching more people with finer material, better images than anywhere, at any time before'.[3] Some were influenced by the theatrical radicals, Joan Littlewood and Bertolt Brecht, and Peter Brook's mesmerising new theatrical methods. Tom Stoppard was identified as a challenging talent.[4] TV drama was

Dennis Potter on set, 1979

'British' – domestic, constrained, immediate – yet could be very powerful. It was a narrative addiction, fed on the privileged market for single plays, the familiar comforts of a long-running series, and the luxurious time and space of a proper serial (with many of the delights of a Victorian novel because of time spent in the company of a story).

Some serials accumulated audiences of 19 million: 10 million was normal. A single play that reached fewer than 4 million was worrying. The mass audience had become highly responsive to the 'quicksilver grammar of film language'.[5] Audience research showed that drama 'has the capacity to unite the national audience in tense anticipation over a series ... People comment that drama is a topic of conversation at work and at home.'[6] People from all classes shared the same arguments or emotions. Yet drama was also 'ordinarily' part of the week's hurly-burly of programmes, just 'what was on'. It encouraged 'audience pleasure, the development of talented artists and technicians, and the honest reflection of contemporary life and mores'.[7]

Television drama had as its primary topic the 'condition of the nation'. In *Tinker Tailor Soldier Spy*, *The Mayor of Casterbridge* and the Christmas retellings of M. R. James's chilling intellectual horror stories, it recalibrated the literary canon for the day. It dealt with the changing role of women. From the sensitive reinterpretation of Vera Brittain's founding World War I memoir *Testament of Youth*, to the caustic, hilarious brio of the feminist science fiction *The Life and Loves of a She Devil*, it was in touch with a shift in female identity and roles. BBC television drama nourished Mike Leigh's alternative realism, where a cadre of actors worked together in a severe and demanding way to produce characters from the ground up: a process through which powerful female performers and roles emerged. Television drama needed strong characters and clear storylines. According to Shaun Sutton, the head of BBC Drama from 1969 to 1981, it was far more broadly based in society than the 'narrow and mono-class' contemporary literature of the period, . But he also said that BBC Drama had been 'a compact family with comfortable family rules moving along contentedly in the mock-paternalistic climate'[8] until independent television shook the whole thing up.

As in the nineteenth-century magazine market, broadcast fictions were made in an omnivorous industrialised process because so much was needed to fill the airwaves. In 1977, a new work by someone who had never previously written for radio or television was broadcast every week. In 1979 alone, the BBC produced 757 dramas, including over one hundred single plays. It sucked up young directors – Antonia Bird came straight from the Royal Court, and Richard Eyre, a theatrical leader, was spotted early in his career. It was also a training ground for writers.

Gerry Mansell's policy paper, 'Broadcasting in the Seventies'[9], led to a creative devolution of drama away from London to Scotland and Wales. (Northern Ireland tried unsuccessfully to get its own centre too.) Sutton sent David Rose, the producer of Z Cars, to become head of Regional Drama in Birmingham, and script units across the country consumed new work voraciously. Sutton believed that BBC drama in this period was successful because 'decisions were being made by a very large number of people and from many different parts of the country. This gave the output a wide variety and taste.'[10] Channel controllers, such as Attenborough, Fox and Cotton, 'didn't ask whether the play would be political, over-sexy or violent, they didn't want to know the content'. They trusted the Drama department to obey unwritten rules of what was appropriate.

Intellectual backbone was provided by Troy Kennedy Martin's perceptive manifesto, 'Nats Go Home', which was published in Encounter magazine in the late sixties, but which only came of age in the seventies and eighties. It argued that television drama needed to break away from the studio version of a stage play and from the rigid conventions of television 'naturalism'. Kennedy Martin had helped create Z Cars, which he saw as the 'zenith' of the attempt to appear realistic. On Play for Today on BBC1, the Corporation had by the middle seventies developed a reputation for a kind of social realism in plays that looked at working-class experience. They had rigidified into a depressingly earnest litany of misery. It was these conventions that Kennedy Martin and Potter had mastered, and then shattered. Steeped in biblical language from his Nonconformist childhood in the Forest of Dean, Potter poetically and shockingly reimagined television and became one of the few authors known simply for his work in the medium. His stark and grand view was always that 'The loss of Eden is experienced by each and every one of us'.

Radio drama was also turned out at a relentless pace, and not just because it was cheap and fast. The art of layering sound, music and voices was endlessly innovative. There were great adaptations, such as *The Lord of the Rings*, but also the creation of splendid hybrids. A strand of anarchic British comedy that had a long pedigree on BBC radio going back to *The Goons*, combined with radio's capacity to realise science fiction convincingly and cheaply, mixed in with an ingenious and gloriously batty individual voice in Douglas Adams, the writer, produced *The Hitch Hiker's Guide to the Galaxy*. Radio was more personal than the shared public experience of television. The head of Radio Drama, Piers Plowright, turned it into a distinct genre almost unique to the BBC and 'the sheer volume into a continual opportunity to experiment'.[11] It was 'fantastic to flop fabulously because next week you could learn from the mistakes'.[12]

Both television and radio were 'radical', with 'Beckett always more significant than *The Mouse Trap*'.[13] A concern with breaking down class and political barriers was part of the temperament of drama at the time. The BBC 'did not have to achieve the closest available correlation of investment and profit: a huge advertising-attracting audience in prime time'. Jonathan Powell said that the holy grail for BBC television drama was 'quality' and the 'justifiably popular',[14] an elusive combination that was understood by all those in charge. Drama 'longed for [popularity] but did not want to be judged by it'. Neither high-minded indifference to audiences nor *ostensible* vulgar audience-chasing were approved of. 'Much was assumed and not spoken': you had to have a police drama on Mondays, a medical drama somewhere, and win the Saturday and Sunday 8 p.m. ratings battle. Anything after 9 p.m. was going 'a bit posh' because it was felt that putting drama in the fiercely competitive earlier slot added public service value. This was 'all in a day's work' for Powell. It was the projects beyond that core which made reputations. Powell was one of the trailblazers, one of the University of East Anglia graduates (Jenny Abramsky was another) to move fast up the BBC. He became head of Serials, head of Drama and then controller of BBC1.

HITS AND MISSES

The 'talented but volatile' Sutton oversaw the filming of every play by Shakespeare, commissioned by Milne – whose wife and family quoted Shakespeare with an easy confidence and love. Sutton's successes had included *Z Cars* and *Doctor Who*, perfectly scheduled late on a Saturday afternoon until, in an almost unique scheduling error, Michael Grade closed it down – 'it was tired. I thought it was dead. I was wrong.'[15] The BBC had done well with *I, Claudius* in 1976, an 'incredibly brave 13-part series, togas, forums, and not much story to go on'.[16] A 26-part series, *Churchill's People*, however, based on the history of the English-speaking peoples, was 'virtually unbroadcastable – but too expensive to shelve'.[17] To add to the BBC's joy, its premises in Ormeau Road were besieged by protesters – the governor for Northern Ireland complaining that the episode 'which had dealt with Derry in 1689, had raised protests, as could have been predicted from the choice of Dominic Behan, a Republican, as the scriptwriter'.[18] The series limped on to the outer circuits of American television.

Another failure was *The Borgias*, a flouncing, hammed-up oddity full of pouting poisoners and swirling capes. Combining 'sex, death and intrigue', it had seemed like a surefire success when proposed. It was an instant failure, with 13-week death throes. It was so dire that the BBC did a deal with ITV that *Brideshead Revisited*, about to become a classic Granada series on ITV, would be scheduled on a separate day so that it didn't have to go head to head with *The Borgias*. Such an arrangement would have been 'inconceivable' between BBC1 and 2 at the time, because they pitched themselves so aggressively against each other. The American co-producers, Herb Schmertz and Frank Marshall of American Mobil, complained that they had not been able to sell it to any US network, not even as 'soft pornography'. Milne told Alastair Cooke, the BBC's great American correspondent, that the BBC had produced 'two dogs' (the other a series on Nancy Astor) and Cooke finally sank them in America as he refused to introduce either.[19] *The Borgias* fiasco jeopardised co-production deals for years. Yet it had a role: *Blackadder* used its conventions mercilessly, cannibalising a disaster for a triumph.

Graeme MacDonald became the next head of Drama in 1981. Clever, sly, 'most untrustworthy', he had 'a wonderful touch for popular drama that sat on the BBC comfortably'. Ideally, dramas were 'heart-warming, accessible, middle ground',[20] but nevertheless intangibly felt 'right' on the BBC. *Shoestring* (the first series shot on film), with its modernist sets, 'film noir' lighting and Trevor Eve as the shambolic journalist sleuth, was an adventurous success. *When the Boat Comes In* explored the North-East during the great depression, with themes of unemployment, community resilience and official hard-heartedness. Mrs Thatcher told a Board of Governors meeting that it was 'a typical example of political bias, and heartstring-pulling, masquerading as art'. This was absurd: it had no pretensions, and although a little sentimental had roots and relevance. *Lovejoy* was a more contemporary example of MacDonald's instincts about British sensibilities. The central character was a 'Jack the lad' antiques dealer, an aspirational chancer, with pretty bits of Britain in the background. At a time when *Antiques Roadshow* was at its height, oldish furniture was part of the eighties zeitgeist, along with puffed-up silk frocks, shoulder pads and swagged curtains. It was all 'put in a lovely BBC envelope' and won high ratings.[21]

Howard's Way overstepped the line. It was a kind of 'cut price British Dallas' about 'gin and Jaguar' people who had recently made quite a lot of money. They had bad relationships and bad taste (anyway, not Hampstead, Crouch End, Ealing, BBC sort of taste).[22] It was a portrait of Thatcher's people – confident, a bit ruthless. They were the same kind of people as those in *Abigail's Party* by Mike Leigh, which had been a BBC success, partly because coming straight from the theatre, directed by Eyre, its split-second comic timing was perfectly rehearsed, partly because there was a strike on ITV and something 'stonkingly' highbrow on BBC2. The play became a classic distillation of an age and a class, observing them from outside, with a savage wit. However, unlike Mike Leigh's play, *Howard's Way* did not so much forensically observe its subjects, it 'went native on them'. Powell said 'it wasn't felt to be quite the BBC: it was faintly distasteful'. A high-minded, disapproving discussion in Programme Review Board worried about its propriety. 'Was it really BBC?' The first episode was a monumental hit. Paul Fox, now the director of Yorkshire Television, phoned up Powell and said, 'You bastards, you've commissioned an ITV programme.'[23] Brian Wenham, the chair of the next Programme Review meeting, reduced the room to hysterics: 'It looks as if the drama department has found a *most distressingly* popular programme.'[24]

Conservatives, who regarded television as a hotbed of revolutionaries, might have been startled to know that 'the tiny, enclosed world of television drama has managed to create for itself a remarkably rigid structure of class distinctions', according to the writer Hugh Whitemore.[25] The 'aristocrats' at the top made single plays, above the makers of 'prestige serials'; both looked down on the 'manufacturers of popular series'; and 'the soap opera manual labourers' languished at the bottom. Many academics have subsequently accepted the definition of single plays as high art at one end of a spectrum, concluding that the 'killing off' of the single play was an act of deliberate cultural vandalism. Single plays had been a training ground. One imaginative and determined producer, Richard Broke (who worked from a wheelchair after a car accident when he was young), made fifty dramas in five years, winning a BAFTA every year. Because a single play did not have to be 'balanced' within itself, it was seen as the best vehicle for political writing, an 'ideological troubadour' which broke down consensus, or the best way of 'getting around the BBC'.

Powell argued that single plays declined not because of a philistine conspiracy, nor because of a political coup against them, but because of a change in broadcasting ecology. It was increasingly hard to find a convincing regular vehicle for them – audiences were flummoxed by the hotchpotch of offerings in a single slot. BBC research showed that audiences, with clearer choices on other channels, were 'for the first time definitely avoiding the uncertainty of the single play'. *Play for Today* and *The Wednesday Play* were steadily losing audiences, and studio-based plays won no BAFTAs after 1970. By 1985 the BBC was making half the number of studio plays that it had in 1980.[26] As people had more entertainment choices – perhaps even as rigid patterns of work broke down – viewing habits changed, as did the dramatic formats that worked.

Yet Alan Bennett's poignant *Talking Heads* monologues exploited the confines of studio production, Dennis Potter revelled in it and Simon Gray crafted powerful works for the studio. Much studio-based drama, however, now looked old-fashioned (and occasionally risible). The cheapest shot followed a character from inside the studio set through a front door to the outside of a real, filmed location; it occurred in almost every play. 'The walls in this production shivered every time a door was unconvincingly shut. They may be made of plywood but the job of scenery is to make plywood behave like brick: not cardboard in a gale!' one exasperated producer commented.[27] Directors and producers, backed by Powell, wanted to move on to film, which made single plays more expensive, while serials and popular dramas replaced single plays as the training houses for new talent.

The period saw the emergence of producers as powerful creators of tele-visual drama. Sidney Newman, the American credited with reinvigorating British television drama at ATV and the BBC, had written of the new breed of drama producers: 'as new as the medium itself ... Unlike the theatre or film, this medium is not kind to the solitary genius, the uncompromising idealist, the vain ass ... the new breed are as tough as commandos, disciplined like Jesuits, and think and act with the speed of lightning.' They spent a good deal of public money, gathered and led production teams, fitted into the huge demands of the schedules and bargained a place for their product.[28] Ken Trodd said the producer was 'half diplomat, half engineer'. The most innovative of them, such as Michael Wearing, reinvented television drama.

In 1982, Wearing produced *Boys from the Blackstuff*, written by Alan Bleasdale, who deployed mordant Scouse wit and an operatic narrative to lay out a classic tragedy of decent men powerless in the face of an overwhelming economic catastrophe, and strong women struggling to protect their families in humiliating conditions. In five interlocking plays, he showed how unemployment wrecked parenting, marriages, individual identity and Liverpool – the decaying city's desolate grandeur captured by the Outside Broadcast unit, who shot the series to save the expense of building sets. Bleasdale wrote to Wearing, 'I think it is very important right now to write about the dole as seen from the point of view of people who are on it ... and to side with them against the people and papers who would like us to believe that ... the majority of the unemployed are malingerers and rogues.'[29] The idea had started in a single play, *The Blackstuff*, about men looking for work laying tarmac, and written as an indictment of the Labour government. It foreshadowed the

Boys from the Blackstuff, 1982: Bernard Hill as Yosser and Graeme Souness as himself

successful Conservative election poster of 1979 with its Saatchi slogan, 'Labour Isn't Working', over a long queue outside an unemployment office. By the time the quintet of dramas was broadcast, unemployment had risen to 3 million under the Conservative government. Working-class industrial work was disappearing.

Just as Shakespeare's plays were rooted in the particular politics and threats of each year of Elizabethan life, so television drama was rooted in its times. Drama was one voice in the busy broadcasting conversation about the world with news, current affairs and other arts. The playwright David Edgar saw it as parasitical on a 'seemingly limitless menu of other forms, mimicking, mixing and cloning with a bewildering fertility'.[30] The arresting emotional storytelling styles of news and current events were appropriated by experimenting dramatists. Potter said that any play might be seen after a shoot-out in Belfast, the antics of a celebrity singer or a 'plastic Prairie western', and although he came to think that these other 'machine-made' programmes did little more than 'feed an addiction for distraction', the strident 'now-ness' of television drama could make it one of the great emancipating social forces.

Wearing's next success, *Edge of Darkness*, came out of anxieties that Troy Kennedy Martin had been circling around for a decade. He felt that by the early eighties the BBC was avoiding political drama. ITV had made an immense success of *The Jewel in the Crown*, based on Paul Scott's edgy imperial lament about Indian partition. Against it the BBC put on *The Thornbirds*, a sentimental

American mini-series. To make matters worse Aubrey Singer had advertised this all over the country on hoardings. Actually, more people watched *The Thornbirds* than *The Jewel in the Crown*, but ITV had broadcast a meaningful original production, and the BBC was matching it with a bought-in 'popular' drama. After this humiliation, Powell was brought in to identify the new and great and get it on screen. 'It was a Penguin classics sort of task' to redefine the canon, and give BBC Drama authority again.

Powell phoned Kennedy Martin to see whether he was writing anything and the writer shambled into his office carrying a cardboard box. Fishing into it, he pulled out one sheet and said dubiously that it might be a beginning. Powell went to MacDonald offering an Austen serial on the principle that 'If you have three flops in a row, do *Pride and Prejudice* – it always works,'[31] on condition that he could do a doom-laden mystery, which would turn into *Edge of Darkness*. The six hour-long episodes metabolised a chilling new mood in the US defence establishment that a nuclear war was winnable: 'It was a time when 30,000 nuclear weapons were thought too old and too few and the whole armoury had to be modernised.'[32] It contained a Russian-doll set of conspiracies within conspiracies, with the whole story framed by James Lovelock's Gaia hypothesis that the planet was a self-regulating system. Later, the Gaia movement made a successful complaint against the BBC, accusing the drama of associating their work with that of terrorists.[33] Yet the serial portrays sympathetically the idealism of the young people who take action against a nuclear conspiracy. Later still, people working with Lovelock saw the drama as an inspired response to his work.

Each episode was ripe with contemporary references – the Falklands, Mrs Thatcher, Nicaragua, Vietnam, and stubborn feminist activism at Greenham Common. It had wonderful visual references. In a classic thriller chase, cloned with a Marx Brothers romp, the police get lost at the Barbican theatre because a lift delivers them on to the roof – a familiar problem in a building notoriously hard to navigate. Filmed just after the miners' strike, the dark, glimmering, barely visible underground scenes are an oblique homage to mining. The 'rush of the real' was distilled into a surreal, Gothic classic. Every element, from the Eric Clapton soundtrack to the use of colour, produced a chilling but inspiring fable of two men choosing self-destruction in pursuit of the public good, as the story spirals to its unsettling, sinister end.

Unfortunately, Kennedy Martin could not think of the right ending. He had wanted the hero to turn into a tree, but the actor Bob Peck refused. So Wearing had to go back to Powell for more money. The whole team was reassembled at vast expense six months after the original shoot had finished to make Kennedy Martin's ending. He wanted snow on a Cumbrian mountain, with black fritillaries blossoming through it. It worked and the series won national and international prizes. Like Potter's work, it was television as art

Edge of Darkness, 1983: Joe Don Baker and Bob Peck as the two altruistic heroes

for a popular audience. This kind of risk-taking with money was manageable, within the period's system of social relationships. People worried about money 'sort of, but on a global scale'. As long as they produced about 250 hours of drama a year, within a budget, no one interfered. Checkland had set up a tightly managed system, but it depended on treating BBC resources as a fixed or non-apparent cost. This was perfectly reasonable given the conditions of the time. But once there were independents making drama and establishing real costs, the whole system became indefensible.[34]

RESPONSIBLE FICTIONS

The two sources of friction sometimes whipped up by the press were taste and 'reality'. Both were refracted through arguments about political bias and had to be managed. The BBC based its reputation on reporting news with even-handed accuracy, and this made it vulnerable to criticisms of bias in fiction.

The overwhelming majority of drama was not remotely radical: it conservatively confirmed values. But some of it did challenge conventions. The border with 'reality' raised two problems. Did 'depicting' reality impose a need for balance? And were there limits that the Corporation could impose on a dramatist's personal visions? The seventies resonated with different answers.

Much depended on the way drama was packaged for the public. In 1975, the BBC put on a series of ten half-hour plays, put together in a week, on topical issues and broadcast live. Cheerily its theme was 'the mood of the country on the brink of a crisis'.[35] Except for David Edgar, whose play was on the absurdity of banking, the writers worked in teams. The topics were unrelentingly gloomy: personal collapse, dystopian scientific experiments, women's exploitation in the sex industry, the increased price of tomatoes.[36] They were hair-raising to make. The only way to get John Le Mesurier on set for the live performance was to tell him that it was a rehearsal. But nobody complained, they caused no rows, and were seen as an interesting experiment despite their immediacy.

Controversy could come from any angle. Mary Whitehouse complained that an episode of *Doctor Who* was too realistic: 'The violence of the Daleks terrified small children in Bolton and Peebles.' The BBC agreed. Ian McEwan's play *Solid Geometry* was banned in 1979, two days before it was due to be made. The head of English regions said, 'How do you think it would look if in the very week Margaret Thatcher was elected we were stupid enough to record a play which featured a twelve-inch penis in a fucking bottle?' This seemed forthright enough to the producer, until he received a memo the next day telling him that if he leaked this information 'he would be sacked'.[37] Negotiation went on all the time. The head of Drama decided David Hare and Howard Brenton's play *Brassneck* needed cleaning up, so in a meeting in a pub he said to the producer, 'I'll swap you two buggers for a shit.' It was tighter when they came to the religious words, the 'Gods' and 'Oh Christs'. Both producer and BBC mandarin accepted it as a necessary evil, or at least necessary for the head of Drama to keep his job.

By the middle eighties the press scented BBC blood. Drama was under attack because everything the BBC did was under attack. Alan Bleasdale's *The Monocled Mutineer*, in 1987, was 'freely based' on a disputed memoir of an insurrection during World War I. It was also part of a debate about the Falklands in the aftermath of that war. The licence that fiction was allowed, however, was eroded when it was advertised in the press and on billboards as a 'true-life story', as if it were documentary, and the advertising campaign designed to enhance the BBC's image accidentally caused another row. The series was a proper thing for the BBC to do, but the way it was managed on to the screens led to an outcry. Bleasdale did not work for the Corporation for several decades after the *Mutineer*, a dispiriting waste of a great talent for which the BBC had helped find a public.

Colin Firth in Tumbledown, 1988, directed by Richard Eyre, produced by Richard Broke

Yet the *Mutineer* combustion, like many others, had an external motor that was only tangentially to do with the drama. Three days before the first episode was broadcast, Stuart Young, the BBC chairman, died. Meanwhile Norman Tebbit was running a monitoring unit scrutinising the BBC for political bias, and 140 Conservative MPs demanded that the Corporation flush out the 'Red Moles' who had infiltrated it.[38] Painting BBC drama as 'left-wing propaganda' was a shot in a larger war,[39] designed to get the right-wing industrialist Lord King, chairman of British Airways, appointed to replace Young. His approach would have been punitively inimical to the BBC. Milne went privately to see Whitelaw in alarm at the prospect of King. 'Please don't worry,' he was assured. But the press did not know this.

The *Mutineer* row was later followed by the *Tumbledown* row (while a *Pennies from Heaven* row about sex, as usual with Potter, rumbled away), which used a sensitive dramatisation of one officer's trauma during the Falklands War to ask wider questions about the way soldiers were treated. It was directed by Richard Eyre, produced by Richard Broke, who had produced *The Monocled Mutineer*, and had a young Colin Firth as the lead.[40] The Ministry of Defence tried to stop it being made,[41] *The Times* thundered that it was treacherous, two members of the right-wing Freedom Association asked Eyre in a public meeting whether the play was political, and his reasonable response, 'of course it was', gave fuel to the press. Unfortunately, it was *not* followed by a play about Mrs Thatcher during the Falklands, commissioned by Milne from Ian Curteis and then shelved. This looked as if the BBC were prejudiced against the prime minister, although there had been creative and political reasons why the play was not made. (It was cut and made successfully much later.) By the time the play had been delayed it was close to an election, and Milne thought it would be biased to show it. The writer, who had written for *The Onedin Line* and pioneered a kind of dramatised documentary form, and who was a close friend of Mrs Thatcher's speech writer, nevertheless believed that a whole tradition of right-wing, positive drama was being excluded from the screens,[42] and that he was being discriminated against. This too caused a festering row.

The conflicts had pre-dated the Thatcher government in 1979, and were made more acute because some of the best dramatists – Ken Loach, Tony Garnett, Trevor Griffiths and David Mercer – did have a political agenda. They saw television as a legitimate tool of social change. Loach and Garnett made hard-hitting 'interventionist' TV drama. Their 'documentary' style looked different, used different voices, had different stories and was frequently based around historical events. It seemed like a slice of reality, more so in the seventies than in retrospect. (The conventions of 'reality', it seems, change.) Television was a very realistic medium, with 'real' pictures in outside broadcasts, 'real' time in game shows, 'real' events in news and current affairs. But current affairs programmes that frequently 'accused' individuals and institutions of injustices (as the plays were to do) were held to some standard of balance and impartiality. These values were not accepted by the dramatists. They were anti-Brechtian in the sense that they sought to hide, rather than expose, the messages they wished to communicate within a realistic form. So, they would have reasonably argued, did the hours of more conventional drama – much of it rigidly, campaigningly, conservative socially – that no one complained about.

If they claimed to be 'real', did they have to be accurate? But if they were fiction, were they granted artistic licence? There was often outrage about BBC drama because members of the public, the Board of Governors, politicians, members of the House of Lords (even the grand and cultured principal of King's College, Cambridge, and author of the influential report on broadcasting, Noel Annan) confused dramatic invention with reality. The press often saw a play as an 'opinion' and bashed the Corporation for holding it, when in fact it merely published it. The BBC struggled to make the terms of dramatic trading clearer, but as David Edgar, a key dramatist of the period, said, 'The press always generalised from the particular, but drama, on the contrary, particularises from the general.'[43]

Earlier, in 1975, *Days of Hope*, developed by Tony Garnett and Ken Loach, took the life of a working-class man and his family, born at the start of the century, through World War I to the General Strike. It was a dismaying story of exploitation told with elegiac romance, through a dreamy shooting style. Simultaneously, another self-consciously 'progressive' drama was shown on BBC2, written by Jim Allen, called *Law and Order*. It revealed every aspect of the

British legal system to be corrupt and unjust. The two dramas caused an outcry. *Law and Order* may have been tough, but it was hardly shocking. The Metropolitan Police Commissioner, Sir Robert Mark, then ruthlessly and effectively rooting out police corruption, said in a BBC Dimbleby lecture, 'Experienced and respected metropolitan detectives can identify lawyers in criminal practice who are more harmful to society than the clients they represent.'[44]

Days of Hope, although seen as 'radical', was an orthodox interpretation (for the time) of the Labour movement's betrayal of its working-class supporters – a view shared in the parliamentary left, the trade unions and universities. The audience for the set of dramas was huge, with the second episode attracting 5 million viewers. Walter Citrine, a former general secretary of the TUC, who had been active during the General Strike, 'was particularly hurt' at being portrayed as a drunkard in it, since he had signed the pledge when he was sixteen. Being teetotal 'was in the bones of the labour movement originally along with Methodism'. But this kind of detail belonged, it was said by its supporters, to a lesser order than the 'broad brush strokes of historical truths' that the drama embodied.

Criticism in *The Listener* said that the plays were driven by a political agenda that they failed to reveal: 'We scarcely got to know the three recurring characters', it said, 'before they were engulfed by events; though they bobbed up occasionally, the most they could do was to wave frantically. They were cyphers for a message.'[45] The *Daily Telegraph* attacked the left-wing consensus in the BBC. 'This is a plea not for censoring left-wingery, but for ending a situation in which this is the dominant philosophy put out by a semi-monopolistic state service.'[46]

There was dismay at the Board of Governors: Lady Avonside enquired whether 'the enemies of the state were moving into Television Drama?'[47] She was worried that 'ordinary folk' might be taken in by the stories. The BBC should make a contribution to national morale by being more careful about how it handled themes central to the nation's confidence in itself.[48] Peggy Jay, a Labour Party activist and wife of the Labour minister Douglas Jay, said that while she admired the quality of *Days of Hope*, it was 'intolerably' inaccurate. 'She had three uncles who were killed within five weeks of reaching the front in 1915, for these men the issue had not been conscription as the play made out, but of volunteering for something they believed worth doing.'[49] The plays had ignored the fact that Britain had been the first country to treat conscientious objectors in a humane and civilised way.[50]

The *Telegraph* was quite wrong: the BBC internal consensus was hardly that of a left-wing conspiracy. Curran replied to a letter protesting about the plays by saying that, since he had become director-general, there had been six plays that had presented the same 'particular problem' (rows about politics) and they had involved only three people: 'The trio of Tony Garnett, Kenneth

Loach and Jim Allen' (producer, director and writer of *Days of Hope*). He described what he saw them doing:

> The treatment has been highly realistic. The background events have been thoroughly researched. The production has been substantially on film and extremely skilful. The emphasis has been on the virtues of the rank and file worker and on the turpitude of management and of formal trades unionism ... In all, the declared approach has been that of the Workers' Revolutionary Party.[51]

Yet Curran also stoutly defended polemical drama – in moderation.

Colin Shaw, the BBC Secretary, was sent away to write a report on radical drama. He was a great guardian of television quality and liberty, both at the BBC and later at the Television Complaints Council, which he set up and engineered into a thoughtful agitator for broadcasting as a public service. His report argued that in the sixties, when the first plays were commissioned specifically for television, 'play-writers turned eagerly to social and sometimes political problems for these were the themes that interested them – whatever their politics'.[52] At first, they were mostly concerned with welfare problems – *Cathy Come Home* and *Edna, the Inebriate Woman*. Shaw pointed out that 'the political play remained a minute part of our output', and that none was 'potentially damaging to the structure of life in this country. The significant thing is probably the *lack* of political drama.'[53] Quoting John Buchan, he concluded: 'Honest, straightforward, well regulated controversy is the only salt which can save the most valuable side of broadcasting from going rotten – and after all we must surely trust the people.'[54] It was a humane and balanced report and defended the radical dramatists.

But this was not how dramatists saw the Corporation. In 1980, when the BBC absurdly banned E. P. Thompson's proposed Reith lectures, David Hare, a rising young playwright, said that he would not write for the BBC because it censored thought. 'A new self-righteous tone has been adopted', said Hare, 'by men who often seem to take a chilling pleasure in the exercise of power. Nobody here likes banning a play, they say, rolling the sentence around their mouths, enjoying the taste.' They believe, he said, 'in something called "editorial control", which I construe as them knowing better than you do, something which as an artist, (I know no other word to use) [I find] hard to accept in a journalist'.[55] Because Milne had worked among 'journalists' (the contempt is palpable), he misunderstood the nature of drama. Hare concluded, magisterially, 'the executive has become deferential to government. They imagine that by placating politicians they will ensure the survival of public service broadcasting. They are wrong.'[56]

The barrage of criticism that the BBC faced from outside was damaging.

In 1977, *Nipper of the Yard* by Barry Keefe, about London's ganglands, ran into legal problems. As a consequence, a committee was set up, chaired by Glenn del Medico, the BBC lawyer, which had to 'approve all dramas based on "real life" issues and ensure that they neither breached libel laws and in a broader way that they did not mislead audiences'. It was a sensible attempt to stop great legal shindigs before rather than after they erupted; it attempted to get some order into the area. In the end, it led to the emergence of an enabling legal intelligence being applied to BBC programmes. But at first it did chill programme ideas, and the process delayed for six years *Our Friends in the North*, loosely based on the charismatic but corrupt leader of Newcastle City Council, T. Dan Smith. Meanwhile a bulging BBC file on the distinction between reality and fiction was set in motion, a legal maw gobbling up precedent. But the 'boundary' with reality went on being contentious even after the BBC had abandoned most of the fertile political writers.

THE POLITICS OF TASTE

The other boundary was taste. In 1963, the 'Lady Chatterley' trial had established that offensive culture could be defended against legal constraint by its 'artistic worth'. The home secretary, Roy Jenkins, had written this thinking into legislation which provided a flexible, contextualised background to policy-making. Rather than any 'index' of proscribed depictions, issues of 'taste' and 'violence' were to be judged by their meaning within the work. Jenkins had said that the BBC's 'interpretation of the public interest had provided one model for my thinking', but while individuals 'chose' books to read and plays or movies to attend, broadcasting went directly into people's homes. In addition to protecting audiences from material they might stumble across, the public service broadcaster had wider, societal obligations to particular audiences – such as children. These responsibilities were enshrined in BBC codes of practice. At times there was conflict – the 'creators' believing they could judge quality better than BBC bureaucrats. Quite often the writers were right in the longer term, but the BBC had to broadcast in the 'here and now'. The BBC was accused of too much sex of the wrong kind and too much graphic violence. Arguments in drama about violence cross-bred with other arguments about real violence on the news.

Television had altered the rules of social distance. The medium could make the viewer a spectator at previously elite and privileged events such as royal weddings, football matches and great news moments. This power to dissolve distance was affecting public understanding of what was 'private' and what was public. For example, children could no longer be protected from adult behaviour. Metropolitan mores were broadcast into homes with more conventional habits. Young people's evolving sexual mores were displayed in front of an older generation's rather different sense of what was permissible in public.

Standing on the new fault line was a redoubtable female Canute, Mrs Mary Whitehouse. Her complaints about 'bad language', blasphemy and the BBC's undermining of traditional Christian sexual values had played a part in causing the resignation of one of the finest directors-general, Hugh Carleton Greene. That a great public servant, with decades of intelligent dedication to the national interest at the heart of government through World War II and on into the Cold War, could be brought down in this way was grievous. But Greene had misjudged her persistence and the resonance of her anxieties, even though they were increasingly at odds with changes in British behaviour. The BBC had treated her with something close to contempt and amusement at first, which was not merely an error, it was wrong. Unpleasantly, the Corporation produced *Mrs Swizzlestick*, a cruel, satirical series parodying her. Many of her preoccupations seem less outrageous now.

Her organisation, the 'Clean Up TV' campaign, which evolved into the National Viewers' and Listeners' Association, saw television as eroding the moral life of the country. An indefatigable publicist, she became a 'byword for affronted decency'.[57] The BBC was bombarded with complaints from this sophisticated campaigning organisation, which encouraged members to complain to the BBC as individuals, with a neat 'Complaint Card' system that alerted the NVLA when a complaint had been made. Although the Corporation queried how 'representative' the complaints were, by the seventies worrying about her response was part of its mental furniture. When Michael Swann became chairman, he and Curran worked hard to engage her, partly because they understood her anxieties and saw she represented a section of the public, partly because they were desperate to mitigate the damage she was inflicting. Swann gave a lecture on violence and TV, agreed to meetings with her, tried to assuage her by giving her attention. But he later concluded that she was not susceptible to reason.

The BBC could be divided over issues of taste. The governors discussed a play by David Mercer: 'Mr Morgan said this play had been truly horrid and obscene, and he was not easily shocked. Mrs Clarke added that Drama Group must have waited until Lady Avonside had retired. The horrid elements mentioned by Mr Morgan (buggery and lesbianism) were just what she had foretold.'[58] It was the camera crew who first objected to Dennis Potter's *Brimstone and Treacle*. They arrived, incensed, at Milne's office when he was controller of Television. Cowgill arrived moments later, agitated by the copy he had just been asked to approve advertising the play in the *Radio Times*.[59] The play had been rushed through editing so that few outside the production team knew what it was about. Potter, Ken Trodd and the director Barry Davies understood perfectly well that it would be seen as offensive, but somehow

*Michael Kitchen as the Devil and Michelle Newey as
the daughter in* Brimstone and Treacle, *1976*

hoped to evade the BBC and have the play broadcast. Potter had said that the 'game' was to 'push' and 'conceal' a work in the BBC system: 'I prefer to see plays in which ideas are not exposed on the surface like basking sharks (or in some cases stranded cod) but arise with the insistence of discovery.'[60]

The play was one of a loose trilogy that included *Double Dare* and *Where Adam Stood*. The latter was Potter's moving adaptation of Edmund Gosse's book *Father and Son*, about Gosse's relationship with his stern, loving and conflicted father. The sombre and affectionately shot film shows the father's struggle to reconcile his pioneering natural history observations and their inexorable argument for Darwin's evolutionary ideas with his fervent, puritanical Christian belief in creation. Mary Whitehouse wrote to the BBC approvingly: she thought it 'exquisite'.[61] She took a different view of *Brimstone and Treacle*, a play about the Devil (played with smoky impishness but chilling evil by Michael Kitchen) infiltrating a suburban home, where the daughter has been brain-damaged in a car accident. The daughter lies, a slobbering, noisy Greek chorus in the corner. The Devil rapes her and she is restored to sentience, after the audience has discovered that her accident had occurred as she ran away after finding a friend and her father in bed together.

The public reason the BBC gave for Milne's decision to stop its broadcast was blasphemy. But it was more visceral than that: the rape scene made Milne feel physically sick. He said that he thought Potter was 'out of the depth of his own psyche and the depth of his own suffering at the time ... he had written a tortured piece that I thought would outrage people ... I thought it was too much'.[62] It remains an uncomfortable play, apparently based on a premise of the restorative power of rape. But its impact lay in dramatic suggestion; there is nothing graphic or violent about the rape scene, just an extraordinary summoning up of a taboo of violation. It embodies a male fantasy in a disturbing envelope of drama. Trodd, a brilliant drama producer who had a famously volatile relationship with Potter, but who produced the greatest of his work, had explored rape sensitively in other drama. But the play was condemned as being likely to outrage public opinion. The ban led to a great outcry that the BBC was censoring writers.

Colin Shaw said that 'Alasdair [Milne] was furious and felt he'd been conspired against', which was true.[63] Curran told a meeting of the Board of Management that year that there was little to be done about Trodd (who had been showing the play, unauthorised, to journalists), although his contract was not renewed.[64] Yet another creative talent made by the BBC was then lost to it, rather than being managed. Milne had then sensibly allowed a showing of *Brimstone and Treacle* at the Edinburgh fringe, 'a useful safety valve'.[65] But he also wrote Potter a careful letter saying it was 'brilliantly written and made, but nauseating';[66] and then a sharp, legitimate reminder to the Drama department:

> Nobody – neither writer or producer or director – should imagine that the act of authorship or producership dictates the act of publication ... Controllers, very occasionally, must be involved at an early stage; otherwise, albeit rarely, the BBC will be forced to intervene, to everyone's sorrow, when it's far too late. These matters are subtle. But it seems that some of the producers and script editors in drama plays don't understand the rules.[67]

The entire BBC Drama department threatened to go on strike. The *Spectator* and the *Mail* fulminated about an insidious left-wing takeover of the BBC, and its corruption of decent standards of behaviour. The *Guardian* worried about the BBC's censorship of dramatists. Yet, when the play was seen in a season of Potter's works in 1987, it was hard to understand why there had been such a fuss. Perhaps the play's scandalous reputation had prepared the audience for what they might find. But the row had an unexpected use: Milne had a propitiating lunch with Potter, who had been suffering from a rare version of arthritis and a skin complaint (psoriatic arthropathy) that were agonising and disfiguring. Milne, a kind man, was 'much moved' by Potter's condition. The BBC wanted to commission something new from him. Over lunch, it evolved into 'something big, something that mattered',[68] which would become *The Singing Detective*. Not only did the disease become the material

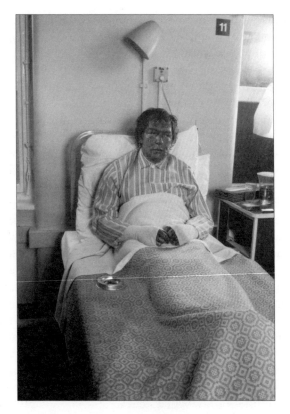

Michael Gambon in The Singing Detective, *1986:*
Potter metabolised his own terrible affliction into great drama

source of Potter's writing, but the tone and outlook of his work were formed by the course of his illness. The ebullience of *The Singing Detective* perhaps came from a new treatment that actually gave him several years of relief from crippling symptoms. Potter became a television celebrity writer in a way that was almost unique, and ploughed everything into that work. He told Joan Bakewell that his sensitive adaptation of *The Mayor of Casterbridge* was written after the death of his father, when 'the grief has been so pitiless that I haven't wanted to turn myself to anything but that'. Potter, said a critic, 'seizes the novel's lines of force converging on the heart of the book'.[69]

By the eighties the harsher political climate was one problem for drama. But so was the competition for quality. 'Everyone was very scared of Granada,'[70] which had been built by Denis Forman and Sidney Bernstein into a formidable creative television machine. ITV had more money to spend, and Granada was spending it on drama that challenged the BBC's core values. *The Jewel in the Crown* had not only beaten the Corporation by creating a contemporary classic, Forman had also innovated commercially, selling it overseas before shooting even began. Many of the BBC's young Turks, among them Powell and later John Birt, had started at Granada. The combination of quality and *Coronation Street* popularity was a stark challenge to the BBC.

Making a success, said Powell, was a cumulative process. Having a good idea was intangible, but people often recognised it. Having a good writer, director and cast all mattered, but was hardly a scientific calculation. It had to be talked about, 'nudged away at', then the project had to become 'an important thing' to the head of Drama and channel controller. Then the 'whole place becomes invested in it'. This 'capacity of the project creates a breeze', which blows in its direction more interest, more resources and a better place in the schedule. None of these factors is preordained in the act of commissioning.

By the early eighties the BBC was facing a brutal crisis, as mass audiences slipped away. Since the introduction of BBC2 in 1964, the Corporation had had an 'inbuilt advantage' over the commercial broadcasters. Wenham said it had enjoyed 'an almost automatic claim to a plurality of delight and excellence, as well as a majority audience share'.[71] When Channel 4 launched in 1982, BBC2's audience share fell from a high of 12.3 per cent to 10.4 per cent in 1984. But the real problem was with BBC1, slumping from 49 per cent in 1981 to a low of 35.9 per cent in 1984, just three years later.[72] Wenham warned that the 'political and public will' to support the BBC was in doubt 'if the BBC failed to serve majorities as effectively as it served minorities'.[73] An internal discussion paper late in 1983 detailed the fate of the Canadian broadcaster CBC, which had been forced to accept advertising on TV, with disastrous results.[74] Competition could only get more ferocious as satellite and cable would offer more channels. What was required was a 'future programming strategy which was essentially political – it was to have, as a prime objective, the maintenance of audience share'.[75] One problem was money. Nigel Pope, a programme planner, said that the early eighties were a 'terrible' period at the BBC and particularly for BBC1.[76] By 1983, ITV companies were spending £300 million a year more on programmes, and by 1984 the BBC was paying artists 35 per cent less than ITV in fees.[77] As the Corporation was making cuts, the commercial companies were using their superior resources to take audience share away from the BBC.

The BBC was not offering programmes in the ways audiences wanted to consume them: the scheduling habits of two decades of television planning no longer worked. When there were only two channels, a strong programme early in the evening such as the *Six O'Clock News* provided a fixed point, from where 'You could pick people up and hold them there for the rest of the evening.'[78] Inertia, as much as anything else, would do the rest. Now there were four channels to choose from, and the schedules were becoming more and more confusing. With the spread of the remote-control 'zapper' in the mid-1980s, people began to flick through channels more frequently.[79] In order to build an audience, therefore, it became imperative for an individual channel to have fixed points at various times in its schedule which the audience could lock on to. The BBC needed something very predictable and regular in the early evenings. But also to battle 'programme by programme, sector by sector, day in, day out, over and over again'.[80] The situation demanded a new relationship to the popular: 'It had to be accepted that the majority of people in the country really did want mass entertainment'; the 'Granadaland' working-class audience had to be won over. Wenham said the BBC had to 'wrench the machine round', even at the cost of other things.

The answer came from the top, and was a BBC management idea. Creative bureaucrats make public service – they are not superfluous. They create structures. Programme makers usually bid for money and a place in the schedule for their ideas. This time the money and the analysis of the need came first. No one knew what would fill the envelope when management created it. Then it broke down production walls, and was made in a new way; it launched a new, uneasy relationship between television and the press, it crossed a BBC Rubicon into the popular, and it reconnected the BBC with its mass audience. In a way, it saved the BBC. It swiftly became the show with the highest ratings on television. At a time when the BBC was widely castigated as 'out of control' and the management seen as inadequate, it was also a powerful example of brave, proper leadership. It was a drama solution that took a long time to put together: and it was called *EastEnders*.

EASTENDERS

By 1983, five of the top six series and serials, in terms of loyalty, numbers and reach, were ITV's.[81] *Coronation Street* 'underpinned the schedules' for ITV two days of the week. The BBC needed to match this place in the collective sensibility and in the ratings. The new bi-weekly drama – it was never called a 'soap' – would be a huge machine of drama production. Powell was enthusiastic, but there was much opposition. 'How could they embrace having a twice-weekly serial which meant having a large chunk of property somewhere and changing the way the BBC worked?' Checkland was the intelligent enabler, he found the money and dedicated it to the project.[82]

The idea was for a regular drama, indeed a never-ending one, but set where, about what? It had to be distinct in some way: a 'public service' soap. Julia Smith, the producer, and Tony Holland, the script editor, were appointed. They had worked together on Z *Cars* and *Angel* (a medical drama series) and understood long-running stories and the relationship between social issues and narrative. Such a drama required a 'community' just as *Coronation Street* had one in the North-West. The first idea was a caravan park. This had the advantage of being cheap and the disadvantage of being miserable: 'We cannot run 52 weeks a year on a place where no one but losers live. It will be unbearably dispiriting,' said Holland. It was rejected. Holland, who came from the East End of London, and Powell thought it should be London. Indeed, Powell had always believed that since *Coronation Street* had a street, they needed an architectural feature, something large and easily imagined, which he thought should be a square. Managing director Bill Cotton was unconvinced that a London setting would work at all. They commissioned research, which found in January 1984 that, apart from a slightly worrying lack of enthusiasm for a new soap opera at all, Southerners would accept a Northern soap, Northerners would accept a Southern soap and Midlanders didn't mind where it was set, as long as it wasn't in the Midlands.

If the programme were going to be made on such a scale, it needed a secure and large set. This was eventually found in Elstree. Smith began long and patient union negotiations for the working hours she needed to get such a great deal of drama out regularly. According to Powell, 'Smith and Holland set off, they wrote scripts, they built a set, they made a programme and it went out.' As far as possible, management did not interfere in the creative process. But much depended on its success.

Smith and Holland wrote long detailed character and plot lines (with secret surprises hidden from writers and casts). Holland worked directly from his own family experience. It had a bit of the Blitz spirit in a mythic 'cockney' world. It consciously intended to tackle social issues. If there were to be a storyline about breast cancer (as there was in the second year) then the coordinating work with health authorities needed to be undertaken, the storyline had to be medically accurate, and if it led (as it did) to a huge increase in women presenting themselves for screening, then the services had to be prepared. It had to 'inform' the public accurately. It was intended to raise 'quite delicate and arresting contemporary problems'. It was consciously 'realistic'. Michelle, the teenage daughter of the family, whose emblematic story started the show, had acne. This was not hidden – it was how she was at the time. It was ambitious theatrically: young directors were appointed straight from the Royal Court. There were top writers, and producers like Michael Wearing.

EastEnders started with a melodramatic death, a dead body in an abandoned house, an unintended teenage pregnancy and some useful practical advice disguised in a plot. It mirrored an earlier smash hit that had been launched 'to help in the most important social issues of the time',[83] which in comparison to rival commercial competitors had been designed to produce 'wholesome instruction and entertainment' for the whole family, and which, while campaigning against injustice, would be 'popular and readable'. Charles Dickens, the editor of *Household Words*, had complained in despair when he saw the preliminary version of the first magazine, saying it read like 'stewed lead', enjoining the new crew of writers to make the magazine more gripping

EastEnders *aspired to be 'public service' soap, 1985*

and compelling. The first words of the eventual issue of the magazine read: 'When Death is present in a house, the very contrast between the time as it now is and the day as it often has been, gives poignancy to sorrow – a more utter blankness to desolation.' The first edition also included a story about the consequences of a teenage pregnancy.[84] In its desire to be 'Dickensian', *EastEnders* had quite unintentionally reproduced the sequence of melodramas and useful family entertainment that had made *Household Words* a publishing sensation in 1850.

And *EastEnders* was a broadcasting sensation. In December 1985, internal research found that the combined weekly audience for the programme had risen from 12 million at the launch to over 20 million within three weeks. A remarkable 50 per cent of the British population watched one episode in a week, and an astonishing 70 per cent watched an episode within a month. This meant, said an internal memo, 'that when they spoke of what people thought of the programme they meant literally, most people'.[85] People found the characters true to life, the plots believable and, in the face of criticism of the content, people watched it together and regarded it as viewing for all the family.[86]

It was to have an uncomfortable symbiotic relationship with the popular press, and it marked a commodification of celebrities as its cast, many unknown until then, became front-page fodder. But crossing the Rubicon to popular drama, and hanging on to public service qualities, put the BBC back fighting ITV and, perhaps more importantly, at the heart of popular pleasure.

SMILEY'S REAL PEOPLE: PUBLIC SERVICE TRADECRAFT

DESMOND MORRIS, the charismatic broadcaster, best-selling author of *The Naked Ape* and head of Research at London Zoo, took its lonesome lady giant panda, Chi-Chi, to Russia in 1966 to see whether the retiring beast could be encouraged to mate with the Moscow Zoo's male, An-An. To his deep alarm the Russians treated him as a spy. His room was bugged; his razor fell apart after being dismantled in a search for recording equipment; he was followed everywhere; most perturbing of all, the Soviets tried to entrap him in a story about a 'secret scientific' factory. The pervading threat and the icy temperatures caused his health to break down. Only a decade later did he realise the Russian behaviour had some bizarre reasoning behind it.[1]

Morris had often worked with Maxwell Knight, a familiar BBC natural history expert, a regular broadcaster on *Animal Parliament, Animal Vegetable and Mineral, The Naturalist, Country Questions* and Peter Scott's bird programmes. Knight was apparently an 'avuncular, friendly old bloke', who had written numerous books about wildlife and domestic pets, from *A Cuckoo in the House*[2] to the often reprinted *Answers for Young Naturalists*. As 'Uncle Max' in *Nature Parliament*, he had exhorted the nation's children to become wildlife detectives, and was part of the Sunday ritual for much of the late 1950s and 1960s – 'roast lamb and mint sauce, Max Knight on the radio, and a wonderful exploration of a pond or wood before tea'.[3]

It was Knight's other professional life which had provoked the Soviets. He had worked for MI5 since 1924, when he had joined the British fascists as an undercover agent, and was employed directly by the Service in the 1930s. He had been head of a unit within MI5 that dealt with Soviet subversion, exposed the Woolwich Arsenal spy ring, bugged the Communist Party headquarters, been suspicious of Anthony Blunt (later unmasked as a spy), and written a paper presciently titled *The Comintern Are Not Dead* in 1945.[4] A sexually ambivalent and often privately unpleasant character (at least to his three wives), Knight was believed to be the model for 'M' in the Bond novels. Both Ian Fleming and David Cornwell (John le Carré) knew him when they worked for the Secret Services.

The mysterious corridors of Broadcasting House in 1932

Occasionally, there was some crossover in Knight's roles. He once asked a Special Branch officer to find a hedgehog that he urgently needed for a programme.[5] In an introduction to one of his books, *The Charm of Birds*, he had written, 'It is because Wildlife is amoral, not troubled by questions of right and wrong, that we find it so refreshing.' His 'tradecraft' in observing people had, he said, in turn been learnt from watching animal behaviour.[6] The Russians concluded that any BBC naturalist colleague of Knight's, let alone one proposing to make a programme about the sex life of pandas in the depths of the Russian winter, was up to no good.[7]

The Corporation's relationship to security was more significant than that of unwittingly providing a retirement job for Maxwell Knight. Since its beginning in 1926, the BBC had been part of the utility infrastructure of the nation. Like water and power, as broadcasting was pushed to the widest possible national audience by the public service principle of universal access, its centrality to the new means of communication made it a pillar of the state's capacity to function. As the provider of authoritative information, with a trusted voice nationally and internationally, it was a vital part of planning for wars, civil emergencies, pandemics, energy crises and civil unrest.[8] Communication was at the heart of all crises.

Some link with the Security Service was inevitable given the BBC's control of transmitters and other technology, but how this relationship was governed and by what principles it operated presented challenges. Democracy is not merely a matter of large principles but lives in small details. The careful husbanding of the editorial independence of the BBC was essential, and it often performed in an exemplary way during acute moments of crisis, drawing lines on principle that it would not cross despite intense government pressure.

The BBC's janus-faced support of, yet critical distance from, the state, faced its toughest test over security issues. Many robust conflicts with governments were caused by infringements of the BBC's citadel – attempts to influence the choice or handling of a story. Conflicts arose because the BBC, sometimes correctly, believed it understood the objectives of policy and how to manage it better than the state. It sometimes, almost despairingly, attempted to use its specialist knowledge to amend and improve the operation of the secret state, as an expert interlocutor rather than a passive partner. It also understood a different side of people. The BBC Secretary had to write 'some very careful good letters: quite sharp, very precise' to the Home Office, and get questions asked in the House of Lords because 'the government were not getting a grip' on what was needed for a warning system in the case of a national emergency – by the eighties more likely to be a 'dirty' bomb on the streets of a city.[9]

The BBC was part of planning for unrest at home and attacks from abroad, while reporting on both. The period from 1974 to 1987 was a time of domestic turmoil and constant external threat, illustrated by a 1975 *Panorama* presented by Michael Cockerell which discussed the British army's plans for dealing with a political coup in the UK.[10] There were paralysing strikes, the Northern Ireland conflict, a spate of security stories, the arrest of several spies and Anthony Blunt's public disclosure (although his treachery had long been known inside the Security Service). The period came to a head in a flurry of attacks on the BBC for being politically subversive.

THE WORLD SERVICE

And there were foreign challenges too. The BBC faced outwards to a turbulent and often oppressed world through the World Service, which had broadcast into occupied Europe during World War II and was broadcasting into the communist Eastern Bloc during the Cold War, as well as into Latin America, Asia and Africa. It was greatly respected by its large audience. Just as the Service had been met with moved gratitude after World War II, so at the end

Nation shall lunch with nation: the World Service canteen in Bush House, 1960

of the Cold War in 1989, when the Berlin Wall came down, the audiences of eastern Europe who had depended on the BBC acclaimed it. In a 1974 survey in ten Indian cities, 25 per cent of adults listened to the BBC in English four times a week, and a majority of those with access to a radio listened to the Hindi service: 'voters, taxpayers, in short Mr Middle India' were regular listeners. The World Service was above all a sinuously attentive news service that brought information to those that were deprived of it, and a nuanced understanding of foreign points of view back to British policy making. It was a priceless (but rather cheap) part of the national need to understand the world it lived within.

Although it suffered punishing cuts throughout the seventies and eighties, the World Service performed as heroically in the Cold War as in World War II. It played a profound role in providing an alternative mental landscape for audiences locked down in repressive regimes. But its information was so reliable that in Russia the political and intelligence elites made sure their dachas were within range of BBC transmitters, while simultaneously ordering that they be jammed so that no one else could listen.

In 1986, the BBC was not the largest but the fifth-largest world broadcaster, with 730–750 hours per week. The Voice of America, Radio Liberty, Radio Free Europe and Russia each broadcast about 2,355 hours per week, and the Chinese 1,554 hours. But the BBC's influence was greater: 'listened to, and trusted … it was the style that had the impact'. Although firmly located in Britain and indeed London, the World Service attempted to understand the condition of the societies it broadcast into. It instilled 'a recognisable voice and tone' in the broadcasters it recruited from all over the world, said the historian Alban Webb, through the 'rigid adherence to BBC editorial procedure'. Arguably, the 'tone' carried all of the values of impartiality and independence. It was editorially independent from the state, but the countries the service broadcast to were 'aligned with the strategic priorities of Whitehall'. At the same time, the broadcasters preserved their precious sympathy with audiences thousands of miles away. BBC broadcasts understood the social fallibilities of the Eastern Bloc – 'which were far deeper than the military failing or the political ones'.[11] The BBC was a place 'where honour could take refuge, where hope could find weapons ready for use'. The success of the World Service did not 'lie on narrowly conceived national self-interest or on the shifting political priorities of the day with their capricious twists and turns but on the importance we attach to the free movement of ideas, to the worldwide dissemination of truth ... so that sanity, decency, truth continue to be held up as a viable way of running a society'.[12]

John Tusa, another great bearer of BBC values (director of the World Service from 1986), said that the Service saw itself as an independent guardian of the national interest, self-appointed but 'not arbitrarily appointed'. Every programme 'smelt of pluralism'.[13] The World Service sounded different because 'the mechanism was different' to other international broadcasters. They were the voice of their governments. The World Service was the voice of the people it broadcast to. People took risks to hear the truth. Sometimes, of course, the BBC failed to live up to these high standards, but far more often it succeeded.

THE BBC AND THE SECRET STATE

The BBC also faced inwards to the nation. The Corporation was related to the secret state not just during periods of clear danger such as World War II and the Cold War. National security had been a factor in the very origins of the BBC, which had been set up in the 1920s in the middle of a panic about the Bolsheviks attempting to incite revolution using broadcasting. The impartiality of the BBC was seen as a bulwark against such propaganda, and since the technology used for entertainment programmes was the same as that needed for security, the BBC engineers who built and managed the transmitters were inevitably involved with the secret state.

The conventionally agreed account of the BBC's victory over proposals for commercial cable stations in the late thirties was most cogently put by the Nobel prize-winning economist R. H. Coase, who said that it was because of the 'Corporation's brute determination to maintain its monopoly'.[14] Coase was a great economist but a very bad historian. The decision was the product not of Coase's 'lazy' civil servants, or the 'monopolistic' BBC, but of security concerns (although it suited the BBC more widely). The cable proposal that concerned the government (and the BBC) was that of Oswald Mosley, the British fascist leader, who in 1936 devised an ingenious scheme to start commercial radio stations based on the Radio Luxembourg model – to be called 'Air Time Ltd'. He planned to bombard British audiences from Iceland, Germany and the Channel Islands with light entertainment, as a 'stepping stone' for his propaganda. But the BBC and the government understood Mosley's intentions, his encouragement of 'Fifth Columns', and the use of propaganda wrapped up in popular music to make the English people sympathetic towards Germany's aggressive policies. As war approached, anxiety about national security became increasingly prominent in the British government's decision to limit the capacity of foreign broadcasting to have a presence in British airspace. Commercial considerations 'provide a convenient smokescreen for an urgent need to act on this mass of proposals'.[15] Mosley was deflected.

In the post-war period, the World Service was financed by a direct 'grant-in-aid' from the Foreign Office which had been voted on in Parliament. Rather than tethering it to the state, this helped keep the Service's editorial values independent: they had their own revenue, they did not have to compete with domestic news agendas. The Foreign Office established the geographical reach of the Service, but Tusa believed it 'failed to understand the very nature of broadcasting', in particular that once programmes were made, they would cost no more to rebroadcast. Information flowed in both directions in regular meetings and briefings, but was carefully fenced around with guarantees of editorial independence. In theory, the Foreign Office had the right, enshrined in the Charter and Licence, to instruct the BBC what to broadcast or not to broadcast abroad, but this was never exercised. In 1979, Mansell said that the Foreign Office had not for many years been in a position to instruct the BBC to 'run a certain line or to omit certain items'.

How was World Service quality assured? Mansell argued that the Service was protected from 'error' but also from interference by the high quality of the central output of news in English, which 'sets the tone for all the language services ... the shop floor level of editors and programme makers keeping a very very sharp and continuous eye on output', and what he called the 'contagion of Bush House spirit, the devotion to the Service, the integrity and high ideals, and they believe it even more when they are under pressure and being criticised because then they discover what makes them exceptional'.[16] The independence of the World Service was also protected by its relationship to what John Tusa called 'the mothership of values' of the larger BBC. It had different news priorities from home news agendas, but the larger decencies of news-making, the proprieties of balance and accuracy and deeper truthfulness

John Tusa, director of the World Service, outside Bush House, 1989

to the context of events, were part of the whole organisation. Then there were shared BBC editorial guidelines: meeting the conditions laid down in them, said Baqer Moin, a young Iranian employed by the BBC in 1976, was a 'wall of protection' for a journalist. If you met them you had done your job, and the BBC mandarins' task was to stop your independence being interfered with – especially by those with power.[17] However, the World Service's distinct ethic and news values were an invaluable corrective to BBC provincialism.

Great political upheavals were the source of crises for the World Service. The BBC came under intense pressure during the Iranian revolution in 1978/79, which it resisted. As Iranian government supporters in London brought intense pressure on the BBC through Whitehall, the British ambassador in Tehran, Anthony Parsons, demanded that the BBC Iranian service be shut down, believing it to be stoking the increasingly violent protests of the supporters of Ayatollah Khomeini.[18] The suspicion was justified by the fact that in 1953, when the elected Iranian leader Mossadeq was brought down by a

US- and UK-inspired coup, the BBC *had* been used to broadcast secret codes to the opposition. The wildest allegation in 1979 accused the BBC of broadcasting instructions for making Molotov cocktails. Mansell received calls from the Treasury, the Cabinet Office and from the permanent secretary at the Foreign Office, Sir Michael Palliser, who called Mansell in. When asked whether they were broadcasting 'inflammatory' material, Mansell replied that they were reporting what was happening, that they had checked every report as fully as they could. Palliser said 'it was very dynamic – the regime thought that the BBC made a material difference to the revolution, but I concluded that the reporting was just that: reporting'.[19] Later Parsons, a diplomat of great distinction, confidentially met the World Service team (which he had tried to silence) and, in a cordial and far-ranging discussion, agreed that the first responsibility of reporting was to deliver as full an account of events as possible, whatever the political consequences.[20] Mansell said that the Service and its reporters, whom he trusted, 'remained very steady'.[21]

The Cold War was 'largely an insiders' affair',[22] according to Peter Hennessy, the innovative historian of the secret state. So the fact that it was often hotter than the public understood was kept secret. It ran, said Palliser, 'like a thread through everything in the post-war period. Within it, the BBC played a surprisingly pivotal role.'[23] From the Cuban missile crisis onwards, a domestic British policy may be discerned of not alarming a British public who, if nuclear attack took place, would be more exposed than some of Europe and certainly more than America. The worry was that 'Once tactical nuclear weapons were used on the battle front, the horror of nuclear war would be seen in practically every home. Truly democratic societies with very limited news censorship would be at a disadvantage over their tightly controlled enemies.'[24]

The Cold War was running 'hot' during the seventies and eighties when a 'potentially lethal combination of Reaganite rhetoric and Soviet paranoia'[25] made America and Russia unstable. Understanding the motivations and intentions of the 'enemy' was not a luxury but an urgent necessity. It was a conflict also conducted within the minds of the population. In 1991, after the Russian coup which finally brought the Cold War to an end, Sir Percy Cradock, the astute and masterful chairman of the Joint Intelligence Committee, ordered champagne for his fellow committee members and toasted the intelligence community: 'We *didn't* have a war. We *did* win.'[26] Intelligence was the most important weapon in the prosecution of that war. Intelligence (both the product and the process), said another expert,

> was the intellectual sitting quietly. It means reviewing known facts, sorting out significant from insignificant, assessing them severally and jointly, and arriving at a conclusion by the exercise of judgement: part

induction, part deduction. Absolute intellectual honesty is essential. The process must not be muddled by emotion or prejudice, or by a desire to please. The skill is largely innate ... the process is as much about synthesis as analysis.[27]

The World Service (in English and multiple languages) and Monitoring were perfect instruments for 'picking up reverberations ... small signs of shifts and feints'.[28] They were the means by which we understood the thinking of our opponents: by being sympathetically alert to how they understood the world.

ENGINEERING

By 1974, the familiar map of regional broadcasting was in effect the map of regional government had nuclear war broken out (or if there had been some kind of coup, which was much discussed in the seventies). The director of Engineering was consulted in the writing of the government War Book, which continually updated instructions for action in the period of mobilisation to war and its outbreak. Regional directors of Engineering (and their secretaries) held the combinations and the safes in which copies of the War Book were kept. The BBC War Books for the period are still classified, although some central government War Books are available. The BBC studio in the government nuclear bunker was enlarged and enhanced in 1984, the only part of the facility that was maintained fully connected and furnished. It was BBC engineers who made the World Service programmes audible in Russia, communist eastern Europe and in oppressive regimes around the world, by building the technical and political coalition needed to evade jamming.

'Security', said Bryce McCririck, director of Engineering from 1981 to 1987, 'was hard wired into broadcasting'.[29] Directors of Engineering were guaranteed a knighthood, were revered authorities in the wider world of engineering, had a security clearance above that of the director-general (and, it was said, above that of the prime minister). Below them were great battalions of BBC engineers whose security clearance was necessary: after all, they built and ran the nation's transmitters. Within the BBC, engineers could 'always bewilder the managers and governors, and because they commanded very large capital expenditure over very long periods of time they had been very powerful'.[30]

Engineers were also the vital early warning system for the Corporation, alerting managers to the next technological survival challenge. Theirs was often a political task rooted in technological ingenuity. When he was appointed director-general, Ian Trethowan told McCririck, 'You just deal with the technology and keep me out of the shit.'[31]

At a time when electrical engineering was at the forefront of scientific inquiry, the BBC's Wood Norton Engineering Research department was at the cutting edge. Chris Clarke, a 'young, self-effacing, geeky, modest chap'[32] from Wood Norton, was taken by Phil Laven, the head of Research, to a very high-powered and very small international technology meeting in New York. They were trying to find a way to link digital equipment to form a complete digital programme chain. There was a belief it would take a decade to solve. Clarke reached into his bag, a bit like a *Blue Peter* presenter, got out a box and said, 'Here is one I made earlier. You're all thinking of it the wrong way ... I have made a digital standards converter.'[33] There was stunned silence. It was a vital part of the arrival at a worldwide agreement on digital video standards known as Recommendation 601, a United Nations-agreed standard. This was just one of a myriad of engineering solutions and inventions pioneered by BBC engineers.

By contrast, the BBC's doomed move into satellite broadcasting, first mooted in 1982 and 'running furiously' by 1983, was 'driven by fear'[34] of being outflanked by other broadcasters in a new broadcasting space, and by a desperate desire to cuddle up to a government that the BBC were at logger-heads with. Mrs Thatcher had influential friends pressing for innovation in satellite technology in order to expose the atrocities they believed Russian forces were committing in Afghanistan.[35] In addition, the government believed that a 'new industrial revolution in communications' could be advanced on the back of the British public's desire to watch more television.

The Broadcasting Unit in the Home Office had little technological capacity; on occasions the BBC found that Home Office officials failed to understand what they were negotiating[36] and 'inadvertently gave away the national interest'.[37] But on satellite policy the BBC failed both itself and the Home Office. Like much connected with technology, satellite policy was 'schizophrenic: on the one side audiences and entertainment and on the other security'.[38] There was no idea how consumers would pay for the service. In a vague way the BBC told the government it would revitalise the British Film Industry. Checkland simply refused to be involved and said it was a moment of 'collective madness'.[39]

It was, however, made worse by the government's determination that the BBC should buy satellite services only from UNISAT, built by British Telecom and British Aerospace. In this, it was driven by the need to keep an advanced industry, with a security angle, in British hands. Paradoxically, the free market government obliged the Corporation to buy the domestic, exorbitantly expensive, British satellite capacity: 'BT was the owner and the user of the services,' said McCririck, 'they had a monopoly and used it against us.' It all came to nothing, and in 1984 the BBC broke its contract with UNISAT, and was forced to pay huge damages after it lost a prolonged court case. Sky had legislation written later to help it launch its service.

VETTING

Given the technical and political interaction with the secret state, it was inevitable that some BBC staff beyond engineers were 'vetted' – their security profile established by MI5 investigation. 'Vetting' was necessary and helpful whenever the nation and the BBC were under hostile threat – if it was done legitimately. The main purpose of vetting in the BBC, as elsewhere, was positive – to rule people out as being a risk. 'It made working more secure, it was essentially positive', said Mike Hodder, the security expert in the BBC from 1982, who also saw himself as 'allaying anxieties'.[40] In 1982, the Diplock Report into the 'Interception of Communications' found that 68,000 people in the country were being vetted. Nevertheless, the British process was a restrained affair. Peter Hennessy calculated that between 1948 and the 1980s, out of the thousands vetted, only 25 British civil servants were dismissed from their posts, 25 resigned and 88 were transferred to less sensitive work. Of these, 33 were later reinstated. None was named.[41] In America, by contrast, 9,500 federal civil servants were sacked, 15,000 resigned, and all were named.

Vetting happened across the Corporation, and in the domestic services much of it was conducted on people who did not know that they were being checked in this way. Nor did the journalists in other organisations who were also vetted. It was a John le Carré kind of business – a bureaucratic affair – conducted in what the beastly Roddy Martindale in *Tinker Tailor Soldier Spy* called 'little reading rooms in the Admiralty, little committees popping up with funny names'.[42] Personnel was the department it ran from. There were a whole series of formal contact points with the Security Service. Stephen Claypole, universally respected and trusted within News, was understood to play such a role: 'he sorted things very astutely'.[43] Claypole said that his job was 'to clear up problems by talking to the right people and keep an eye on issues, be sensitive to things emerging in news, current affairs, and make sure we understood what we were saying'.[44] Much was denied: only in 1985 was it admitted that MI5 regularly briefed BBC management on subversives in industry.[45]

The Corporation had its own George Smiley-like codenames for security. 'Deferred Facilities' meant Civil Defence or any emergency. MI5 was called 'College' and the vetting process 'Colleging' because during World War II part of MI5 was based in Bedford College in Bedford Square (and later Regent's Park).[46] The procedure was more properly called 'formalities'.[47] The people to whom papers were sent for 'Colleging' were called 'Box 500' after the Oxford postbox number originally used during the war. The BBC wanted a way of identifying the files of those who had been vetted which would not reveal it to the individuals concerned, so they stamped 'Formalities Cleared' on the back of files. It looked to non-insiders like just another bureaucratic procedure.

Those who had not passed the process had a tag resembling a Christmas tree attached to their files.

There was a general awareness of the issue. When Giles Oakley was offered a job on the Community Broadcasting Unit, 'his boss had to nip into Lime Grove to use the phone' to check that Giles's security vetting had come through.[48] Paul Bonner, editor of *Open Door*, was told he should not employ a particular journalist, because the brother of this journalist, a Reuters correspondent in Berlin, was believed to have 'gone over the wall to the East'. Bonner objected that this was ludicrous and unfair, and was told he could give the journalist a temporary contract.[49]

The BBC system of internal vetting was unique. Journalists in other media were vetted, but not systematically, and not within their own organisations. There was no such vetting at ITV, or at least, the official historians of the commercial system could find no record of it.[50] But 'Thames was the big security worry', said Denis Forman of Granada TV. At the inception of ITV there had been a worry about security, but it was dealt with, said Forman, by making sure that those at the top of the organisation could provide an overseeing eye.[51] The first director and chairman of ITV, Sir Robert Fraser and Sir Kenneth Clark, had both worked in the Ministry of Information during World War II and knew all about intelligence concerns. When Channel 4 was launched in 1982, there was similar anxiety, but again only, it appears, about the very top of the organisation. Phillip Whitehead, the Labour MP who on the Annan Committee had been one of the architects of the new channel, insisted that the chairman of Channel 4 had to be a Privy Councillor, in order to deal with security: Edmund Dell, a Privy Councillor, was duly appointed to deal with 'things that mattered that were not everyday running issues'.

In 1987, after the *Observer* broke a story about vetting in the BBC, Michael Checkland, by then director-general, told the Board of Governors in good faith that vetting had begun in 1937, 'at the request of the BBC as a protection against fascist infiltration'.[52] This was the best knowledge available to the BBC from its own papers at the time. Actually, the BBC was not entirely sure when it had started, and in 1984, Ronnie Stoneham, the BBC head of Security, said, 'I cannot give you a definitive answer to the question "Who originated the request for vetting of BBC staff."'[53] Ahead of a meeting with the Security Service, he suggested that the BBC should let them 'make the running' if they discussed the 1930s and 1940s, 'in order to see if they have more detailed information'.

In fact, more recently released government papers which were not then accessible to the BBC or the public show that an informal practice went back to September 1933. The story is one of movement from a totally covert and informal scrutiny to an increasingly formal system. It had left from the very early days barely a trace even in government papers, and none at all in BBC papers. The system began when Colonel Alan Dawnay was appointed to the BBC as controller of Programmes in 1933, officially in charge of developing BBC administration. Half of his salary was paid by the War Office, and he started an informal checking process, which also considered those who broadcast and what they said. It is not clear whether Reith knew this. Dawnay was in charge of 'careful and detailed examination of the role of every officer in the BBC'. And the first concern was not, as Checkland later understood, with fascists, but with potential communist infiltration of the Corporation.

In 1933, Dawnay met the head of MI5, Sir Vernon Kell, who, according to a colleague, was 'able to smell a spy like a terrier smells a rat', and agreed that they would tell Dawnay 'if undesirable persons were obtaining employment with his organisation'. Communication would 'be sent to Dawnay's private address – 3 Eaton Terrace SW1'. Kell said of the agreement, 'I think I have effected a satisfactory liaison.'[54] At further meetings between Dawnay and the MI5 official 'B',[55] they discussed possible 'treachery on the part of the staff inside the BBC', and Dawnay said he believed there was none, but if anything came to light he would inform 'B', who would in turn warn Dawnay of problems.[56] 'B' commented that 'it was most undesirable that Colonel Dawnay's contact with me should be generally known', but that from the Security Service point of view the relationship so far was working 'quite satisfactorily'.[57]

Engineering was a worry from the beginning. Charles Carpendale, Dawnay's more efficient replacement, 'was very alive to the fact that owing to the majority of the staff of the BBC being employed as engineers on the technical side, any undesirable member of the staff could at any time sabotage the whole show – this point being especially applicable to a period of crisis within the country'.[58] During the 1930s, as the threat of war increased, the procedure was regularised, and became known by senior BBC executives, with a formal and written agreement implemented in 1937 (the document Checkland referred to in 1987).

By 1940, all staff records had to bear the mark 'Credentials OK', showing that any member of staff had been through what was then called 'College'.[59] And a standard 'vetting form' was created.[60] The process was kept secret, both from those subject to it and the public: 'On principle, we cannot ever agree to any information we supply regarding an individual, or the fact that we have been, or are to be consulted about him, ever being mentioned to the individual concerned.'[61] The maintenance of secrecy was reaffirmed, but also the nature of vetting. An MI5 official said that 'the difference between MI5 and the [Soviet] OGPU or [Nazi] Gestapo was that MI5 did not insist but merely advised, and responsibility was with the person receiving the advice'.[62] The BBC, not the government, was to decide what to do about any individual.

Returned vetting correspondence was to be marked 'SECRET AND PERSONAL. NOT TO BE PLACED IN A DEPARTMENTAL FILE'. The fact that the Security Service was involved should never be mentioned, nor was anyone to be told that the Security Service had warned against their employment. If the BBC wanted to employ the candidate despite a security threat being uncovered, they could, but should give a reason.[63] Later, it was formally agreed that the Security Service would make efforts to weed out 'spiteful or frivolous accusations'.[64]

After World War II, the Security Service wanted to restrict vetting to those who were to be promoted. But the BBC repeatedly asked for vetting to take place at entry level.[65] During the 1950s and 1960s, the BBC battled both to keep vetting and to keep it secret at a time when other forms of vetting were beginning to be publicly acknowledged. The Corporation argued that the porous nature of the organisation, and its odd internal structure, meant that it needed vetting at entry. Anyone coming into the BBC in one area could move to another as they moved up the organisation – Light Entertainment, News, Current Affairs, Drama, and even Engineering had permeable borders. MI5's view, perhaps unexpectedly, was that the BBC was in danger of depriving itself of talent.[66] Roger Hollis, the director-general of MI5, said it was not the policy of government 'to exclude Communists and other potentially subversive types from public service but only from those occupations where "unreliability" could have security implications'. The result of this was that at a time when communists were not barred, for example, from teaching, those working on children's programmes would be vetted. The anxiety was of 'an unhindered' opportunity to slant broadcast material for a politically subversive purpose.

The BBC wanted all newsroom staff vetted ...

in view of the overriding requirement of impartiality and integrity in its news services, the importance of the reputation which it has built up in this sphere and the great practical difficulty of guarding against unreliable sub-editing in the conditions of a broadcasting newsroom: the BBC feels it is essential that the political reliability of all newsroom staff should be beyond question ... It is the BBC's view that security is jeopardised, even in peacetime conditions, by occasional lapses of political judgement in BBC news broadcasts which might be thought to indicate a pro-Communist bias, precisely because such lapses undermine public confidence in an institution and a service to which everyone turns for stability and encouragement in an emergency such as war.[67]

The Security Service replied that it was up to the BBC to make its editorial processes secure.[68] Hollis was concerned that the BBC was pushing him to exceed his brief. But the Corporation argued that without vetting it would 'gradually accumulate into the Corporation communists or near communists at the rate of about four or five a year, and that many of these would become disgruntled when not promoted beyond a certain point'. In 1959, the BBC offered a bargain: if they could maintain vetting levels, they would go on providing general information and photographs about artists and contributors, about staff, programmes, use of rooms on BBC premises, special liaison with the Monitoring Service, and general assistance to Special Branch. Hollis was 'surprised and impressed' by the amount of cooperation being offered.[69]

On and on the argument went. The BBC wanted Finance, Audience Research, News Information and Light Entertainment (perhaps for subversive satire?) vetted.[70] Hollis wrote, 'we are vetting for security whereas the BBC, in part, wish to vet in order to avoid embarrassment'.[71] In government departments the only staff vetted were those with access to secret work.[72] The BBC replied that it employed 5,500 engineers, and the service could not operate if there was an emergency (and emergencies were much at the forefront of administrators' minds) unless the vetting was complete. It was the access to microphones – and consequentially the nation – which worried the BBC. Moreover, its transmitters were top priority on Cabinet Office anti-sabotage lists.[73]

The BBC did not want vetting to become public, 'because of the fierce parliamentary and public criticism which would inevitably result ...'[74] The World Service existed as 'one of the main instruments in this country's efforts to combat the ideologies of the Iron Curtain countries ... to project the ideals of western democracy and effectively to refute the continuous flow of propaganda from the Iron Curtain countries'. The BBC argued it needed wide vetting as staff could pass on details of other staff members, increasing threats to families behind the Curtain. Details of recruitment procedures might get out, allowing the possibility of manipulation, 'as in the recent attempt by the Yugoslav Government'. Several dictation typist candidates had been revealed as agents, one for the Egyptian secret services, one Czech, and one close to the Bulgarian delegation.[75] A Chinese spy had been uncovered in the World Service; a member of ACCT was a communist agent; a member of the Romanian staff was subject to a trap;[76] and in 1978, Georgi Markov, a respected journalist on the Bulgarian Service, was poisoned by a pellet injected from the tip of an umbrella, while walking on Waterloo Bridge. He died four days later. Helen Rapp, who had been smuggled out of Russia as a baby in 1917 and had worked for the World Service before the Open University, was a member of a BBC educational delegation in Bulgaria itself when the murder occurred. The news of Markov's death was held up for 24 hours to enable the Foreign Office to get the delegation back home.

The BBC publicly denied vetting, saying in 1968, 'it can be stated categorically that BBC staff are not subject to security clearance as a prerequisite for employment'. People were very carefully checked because the BBC's reputation depended on 'the probity of the individual ... A point to be stressed is that the BBC asks no questions either about religion or political beliefs.'[77] Strictly this was true: MI5 asked the questions, not the BBC. In 1977, an article in the *Evening Standard* mentioned the use of 'Christmas trees' on the back of personal files signalling the existence of a separate security file on a staff member. Peter Hardiman Scott, controller of Administration, where the security contacts within the BBC were then housed, reminded the director-general of the form of words should the affair resurface and the BBC be 'forced to utter' on the matter:

> In carrying out our editorial policy we are concerned only with the professional ability of staff to perform their duties, but it would only be reasonable to take account of what people have said and done in public. Because in any state of emergency the BBC would be the most important means of communication with the public, certain members of staff of necessity are privy to some security information; these few people are subject to the same kind of security vetting as anyone in a comparative position in the Government's service.

Hardiman Scott noted to the director-general that this defence 'should be discussed with our "friends" before it is used'.[78]

The BBC put forward about 1,400 people a year for vetting. On average, about ten were identified as a 'risk' and not employed, but the majority of those even with adverse reports were employed. In 1976, for example, 1,257 people were vetted, and of the 80 adverse reports on new members of staff, 33 were offered jobs and only 14 turned down.[79] A higher number of people were not cleared in the World Service, but were still employed.[80] But it was a different situation: 'Of course people could not be cleared ... it merely reflected the problems of the political systems from which they came. Their "uncleared" situation was frequently open knowledge.'

Vetting gave the BBC a valuable shield, however, made of hard evidence in a world of swirling accusation. In January 1980, Mrs Thatcher forwarded the BBC a letter accusing it of left-wing bias because of a sequence on *Nationwide* about flying pickets in a steel dispute. Swann replied, acutely wielding vetting against her.

> Finally a difficult point that disturbs me very much ... the remarks about clearing these 'saboteurs' out of the BBC. I expect you will know that anyone with access to programme decisions, and in certain other sensitive areas (about 40% of staff), is vetted at our request by the Security Service. If therefore any ideological extremists slip through it is hardly our fault. In reality, I am quite sure that very few do and I know from personal experience that we are much less plagued by such people than the educational world.[81]

In the eighties, 'spooks' were in the air. In 1982, Geoffrey Prime, a code-breaker at GCHQ, who had at first been arrested for child abuse, was revealed as a Russian agent. Books like *The Climate of Treason* by the BBC's Andrew Boyle – which publicly exposed Anthony Blunt – sold several million copies. Milne (whose older brother Tom had worked for the Secret Service) tried to rationalise the BBC system. A set of new security brooms at the BBC were appointed, all ex-soldiers. Their object was to reduce the number of vettings and make the system clearer. Christopher Martin recognised that the BBC process was 'ridiculous, and gone about in the wrong way'.[82] In 1983, Ronnie Stoneham became the security expert in the BBC. He was caricatured unfairly in the press, according to one BBC official, 'as if he were some crusty hard-line brigadier of right-wing views and repressive tendencies'. He was a gift to *Private Eye*. Someone in News leaked stuff about him and was 'torn off a strip' by Larry Hodgson. Yet he had been appointed to reduce numbers.[83]

Security was an area where character and personal contacts remained intangibly important. Mike Hodder, Stoneham's successor, said, 'some things were too important or delicate to write down ... they were sorted on the hoof. A visit to someone's offices could do more work than any number of memos,' and indeed there were things it was wise not to write down. Much of what Hodder did was allay unreasonable fears. A candidate for one job felt that she would not be appointed because she was a lesbian; he assured her this was a ridiculous anxiety. Anything that was in the open was not a source of worry: if somebody was in a political party, even an extremist one, then, as long as the editor or producer knew, News and Current Affairs were 'actually enriched by as wide a range of views as it is possible to canvass'. The idea of spy 'cells' came from the spy fiction of the period, and was 'poppycock'. But the government needed 'calming'.[84]

Beyond the BBC, the interests of the security services were occasionally badly informed. During the seventies and eighties there were radical ideas in the firmament about the media. Very bright (and about to be very eminent) broadcasters and journalists – such as Anthony Smith, Neal Ascherson, Michael Darlow, Nick Garnham and James Curran – developed these ideas. The Rowntree Foundation put some of its charitable money into communications policy and produced, from its office at 9 Poland Street, a stream of proposals for community radio, radical distribution networks and 'the Right of Reply' campaign. This was ahead of its time, demanding that if you could prove you had been unfairly traduced by a newspaper then you had the right to reply in the paper. In the early seventies, the Free Communications Group produced a stream of original pamphlets concerned with content and management, ethics and economy.[85] Darlow said that, after most meetings of the group, the game was to identify 'the spook at the back'.[86]

While vetting may have helped the BBC defend itself against infiltration and attacks from the government, negative vettings could be damaging, and shocking if applied in error. Isabel Hilton had read Chinese at Edinburgh University and, in 1973, been one of the first British students to spend a year in China. Hilton had caused person and bicycle jams everywhere she went – most Chinese had never seen foreigners before, let alone elegant beauties with long blonde hair. When she returned, John Chinnery, the head of her department, asked her to be the secretary of the Scotland/China Association (the English branch of which was chaired by Asa Briggs, the eminent historian and Provost of Worcester College, Oxford, later Lord Briggs). Chinnery was, as everyone knew, a member of the Communist Party. Hilton was asked to apply for a BBC Current Affairs job by Alastair Hetherington, the ex-editor of the *Guardian* and controller of BBC Scotland. Her application was followed by a very long silence. In the meantime, Bruce Page offered her a job on the (briefly) upmarket *Daily Express*. She rang Hetherington as a courtesy, and he was surprised when she told him that she had never been offered the BBC job. He said he would talk to the head of Personnel.

Hilton moved south and to a string of impressive jobs in foreign journalism. She was never a 'joiner' of anything, and the idea that she was in any way 'subversive' was laughable. Out of the blue in 1985, David Leigh phoned her from the *Observer*, saying that Anthony Howard, the political commentator, had told him a 'shocking story' about a negative vetting. Leigh deduced that the victim must be a woman because Howard had not used any personal pronouns. Leigh wondered whether she could think of anyone it might have been. Hilton, startled, realised that it must be her. She was furious, and after she had consulted a lawyer, the case was taken up by the NCCL.[87] The BBC's public response to enquiries was dismissively inadequate. Isabel Hilton, 'one of the "victims" of vetting', went a memo, 'has written asking for access to the file on her as it had contained inaccurate information'. Roger Johnson, controller Personnel TV, replied: 'We have been unable to trace any information on file relating to your application, and as far as I can ascertain, no files now exist concerning these events. I regret therefore that I cannot help you with your request, having satisfied myself that your assumption that files relating to this matter may be held here is incorrect.'[88]

When the case went to a European court, the government admitted that there had been vetting and said it was a justified procedure, but it had done 'no harm' to Hilton because she had got another job. In a broad sense, this was a lie. It is hard to calculate what harm a negative vetting would have on a journalist's career, or who might have been informed about it. In a narrow sense, it was also a lie, as it certainly caused 'harm' – she did not get the BBC job. The BBC has never apologised, nor explained what the issue was. Mike Hodder did, however, say, 'it was all a mistake'. Hilton's best guess is that in the febrile atmosphere in the run-up to the referendum on Scottish devolution, the

Secret Service was interested in Tom Nairn, Neal Ascherson and Hetherington himself, all clever, passionate devolutionists, whom she was close to.

The story broke in the *Observer*, and David Leigh wrote a book including the affair. All the other papers carried reports of the *Observer* revelations.[89] The Soviet news agency Tass chirpily reported that 'permanent political control' was being introduced at the BBC.[90] Roger Bolton, who had just returned from the Edinburgh TV festival, said that you could be a 'Cabinet member who had once upon a time been in the Communist party, but not an assistant film editor in the BBC'. Milne said, 'the final decision in the vetting system rests with the BBC. We take the decision, we invoke the procedures or not. We do it ourselves on the best advice ... This story is 50 years old and it has taken the Press that long to find it.'[91] He hoped to be able to announce publicly the posts which would continue to be vetted – but was determined to reduce the numbers.[92] The story was not merely embarrassing for the BBC. Coming close on the heels of the banning of *Real Lives*, it set in motion another toxic wave of distrust. This time it was a suspicion not that the Corporation was 'opposed' to the government, but, on the contrary, that it was unhealthily in its pocket. Vetting was defensible and proper, but the BBC failed to make a case for it.

TINKER TAILOR SOLDIER SPY

Christmas trees finally ceased to be used in August 1984.[93] At the same time, against the stark background of the Cold War, treachery was in the air. The government accused the BBC of it, politicians were darkly aware of it, and staff were suspicious that the BBC might have betrayed them.

'The avenger stole upon the citadel and destroyed it from within,'[94] wrote John le Carré of Kim Philby, one of the 'Cambridge' spies, whose betrayal was the basis of his book *Tinker Tailor Soldier Spy*, published in 1974. Le Carré said that he had entered the intelligence services in the spirit of Buchan and left in the spirit of Kafka; both moods survive in the 1979 BBC adaptation of the book. This translated the temperature of the story of the corruption of the British establishment into a hauntingly affecting thriller and great modern classic about the condition of Britain. Le Carré wondered whether the spies revealed the nation to be 'so far past the peak of our national and emotional energy' that 'its members collectively and individually had abdicated the responsibility to develop'.[95] The narrative suited the new political climate as Mrs Thatcher came to power, describing, as she did, the hollowing out of the nation by those who were supposed to know best and keep it safe. Yet the series also provided a stark challenge to that narrative, for in it honour and truth were saved by George Smiley, the arch-mandarin. A clever, weary, sullied man whose journey from darkening autumn into bleak winter dictates the pace, Smiley is no Thatcherite.

John le Carré in 1966

After years of negotiating to make a series of *Brideshead Revisited*, the BBC was dismayed to discover that Evelyn Waugh's estate had given the rights to Granada, the only commercial company that really frightened it. The producer Jonathan Powell was working in his little office overlooking Shepherd's Bush Green ('quite MI5ish') when Graeme MacDonald, head of Series, came in despondently to tell him the *Brideshead* news. Powell had recently read *Tinker Tailor* and suggested it as a replacement. MacDonald replied gloomily that London Weekend Television already owned the rights. But Powell checked, and discovered that the commercial broadcaster had let the option go – the day before.[96] When they asked le Carré, he agreed to meet them, and the class team of the era was assembled – Arthur Hopcroft to do the scripts, John Irving to be director, with Michael Wearing, the great producer of subtle and thoughtful drama, in charge. When they met in le Carré's Hampstead house, le Carré said that since 'the plot, narrative, heart of all' was sustained by one character, 'if we were to cry for the moon we would cry for Alec Guinness as Smiley'.[97]

Guinness was known to refuse television, so le Carré wrote him a careful letter, the beginning of a seductive gavotte. For eight or nine hours of broadcasting, he wrote, 'Smiley is the "motor" – as the Germans call it' of every episode. Guinness, he said, had the right existential manner for Smiley. By return of post, Guinness replied that perhaps he was too old, that 'although thickset' he was 'not really rotund', and that as his powers were failing he needed scripts 'hopelessly early'.[98] Back bounced le Carré with an extraordinarily perceptive reply: analysing both Guinness's performance and Smiley's character together. Guinness was just the right age, he said, and would bring to Smiley 'a mildness of manner, stretched taut, when you wish it, by an unearthly stillness and an electrifying watchfulness. In the best sense, you are uncomfortable company, as I suspect Smiley is.' An audience wishes, 'when you wish it – to take you into its protection. It feels responsible for you, it worries about you.' When either Smiley or Guinness 'gets their feet wet', he said, 'I can't help shivering'. Smiley, he observed is 'an abbey, made up of different periods, fashions and even different religions, not all of them necessarily harmonious'. Smiley becomes indeed a metaphor for the nation, he is 'a guilty man, as all men are who insist on action'.[99] Guinness would be the perfect vehicle for Smiley's solitude, moral concern, humanity. The letter talked of religion, and Nietzsche.

Guinness agreed to meet them to discuss the project, suggesting the Mirabelle restaurant (where he said he usually lunched when in London). Powell, consumed with excitement, coup in hand, rushed down to MacDonald, who promptly told him that he could not take anybody, not even the most distinguished actor of his generation, to lunch at the Mirabelle on licence fee-payers' money. They went to the Etoile in Charlotte Street instead. Guinness succumbed.

So began the extraordinary process of creating Smiley: Guinness took the excellent scripts by Hopcroft and bore down on the logic of performing them. 'I am very impressed by them – I am full of admiration for what has been done,' he said, but he felt that 'Smiley begins too weakly and too passively'. There needed to be some 'swift glimpse' of his professional authority before he starts to listen to Martindale. Powell, Guinness, Wearing and the director spent two weeks in the Connaught hotel – in a process Powell had never seen happen before. Guinness claimed that he could not memorise long scripts any more, so ruthlessly savaged the script: 'in a way the shooting plan was made – Guinness was extraordinary – inhabiting the rooms and corridors of the script in his mind'.[100]

Tinker Tailor became a state-of-the-nation piece about destruction and loss. The poignantly lovely music by Geoffrey Burgon pitched the tone as a lament for innocence. In order to get it all approved, Powell had said it would be made conventionally in the studio, but as the project gained status he knew

*Alec Guinness as George Smiley: an elegiac performance
concerned with the condition of the nation*

he could bump it up to film. Guinness was encouraged to say that he could only really work in the fluid medium of film, and he had his way.

The BBC production worked very hard to get at something deeper than the 'look' of the Secret Service – researching intelligence processes that lay behind on-screen actions. Le Carré briefed the BBC, including how 'one-time' encryption pads were used based on random numbers that 'a computer can throw up till it is sick in the face'. He described MI6 files: 'Operational files are green. Green being a much used colour for intelligence documents.' In other films, secret files were always too brightly coloured. Real 'red hot files', containing top-secret material, were handwritten and with only one copy. They would be distinguished only by a small label saying something like 'To be distributed strictly according to Classification' and marked perhaps 'Guard', 'Whitehall code for "Do Not Show to Americans"'.[101]

Le Carré had invented a jargon – 'lamplighters' and the 'circus' – that infiltrated the world of spies. Later, he distinguished between reality and his narratives: 'The disciplines require that I shape out of the monotony and everyday life of espionage something that has a beginning a middle and an end,' but 'In the authentic world, almost no espionage case is ever resolved.'

After the first episode, Brian Wenham, managing director of Television, said at the BBC Board of Management, 'part of the fascination lay in the striking similarity between "The Circus" and the BBC'.[102] Presumably he was referring to the conspiracies and deceits, the rise and fall of competing barons. Perhaps it was also the sense of a beleaguered moral code, or indeed the BBC's feeling at that moment that it represented something of the nation against the odds. He might have been referring to the Corporation's own heritage of spying. Le Carré said that he used BBC Monitoring reports as source material, and of course there were the World Service spies, and Guy Burgess, who had worked for the BBC – twice. Smiley's tortuous dealings with Whitehall and ministers may have seemed familiar. Certainly the traffic of files and humdrum bureaucratic record with which Smiley painstakingly unravelled the treachery were Corporation tradecraft too.[103]

But Wenham may have recognised something more basic in the programme. John Irving, the director, had been a documentary maker and brought a hunger for veracity to the series. Much filming was done in the winter (expensively, as the days were shorter and less filming could be done) to capture the dying light.[104] But Irving was also worried about what Secret Service buildings looked like, asking whether he could get into any to see. There was no need, said le Carré. The dusty offices, the corridors, the elderly office furniture and even the anxiously cranking lifts of MI5 felt like, looked like and had some of the same kinds of people – as the BBC.[105]

13

ENDGAME

ALL BBC CRISES have an 'element of St Sebastian', said a great BBC enabler, Mark Damazer, who had become editor of *Newsnight* in 1986. 'There is nothing to be done but endure the arrows.' Emergencies tested the BBC's constitution to destruction, because the external onslaught was relentless. Within the BBC, they provoked nervous breakdowns and latent civil war as Corporation barons clashed. Then, as a matter of honour, BBC news would savage the Corporation. There was no training for such a conflagration. They were 'without rules' and, as the BBC was a 'dissenting place',[1] it leaked. The tools of horse trading used, for example, by politicians were useless. The pace was pushed by merciless press hostility. The BBC made good copy with its combination of celebrities, political misdemeanours and popularity. Margaret Thatcher's power was at its zenith when Ben Pimlott wrote in the *New Statesman*, 'This is a government, and above all a prime minister, that now believes it can break any convention, dispatch any sacred cow to the abattoir, with absolute impunity. In the present mood of exuberant iconoclasm, change has become an end in itself.'[2] Pimlott had seen the importance of the Thatcher revolution – but said that, by the late 1980s, it was 'entering its Maoist phase'. The new radicalism was sundering the previous compact between industry and the state; it was called 'privatisation' but was grander (and perhaps less intentional) than that. If the unthinkable was possible, perhaps the BBC – an industry with a relationship to the state – could also be dispatched?

The real threat was ideological exhaustion: the intellectual case for the BBC had frayed. It did not defend its values convincingly, and could not defend its management style. Public service, impartiality, quality, fairness and independence were priceless, but in the new climate simply asserting them was no answer to the evangelical belief, shared by the Thatcher and Reagan governments, in market competition as the only guarantee of freedom. In 1987, in the USA, the Fairness Doctrine which had guaranteed political balance in broadcast news was abolished in the name of 'freedom of choice'. It wrecked the mighty machines of American news, CBS, NBC, and responsible broadcast news across the USA. In order to avoid this fate, the BBC would need to think strategically about its legitimacy.

By the 1980s, an inevitably fallible organisation felt, at the centre, near meltdown. 'Things are so bad at the BBC', said John Cleese, 'that they are stabbing each other in the front these days.' Externally, it was 'everyone's Aunt Sally';[3] internally, there was trench warfare between the governors and management. Michael Grade said the director-general's office 'was like a guarded fortress'. David Holmes, the BBC Secretary from 1983 to 1985, said, 'In any normal sense, the BBC was not, by 1984, actually managed at all.'[4] The BBC was 'sick', said Hodgson, who came later. There had been a 'change of culture in the nation', and 'the BBC was out of step and antagonistic to it'. The BBC was not a venal place: salaries were modest, although there was a reek of a sense of entitlement, and expenses could be too high. It was 'corrupt in a different way', said Hodgson. People treated it as a 'fiefdom for their prejudices. They couldn't see that the nation might want something different, and that a perfectly reasonable alternative view to their own existed.'[5]

Of course, the BBC had just created *EastEnders*, remade all of Shakespeare, and demonstrated its journalistic integrity by employing Charles Wheeler, and the World Service was recognised as having the best understanding of the emergence of the Solidarity movement in Poland of any international news organisation. That was brilliant achievement, not failure. The Corporation was various. Yet ultimately, it depended on the coherence at the top.

BBC managers in the 1980s had little sense of 'collegiality', viewing all 'negotiations as zero-sum games', observed John Tusa, who joined the Board of Management in 1986 as director of the World Service. An attempt to make the World Service available domestically was absurdly crushed because it would increase competition with the BBC's domestic radio stations. *Newsnight* was left without a fixed place in the schedules. Collaboration between the early pilots for BBC World TV and a domestic 24-hours news channel was killed off. BBC1 and BBC2 fought each other. The reorganisation of Radio 3 and the Proms was delayed. BBC managers operated out of 'splendid silos' and controllers 'defended their bailiwicks, and never joined together to consider whether there was a better way of doing things', said Tusa.[6] The governors, who had none of the necessary skills, began to behave as if they were running the BBC. Neither governors nor Board of Management discussed the ideas that were transforming the nation. It had become 'a two-track place', said Grade. There were the people making programmes and sorting schedules, and the people 'somewhere else having rows'. The whole machine of 'referring up' difficult issues happened in the wrong place and at the wrong time – after a programme was made. By then 'you had got yourself into a terrible muddle', said Grade.[7] Once a programme was finished its makers were likely to regard any intervention as censorship, which by then it was.

*Douglas Hurd with Lech Walesa, the leader of Solidarity, in 1989.
Walesa said, 'The BBC World Service was our lifeline to the world'*

MILNE AND THE CHAIRMEN

Milne's appointment as director-general in 1982 had seemed so positive. 'The first ever professional broadcaster to get to the top,' said Alwyn Roberts, the governor for Wales, a guardian of public service values.

Milne was from the last generation of an extraordinary thread of British public life, which regarded service all over the British Empire as a natural destiny. Like William Beveridge and George Orwell, he was born in India, an 'imperial orphan', sent home to Edinburgh after a brother died. He did not see his father until he was five. Coming from the periphery, such families wanted to be in charge at the centre. Milne was at his best dealing with India, where the Corporation had a vast audience. He dealt adeptly with Indira Gandhi's attacks on the BBC and invested in reporting that connected the two nations more closely.[8] This careful fostering of relationships with the world's largest democracy, which served British national interests, was absurdly destroyed by his successors in the name of efficiency.

Milne was proud of his Winchester scholarship, proud of current affairs cleverness and proud of the BBC. But that justifiable pride had to be translated into terms that convinced others. He had created programmes that made television into an art. He was a gifted manager of creative people. 'Warm-hearted under a prickly exterior', said Joan Bakewell,[9] he could be compassionate, touching and, when on form, clever, particular, impressive and authoritative. But he could also be abrupt, impatient and rude. He disposed of Aubrey Singer and Dick Francis awkwardly (perhaps because he found it so hard), failed to protect able producers like John Gau, and failed to back people up. With such a mercurial temperament, it was as if the electric current of 'being Alasdair' broke down on occasions. One visit to the World Service left people demoralised, he seemed so uninvolved; the next he was tremendous, far-seeing, encouraging. He stood up for the BBC, which he loved, in a harsh political environment, but failed to grasp fundamental problems within it. Marmaduke Hussey said he 'understood how to make programmes – but didn't understand people; the last person you'd choose to run a big organisation in a hostile climate'. He was at his best sparkling and sparring with Anthony Jay, the incomparable writer of *Yes Minister* and *Yes Prime Minister*. Milne fostered both series with an unerring eye. But he had a short attention span, no stomach for the patient talking round of his boards, no appetite for papers: 'you always knew when you had lost Alasdair ... he took a shoe off'.[10]

What did a director-general have to do? Michael Checkland said, 'Make sure that public money is well spent and demonstrate it, relate to his governors and his chairman, get the right programmes made, think about the long term, get the right people with real ability in the right places and make sure new talent is being brought on, sort issues before they get out of control, deal with mistakes fast, articulate a decent reason why the BBC ought to exist.'[11] Once Milne lost the capacity to appoint the people he needed, because the governors distrusted him, power drained away. He was managing very little of what he needed to.

Although he had always wanted to be director-general, Milne did not know what to do with the position when he got it. He had arrived as controller in Scotland with a masterly vision and had brilliantly delivered it. Yet he seemed to have no plan as director-general. He was bored, uneasy, missing the buzz of Lime Grove. 'Like a caged animal, pacing around Broadcasting House, he longed to escape.' He refused to look at the audience complaints that arrived in his office, even though all previous directors-general had seen them as a useful early-warning system. He went on a tour of the regions with Sheila, a 'good DG's wife, not pompous, kind, clever, his rock', and heartened them all.[12] But there he appeared as chief among his own tribe – programme makers.

The times were wolfish. One reason for the internal BBC incapacity to deal with the crises was that the new free market radicals saw impartial and independent institutions as opposed to them. The times were challenging for the monarchy, the Anglican Church, the arts and the civil service, as well as for the BBC. Although the Conservative government had calmed the licence-fee frenzy and extended its Charter, Margaret Thatcher 'did not like the BBC because she thought that it did not like her', said Douglas Hurd. Hurd believed she 'was strong-minded but confused over broadcasting. She wanted Lawson's free market, thought that the licence fee was morally wrong and intellectually disapproved of it'. However, she also wanted to be able to command broadcasting to kick-start a social and industrial revolution by providing content for cable and satellite TV as the Trojan horse for a revolution in commerce. It never worked. Hurd went on, 'She knew that she didn't want a "state" broadcaster, but she did want control of the content.'[13] It was a muddle.

John Cole, the BBC's wise political correspondent, whose rich Northern Irish accent distinguished him from the metropolitan BBC, endowing both with enhanced authority, wrote in *The Listener* that 'working journalists' saw the governors as 'shock absorbers'. It was an honourable role. 'The existence of governors interposed between politicians and broadcasters is what makes the BBC a *public service* broadcasting organisation, rather than a *state* one.'[14] Mrs Thatcher said, 'My view of the Boards of Public Bodies is that they are there to do things, not represent things.'[15] She believed that the governors had gone native on the BBC, so she tore up the traditional compact. Previous informal conversations between government and the BBC about suitable governors ended abruptly. All governments had wanted friends on the board, but had sought political balance. The BBC needed critical, able, independent governors from all sides of politics. Now there was a change in principle. George Howard was sent by the board of governors to tell William Whitelaw that the next chairman ought to be the liberal Mark Bonham Carter, who had just produced a careful report on broadcasting in Northern Ireland. He came back beaming and said: 'It's going to be me!' Whitelaw thought Howard would be more acceptable in No. 10. Howard was a resolute defender of the BBC, but 'had no method', said Trethowan. The BBC depended on the canniness of its directors-general and relied on having a chairman of the governors who could hold their own council, yet be in touch with the political temper of the times, and manage the board. The relationships between these bodies were crucial. The governors chose the director-general and the government chose the chairman. It was moreover governed by a Royal Charter, which gave it added independence. Although the governors and the chairman were in some constitutional sense 'the BBC', who was in charge?

Yet some of what Milne called the 'foul contagion' (by which he meant opposition to him) was really the infection of a corrosive dissembling at the top of the BBC, some of which was nevertheless beyond the Corporation's control. William Rees-Mogg, the vice-chairman, despite his background in news, was vindictively hostile to the BBC. Howard, despite his valiant willingness 'to literally sweat out the case' for the BBC in front of aggressive MPs, and despite his direct line to Whitelaw (going back to a brave war record in Burma), presented two problems that the BBC had somehow to manage: money and sex. The Corporation had never encountered such problems in a chairman before, although 'creativity' around expenses was rife throughout Fleet Street.

'Dealing with his expenses was a constant nightmare,' said David Holmes. He wanted programmes made and meetings held at Castle Howard. He shouted down a proposal to centralise expenses that had been deliberately designed to rein him in. A widower, he was determined to take anyone he wanted on BBC business trips. At the Montreux film festival, Michael Bunce, the head of press, went up to Howard's suite to get it ready for thirty-five journalists who were to interview the chairman about BBC successes. With minutes to go before the press arrived, Bunce had to bundle underwear and a young woman out of the room.[16] BBC managers had to manage, muffle, absorb this behaviour. Why didn't they stop it? It was partly the times, which were more deferential, partly that feminism was transforming but had not yet transformed expectations, partly that Howard was grand and so well connected. It was corrosive.

The next chairman was Thatcher's own: Stuart Young was a successful businessman, whose brother David was in cabinet, and who had originally been in favour of funding the BBC by advertising. He became a passionate BBC advocate, but was not used to the delicate political business of chairing boards. He had robust rows with Checkland, but they trusted each other. Checkland had successfully seen off a Norman Foster building planned by Milne and Howard for the Langham site opposite the BBC. 'A massive landmark project, which those of us in television were moody about. We wanted the money to go into programmes.'[17] As chairman, Young was a courteous, proper man, 'no knuckler down to No. 10 or any minister'.[18] Within a fortnight, he had written Milne a note: 'Dear Alasdair, We cannot go on like this. Yours, Stuart.' Soon after, he was diagnosed with cancer. Often in pain, he was courageous, yet disturbed by the sense that 'things were going wrong within him'.[19] Milne could be warm and intuitive: 'if Stuart was in pain or worried then great waves of support would flow out of Alasdair'.[20] These moments of rapport never lasted long.

MAGGIE'S MILITANT TENDENCY

Yet what looked like a landslide of crises about programmes was really about how the BBC handled problems. At the end of January 1984, Michael Cockerell was tweaking the script for the last cut of a *Panorama* called 'Maggie's Militant Tendency'. Ever more laconic as he added words to pictures with deadlines approaching, Cockerell was a great public service reporter, whose mischievous and patrician understanding of the chemical interaction between personality and politics was to hold the British political system to account, and keep the public gripped, for decades. He was part of a gang, including Tom Bowyer and Tom Mangold, who had worked on *24 Hours*. They shared a magnificently irreverent relationship to power. The BBC lawyer, Glenn del Medico, had been called in from a children's birthday party to view the rough cut of the programme on the previous Sunday. He had talked about it with them earlier,

Michael Cockerell in 1978: always asking what made the powerful tick

challenged evidence and cut several questions out of the film. Peter Ibbotson, the editor of *Panorama*, says that earlier he had taken out allegations made in the programme, because he was insecure about the identity of the sources.[21] Together, del Medico and Ibbotson reviewed the programme and asked for a further recut.[22]

The programme revealed the views of, and associations between, right-wing groups clustered around the Conservative Party. But it went too far. The catchy title was misleading: whatever their connections, they did not add up to a dedicated entryist organisation like the real Militant Tendency, which was trying to subvert the Labour Party from the inside. The broader idea was defensible, however. There certainly was a group of right-wing MPs who were defined by their social rather than economic opinions. Harvey Proctor, one of the MPs discussed in the programme, had won a surprise election victory in 1979, having argued for a reduction in the number of 'coloured' immigrants. He was chairman of the right-wing Monday Club's Immigration and Repatriation Committee (later renamed, under him, the Immigration and Race Relations Committee). He opposed the Anglo-Irish Agreement and voted for the return of capital punishment.

Neil Hamilton was a colourful MP. He was shown in the film giving a Nazi salute. But this later turned out to be a joke as he was apparently 'messing around' on a 1983 trip to Berlin.[23] Hamilton lost his seat to the former BBC correspondent Martin Bell in the 1997 election over 'sleaze', having been accused of taking cash for parliamentary questions, and he also lost the ensuing libel case.[24] *That's Life* had already drawn attention to the fee he had received for supporting (a potentially cancer-forming) chewable tobacco in Parliament.

The third man named, Gerald Howarth, 'was a respectable, standard right-wing MP'.[25] He had been filmed attending a vintage rail enthusiasts' meeting in Didcot, where everyone was cheerily sporting railway uniforms and hats. He had also, when a young man, attended a right-wing rally in Italy. The programme ran a clip of him in railway uniform with a line of text that said that he had been to a fascist rally, implying that the film was recent evidence of this. It had not occurred to Ibbotson (who was new to *Panorama*) to interrogate the origin of the clip when he reviewed the film; he read it as evidence of attendance at a rally.

John Gummer, a reformist chairman of the Conservative Party, who had himself initiated an inquiry into right-wing groups and the party because he was anxious about them, was interviewed live on the programme by an oddly detached Fred Emery. Gummer said 'it felt like being Agatha Christie', as he itemised what he said were the programme's seventeen errors and emphasised that there was no evidence for any kind of entryism. Calling himself a 'one nation' Conservative, he said later that the BBC 'is one of the great, enduring British achievements – and makes the world better'. He added, the 'exposure of obnoxious people is an entirely proper part of political decency. I applaud the BBC's work on this.' But he said that the film had edited clips carelessly (muddying the reputation of one of the MPs by using his mother's political affiliations) – claims the programme makers deny. Gummer was 'absolutely furious' at one of the edits, which apparently showed an enthusiastic response to a speech by Harvey Proctor, but had used shots taken from a speech by Gummer: 'It was MY audience – not his!' Most seriously, the way in which the BBC 'prevaricated and handled the complaints was dishonest'.[26]

The MPs sued for libel. Anthony Jennings, the BBC lawyer, Alan Protheroe, Milne and Margaret Douglas, his political adviser, looked at the film, understood that some of the detail seemed 'insecure ... although the wider story was an important one'.[27] They looked at it in a rose-tinted-spectacles kind of way – substituting hopes for hard scrutiny. But of course Jennings was still assuring them that the case would be won in court. Yet in March, Milne told the governors that although there had been 'questions of taste and style' the evidence stood up and he backed the programme.[28] Researchers for the programme were pursuing further evidence in Italy[29] and among Conservative MPs who had been on the trip with Hamilton.[30] 'They kept telling us that there would be clinching material,' said Protheroe, 'but it melted away.'[31] Milne repeatedly assured the governors that the evidence was 'bomb-proof'. Asked later whether everything in the film was true, he replied it was, except for two minor details.[32] Milne was defending the wider story yet obfuscating the problems. More damagingly, in effect he was misleading the governors about how he was dealing with the issue – which was to prevaricate. But he still believed that clinching evidence was coming in.

But there was dissembling all around. As Milne failed to get things through the governors, he tried to avoid them, which meant *they* suspected conspiracy even where there was none. As some programme makers suspected interference, *they* tried to avoid management scrutiny. Generally, Trethowan had said some in Current Affairs were '22 carat shits'. Birt said 'they misunderstood who had the right to decide what was broadcast: it was a fundamental error'.[33] Then the governors intended to sack Milne, but did not act for three years. People knew that he was doomed, but it was never mentioned. Although important and good programmes were being made, few people at the top of the BBC were being frank with each other, and work and relationships were insidiously undermined by distrust. The plan discussed between Milne, Jennings, Douglas and Protheroe was to keep the libel case going through the courts as long as possible, partly on the grounds that the BBC could outspend the MPs as their legal costs mounted,[34] but equally because they hoped the research would unearth more material.[35] Hodgson said that they saw this as having the added advantage of forestalling attempts by the MPs to go to the Broadcasting Complaints Commission (BCC). The Commission mechanism offered free redress and would (lethally, she thought) have examined the film footage scrupulously, but it could not consider complaints that were *sub judice* to the libel case. This too was expected to prolong the case until it withered away. As the composition of the governors changed, however, it was also suspected that evidence from meetings was being leaked by governors to press opponents of the BBC. Meanwhile, Ibbotson and Cockerell were told that pressure was being applied to witnesses;[36] Milne was told they were being 'bought off or bullied'.[37]

Hodgson, as a quite humble deputy secretary, minuted both boards, but was also the liaison with the BCC for the Corporation. She was instructed not to take a minute at several management meetings at which the BBC's approach was planned. She thought that Milne and Protheroe were consciously misdirecting the governors, trying to 'price the MPs out of the market', which might ruin Howarth's reputation and finances – despite knowing that the basis of his complaint was correct. Privately dismayed, but neither part of the inner sanctum, nor near enough to the programme makers to affect matters, she consulted her own senior and well-connected solicitor. He told her to wait for the case to reach the courts. Meanwhile, Hamilton personally assured Michael Heseltine and Gummer that all the allegations against him were a BBC conspiracy against the Conservative Party. Hamilton and his wife came into the BBC and 'ranted at the DG'.[38]

Norman Tebbit, who in October 1984 was heart-wrenchingly extracted from the ruins of the Grand Hotel in Brighton after the IRA bombing, his desperately injured wife beside him (under TV lights borrowed from the BBC),[39] brought Young 55 complaints against the programme. Young questioned Protheroe and Milne, and again they assured him both in private and publicly in meetings that the BBC's evidence was watertight, that more evidence was coming in and that the case would be won in court.

Young's position was special, because at the heart of the programme was an allegation of anti-Semitism in the Conservative Party. Young and his brother were prominent Conservatives, and Young was the first Jewish chairman of the BBC. Grade, who met Young frequently outside the BBC, said that the chairman had his own sources on the story, and would get 'a phone call each week' from the Jewish Board of Deputies and his Israeli contacts, assuring him that the programme was right: 'when he wavered they would secure him again'.[40] Young was convinced that the general argument of the programme was correct but did not appreciate the problems with how the television story was told. Milne said, 'we were confident he backed the story: he was with us on this one'. So while Milne and Protheroe had lost the trust of the Board of Governors, 'who had become very panicky', they felt that ultimately they had the personal, solid backing of the chairman.[41] Indeed, the BBC's plan seemed to be working, as the libel case quietly rumbled on and disappeared from view. Then, in 1985, the *Real Lives* crisis erupted. This was an entirely different problem.

REAL LIVES

Paul Hamann's innovative documentary probed the psyche of extremism within the normality of Northern Ireland. Hamann was a subtle, responsible programme maker, trusted by officials. Earlier, the Northern Ireland Office had agreed to 'give him any assistance' to make a programme on the SAS, after an official 'spoke to Mr. Hamann and considers him to be an intelligent and objective producer who knows Northern Ireland, the political situation, the police and the army well'.[42] *Real Lives* showed Sinn Fein's Martin McGuinness and the Democratic Unionist Gregory Campbell at home with their children. Within Northern Ireland, it represented a BBC achievement, in bringing local audiences to a level of maturity where they accepted the insights of such programmes. *Real Lives* was 'elegiac like a David Lean movie'.[43] It was an essay in alternative child-rearing models: McGuinness looked like a middle-class affectionate father; Campbell was from a different style of Unionist propriety. Both were teetotal, loving parents who hated each other, and were sworn enemies of each other's communities.

Jimmy Hawthorne, the director of the BBC in Northern Ireland, had passed it without even warning Lucy Faulkner, the Northern Ireland BBC governor, as he saw no problem with a programme that was 'normal' in Northern Ireland, within the law, within the BBC's guidelines, and gave a 'fair if chilling insight' into men who were elected representatives. But this was to misread the febrile atmosphere around Northern Ireland, with politicians in Britain under constant physical threat. It was to miscalculate the values of the London-based press nosing around the BBC, knowing that Conservative hostility to the Corporation was high. Barrie Penrose of the *Sunday Times* was writing an article on the BBC and Northern Ireland, and had alerted the home secretary, Leon Brittan, and Bernard Ingham at No. 10 to the programme. He needed a quote from Mrs Thatcher, who had recently made a speech saying that broadcasters must starve 'terrorists of the oxygen of publicity'. She was in America, so it was arranged to ask her a hypothetical question about her view of a television interview of an IRA chief of staff (which McGuinness is said to have been). She said that 'she would condemn it utterly'. The *Sunday Times* had a scoop. When No. 10 phoned the BBC demanding to know about 'an interview with a terrorist', it took hours to even find out what programme they were talking about.

Then Leon Brittan changed the terms of the row by publishing a letter saying the programme was too dangerous to broadcast. Brittan said that an interview with an 'apologist' for the 'murder and maiming of innocent people' would cause 'profound distress' and 'materially assist the terrorist cause'. What had started as a controversy about a programme was changed by what Milne called 'Brittan's wretched letter'[44] into an unprecedented confrontation between the BBC and the government over a heartland issue of Corporation independence. The Corporation replied sharply that 'the home secretary appeared to have been seeking to shift the constitutional position towards an acceptance of his right to influence BBC decisions'.[45] All governments possessed the right to direct the BBC to show some things and prohibit it from showing others. This large, looming power was written into the Charter and licence, but only to cover the exceptional circumstances of the transition to war, and it was so powerful it had never been used since World War II. Indeed, behind the scenes civil servants had been busy repudiating attempts to use some version of it over Northern Ireland for over a decade. The Broadcasting Ban imposed in 1988 was in part a pragmatic, vague, ridiculous reinterpretation of it designed to stave off the far more damaging imposition of this right.[46]

Brittan (who was busy defending the BBC elsewhere) backed off, saying the letter expressed a 'personal view', not an official attempt to widen the scope of his formal powers. As he had said that the programme raised issues of national security, however, the governors agreed they should call an emergency meeting. Milne was away in Sweden. Young had been to the opera the previous evening with his brother and Mark Bonham Carter, who had braced his resolution to make sure the programme was shown. Young told Barlow as he left his office to chair the meeting that 'he knew what he had to do'.[47] Most governors began the meeting assuming they would decide that *Real Lives* should be shown. Because of the security dimension, however, they broke the strong convention that they ought never to *pre*view a programme.

Watching it collectively produced an unnatural mood. Tutting, the governors reacted with disapproval. Rather than concluding that its topic was unsettling, they worked themselves into a state of righteous indignation and decided that the programme itself was wrong. David Holmes, BBC Secretary at the time, said that the governors found it hard to divorce themselves from their subjective view of programmes and stand back professionally. 'You need to say I am offended, upset, disagree with this programme but in the interests of public service broadcasting, the nation and public information, I would support it.'[48] Alwyn Roberts defended it perceptively, saying that *Real Lives* was educative: 'It showed us that we don't need all the good guys to wear white hats and all the baddies black hats. My confidence in parliamentary democracy depends on a better-informed electorate that discriminates and can bear complexity. The BBC was there to turn crude views into better-informed ones.'[49]

After coffee, William Rees-Mogg broke another convention that the vice-chairman would speak last, summing up the views expressed in the room. Instead, he spoke first and fanned self-righteous collective dismay. He began the discussion with waspish hostility. (Sloboda asked him at a dinner, 'Do you actually like the BBC?' He never answered.) He said *Real Lives* was 'vile propaganda for the IRA'.[50] Faulkner, who had formally just retired, said that it 'was a kind of Hitler-loved-dogs programme', and the governors refused to take advice from any BBC expert on Northern Ireland. The venomous distrust between the governors and BBC managers set a tone. In this case, entirely mistakenly, they saw it as a duplicitous attempt to get something past them. Daphne Park, a doughty, pugnacious governor, who had been the most senior woman ever in MI6, said the 'programme makers had not behaved properly'. They decided that the programme should not be broadcast. It was a misjudgement. When the decision was announced, the press mauled the BBC for being intimidated.

When Milne returned, he told the governors that journalists interpreted their decision as an infringement of BBC independence and that the Board of Management had agreed that the programme must be broadcast. Yet, remarkably, he admitted that the BBC was 'out of control in many respects'. Young told him that if he 'wanted to state publicly that he believed *Real Lives* should be broadcast, that would be a "resignation statement or a firing statement"'. The governors said that, because management in Northern Ireland had not referred the programme up to the director-general's office as required by guidelines, it could not be broadcast. At the centre of the storm, Milne wrote a luminous exposition of the role of the BBC: 'In all programme matters, we all seek the truth in a forthright and even-handed manner, that is the BBC tradition. It transcends and overrides the particular views of any member of staff. It transcends any external pressures. It transcends the attitudes of any Board of Management or any Board of Governors.'

For the first time, all BBC journalists came out on strike on a matter of principle, and they were joined by most journalists from commercial TV and radio news. It showed how important the BBC was to British journalism. But it made dealing with the problems that had caused the *Real Lives* crisis worse. Later in the year, the programme was broadcast after minor changes that Milne called 'additions', and Young called 'amendments'. Brittan later said, 'The BBC should have been more confident, not so anxious about politics the whole time.'[51]

The roof did not fall in. It was a model of public service journalism. Meanwhile, Brittan had been replaced as home secretary by Hurd, who went out of his way in a speech in Cambridge to be positive about the programme and indeed the work of Hawthorne, who, a dedicated public servant, was heartbroken about the row, and had resigned. Hurd visited the BBC privately, and fences were mended.[52] The governors had already decided that Milne should go when Young became chairman, but any decision could not be formally made for at least a year after the *Real Lives* crisis, as it would look as if the BBC were submitting to pressure. To those at the centre of the dispute, the disagreement had been at least a principled one. Roberts said it was 'honourable – it may have gone the wrong way but it was about serious principles', unlike the 'Maggie's Militant Tendency' libel case, which 'was crawling disreputably along'.

Other rows broke out like wildfire. Before *Real Lives*, a young researcher, Allan Little, had no reply to an invitation to Gerry Adams to appear on *Open to Question*, a programme in which Scottish teenagers interrogated a figure in public life. As the scandal broke, Danny Morrison from Sinn Fein headquarters telexed to accept the invitation. 'All hell broke loose,' said Little. The tabloids alleged that the BBC was letting a murderer indoctrinate schoolchildren. Protheroe told the controller of BBC Scotland, 'there is an easy answer – sack the researcher and issue a statement blaming him'. Pat Chalmers, the decent controller, refused to cover management's backs unjustly at the expense of a junior.[53] Little had behaved scrupulously and kept his job.

Real Lives was accompanied by a controversy over BBC coverage of the divisive miners' strike – when men from an historic craft led like lemmings over the cliff immolated themselves, threatened national order, and were often punished unjustly. It was followed by an avoidable row about *The Monocled Mutineer*, World War I fiction dressed as fact, and a noisy fracas over a play about Mrs Thatcher during the Falklands War, by Ian Curteis, who claimed that the BBC was biased against patriotism.[54] There was also a scandal about a programme in the *Rough Justice* series that got an innocent man out of jail, but had, the judge said, interviewed the key witness in a misleading way. Then a series about the 'Secret Society' alarmed the governors. Park, a suspicious guardian of the secret state, was outraged. The chairman said the question 'was not the political views of Duncan Campbell [the presenter] but his declared belief that anything secret should be exposed'.[55] Milne floundered; again Protheroe tried to blame Chalmers. Later, BBC offices in Scotland were raided over an episode on the use of computer surveillance; it was called the Zircon affair. The BBC was punch drunk with crises.

Meanwhile, to add to the gaiety of nations, the Conservative MP Winston Churchill introduced a Private Member's Bill to bring the BBC under the provisions of the 1959 Obscene Publications Act. Loudly backed by Mrs Thatcher, who trooped through the 'Yes' lobby for the Bill's second reading, it proposed restrictions on broadcasters that the Lord Chamberlain had long abandoned in theatres. At a public meeting at BAFTA, David Attenborough said that every day a praying mantis committed all of the itemised behaviours the Bill proposed to prohibit – and *ate* its mate. The Bill would be the end of natural history programmes. It was defeated.

THE PEACOCK REPORT

In the middle of the mayhem, the Conservative government moved a threatening tank on to the BBC's lawn. The Peacock Committee was to look at the case for replacing the licence fee with advertising revenue, seen as the first step in the dismemberment of the Corporation. Advertising had been known to be the prime minister's favourite answer to bringing the disciplines of the market to the Corporation.[56] The incomparable Sam Brittan, at the height of his authority as an impeccably 'dry' economic commentator, but a man of great humanity, was a decisive member of the Committee. He saw the BBC as a national institution in the way that an individual newspaper was not. This special and valuable place led to the 'vitriol' and 'feeling' which characterised politicians' reactions to the BBC. Brittan thought 'that the idea of a national broadcasting corporation whose every deed and every saying was a matter for the Cabinet and for high political talk … belonged to *1984*', and in the light of this Orwellian insight his 'immediate objective was how to depoliticise relations between Government and the BBC'.[57] Leon Brittan, the home secretary (and Sam's brother), had said that he meant 'the committee to interpret their brief very widely'. This sounded dangerous. Another member was Peter Jay, the author, with John Birt, of an influential proposition that broadcast news had a 'bias against understanding'.[58]

Sir Alan Peacock,[59] the chairman, had been a pioneer of liberal economics long before they were fashionable, and had done much to train a more open-minded generation of government economists. But, despite a particular interest in the economics of the arts,[60] he had little interest in what the BBC actually did, saying that 'making programmes was utterly irrelevant' to their deliberations. Alastair Hetherington (who was a BBC 'deep throat' on the Committee) told Janet Morgan that 'he had been cut short by the Professor' when he asked about the effect proposals might have on the news, the arts and music.[61] Hurd told the prime minister that Peacock's interpretations of the concept of public service 'appear to exclude the whole of Radios 1 and 2, but include Radios 3 and 4, which Professor Peacock enjoys'.[62]

The Peacock Committee found Milne offhand, unconvincing and arrogant, when he appeared before them. He was resistant to practising in advance,[63] stumbled in the rehearsal,[64] and when asked how much of the BBC's output could be described as public service broadcasting gave what may have appeared to him the satisfyingly succinct answer: 'All of it'. It was probably the worst answer he could have given. His colleagues were in despair.[65] The first on a list of 27 questions the Committee wished the BBC to consider was an equally terse invitation for him to expand on this.[66] He thought he had been polite,[67] and probably felt bullied, but it seemed to epitomise an ostrich-like refusal in the BBC to realistically consider economic and political developments.

However, behind the scenes, the BBC had brought institutional intelligence to bear on understanding the problem. Brian Wenham, a close personal friend of Peacock member Peter Jay, chaired the response with great wit and forensic thinking, and Milne helpfully told them to commission some 'genuinely' independent work.[68]

Wenham was a subtle, able man, with a sardonic turn of mind. Typically he gave the Committee a nickname, 'The Magnificent Seven'.[69] He saw the challenge as 'an interesting intellectual problem', about which the BBC had opinions, but had not tested the arguments.[70] Andrew Ehrenberg and Paddy Barwise at the London Business School were told to research the feasibility of funding the BBC by advertising. Their work showed that putting advertising on the BBC would not only squeeze revenue for the commercial companies but, more unexpectedly, the overall investment in advertising would decline – more advertising space would lead to a decrease in advertising spending.[71]

Their research was empirically founded and theoretically sophisticated and convinced the Committee, which dismissed the question of funding the BBC by advertising in the first section of its report – despite that being the main reason it had been set up. The BBC work was backed up by even gloomier evidence from elsewhere about the consequences of the Corporation carrying advertising.[72] Furthermore, Peacock depoliticised the argument about the licence fee by recommending that it be indexed on an annual basis to the general rate of inflation – an olive branch that Hurd, by now home secretary, had agreed, but which Milne had bizarrely turned down.

The Peacock Report did what the Corporation had been unable to do for itself: refreshed the legitimacy of the idea of the BBC. But Wenham and his team had helped the report get there. In a tour de force of argument, the report re-engineered a convincing case for the economic rationale of public service broadcasting. Although it was interested in the long-term 'free market of subscription', it said that in the immediate conditions of imperfect competition, public service broadcasting compensated for market failure by delivering programmes that the market could not. Even large, popular programmes with public service values fell into this category. The Peacock Report marked a decisive moment in the Corporation's survival and success for the next twenty years. Checkland was flooded with relief when he saw it: 'Maynard Keynes once said, "In the long run we are all dead." When I read the report, I knew we were fine … yes, something was due to happen in twenty years – well, lots might happen in twenty years.'[73] Sam Brittan said in exasperation, 'Somebody had to save the BBC!'[74]

A NEW CHAIRMAN

Young returned from China with cancer 'racing through him', said Hodgson, now Secretary. By 1986, with the chairman mortally ill, and with two of the most experienced governors, Roberts and Rees-Mogg, due to retire, she knew the governors were rudderless. She went to see Hurd, and Joel Barnett, a sharp and effective former Labour minister, was appointed vice-chairman the next day. It was a careful reopening of proper BBC relations with government. When Young died in harness, Milne knew that he was on perilous ground with the rest of the governors over 'Maggie's Militant Tendency', but was still assuming that the problem would be solved by more evidence.

Hurd wanted a chairman 'who was not a Government puppet, from outside the frame, who would listen to our complaints without feeling sacrilegious'. A chairman needed to be politically well connected. He also needed an array of skills: the capacity to apply sociable solvent to intractable problems, the ability to chair a board, an understanding of the role of journalism in a free society, a streak of ruthlessness and a dedication to public service decency. According to Hurd, William Waldegrave suggested Marmaduke Hussey, who was married to his sister, Susan. Hurd 'asked Margaret' informally, and she thought it a good idea. Hodgson said that Hussey emerged out of a discussion

Patricia Hodgson became the first woman BBC Secretary

of candidates with Brian Griffiths (head of staff in No. 10), whom she knew.[75] After a decade of relating to Mrs Thatcher, since their first meeting at the Bow Group dinner, she was trusted in No. 10. Hurd was right, Mrs Thatcher was confused about broadcasting. Yet out of the contradictory impulse, on this occasion, Hurd, Hodgson and Griffiths helped produce a chairman who would lead the BBC and inspire confidence outside. Griffiths had been to see Hussey about likely candidates and then, Hussey said, Griffiths's wife suggested that Hussey himself was the right man. Mrs Thatcher agreed.

On one extraordinary point all of the differing accounts agree: that Mrs Thatcher, before making her mind up, consulted Rupert Murdoch, who said, 'He's your man.' Mrs Thatcher may have been full of anxious proprieties about the BBC, and Hussey had worked for Murdoch, but nevertheless it was a peculiar move to seek the approval of the Corporation's most committed commercial and political enemy. Hussey became the surprise appointment.

A large, handsome man with a bluff manner artfully deployed to conceal intelligence, 'sharp as a button',[76] Hussey was Milne's nemesis. Like Milne,

Marmaduke Hussey, BBC chair of the governors

he was from a colonial family, and he had lost a leg in his first battle during World War II. He spent five years with an open wound which was expected to kill him, until a risky operation solved the problem. He bore the tension of disability with fortitude. Managing the pain gave him a belief in himself, a streak of hardness and a need to conceal his inner feelings. Once at a dinner party the foot fell off his false leg and the concerned host wondered whether he should call a doctor. Hussey replied, 'A blacksmith would be more helpful!' He had been managing director of Times Newspapers, when the print unions were holding the press hostage. In 1978, *The Times* stopped publication for a year when the printers went on strike after Hussey threatened to close unless they accepted staff cuts and flexible working hours. If his regime at *The Times* had ultimately been a failure, he had learnt much from it. Anxious to make his appointment credible across the party divide, Hussey went to see Harold Lever, the immensely clever and fabulously rich Labour peer who had been a key economic adviser to successive Labour governments. Lever lived in Eaton Square, with a priceless collection of modern art and a beautiful Lebanese princess for a wife. He entered wearing a silk embroidered dressing gown, and waving a stick. 'Sack the man,' he said, 'do what you have to. The fucking unions are fucking up the country.'[77]

Hussey was strong and snobbish. This was his last great job and he was determined to get order into the BBC – 'the trick is to be a shit if you need to be'. He inspired affection and devotion in many. His charming wife (he had a great respect for wives in general) was a lady-in-waiting to the Queen, and together they would 'take the BBC out into the real world again: make it friends, give it confidence'. Hurd said, 'He certainly did not "behave" compliantly at all!' Hurd had a lunch with him when they agreed Milne must go. Hussey and Barnett agreed on it over another lunch.[78] No one discussed it humanely with Milne.

THE END OF MILNE

Then 'Maggie's Militant Tendency' stormed unexpectedly back on to the BBC stage. Anthony Jennings, who died in early 1986, had begun to warn the board that it ought to settle the libel case with the MPs, but Milne and Protheroe hoped to spin the case out as they believed more evidence would arrive to support the programme's claims. The MPs were demanding a 'grovelling apology'. There was a meeting at No. 10 with Ingham, Gummer and Mrs Thatcher, designed to ease the problems between the BBC and the government. But it was, Ibbotson believed, blown away by an intemperate attack on the prime minister by Robin Day, who had come with them to discuss political interviewing. Then in October, Protheroe, who had been trying to arrive at a settlement with the MPs, burst back into the BBC, from court, ashen-faced, and said, 'They are going to go all the way.' His panic showed how weak some in the BBC feared its case to be.

Jimmy Goldsmith had run what *Private Eye* called the 'Goldenballs appeal', and raised enough money for the MPs to continue their legal battle. Barnett had not even been told that the case was coming to court and learnt about it from the *Guardian*.[79] If Barnett 'expressed concern that neither he nor the chairman-designate had been consulted about developments in this case', it was Alwyn Roberts, Milne's surviving supporter on the board, who raised the real problem. 'At the time it had been broadcast, the Board had been assured that it was "fireproof" as far as the facts were concerned. Now it appeared the Board was being told it was not fireproof after all.' Milne replied that 'at the time it had been his understanding that the programme was sound', but Protheroe said some of those who had 'provided the evidence on which the programme relied were now going back on what they had said'.[80] The Corporation's case was unravelling. At the next meeting with Hussey (who had now become chairman), the governors were incandescent. They ordered the BBC to settle the case.

Hussey would have acted swiftly to sack Milne, but a loose Conservative cannon forestalled him. Norman Tebbit had attacked Kate Adie's reporting on the effects of American bombing in Libya. He argued that 'The word "conservative" is used by the BBC as a portmanteau word of abuse for anyone whose views differ from the insufferable, smug, sanctimonious, naïve, wet, pink, orthodoxy'[81] of the Corporation. Six months after the bombing, Tebbit produced a dossier of evidence, saying that the BBC's coverage was 'riddled with inaccuracy, innuendo and imbalance', and called for a review of managerial and editorial standards.[82] The press loved Tebbit, who was indeed a kind of national hero, and clamoured against the Corporation.

At first, the BBC was paralysed. Tony Byers told Adie that Tebbit had accused her of treachery at midday. Milne was in a meeting with Tebbit's evidence going through the broadcasts line by line, but no one talked to Adie. As the day wore on, there was still no BBC statement, nothing on the *Six O'Clock News*. Adie felt that news management had left her to her own devices, and she was 'going through the roof'.[83] Then Grade found her – 'What are we saying?' – and issued a strong defence of Adie, told the *Nine O'Clock News* to carry it, and sat personally fielding the incoming press calls. Meanwhile, Stephen Claypole had talked to Hussey – 'Very straight and strategic – proper sort of man,' said Hussey. (Adie called Claypole and Grade 'heroes'.)[84] The BBC responded with point-by-point rebuttals which Tebbit claimed were 'statistical gymnastics'. Hussey came out fighting, defended Adie, said the Corporation 'would not be intimidated'. It was a hiccup – but a gift to Hussey. It allowed him to stand up for the BBC in public. The crisis melted away. But it meant that he could not act on Milne.

Hodgson, who as assistant secretary had attended both boards in 1984, believed that there had been something close to an intention to misrepresent the case to the governors (the mutual distrust having risen to acute levels), combined with an intention to outspend the claimants and prolong the case.[85] By 1986, promoted to Secretary, she had different responsibilities. Any BBC Secretary had obligations both to the director-general and to the chairman, which took the form of strong personal relationships (when things were working). Milne had attempted to move her to another job. Yet the BBC Secretary also had an overriding duty to the BBC – as a kind of platonic ideal. Ultimately, they served the enduring institution – not the individuals in office. This was an example of it. She said she had 'the smoking gun', which she gave to Hussey. Milne had fumbled telling Young and the governors about what he knew of the programme but also, more damagingly, about how the Corporation was dealing with the libel case. Hussey decided that the case had to be settled fast. There was a very large out-of-court payment of nearly £1,000,000. The programme makers felt aggrieved.

Hussey and Barnett demanded formal, written replies from Milne to a list of questions. They wanted evidence of professional incompetence to avoid the charge that their move to sack Milne was politically motivated. Margaret Douglas, out of her depth, drafted reply after reply. Bill Cotton said, 'Al had been dead in the water for 18 months.' From September 1986, Tusa wrote in his diary, 'we reeled under a series of self-inflicted wounds opened up and mercilessly probed by the press who like sharks gathered around the smell of blood in the water'. Just before Christmas, there was a Board of Management dinner: 'Alasdair gave another revealing indication of his reckless attitude.' In a speech he said 'Happy Christmas', and that he intended to remain as director-general until 1990. 'There was no response, neither applause, hear, hear or anything.'[86] The Board of Managers shifted uneasily in their chairs. It was bluff, or delusion. It was tragic.

Although Milne had been living on the edge of a precipice for so long, he seemed oblivious. In December, Mrs Thatcher, he noted in his diary, 'cut' him at Stuart Young's funeral.[87] After Christmas, Hussey phoned the Secretary formally: the governors had decided to fire Milne the following Thursday, at the board meeting in the morning. Then Barnett said that would give Milne and Wenham time to go to the press, and by the afternoon it would have become a scandal all over Prime Minister's Questions (PMQs) about the Conservative government trampling over the Corporation. Barnett said that it had to be delayed until after the start of PMQs at 2.30 p.m. The sacking was meticulously planned like a coup. The night before the meeting, there was a Board of Governors dinner for Alwyn Roberts's retirement. He knew that 'Alasdair just had to go' (but knew nothing of the plan). Yet Roberts admired Milne and was touched and proud to work with him. Roberts gave an inspiring, reasoned speech, warning properly that the governors must not attempt to run the Corporation, whose duty was to make challenging programmes. It was 'immensely heartening' for embattled programme staff and offered some idealism and encouragement in a dismal time.

The next morning's meeting was surreal as the governors dallied their way through business. After lunch, Milne was brought up to Hussey's office. Hussey had a letter prepared. They offered Milne a deal – if he chose to resign he could go with honour; they would deal with his pension rights (which were not generous), and no one would be told. He was given 'no chance to talk to a lawyer, no chance to talk to anyone, no chance to consider my financial position'.[88] If he resisted, then they would make it public. They had sacked him. Hussey went into the joint meeting with the two boards and announced that Milne had resigned 'for personal reasons'. 'Why did no manager ask a question?' Tusa wrote. 'Not because we were cowed', but because 'it was both a staggering surprise and yet no surprise at all'. Sloboda wept, despite having been close to how far it was all unravelling. Sloboda and Michael Bunce arrived at Milne's house – he had come home entirely unprotected and was in

Trog's cartoon captured what many believed: Milne bought the cartoon for himself

shock. It was cruel. The BBC consumed its own – cutting off the head renewed it; that was how it survived. It was the reassertion of reality out of a fog of dissembling.

Tim Orchard was editing *Newsnight* and thought that the public should be told what the Corporation knew, that Milne (although they could not put their finger on the precise reason why) had been sacked. Needing clearance for such a risky story, he rang Robin Walsh, who asked, 'Do you have any evidence?' 'No,' said Orchard. 'Well, if you can find some, tell me and do it.' Later, Bill Cotton put his head around Orchard's door. 'Be kind,' he said. *Newsnight* ran the story: an example of the BBC and the autonomous empire of Lime Grove acting on its own. But was it the right story to carry? Surely it must have been.[89]

The next day, Bernard Ingham wrote to Milne from No. 10: 'I am anxious to express my sorrow at the unhappy turn of events … My only concern is whether I might have done more in all the circumstances to promote closer contact and understanding.' Roy Jenkins wrote, 'I have long had a high regard for your good sense and firm standards. You are the honourable casualty of dishonourable political warfare.'[90]

SURVIVAL

Many had 'saved' the BBC. The task of reforming it had begun (and it would have to be reinvented again and again). Checkland, decent, effective, became the next director-general. He was part of the answer. Hussey, a resolute, charismatic chairman, brought a new grip to the task, but was not easy for everyone to get on with. He was another part. Paul Fox, a life force, who also brought

John Birt into the BBC, Wenham (who was hardly thanked for his key role) and Hodgson, strategically accomplished: all played their part. So, surprisingly, did home secretaries and their permanent secretaries, big, experienced Whitehall players determined to protect an institution whose values they recognised as precious in bellicose times. The Corporation bustled with gifted managers: Grade, Tusa, Wyatt, Hall, Thompson, Damazar, Abramsky, Yentob, Powell, moving on and up.

In an odd way, Milne's last valiant service to the Corporation to which he had given his life was to be sacked. He gave it the capacity to alter its direction by giving it a new director-general, one of the mechanisms of public account-ability that secure its survival.

Indeed, these large, combustible affairs were only a fragment of the BBC. What mattered was its place in British lives. It was the administrators guiding the pilot ship of BBC news values out into the world from the World Service; the BBC mandarins, programme makers, journalists and thinkers who caught the mood of the nation, broke stories, gave a voice to the less powerful; who expressed the romance of news, made programmes that sparked children's imaginations, created compelling drama, made funny, delightful, challenging broadcasts which advanced rational debate; who had in their DNA the duty to inform, educate and entertain – these were the people who kept the mother ship of values in the BBC at home moving forward. In the bowels of the Corporation, clever men and women had the time of their lives.

John Birt said, 'the miracle was that in this paranoid, untrusting, ungen-erous environment the BBC still made astonishingly good programmes. The powerful creative incubus at the heart of the Corporation could not be suppressed.'[91] The BBC was still alive, busy about its work in the British consti-tution and in the lives of the British and indeed the world.

★ ★ ★

As Prospero, surveying his creature Ariel from the front of Broadcasting House, says:

> Gentle Breath of yours my sails
> Must fill, or else my project fails,
> Which was to please.

William Shakespeare, The Tempest, Act 5, Epilogue

Prospero and Ariel *by Eric Gill, 1933: presiding spirits over Broadcasting House*

APPENDIX: BBC DIRECTORS-GENERAL AND CHAIRMEN

DIRECTORS-GENERAL

1960–69 Sir Hugh Carleton Greene
1969–77 Sir Charles Curran
1977–82 Sir Ian Trethowan
1982–87 Alasdair Milne
1987–92 Sir Michael Checkland

CHAIRMEN

1967–72 Lord Hill of Luton, Charles Hill
1973–80 Lord Swann of Colne St Denis, Sir Michael Swann
1980–83 Lord Howard of Henderskelfe, George Howard
1983–86 Stuart Young
1986–96 Lord Hussey of North Bradley, Marmaduke Hussey

NOTES

Illustrative clips, a bibliography and an essay on the writing of this book can be found at bbc.co.uk/historyofthebbc.

All interviews are by the author and for this book unless otherwise stated. The author has had access to the BBC's own immensely important Oral History interviews. All cited papers are from the BBC Written Archive Centre (WAC) unless otherwise indicated. Other papers are from the National Archive Office (NAO), the Public Record Office (PRO), the Cabinet Office and university collections and private papers. N&CA is the News and Current Affairs division, CMAC is Central Music Advisory Committee, NI is Northern Ireland, BOM is Board of Management, BOG is Board of Governors, and HO is Home Office.

Reference is also made to Witness Seminars. These brought together previous participants in events discussed in the book, from within and on occasions from outside the BBC. Six seminars were organised in collaboration with Michael Checkland: two on resources, others on planning, finances, the licence fee and the unions; others were on the role of the BBC Secretary (whose task was to liaise between the board of management and the board of governors), BBC engineering, women in the BBC, drama and *EastEnders*, the reporting of the famine in Ethiopia, BBC handling of complaints and BBC governance. They informed the whole book.

INTRODUCTION

1. John Stuart Mill, *On Liberty*, CUP, Cambridge, 2004, p. 157.
2. Interview, Asa Briggs.
3. Interview, Anna Home.
4. George Orwell, 'The freedom of the press' (Orwell's proposed Preface to *Animal Farm*), in Peter Davison (ed.), *Orwell and Politics*, Penguin, London, 2001. p. 76.

CHAPTER 1: MRS THATCHER AND THE BBC

1. Secretary of the BBC (Colin Shaw) to the chairman of the governors, 18 February 1976, R78/2,184/1.
2. Interview, Brian Griffiths.
3. Quoted in Humphrey Carpenter, *Dennis Potter*, Faber & Faber, London, 1998, p. 339.
4. Interview, Patricia Hodgson.

5.   Margaret Thatcher, *The Downing Street Years*, HarperCollins, London, 1993, p. 632.
6.   Sarah Curtis (ed.), *The Journals of Woodrow Wyatt*, vol. 2: *Thatcher's Fall and Major's Rise 1989–92*, Macmillan, London, 1999, p. 183.
7.   Director-general Charles Curran to Mrs Thatcher, MP for Finchley, 21 January 1960, R78/2,184/1.
8.   Curran to Mrs Thatcher, 8 December 1969, R78/2,184/1.
9.   Copy of letter from the chairman of the BBC to the Postmaster General, 1 June 1964.
10. Canadian Hansard, Commons debate, 1 November 1967, p. 3754, col. 2.
11. Thatcher to Curran, 18 December 1969, R78/2,184/1.
12. Thatcher to Curran, 6 November 1969; Curran to Thatcher, 28 November 1969, R78/2,184/1.
13. Complaint about *24 Hours* programme on hijacking, 23 September 1970, R78/2,184/1.
14. Geoffrey Ogle, letter to Mrs Thatcher, 11 April 1976, R78/2,184/1.
15. Mrs Thatcher, speech to the parliamentary press gallery, 10 July 1981.
16. John Campbell, *Iron Lady*, Jonathan Cape, London, 2003, p. 225.
17. Curran to controller Educational Broadcasting, 6 August 1971, R78/2,184/1.
18. Mrs Thatcher, 12 November 1974, RAPIC A2585.
19. Mrs Thatcher, 16 October 1984, RAPIC A2585.
20. Interview, Bernard Ingham.
21. Nigel Lawson, *The View from No. 11*, HarperCollins, London, 1994, p. 127.
22. Carol Thatcher, *Below the Parapet*, HarperCollins, London, 1996, pp. 143–8.
23. H.C.A.G. Tel. to the chairman, 31 January 1974, R78/2,184/1.
24. Chairman of governors to Mrs Thatcher, 14 February 1974, R78/2,184/1.
25. Desmond Wilcox and Esther Rantzen, *Kill the Chocolate Biscuit*, Severn House, London, 1982, p. 23.
26. Mrs M. Parker to the director-general of the BBC, cc Mrs Thatcher, 6 November 1974, R78/2,184/1.
27. Curran to Thatcher, 16 December 1974, R78/2,184/1.
28. Interview, Douglas Hurd.
29. Percy Cradock, *In Pursuit of British Interests*, John Murray, London, 1997, p. 20.
30. Ibid., p. 23.
31. Interview, Bernard Ingham.
32. Chief assistant to the director-general to head of Religious Programmes Radio, 14 May 1976, R78/2,184/1.
33. The *Sun*, 20 October 1983.
34. Letter from Peter Hardiman Scott (copied to the political editor and the director of Local Radio) to Mrs Thatcher.
35. Board of Management, 25 October 1976, RS5,N926.
36. BBC WAC: Radio Weekly Programme Review Board, December 1976.
37. Robert Harris, *Good and Faithful Servant*, Faber & Faber, London, 1990, p. 71.
38. Sir Michael Butler, *Europe*, Heinemann, London, 1986, p. 116.
39. Director-general's Report G80/80, 2 May 1980.
40. Interview, Bernard Ingham.
41. Margaret Thatcher, *The Downing Street Years*, Penguin, London, 2000, p. 634.
42. William Whitelaw, *The Whitelaw Memoirs*, Aurum Press, London, 1989, p. 217.
43. BOM 21/5/1979 378.
44. G168/79, 14 June 1979; note by the secretary, 19 June 1979.
45. Interview, Anthony Smith.
46. Ian Aitken, William Whitelaw obituary, *Guardian*, 2 July 1999.
47. Charles Curran, BBC Oral History.

48. Interview, Sir John Chilcot.
49. Aitken, William Whitelaw obituary.

CHAPTER 2: THE LICENCE FEE AND BBC INDEPENDENCE

This chapter is based on six Witness Seminars conducted for the history, on the BBC's finances and organisation.

1. Interview, Patricia Hodgson.
2. Interview, Robert Hazel.
3. Interview, Lord Hurd.
4. BOM 23/2/76 107.
5. BOM 27/11/1978 839.
6. Philip Whitehead, *The Writing on the Wall*, Michael Joseph, London, 1985, p. 45.
7. Ben Pimlott, *Harold Wilson*, HarperCollins, London, 1990, p. 178.
8. BOG 24/10/1974 664.
9. Pimlott, *Harold Wilson*, p. 181.
10. NAO Treasury memo, PM Rayner to CD Butler, 29 September 1978.
11. BOG 10/10/1978 638.
12. NAO TNA PRO H0256/861, letter M Swann to Lord Harris, 13 December 1974. Interview, Roy Jenkins.
13. BOM 20/1/1975 29.
14. BOG 5/12/1974 757.
15. Charles Curran, *The Seamless Robe*, Collins, London, 1979, p. 276.
16. NAO TNA PRO H0256/861, Note of meeting, 26 November 1974.
17. NAO NA T319/2616, Increase in BBC licence fee 1975, PM's Personal Minute No. M129174, 30 October 1974.
18. NAO NA T319/2616, Increase in BBC licence fee 1975, Letter RT Armstrong PM's office to Hayden Phillips HO, 13 November 1974.
19. BOM 11/11/1974 526.
20. NAO NA T319/2616, Increase in BBC licence fee 1975, Memo PJ Kitcatt to Harrop, 17 October 1974.
21. BOM 7/3/1977 126 (b); BOM 14/3/1977 138 (b).
22. Managing director Television's Meeting, 18 May 1976, Ian Trethowan.
23. *Evening News*, 18 May 1976.
24. Dominic Sanbrook, *State of Emergency*, Allen Lane, London, 2010, p. 175.
25. Michael Grade, *It Seemed Like a Good Idea at the Time*, Pan Books, London, 1999, p. 391.
26. Interview, Ros Sloboda.
27. BOG 26/9/1974 592.
28. Curran, *The Seamless Robe*, p. 275.
29. Ibid., p. 273.
30. Eighty per cent was spent on wages, 10 per cent on capital projects and 10 per cent on everything else, Curran estimated.
31. R78/209/1 Finance BBC 1970–75. Paper by Paul Hughes, p. 7.
32. R78/209/1 Finance BBC 1970–75, p. 12.
33. R27/1043/1 Artists' payments and fees, Policy.
34. Ian McIntyre CR3 wrote to MDR 1/3/82 BBC R27/1043/1 Artists' payments and fees, Policy.
35. R134/752/1 Artists' payments and fees, File 2, Tony Palmer, 24 September 1979.

36. Michael Checkland, Industrial Disputes Seminar.
37. Ibid.
38. BOM 1977 The effect of pay disparity.
39. BBC, General Advisory Committee, 20/7/1976.
40. TNA PRO H0256/861 Letter Paul Hughes to NM Johnson, 23 July 1975.
41. Geoff Buck, Finance Seminar.
42. NAO TNA PRO H0256/861 Memo J Dromgoole to Miss Jones, 24 July 1974.
43. Interview, Donald Slater.
44. Industrial Disputes Seminar.
45. Industrial Disputes Seminar.
46. R78/2016/1 Conditions of Service Policy, Non-manual staff, part 3.
47. Ibid., Alasdair Milne to Ian Trethowan, 10 October 1977.
48. Ibid., CDP Kinchin Smith, 3 May 1978.
49. R78/405/1 Conditions of Service Policy, Non-manual staff, part 1, N&CA meeting, 2 October 1970.
50. Ibid., Note 'Conditions of Service' CR East, 6 August 1971.
51. R78/20 1601 Memo from Andrew Todd Dep Dir N&CA to DCNA, 5 April 1978.
52. Phillip Whitehead in a Channel 4 series, *The Writing on the Wall*.
53. BBC *World at One*, 15 July 1976.
54. Interview, Tony Hearn, general secretary, ABS.
55. ABS membership in December 1982, for example, was strongest among 'Professional Conditions Staff' at 55 per cent of total numbers.
56. Aubrey Singer, BBC Oral History.
57. BOM 26/6/78; GAC 19/10/77 845 The BBC's Finances.
58. Interview, David Allen.
59. Callaghan memoirs.
60. BOG 21/3/1975.441, 12.
61. Bernard Donoughue, *Downing Street Diaries*, Jonathan Cape, London, 2008, p. 302.
62. BOG 11/3/1976, 321.17.
63. NAO TNA PRO H0256/861 Letter P Hughes to J Dromgoole, 20 December 1974.
64. BOG 27/5/1976 401.
65. NAO, NAO PRO HO BD/H Merlyn Rees to Denis Healey, 31 January 1977.
66. NAO, BD/A/3093 Memo DJ Trevelyan to RT Armstrong, 10 January 1977.
67. BD/A/3093 Internal HO memo DJ Trevelyan to RT Armstrong, 23 February 1977.
68. NAO PRO BD/A Merlyn Rees to Denis Healey, 14 March 1977.
69. NAO PRO BD/A/3093 Note of meeting held on 30/3/1977, by C Farrington private secretary to home secretary, 1 April 1977. In the event the 'one-year' settlement was repeated during the next two years.
70. Letter Denis Healey to Merlyn Rees, 13 April 1977.
71. NAO PRO BDA/A/3093 pt II Internal HO memo DJ Trevelyan to RT Armstrong, 20 April 1977.
72. BOM 2/5/1977 215 (b).
73. G97/77 Note by the director-general of a conversation at the Home Office on 4/5/1977.
74. BOG 12/5/1977 309.
75. Peter Fiddick, *Guardian*, 27 June 1977.
76. Managing director Television's Management Meeting 5/7/1977 206.
77. BOM 27/6/1977 323.
78. 'Television licences: up and often?', *The Economist*, 2 July 1977.
79. Ian Trethowan, *News of the World*, 21 May 1978.

80. *Guardian*, 18 May 1978; Broadcast, 29 May 1978.
81. BOM 16/10/1978 715.
82. NAO Internal Treasury Memo Perry to chief secretary to the Treasury, 22 July 1977.
83. NAO Treasury, Letter DW Healey to J Callaghan PM, 6 November 1978.
84. NAO BD/A/ 3093 Note Merlyn Rees to James Callaghan, 21 July 1977.
85. NAO Memo AJ Perry to P Hinckley (Treasury), 1 August 1977.
86. NAO BD/A/ 3093 Letter AJ Perry Treasury to D Peach HO, 8 July 1977.
87. NAO BD/A/3590 ptII Internal HO memo SR Muir to S Littler, 23 June 1978.
88. NAO Letter D Healey to J Callaghan, 16 November 1978.
89. Norman Tebbit, *Upwardly Mobile*, Weidenfeld and Nicolson, London, 1988, p. 99.
90. BOM G7/79 The Financial Situation: note by director of finance Paul Hughes, 5 January 1979.
91. Geoff Buck, Resources Seminar.
92. BOM (77) 155 Review of the Financial position to 31 March 1979.
93. NAO BD/AY/760 Part II Internal HO memo, Shirley Littler to Chilcot, 28 February 1979.
94. Interview, Robert Banks Stewart.
95. Nigel Willmott, 'Changes certain but Old Guard holds on', *Television Weekly*, 24 February 1984.
96. Interview, Michael Checkland.
97. Interview, John Birt.
98. BBC Resources Seminar.
99. Evidence in all of this section from six Witness Seminars.
100. BOM 29/10/79 711g.
101. David Goodhart, 'BBC puts on a show of strength', *Financial Times*, 23 March 1984.
102. Interview, Gerry Morrissey.
103. Scenic Construction/Scenic Reorganisation Feb 1984–April 1984, File 5, Tony Hearn, 2 February 1984, RAPIC A1218.
104. BBC Industrial Disputes Seminar.
105. Memo 15/3/84 Dick Grey SPO Design Television 1 to director, Television.
106. Interview, Duncan Thomas.
107. Ibid.
108. BOM 22/9/80 505, DJ Webster, director of Public Affairs.
109. Michael Moran in H. Drucker and A. Gamble (eds), *Developments in British Politics 2*, Macmillan, London, 1986, p. 281.
110. Scenic Construction/Scenic Reorganisation Feb 1984–April 1984, File 5, Tony Hearn, 2 February 1984, RAPIC A1218.
111. Memo Mike Chattin SPO Scenic Operations to John Needle, 15 March 1984, Scenic Construction/Scenic Reorganisation Feb 1984–April 1984, File 5, RAPIC A1218.
112. Memo head of Press and PR to director, Television; director of programmes, Television, 21 February 1984.
113. Interview, Duncan Thomas.
114. Goodhart, 'BBC puts on a show of strength'.
115. John Foster letter, *Guardian*, 27 February 1984.
116. BOM 19/3/84 180 26/3/84.
117. Colin Crouch, in C. Crouch (ed.), *The Resurgence of Class Conflict in Western Europe since 1968*, Macmillan Press, London, 1978, p. 204.
118. Interview, Tony Hearn.
119. Ibid.
120. Dennis Barker, 'Golden deal on TV overtime', *Guardian*, 27 April 1984.

121. Max Hastings, 'Why the Likely Lads get out', *Evening Standard*, 9 February 1984; Paul Johnson, 'Clattering BBC train', *Spectator*, 18 February 1984; 'What is the BBC for?', *The Economist*, 18 February 1984.
122. George Gale, *Daily Express*, 24 February 1984.
123. Scenic Construction/Scenic Reorganisation Feb 1984–April 1984, File 5, Letter C Chope to Alasdair Milne, 30 April 1984, RAPIC A1218.
124. Julia Haviland and David Hewson, 'Thatcher favours some ads on BBC', *The Times*, 13 December 1984; David Hughes and Jane Adams, 'Advertising on BBC?', *Daily Mail*, 13 December 1984.
125. 'Say no to the BBC', *Daily Express*, 13 December 1984.
126. From 29,672 in 1983 to 26,189 in 1984.
127. Interview, Mark Thompson.

CHAPTER 3: NORTHERN IRELAND

1. Interview, Denis Murray.
2. Interview, Jonathan Powell.
3. Interview, Austin Hunter.
4. Interview, Denis Murray.
5. BOM 5/4/1975. 189(b).
6. Interview, Austin Hunter.
7. Interview, Mark Adair.
8. Interview, Mark Adair.
9. John Reith, *Into the Wind*, Hodder and Stoughton, London, 1949, p. 135.
10. Interview, Pat Loughrey.
11. Interview, Robin Walsh.
12. *Cabinet Office* (NAO CAB) *Northern Ireland Broadcasting and Press; Policy*, NI34/118/16 RJ, Cudlipp, 17 March 1975.
13. Interview, Robin Walsh.
14. Seamus Heaney, 'The State of Ulster', *New Statesman*, 1 July 1966.
15. Interview, Sir Paul Fox.
16. Simon Winchester, *In Holy Terror*, Faber & Faber, London, 1974, p. 142.
17. Roy Foster, *Modern Ireland*, Penguin, London, 1988, p. 27.
18. Roy Foster, 'History and identity in modern Ireland', Bindoff Lecture, QMW, 1997, p. 17.
19. NAO CAB (TNA)BD/A/3590 pt II HO Extract from notes of a meeting between Mr Armstrong and Sir Anthony Rawlinson, 26 January 1978.
20. Interview, Austin Hunter.
21. Interview, Sir Kenneth Bloomfield.
22. R78/1407/1, 1 December 1976.
23. BOM 5/4/1976 189(b) N&CA 21/7/1972 436.
24. Charles Curran, *A Seamless Robe*, Collins, London, 1979, p. 11.
25. Interview, Lord Briggs.
26. Cameron Report, *Disturbances in Northern Ireland: Report of the Commission Appointed by the Governor of Northern Ireland*, Her Majesty's Stationery Office, Belfast, 1969, p. 271.
27. Hansard, 22 October 1968, cols 1088–90.
28. See Jean Seaton, *Carnage and the Media*, Penguin, London, 2005, ch. 10.
29. *Observer*, 17 August 1969.

30. Interview, John Simpson.
31. Interview, Pat Loughrey.
32. Interview, Chris Langton.
33. *Operation Banner: an Analysis of Military Operations in Northern Ireland*, MoD, 2006, p. 123.
34. N&CA 1/9/1972 516.
35. *Operation Banner*, p. 3.
36. Charles Curran, BBC Oral History.
37. 1981, BL, Special Collection.
38. BOM 5/4/1976 189(b).
39. R78/1303 ACNI to ENCA, 21 February 1973.
40. Simon Winchester, *In Holy Terror*, Faber & Faber, London, 1974, p. 142.
41. TNA CAB NI 34/110/01 6194A Broadcasting, 17 March 1974.
42. R78/696/1 Northern Ireland civil disturbances part 1 1967–70: Ian Paisley N&CA, 20 December 1968.
43. Ibid., part 3, 1976–82, Ian Paisley.
44. Brian Faulkner's widow, Lucy, was later a remarkable and effective BBC governor.
45. Ben Pimlott, *Harold Wilson*, HarperCollins, London, 1992, p. 231.
46. BBC, *The World at One*, 10 August 1971.
47. Transcript of item 'Report on the Death of Roman Catholic Priest', *The World at One*.
48. R78/696/ 2 Northern Ireland civil disturbances part 2 1970–1974.
49. Interview, Jonathan Dimbleby.
50. Reported in *Ariel*, 15 August 1975.
51. BOG 1975. 705 Transmitters in NI.
52. Interview, Austin Hunter.
53. N&CA 25/2/1972 1041.
54. Interview, Jonathan Powell.
55. Interview, Peter Hennessy.
56. Hugo Young, *The Hugo Young Papers*, Allen Lane, London, 2008, p. 68.
57. N&CA 3/7/1972.
58. N&CA 19/4/1972.
59. NAO CAB NI Off the record discussion Stuart Wynton and Whitelaw, 2 February 1973, 6 February 1973, sent to ENCA.
60. Frank Field, Lord Bonham-Carter obituary, *Independent*, 7 August 1994.
61. NI 34/110/01 6194A.
62. Interview, Anthony Campbell.
63. Bomb scares in BH Belfast R78/696/ 2 8/2/74.
64. Broadcasting Council Northern Ireland 11/1982.
65. Interview, Denis Murray.
66. NAO, CAB, NICIOs, NI Deputy, 21 February 1974.
67. David McKitterick, *Lost Lives*, Edinburgh University Press, Edinburgh, 1999, p. 143.
68. Richard Rose, *Northern Ireland*, Macmillan, London, 1975, p. 25.
69. CAIN ulst.ac.uk.
70. Pimlott, *Harold Wilson*, p. 634.
71. Ibid.
72. NAO CAB NICIO/ ENSA Meeting, 21 February 1974.
73. NI 34/110/01 6194A.
74. NI 34/110/01 6194A Broadcasting: Television and Radio General File on policy.
75. NI 34/110/01 6194A Francis to director-general, 10 June 1974.

76. Curran in *Ariel*, 18 September 1974, p. 1.
77. N&CA, 17 March 1972, 160.
78. Interview, Paul Bew.
79. Liz Curtis, *Ireland: The Propaganda War*, Shasta, Belfast, 1998, p. 68.
80. F. S. L. Lyons, *The Burden of our History*, the W. B. Rankin Memorial Lecture, Queen's University Belfast, 1978, p. 27.
81. Richard Francis, *Broadcasting to a Community in Conflict*, Chatham House, London, 1977, p. 7.
82. Douglas Hurd, *Memoirs*, Abacus, London, 2004, p. 329.
83. NAO CAB NI 22/4/1975 NI 34/110/01 6194A Broadcasting: Television and Radio General.
84. Interview, Roger Bolton.
85. NAO CAB NI 34/110/01 6194A Broadcasting: Television and Radio General memo 'The Misdemeanours of the BBC' JHG Leahy to Mr Roberts [T Roberts director Information Service NI Dept] and Mr Gilland, 3 February 1976.
86. BOM 18/10/1976 536(c); 25/10/1976 551 (d).
87. Kenneth Bloomfield, *The BBC at the Watershed*, Liverpool University Press, Liverpool, 2008, p. 21.
88. Sir Kenneth Bloomfield, BBC Oral History.
89. BOM 27/6/77 322f.
90. The account of this meeting is taken from Richard Francis's paper for the Board of Governors of 24 November 1976. Previous versions have depended on the press record. G260/76 24/11/1976.
91. BOM 8/11/1976 588 (c).
92. BOG 2/12/1976 883.
93. R78/1407/1 Northern Ireland Civil Disturbances part 6 16/1/1976–9/2/77 BOM 24/1/1977 43.
94. BOG 2/12/1976 883.
95. R78/1407/1 NICD part 6 16/1/1976–9/2/77 memo C Curran to RT Armstrong HO, 1 December 1976.
96. R78/1407/1 NICD part 6 16/1/1976–9/2/77 BOM 8/11/1976 588(c).
97. BOG 18/11/1976 847.
98. R78/1407/1 NICD part 6 16/1/1976–9/2/77.
99. R78/1407/1 NICD part 6 16/1/1976–9/2/77 BOM 8/11/1976 588.
100. R78/1407/1 NICD part 6 16/1/1976–9/2/77 memo CIS to director-general, 6 January 1976.
101. NAO CAB He also said he would talk to Mrs Thatcher. (NI 34/118/24 CN 11759B Broadcasting: Television and Radio Note for the record R Ramsay, 15 December 1977.)
102. NAO CAB NI 34/118/24 CN 11759B Broadcasting: Television and Radio Note for the record R Ramsay, 20 December 1977.
103. R78/1408/1 NICD part 7 10/21/1977–31/1/1978 Note on a meeting with Airey Neave MP, 9 March 1977, Michael Swann to Charles Curran, 9 March 1977.
104. Hansard, 27 September 1976.
105. Brian Harrison, ODNB entry on Airey Neave, 2004.
106. Airey Neave, *They Have Their Exits*, Leo Cooper, Barnsley, 1953, p. 179.
107. *Irish Times*, 31 March 1979.
108. Hansard, 17 December 1976.
109. NAO CAB NI 34/110/01 6194A Broadcasting: Television and Radio General memo JG Pilling [PS Sof S] to Mr Corbett, 15 January 1979.

110. NAO CAB NI 34/110/01 6194A Broadcasting: Television and Radio General memo, 15 December 1977.
111. Interview, Stephen Claypole.
112. NAO CAB NI 34/110/01 6194A Broadcasting: Television and Radio General.
113. Interview, Ros Sloboda.
114. NAO CAB NI 34/110/01 6194 Note of telephone complaint.
115. NAO CABNI 34/110/01 6194.
116. NAO CAB NI 34/110/01 6194A Broadcasting: Television and Radio General Letter Humphrey Atkins to I Trethowan, 12 July 1979; Reply I Trethowan to H Atkins, 17 July 1979.
117. NAO CAB NI minuted SofS [W Whitelaw] on July 20th, copied to Messrs Allison Rossi, Goodhart and Lord Elton, with 'hidden copies' to PS/PUS (L&B), Mr Stowe, Mr Lane, Mr Gilliland, Mr Corbett [NIO the last two IO].
118. Interview, Pat Loughery.
119. Gillian Reynolds, *Daily Telegraph*, 5 September 1979.
120. Rose, *Northern Ireland*, p. 139.
121. Interviews, Stephen Claypole, Roger Bolton, Chris Langton.

CHAPTER 4: ARTS AND MUSIC

1. William Glock, *Notes in Advance*, OUP, Oxford, 1991, p. 104.
2. Minutes of CMAC meeting, 09/1960, R27/1,027.
3. See Jenny Doctor and Nicholas Kenyon (eds), *The Proms*, Thames & Hudson, London, 2007.
4. Gerard Mansell, BBC Oral History.
5. David Pountney, 'If we ran the proms', *Guardian*, 12 July 2002.
6. Simon Reynolds, *Rip It Up and Start Again*, Faber & Faber, London, 2005.
7. Interview, Christopher Hogwood.
8. Interview, Nicholas Kenyon.
9. Hans Keller, 'Broadcasting in the Eighties', *Spectator*, 10 July 1976.
10. Glock, *Notes in Advance*, p. 115.
11. BBC Proms prospectus, 1977.
12. Interview, Humphrey Burton.
13. Pierre Boulez, *The Listener*, 3 April 1973.
14. Robert Hughes, 'The shock of the new', *The Listener*, 2 October 1980, p. 446.
15. Ben Pimlott, 'Should the Arts be popular?', Lloyds TSB Forum Lecture, 2003.
16. Joan Bakewell and Nicholas Garnham, *The New Priesthood*, Faber & Faber, London, 1972.
17. BBC Board of Governors, 742 4(i) 1976.
18. Interview, Humphrey Burton.
19. John Myerscough, *The Economic Importance of the Arts in Britain*, Policy Studies Institute, London, 1987.
20. Hughes, 'The shock of the new', p. 446.
21. Interview, Humphrey Burton.
22. Interview, Roy Tipping.
23. Minutes of CMAC, 28 October 1977. R27/1,033.
24. Minutes of CMAC, 30 October 1986. R27/1,034.
25. Interview, Humphrey Burton.
26. Listening Panel, R9/1,038/1.
27. Listening Panel, R9/1,046.

28. Interview, Robert Ponsonby.
29. Interview, Arnold Whittall.
30. Hans Keller, speech to Composers Guild of Great Britain, December 1975, reprinted *The Composer*, Summer 1976.
31. Ernest Warburton, 'Music on Radio 3'. B12–1.
32. Meeting to discuss 'The broadcasting of advanced music', c. 1973. R27/1,039/1.
33. Robert Ponsonby in conversation with Richard Stoker, *The Composer*, Summer 1975.
34. Memo from Singer to Ian McIntyre, 27 November. B12–1.
35. Minutes of CMAC, 30 March 1984. R27/1,033.
36. 14 November 1986. B12–1.
37. Audience research in 1980 indicated that the majority of listeners to music on Radio 3 were men, and over fifty. From 'Estimate of audiences for music programmes', 19 March 1980. GAC 587.
38. Memo from Hearst to Singer, 20 November 1979. B12–1.
39. Stephen Hearst, 'Radio 3 – some points for discussion', 8 September 1978. R70/3911.
40. Singer to Ponsonby; 15 May 1979. B430–1.
41. Ponsonby to Singer; 27 June 1979. B430–1.
42. Tony Stoller, *Sounds of Your Life: The History of Independent Radio in the UK*, John Libbey Publishing, 2010, pp. 171–2, 208–16.
43. Minutes of CMAC, 15 April 1983. R27/1,033.
44. Memo from Ponsonby to Burton, 29 March 1976. C129.
45. Memo from Pamela Reiss, research output editor, Minutes of CMAC, 12 February 1980, R27/1,034.
46. Memo from Roy Tipping to Alan Yentob, Minutes of CMAC, 12 November 1986. R27/1,033.
47. Minutes of the Board of Governors, 15 November 1984, minute 367. R1/51/5.
48. 'Audiences for youth programmes', October 1987. R 15/21/3.
49. Minutes of CMAC, 27 October 1978. R27/1,033.
50. B430–2.
51. Yentob to Bill Cotton (managing director, Television), 6 November 1985. B430–2.
52. Interview, Nicholas Kenyon.
53. Leo Black to Ponsonby. R27/1,057/1.
54. Ponsonby to Peter Gould, 11 March 1975. R27/1,057/1.
55. Interview, Christopher Hogwood.
56. Joseph Kerman, *Contemplating Music*, Constable, London, 1985, p. 192.
57. Robert Donington, *The Interpretation of Early Music*, Faber & Faber, London, 1974, p. 49.
58. Ibid., p. 80.
59. R15/21/3.
60. See Humphrey Carpenter, *The Envy of the World*, Weidenfeld & Nicolson, London, 1996, pp. 265–7.
61. Will Crutchfield, 'A report from the musical battlefield', *New York Times*, 28 July 1985.
62. Aubrey Singer, BBC Oral History.
63. Michael Checkland, BBC History Seminar.
64. The Annan Committee, *Report of the Committee on the Future of Broadcasting*, HMSO, 1977, ch. 3: 'The arts and broadcasting'.
65. Minutes of CMAC, 27 April 1979. R27/1,033.
66. Interview, Giles Oakley.
67. Interview, John Drummond.
68. Interview, Robert Ponsonby.

69. Aubrey Singer, BBC Oral History.
70. Ibid.
71. Managing director, Radio BOM 434, 28 July 1980.
72. Interview, John Morton.
73. *The Times*, 10 March 1980.
74. BOM 10/3/1980, 110d.
75. Aubrey Singer, BBC Oral History.
76. BOM 30/6/1980, 356b. Strictly confidential full version of minute.
77. Interview, Robert Ponsonby.
78. Swann Papers, Edinburgh University. Letter from Michael Swann to Lord Goodman.
79. Michael Checkland, BBC History Seminar.
80. *Observer*, 26 April 1987.
81. Interview, Robert Ponsonby, 'Conflicts of sound and vision: Nicholas Kenyon talks to Robert Ponsonby', *The Times*, 15 September 1984.
82. Interview, Stephen Plaistow.
83. David Wright, 'Re-inventing the Proms', in David Wright, Jenny Doctor and Nicholas Kenyon (eds), *The Proms*, Thames and Hudson, London, 2009, p. 168.
84. Drummond, *Tainted by Experience*, pp. 315–16.
85. John Drummond, *Music and the BBC*, BBC, 1985, p. 12.
86. A new opera, *Yan Tan Tethera*, commissioned from Harrison Birtwistle by BBC2 and then dropped, was transmitted in a simultaneous broadcast by Channel 4 and Radio 3 in 1987.

CHAPTER 5: ATTENBOROUGH

1. ARKive Wildfilm Film Oral History interview with Richard Brock.
2. Christopher Parsons, *True to Nature*, Patrick Stephens, Cambridge, 1982, p. 318.
3. ARKive interview with Richard Brock.
4. Interview, Mike Salisbury.
5. R. A. Hinde and W. H. Thorpe, 'Nobel recognition for ethology', *Nature*, 245, 1973, p. 346.
6. Interview, Mike Salisbury.
7. Charles Darwin, 'A fragment of autobiography: 1838', in Gavin de Beer (ed.), *Charles Darwin, Thomas Henry Huxley*, Oxford University Press, Oxford, p. 5.
8. Introduction by David Attenborough, in Parsons, *True to Nature*, p. 9.
9. Interview, Mike Salisbury.
10. Interview, Professor Patrick Bateson.
11. Aubrey Singer, BBC Oral History.
12. Richard Attenborough, *Entirely up to You Darling*, Hutchinson, London, 2008, p. 11.
13. Interview, David Attenborough.
14. Ibid.
15. R. Burkhardt, *Patterns of Behaviour*, University of Chicago Press, Chicago, IL, 2006, p. 76.
16. David Attenborough, *Life on Air*, BBC, London, 2002, p. 18.
17. Ibid., p. 76.
18. Ibid., p. 77.
19. David Attenborough, *Journeys to the Past*, Lutterworth Press, Guildford, 1981, p. 7.
20. Interview, David Attenborough.
21. Interview, Desmond Morris.

22. ARKive, Wildfilm Oral History interview with Desmond Morris.
23. Will Wyatt, *The Fun Factory*, Aurum Press, London, 2003, p. 48.
24. T41/520/1Treatment for *Life on Earth*, sent from Bristol to BBC2, p. 3.
25. SW3/32/1 Life on Earth: Natural History, 1st draft.
26. David Attenborough, *Life on Earth*, Collins BBC, London, 1979.
27. David Attenborough in Anthony Huxley, *The Green Inheritance*, Harvill, London, 1984, p. 11.
28. T41/520/1 Frank Gillard, 'Natural History: the Western Region'.
29. Desmond Hawkins interview with Christopher Parsons, ARKive.
30. Desmond Hawkins, First Five Years of the BBC Natural History Unit, BOM (62) 119, 1962.
31. BBC Wildlife Programmes, WE17/2/1 Natural History Unit, 1962.
32. ARKive interview with Richard Brock.
33. WE8/83/1, David Attenborough to Alasdair Milne, 20 September 1975.
34. Interview, Mike Salisbury.
35. Attenborough, *Life on Earth*, p. 312.
36. Parsons, *True to Nature*, p. 308.
37. Interview, Mike Salisbury.
38. Ibid.
39. Interview, David Attenborough.
40. Parsons, *True to Nature*, p. 310.
41. Parsons, *Life on Earth*, 24 August 1972, T41/520/1.
42. Parsons, *True to Nature*, p. 310.
43. Parsons, *Life on Earth*, 11 February 1977, T41/520/1.
44. Interview, Edward Williams.
45. *Life on Earth: Natural History*, draft job description, 15 December 1975, SW3/32/1.
46. WE8/83/1 26/09/1975, Mick Rhodes to Attenborough.
47. Rhodes to controller, BBC2, 7 October 2010, BBC WAC.
48. Rhodes to controller, BBC2, 25 October 1977, T41/520/1.
49. 25 October 1977, SW/32/1.
50. ARKive interview with Richard Brock.
51. BBC2, 06/1977, T41/520/1/ NHU.
52. Interview, David Attenborough.
53. ARKive Wildfilm interview with Gerald Thompson.
54. P. S. Crowson, *Animals in Focus*, Caliban Books, Oxford, 1981, p. 24.
55. Attenborough, *Life on Earth*, pp. 290–91.
56. Interview, Steve Jones (Professor of Genetics, UCL).
57. James Secord, *Victorian Sensation*, University of Chicago Press, London, 2000, p. 510.
58. Parsons, *True to Nature*, p. 10.
59. Interview, David Attenborough.
60. Attenborough, *Life on Air*, p. 328.
61. Interview, David Attenborough.
62. Interview, Patrick Bateson (Provost of King's College, Cambridge).
63. Attenborough, *Life on Earth*, p. 97.
64. Gillian Beer, *Darwin's Plots*, Routledge, London, 1983 (this came after the Attenborough series).
65. Milton, *Comus, Collected Works*, CUP, Cambridge, 11. 710–14, p. 76.
66. J. M. Keynes, *Essays in Biography*, Hodder and Stoughton, London, 1933, p. 120.

CHAPTER 6: THE ROYAL WEDDING

1. *Daily Express*, 14 June 1981.
2. Nigel Dempster, *Daily Mail*, 17 September 1980.
3. Interview, Brian Hanrahan.
4. *Guardian*, 8 June 1977.
5. Andrew Morton, *Diana*, Little, Brown, London, 1992, p. 46.
6. *The Times*, 25 February 1981.
7. *Guardian* Diary: Royal Wedding, The Prince of Wales (1), RAPIC 10136256, Box A2614.
8. *Blue Peter*, 25 June 1981.
9. Walter Bagehot, 'The Monarchy', in Norman St John-Stevas (ed.), *The Collected Works of Walter Bagehot*, vol. 5, The Economist, London, 1974.
10. Ben Pimlott, *The Queen*, HarperCollins, London, 1996, p. 379.
11. Ibid., p. 381.
12. Richard Cawston, *The Royal Family*, BBC TV and Independent TV.
13. T70/3/1: Royal Interviews Declined.
14. Will Wyatt, *Life in the Fun Factory*, Aurum Press, London, 2003, p. 316.
15. Interview, Dickie Arbiter.
16. Interview, Samantha Cohen.
17. Frank Gillard, in Caroline Elliot (ed.), *The BBC Book of Royal Memories*, BBC Books, London, 1991, p. 21.
18. Jonathan Dimbleby, *Richard Dimbleby*, Hodder and Stoughton, London, 1975, p. 244.
19. John Snagge, *The BBC Book of Royal Memories*, p. 43.
20. Royal Wedding, The Prince of Wales (1), 16 April 1981, RAPIC 10136256, Box A2614.
21. BBC The Coronation 1937, Gerald Cock to Hardinge, 13 April 1937.
22. Interview, Will Wyatt.
23. Royal Wedding, The Prince of Wales (1), head of Entertainment, 8 April 1981, RAPIC 10136256, Box A2614.
24. T43/46/1, Phil Lewis to HOBG, 30 April 1981.
25. Christopher Andrew, *The Authorized History of MI5*, Allen Lane, London, 2009, p. 233.
26. Phil Lewis to HOBG, 30 April 1981, T43/46/1.
27. Royal Jubilee File 1: A Day of Celebration. Phil Lewis to head of Artist's Contracts, 11 February 1977, T14/3368.
28. Managing director, Television meeting, 22 February 1981, B223-5-4, R78/1, 403/1.
29. Director-general to the Palace, 15 May 1981, B223-5-4, R78/1, 403/1.
30. Roy Norton, Pebble Mill, to RJ Stanley Resident Agent Althorp, 13 July 1981.
31. 'Royal wedding' Local Radio Programme service organiser, 13 July 1981, R102/33/1: RAPIC A6127, B223-5-4.
32. Manager of Radio Leeds, 27 July 1981, R102/33/1: RAPIC A6127.
33. Television Weekly Programme review, 5 August 1981, R78/1.403/1: B 223-5-4.
34. Ibid.
35. Ibid.
36. Phil Lewis to HOBG etc., 22 September 1981, T43/46/1.
37. Humphrey Carpenter, *Robert Runcie*, Hodder and Stoughton, London, 1996, p. 223.
38. Robert Lacey, *Majesty*, Little, Brown, London, 2002, p. 283.
39. Major General Krunyawath to George Howard, 6 August 1981, R78/1.403/1, B 223-5-4, HSTV.
40. BBC Broadcasting Research: 'The Royal Wedding' Special Report.
41. Viewing Panel Report *The Day Begins*, 14 September 1981, VR/81/267.
42. Programme Review Board, 4 August 1981, T43/46/1.

43. Television Weekly Programme review, 5 August 1981, R78/1.403/1 B 223–5-4.
44. N&CA Meeting, 4 August 1981, T43/46/1.
45. Ferdinand Mount, *The British Constitution Now*, Heinemann, London, 1992, p. 111.
46. Interview, Dickie Arbiter.
47. BOG, 31 October 1985, 374.
48. BOG, 13 November 1985, 399.
49. Lord Chamberlain's Office to Sir Michael Swann, 23 January 1974, T62/294/1.
50. Peter Dimmock to Paul Fox and general manager Enterprises, 6 February 1974, T62/294/1.
51. Richard Cawston to head of Doc, 19 June 1974, WAC T62/294/1.
52. Prince Philip to Cawston/Swann, November 1974, T62/294/1.
53. Gill to head of Doc and managing director, Television, 5 November 1974, T62/294/1.
54. Paul Ferris, *Sir Huge*, Michael Joseph, London, 1990, p. 263.
55. Interview, Will Wyatt.
56. Interview, Michael Cole.
57. Kate Adie, *The Kindness of Strangers*, Headline, London, 2002, p. 132.
58. Jennie Bond, *Reporting Royalty*, Headline, London, 2001, p. 4.
59. Interview, Dickie Arbiter.

CHAPTER 7: THE FALKLANDS

1. Interview, Tony Byers.
2. Lord Carrington, *Reflect on Things Past*, Collins, London, 1988, p. 351.
3. John Campbell, *Iron Lady*, Jonathan Cape, London, 2003, p. 165.
4. Ibid., p. 173.
5. Ibid., p. 312.
6. Interview, Sir Frank Cooper.
7. Sir John Nott, 'The Falklands: 30 years after', Conference, University of Kent, 2012.
8. Charles Moore, *Mrs Thatcher: the Authorized Biography*, Allen Lane, Penguin, London, 2013, p. 501.
9. William Whitelaw, *The Whitelaw Memoirs*, Aurum Press, London, 1989, p. 268.
10. Carol Thatcher, *Below the Parapet*, HarperCollins, London, 1996, p. 201.
11. Lawrence Freedman, *The Official History of the Falklands*, vol. I, Routledge, London, 2005, p. 223.
12. Interview, John Cole.
13. Alan Clark, *Diaries*, Weidenfeld and Nicolson, London, 2000, p. 313.
14. The *Sun*, 6 April 1982.
15. James Cameron: BBC 4 Views of the Week, 22 April 1982.
16. *The Listener*, 6 May 1982.
17. N&CA Meeting, 10 April 1982, B405–7-2 TD15.
18. Ibid.
19. Ibid.
20. Ibid.
21. Interview, Michael Cockerell.
22. Alan Protheroe, BBC Oral History.
23. Interview, Stephen Whittle.
24. Report on the Government and the media, Protheroe B405–7-26682, 10 May 1982.
25. Interview, Brian Hanrahan.
26. Interview, John Shirley.

27. Interview, Sir Frank Cooper.
28. Interview, Robert Fox.
29. Interview, Brian Hanrahan.
30. Hanrahan, in evidence to the Media Select Committee, 15 October 1985.
31. Falklands File B. 405–33. R55: Falkland Islanders letter to the BBC, July 1982.
32. Interview, John Tusa.
33. Robert Harris, *Gotcha!*, Faber & Faber, London, p. 83.
34. Interview, Will Wyatt.
35. Weekly Radio Review Board B405–33, 14 April 1982.
36. Interview, Robert Fox.
37. Thatcher, *Below the Parapet*, p. 196.
38. Falklands File B. 405–33. R 55.
39. N&CA B 405–33–2, 26 April 1982.
40. Letter DRB in R34/490/2 Policy Nomenclature File, 1B 1943–6, 23 April 1943.
41. The Scottish press officer AP Lee to PRO Scotland copied to C(H) and C(P) in ibid., 16 July 1940.
42. S.J. Lotbiniere r34/490/1 policy, nomenclature, 1935–42, 23 January 1942.
43. BBC Publicity Press Cuttings Falklands, 4 May 1982.
44. Richard Francis, 'Reporting the War', 2 May 1982.
45. Simon Jenkins and Max Hastings, *The Battle for the Falklands*, Pan, London, 1982, p. 125.
46. Capron to director-general designate, Falklands 2, 14 May 1982.
47. Peter Hennessy and Michael Cockerell, *Sources Close to the Prime Minister*, Jonathan Cape, London, 1986, p. 166.
48. Defence secretary John Nott to George Howard, 13 May 1982.
49. BBC Listening Report SU/702/A1/1, 15 May 1982.
50. *Today*, 13 May 1982.
51. *The Times*, 14 May 1982.
52. Richard Lindley, *Panorama*, Politicos, London, 2002, p. 73.
53. Interview, Jenny Abramsky.
54. Interview, Brian Hanrahan.
55. B405 33 Programme Policy Committee Minute 3, 27 May 1982.
56. Alan Protheroe wrote to MDXB D Muggeridge about the original report on the transmitters, and Cabinet responses, 16 February 1983.
57. Bernard Ingham, *Kill the Messenger*, HarperCollins, London, 1991, p. 175.
58. R Radio Atlantico del Sur, BBC RAPIC AOO 10233, 22 May 1982.
59. Programme Policy Committee, 27 May 1982.
60. Freedman, *The Official History of the Falklands*, vol. I, p. 47.
61. Robert Fox, *Eyewitness Falklands*, Methuen, London, 1982, p. 74.
62. Freedman, *The Official History of the Falklands*, vol. I, p. 250.
63. Hennessy and Cockerel, *Sources Close to the Prime Minister*, p. 166.
64. R Radio Atlantico del Sur, BBC RAPIC AOO 10233, 21 May 1982.
65. Andrew Walker, B40/ B 10–16, 4 June 1982.
66. N&CA, B 405–7-2, 29 June 1982.
67. Ibid.
68. B 405–7-2, R55.
69. Mathew Parris in Campbell, *Iron Lady*, n. 90.
70. Mrs Thatcher, 3 July 1982, quoted in Moore, *Mrs Thatcher*, p. 754.
71. N&CA, B405–7-2, September 1982.

72. William Whitelaw, in David L. Edwards and Peter Smith (eds), *Robert Runcie*, Fount, London, 1990, p. 260.
73. Interview, Brian Hanrahan.
74. Martin Harris, in D. Butler and T. Kavanagh (eds), *Nuffield Election Study 1983*, OUP, Oxford, 1983, p. 167.
75. Interview, Lord Briggs.
76. Witness Seminar, BBC Secretaries.
77. B405–7-2 TD15, 1 May 1982.

CHAPTER 8: ETHIOPIA

This chapter was informed by a Witness Seminar on the reporting of the famine and the organisation of Live Aid. For a richer account of the relationship between aid and the media in this story, see Suzanne Franks, *Reporting Disasters*, Hurst, London, 2013, written as part of the research project that produced this book.

1. Bob Geldof (with Paul Vallely), *Is That it?*, Sidgwick and Jackson, London, 1986, pp. 212–14.
2. Michael Buerk, *The Road Taken*, Hutchinson, London, 2004, p. 293.
3. BBC *Six O'Clock News*, 23 October 1984.
4. Interview, Ron Neil.
5. Tony Vaux, *The Selfish Altruist*, Routledge, London, 2001, p. 52.
6. Amartya Sen, *Poverty and Famines*, OUP, Oxford, 1981, p.120.
7. Amartya Sen and Jean Dreze, *Hunger and Public Action*, OUP, Oxford, 1989, p. 231.
8. BBC Broadcaster's Audience Research Board Reports, R 9/1, 147/5.
9. The combined audience for the three daily bulletins on 23 and 24 October 1984 was 17.4 million and 18.1 million respectively. BARB Reports, R 9/1, 147/5.
10. Paul Harrison and Robin Palmer, *News out of Africa*, Hilary Shipman, London, 1986, p. 101.
11. Ibid., p. 123.
12. Interview, Chris Cramer.
13. David Rieff, *A Bed for the Night*, Vintage, London, 2002, p. 38.
14. Dawit Wolde Giorgis, *Red Tears*, Red Sea Press, New Jersey, 1989, p. 188.
15. Harrison and Palmer, *News out of Africa*, pp. 105–6.
16. Interview, Michael Buerk.
17. Interview, Paddy Coulter.
18. Buerk, *The Road Taken*, pp. 271–4.
19. *Emergency Appeals Case File*. Script for DEC TV Famine Appeal broadcast on BBC 19 July 1984 by Frank Bough, RAPIC B 420–4-3.
20. *Emergency Appeals Case File*. Letter from Pam Pouncey DEC secretary to Dennis Mann BBC appeals secretary 4 September 1984, RAPIC B 420–4-3.
21. Interview, Peter Gill.
22. Interview, Chris Cramer.
23. Ibid.
24. *Six O'Clock News*, Press Statement, T67/370/1, 8 June 1984.
25. Interview, Ron Neil.
26. *Six O'Clock News*, Memo from Andrew Taussig, chief assistant Current Affairs Television, to Chris Capron, head of Current Affairs, T67/370/1, 17 May 1984.
27. Buerk, *The Road Taken*, p. 157.
28. Interview, Mike Appleton.

29. Harrison and Palmer, *News out of Africa*, pp. 52–67.
30. Brian Phelan, 'Dying for news', *The Listener*, 28 February 1985.
31. *Emergency Appeals Case File*. Script for Famine Appeal by Esther Rantzen, RAPIC B 420–4-3, 31 October 1983.
32. *Emergency Appeals Policy 1965–1985*. Summary of Results from Radio and Television DEC Appeals (1966–83), B420–4-1.
33. *Emergency Appeals Case File*. Minutes of DEC meeting, B 420–4-3, 25 March 1983.
34. Interview, Mike Wooldridge.
35. Interview, Libby Grimshaw.
36. Ibid.
37. William Shawcross, *The Quality of Mercy*, Fontana paperback edn, London, 1985, p. 432.
38. Africa Watch Report, *Evil Days*, Human Rights Watch, New York, 1991, p. i.
39. Interview, Mike Wooldridge.
40. Giorgis, *Red Tears*.
41. Ibid., p. 141.
42. Vaux, *The Selfish Altruist*.
43. John Campbell, *Margaret Thatcher*, Jonathan Cape, London, 2003, vol. 2, p. 339.
44. Hugo Young, *One of Us*, Macmillan, London, 1989, p. 173.
45. Campbell, *Margaret Thatcher*, vol. 2, p. 340.
46. The National Archive, ODA 53/2: Letter from Michael Smith, British Embassy, Addis, 8 December 1982.
47. The National Archive, Public Record Office (TNA PRO) OD 53/5: Minutes of meeting between Save the Children and ODA officials, 5 October 1984.
48. TNA PRO OD 53/7: Memo from Denis Osborne to Sir Crispin Tickell, 29 October 1984.
49. Hansard, 22 November 1984, col. 418.
50. Letter from Charles Powell to FCO headed 'Ethiopia: Famine Relief', 29 October 1984. Obtained under FOI.
51. In her book *Statecraft* (HarperCollins, London, 2002, pp. 442–4) Mrs Thatcher makes very clear her hostility to foreign aid as a means of assisting development in poor countries.
52. Interview, Timothy Raison.
53. *Observer*, 18 November 1984.
54. Christopher Bosso, in Michael Margolis and Gary Mauser (eds), *Manipulating Public Opinion*, Brooks/Cole Publishing Co., Belmont, CA, 1989, pp. 153–74.
55. Africa Watch Report, *Evil Days*, p. 178.
56. Kissinger, quoted in Randolph C. Kent, *Anatomy of Disaster Relief*, Pinter, London, 1987, p. 81.
57. Alex de Waal, *Famine Crimes*, African Rights, Oxford, 1997, p. 164.
58. TNA PRO ODA 53/6: Report by Barder on the 'September Events' dated 5 October 1984.
59. FCO confidential paper 'The Ethiopian Famine: Policy Problems', 29 October 1984. Obtained under FOI.
60. TNA PRO OD 53/9: Telegram from UK Moscow embassy, 16 November 1984.
61. Giorgis, *Red Tears*, p. 158.
62. Ibid., p. 136.
63. Interview, Sir Crispin Tickell.

64. See *The Story of Band Aid*, Channel 4, December 2004, where the archive news footage of Geldof confronting Mrs Thatcher is shown and Geldof is then interviewed about the incident. See also Geldof (with Vallely), *Is That It?*, pp. 314–15.

65. TNA PRO OD 53/3: Transcript of news interview given by the prime minister to John Simpson, 31 March 1983.

66. Channel 4 documentary, *The Band Aid Story*, December 2004.

67. Grade, *It Seemed Like a Good Idea at the Time*, p. 196.

68. 'Do They Know It's Christmas?' continues to sell in various different versions; http://www.bobgeldof.info/Charity/bandaid.html, accessed 12 February 2007.

69. Mark Duffield, *Global Governance*, Zed Books, London, 2001, p. 76.

70. BBC History Seminar, 'Famine, Aid and the Media', 14 November 2004.

71. The draft title that appeared on the front cover of *Radio Times* for an event that never actually occurred.

72. BBC History Seminar, 'Famine, Aid and the Media'.

73. When BBC2 had to return to its mandatory Open University schedules during the night.

74. Interview with Trevor Dann in 'The inside story of the day rock changed', *Word*, November 2004.

75. Grade, *It Seemed Like a Good Idea at the Time*, p. 197.

76. Outside Broadcasts, B 220–002 1973–89. The director of programmes (TV) reported to the Board of Management on 22 July 1985 that UK TV viewing figures for the Live Aid concert had been over 30 million. A BBC press release claimed an estimated one and a half billion viewers in over one hundred countries. See Graham Mytton, head of International Audience Research, BBC World Service, 'A billion viewers can't be right', *Intermedia*, 19(3), May/June 1991.

77. Audience Research TV Audience Reaction TV/85/89, 'Live Aid for Africa'.

78. Peter Burnell, *Charity, Politics and the Third World*, Harvester Wheatsheaf, London, 1991, pp. 203–4. By the time Band Aid was wound up in 1987 it had raised a total of £174 million; Duffield, *Global Governance*, p. 76.

79. As Frank Prochaska showed, in the nineteenth century, women and children were the bedrock of philanthropic institutions.

80. Duffield, *Global Governance*, p. 76.

81. Burnell, *Charity, Politics and the Third World*, p. 12.

82. Central Appeals Advisory Committee (CAAC) Agenda and Papers D34-4-6, paper on 'Broadcast Appeals: Policy and Research Issues', presented 25 September 1986.

83. BBC Annual Report 1987, p. 108.

84. Greg Philo, 'From Buerk to Band Aid', in John Eldridge (ed.), *Getting the Message: News, Truth and Power*, Routledge, London, 1993, p. 122.

85. *Emergency Appeal Case File*, BBC WAC: RAPIC B420–4-3.

86. CAAC, paper on 'Broadcast Appeals: Policy and Research Issues'.

87. Geldof (with Vallely), *Is That It?*, p. 392.

88. Cathy Walker and Cathy Pharoah, *A Lot of Give*, Charities Aid Foundation, Kent, 2002, p. 107.

89. Mark Ellen, 'The longest day', *Word*, November 2004. Ellen had been one of the presenters of Live Aid.

90. BBC report, *From Seesaw to Wagon Wheel: Safeguarding Impartiality in the 21st Century*, June 2007.

91. *Emergency Appeals Case File*. Memo from appeals secretary to director of Public Affairs, RAPIC B420–4-3, 17 June 1982.

92. BBC Summary of World Broadcasts ME 7788, 31 October 1984.

93. Africa Watch Report, *Evil Days*, p. 177.
94. De Waal, 'African encounters', *Index on Censorship*, vol. 23, November/December 1994, p. 15.
95. J. Clay and B. Holcomb, *Politics and the Ethiopian Famine*, Cultural Survival, Cambridge, MA, 1986, p. 193; see also Donald Curtis, Michael Hubbard and Andrew Shepherd, *Preventing Famine: Policies and Prospects for Africa*, Routledge, London and New York, 1988.
96. Geldof (with Vallely), *Is That It?*, p. 339.
97. Ibid., p. 14.
98. Letters to the Editor, *The Times*, 7 November 1984.
99. Interview, David Loyn.

CHAPTER 9: WOMEN IN THE BBC

1. This chapter depends on a Witness Seminar attended by 27 women, organised by Dr Suzanne Franks, and chaired by the author.
2. Joan Bakewell, *The Listener*, 27 September 1974.
3. Rhona Rapoport (ed.), *Women and Top Jobs*, PEP, George Allen and Unwin, London, 1971.
4. Isabel Allen, 'Women and employment in the BBC', in *Women and Top Jobs*, p. 170.
5. Ibid.
6. There were fewer in the highest grade in 1979 than in 1969.
7. R34 T/1–2. J. Reith to station director, 26 July 1926.
8. *Women's Leader*, 2 January 1931.
9. Sally Feldman, Seminar.
10. Kenneth Adam, in John Grist, *Grace Wyndham Goldie*, Authors OnLine, London, 2006, p. 3.
11. Aubrey Singer, BBC Oral History.
12. Interview, David Attenborough.
13. David Hendy, *Life on Air: A History of Radio 4*, OUP, Oxford, 2007, p. 57.
14. Anthony King and Anne Sloman, *Westminster and Beyond*, Macmillan, London, 1973, p. 79.
15. Jonathan Lynn and Anthony Jay, *The Complete Yes Minister*, BBC Books, London, 1989, p. 360.
16. Interview, Elspeth Howe.
17. R 78/3 984/1.
18. Women's Monitoring Network, Report No. 2, 27 February 1982.
19. CPBE, *Women in Focus: Guidelines for Eliminating Media Sexism*, London, 1985, p. 15.
20. R78/2 257/1.
21. Report BM(73) 31: Limitations to the Recruitment and Advancement of Women in the BBC.
22. Women in the BBC, note by director, Personnel 1970 R2/70/3 B.M. (73) 31, p. 3.
23. Women in the BBC, One Year Later, BM(74) 96.
24. Interview, Jenny Abramsky.
25. Margaret Drabble, *Jerusalem the Golden*, Penguin, London, 1978, p. 15.
26. Seminar.
27. Interview, Thena Heshel.
28. Paul Donovan, *All Our Todays*, Jonathan Cape, London, 1997, p. 22.
29. Interview, Joan Bakewell.

30. Angela Neuberger, Seminar.
31. Caroline Millington, Seminar.
32. Susan Brownmiller, 'In our time', *Guardian G2*, 10 October 2012.
33. Interview, Susan Davies.
34. Interview with anonymous BBC correspondent.
35. Interview, Patricia Hodgson.
36. Caroline Millington, Seminar.
37. Seminar.
38. Richard Lindley, *Panorama*, Little, Brown, London, 2002, p. 269.
39. Anna Carragher, Seminar.
40. Sandra Chalmers, Seminar.
41. Interview, Ros Sloboda.
42. Angela Neuberger, Seminar.
43. Interview, Gwyneth Williams.
44. Interview, Naomi Sargant.
45. Gillian Reynolds, 'Women's place', *Broadcast Magazine*, 19 February 1979.
46. Lindley, *Panorama*, p. 273.
47. Monica Sims, *Women in BBC Management*, BBC, London, 1984.
48. R78/2 257/1.
49. BBC Seminar.
50. Morwenna Banks and Amanda Swift, *The Joke's on Us*, Pandora, London, 1987, p. vii.
51. Ibid., p. 245.
52. Interview, Francesca Kirby-Green.
53. Ibid.
54. BBC Seminar.
55. Interview, Francesca Kirby-Green.
56. Claire Dickson Clarke, BBC Oral History.
57. Interview, Sally Feldman.
58. Roger Bolton, *Death on the Rock*, W. H. Allen, London, 1990, p. 76.
59. Sims, *Women in BBC Management*, p. 11.

CHAPTER 10: LIGHT ENTERTAINMENT

1. *Daily Mail*, 6 June 1984.
2. Summary of meeting with Leon Brittan, chairman, director-general and director, Finance, 7 March 1985.
3. *The Listener*, 1 August 1974.
4. *Observer*, 11 June 1971.
5. BBC1, 25 December 1974.
6. Research, Chris Dunkley, *The Listener*, 4 March 1982.
7. Interview, Michael Grade.
8. Michael Grade, speech at Bill Cotton's memorial service, 2009.
9. Michael Grade, *It Seemed Like a Good Idea at the Time*, Macmillan, London, 1999, p. 239.
10. Interview, Sir Bernard Ingham.
11. *Yes Minister*, T62/323/1, C127, 1 November 1974 to 31 March 1989.
12. Interview, Alasdair Milne.
13. Interview, John Howard Davies.
14. Tom Sloan, 'Television and light entertainment', BBC Lunchtime Lecture, 1969.
15. Paul Fox, 'This is BBC1', BBC Lunchtime Lecture, 19 February 1969.

16. BOG 8/5/75 320 (c) Discussion of G176/75.
17. B650–5-2 Standards of Taste Part 2 General (attached to B650–005–002 Standards of Taste General Part 2 09/01/1974 – 31/12/1987, 10124347).
18. Interview, Will Wyatt.
19. Interview, Gareth Gwenlan.
20. 'A+ salaries' were approved for John Howard Davies and Terry Hughes in 1977. BOG June–September 1977, R1/45/3. Light Entertainment Group, Television: Senior Management.
21. TWPR, 20/0679. Minute 189 cont.
22. Interview, Will Wyatt.
23. Bill Cotton, obituary, *The Times*, 12 August 1998.
24. Grade, *It Seemed Like a Good Idea at the Time*, p. 301.
25. Interview, John Howard Davies.
26. Bryan Cowgill, BBC Oral History.
27. Grade, *It Seemed Like a Good Idea at the Time*, p. 175.
28. TWPR, 12 January 1980. Minute 341. Mr Bill Cotton.
29. Interview, Alasdair Milne.
30. Bill Cotton, BBC Oral History.
31. Huw Wheldon, *Competition in Television*, BBC, 1971, pp. 9–10.
32. Ibid.
33. Ibid.
34. Interview, Alan Yentob.
35. Purchase of Programmes – General, Part 1, 1 March 1977. Draft GAC paper: 'Acquired Programmes' G93/90, 5 October 1990. BBC RAPIC 10116535, D371–002.
36. Aubrey Singer, obituary, *The Times*, 29 May 2007.
37. Interview, Anna Home.
38. Purchase of Programmes Policy, Part 1, 01/04/1969–31/12/1992. 'Bought In Programmes' 22/07/1977. BBC RAPIC 10176560, A5779, D371–001.
39. Ibid.
40. Interview, John Birt.
41. Ibid.
42. *Daily Mail*, 30 July 1977.
43. Sean Day-Lewis, 'BBC to spend £2m on TV light shows', *Daily Telegraph*, 24 July 1970.
44. Memo from head of Commercial Operations USA on the subject of BBC Television in America, 11/11/1980. R104/197/1, F369–4-2, 10070703, DP20. BBC Enterprises USA, 1980.
45. Will Wyatt, *The Fun Factory*, Aurum Press, London, 2003, p. 102.
46. *Blankety Blank* Pilot, 07/08/1978; Letter 06/07/1978, from Gil Fates, Goodson-Todman Productions, to Alan Boyde (producer *Blankety Blank*), T70/15/1, 10031068.
47. Interview, Jon Plowman.
48. *Blankety Blank*, TWPR, 25 April 1979.
49. Ibid., 4 April 1979.
50. Ibid., 16 May 1979.
51. Ibid., 2 January 1980. Minute 7 cont.
52. *Sunday Times*, 22 January 1995. Cited in Antony Easthope, *Englishness and National Culture*, Routledge, London, 1999, p. 160.
53. Horace Newcomb and Robert S. Alley (eds), *The Producers' Medium*, Oxford University Press, New York, 1983, p. 11.
54. Norman Lear, in ibid., p. 194.

55. Interview, Jon Plowman.
56. See Jeremy Tunstall and David Machin, *The Anglo-American Media Connection*, OUP, Oxford, 1999, p. 94.
57. Interview, Richard Briers.
58. Memo from managing director, Television Paul Fox to controller, BBC1, H.L.E.G., H.C.L.E.G. and Dir. Co-prod. 19/10/1988. BBC RAPIC 10122207, A2451. Columbia Broadcasting Systems, Part 2. 01/09/1983–31/05/1990. N107.
59. Interviews, John Howard Davies, Susan Belbin, Colin Gilbert.
60. Interview, Susan Belbin.
61. Interview, Jimmy Gilbert.
62. Compiled by the comedy script editor, Ian Maine.
63. 'First Draft: Comedy Writing', Producer Tom Alban. PLN016/00FK8160.
64. Interview, Geoffrey Perkins.
65. Stephen Wagg, 'At ease Corporal': social class and the situation comedy in British television', in *Because I Tell a Joke or Two*, Routledge, London, 1998, pp. 20–21.
66. Interview, Jon Plowman.
67. *The Marti Caine Show*, TWPR, 24 January 1979. Minute 50 cont.
68. Shirley Bassey, TWPR, 31 October 1979. Minute 313 cont.
69. *Three of a Kind*, TWPR, 15 December 1982. See also TWPR, 17 April 1985.
70. Peter Black, 'Comedy Styles', *The Listener*, 15 June 1983.
71. Barry Took, *Star Turns*, Weidenfeld and Nicolson, London, 1992, p. 48.
72. Editorial Control of Programmes Policy, Part 4. January 1973–September 1980. B650–1-1, R78/1210/1.
73. Interview, Bill Cotton.
74. *The Black and White Minstrel Show*, TWPR, 16 June 1976. Minute 202 cont.
75. Ibid., 21 June 1978. Minute 178 cont.
76. Ibid., 2 July 1975.
77. Ibid., 21 June 1978.
78. Ibid., 21 June 1978. Minute 178 cont.
79. *IBA Television and Radio Journal*, 1977 (Guide to ITV and Independent Local Radio), p. 51.
80. General Entertainment Programme Policy – Minutes of meeting held 2/11/1982. R78/2551/1.
81. Simon Edge, *Daily Express*, 25 May 2004.
82. Bill Cotton, BBC Oral History.
83. Television Management Registry, Part 1. Light Entertainment – General, July 1974–October 1992. RAPIC A2207, B200–2.
84. Interview, Sarah Caplin.
85. Interview, Esther Rantzen.
86. Audience Research Report Jan–Jul 1986, T67/395/1.
87. Esther Rantzen, *Esther*, BBC, London, 2001, p. 185.
88. *That's Life* – General C008–002 01/09/80 to 13/12/1984, 13 October 1982 (Manager Current Affairs Programmes) Esther Rantzen T67/374/1.
89. *That's Life* – General C008–002 01/09/80 to 13/12/1984, T67/374/1.
90. Private information.
91. *That's Life* – General C008–002 01/09/1980 to 31/12/1984.
92. *That's Life* – General C008–002 01/09/1980 to 31/12/1984, 10/11/1980, T67/374/1.
93. Esther Rantzen, *The British Way of Birth*, Pan Books, London, 1982, pp. 1–10.
94. Interview, Esther Rantzen.
95. Interview, Catherine Crowther.

96. The 'Battered Baby' Syndrome, Department of Health, London, 1972, p. 15.
97. Arnon Bentovim (ed.), Child Sexual Abuse Within the Family: Assessment and Treatment, Wright, London, 1978, p. 44.
98. David Hare, 'Jimmy Savile', Guardian, 9 July 2014.
99. N18/3,6641, Artist file, Jimmy Savile, 1959–65, 13 December 1965.
100. N18/6,391. Artist file, Jimmy Savile, 1972–4.
101. Ts51/281/1.
102. Interview, Helen Pennant-Rae.
103. Andrew O'Hagan, 'Light Entertainment', London Review of Books, 8 November 2012, p. 27.

CHAPTER 11: DRAMA

This chapter was informed by a Witness Seminar on BBC Drama and the creation of *EastEnders*.

1.   Dennis Potter, Preface, in Robert Muller (ed.), The Television Dramatist, Elek, London, 1973, p. 304.
2.   V. Gras and J. Cook (eds), The Passion of Dennis Potter, St Martin's Press, New York, 2000, p. 113.
3.   Ken Trodd, Introduction, in The Trodd Index, Faber & Faber, London, 1977, p. 53.
4.   All of the above in Howard Newby, 'Radio, television and the arts', BBC Lunchtime Lectures 10th series, 15 January 1976, pp. 3–16.
5.   Trodd, Introduction, The Trodd Index, p. 53.
6.   Audience Appreciation Report: Drama R.37, December 1981, BBC WAC.
7.   'Drama in National Life', Drama, T72/311, 15 May 1979.
8.   Shaun Sutton, BBC Oral History.
9.   Gerard Mansell, 'Broadcasting in the Seventies', BBC, 10 July 1969. Mansell's radical report led to protests in the press and by BBC staff.
10. Shaun Sutton, BBC Oral History.
11. Interview, Richard Broke.
12. Interview, Ken Trodd.
13. Interview, Margaret Heffernan.
14. Interview, Jonathan Powell.
15. Interview, Michael Grade.
16. Shaun Sutton, BBC Oral History.
17. Churchill's People, BOG papers, 320(b).
18. James Hawthorne Papers, JH-041BC.
19. Memo MD Aubrey Singer to DRTel, 19 April 1982. He wrote to the director-general, 22 September 1982. BBC Programme Policy T62–223–1.
20. Interview, Jonathan Powell.
21. Interview, Will Wyatt.
22. Interview, Jonathan Powell.
23. Interview, Paul Fox.
24. Programme Review Board, director, Television, 19 October 1982.
25. Interview, Hugh Whitemore.
26. Interview, Peter Goodchild.
27. Televised Drama, T72/233/4, 15 May 1979.

28. Helen Wheatley, 'Experimentation and armchair theatre', in L. Mulvey and J. Sexton (eds), *Experimental British Television*, Manchester University Press, Manchester, 2007, p. 34.
29. BFI Dossier no. 20, ed. R. Patterson.
30. David Edgar, 'Playing shops: shopping plays', in J. Bignall (ed.), *British Television Drama Past, Present and Future*, Palgrave, Basingstoke, 2000, p. 76.
31. *Edge of Darkness*, C037, 1 January 1985 to 31 May 1992, T62/256/1.
32. Troy Kennedy Martin, *Edge of Darkness*, Faber & Faber, London, 1990, p. vii.
33. *Edge of Darkness*, C037, 1 January 1985 to 31 May 1992, T62/256/1.
34. Interview, Jonathan Powell.
35. Memo, Graeme MacDonald, 'Eleventh Hour', T72/233/1.
36. Programme Review discussed them, TVWPR, 30 July 1975, 211.
37. David Hare, *Guardian*, 15 August 1981.
38. Eldon Griffiths, MP, *Sunday Express*, 23 March 1980.
39. Interview, Alasdair Milne and Richard Broke.
40. Interview, Richard Broke.
41. *Tumbledown*, MoD Robert A. D. Lawrence to Richard Broke.
42. Interview, Ian Curteis.
43. Interview, David Edgar.
44. BBC Dimbleby Lecture, 3 November 1973.
45. Peter Buckman, 'Urgent messages', *The Listener*, 9 October 1975.
46. D.A.N. Jones, 'Citrine on Days of Hope', *The Listener*, 9 October 1975.
47. BOG papers, 25 Sepember 1975, *Polemical Drama*.
48. General Advisory Council Minutes, 22 October 1975, p. 2, R6/290/11.
49. Ibid.
50. Programme Policy Drama, T62/223/1, Colin Shaw, 29 September 1975, R78/2,503/1.
51. Programme Policy Drama, T62/223/1, B170–001. Colin Shaw, Committed Drama.
52. Ibid., Committed Drama, 1975, p. 9.
53. Ibid., p. 10.
54. Ibid., p. 12.
55. David Hare, *Ah! Mischief*, ed. Frank Pike, Faber & Faber, London, 1982, p. 42.
56. Ibid.
57. Ben Thompson (ed.), *Ban this Filth! Letters from the Mary Whitehouse Archive*, Faber & Faber, London, 2012, p. 32.
58. BOG 385 2(d) Play Things, 13 May 1976, 350(b).
59. Interview, Alasdair Milne.
60. Dennis Potter to Milne, T62/233/1 Drama DG.
61. Mary Whitehouse, 23 April 1976, in Thompson, *Ban This Filth!*, p. 32.
62. Alasdair Milne, *DG: The Memoirs of a British Broadcaster*, Hodder and Stoughton, London, 1988, p. 114.
63. Colin Shaw, Witness Seminar, University of Westminster, 23 February 2004.
64. 'He [director-general Curran] and MDTel recognised that there was little to be done in this instance because the producer concerned was leaving the BBC in a few months time in any case' (BOM, 29 March 1976, 173(d)).
65. Television on the Fringe, BOG 274, 13 April 1978.
66. Alasdair Milne to Potter, T62/244/1, Drama DG.
67. Alasdair Milne, Drama Programmes Policy, 27 February 1978, T62/233/1.
68. Interview, Alasdair Milne.
69. Christopher Ricks, *The Listener*, 10 October 1978.
70. Interview, Jonathan Powell.

71. TWPR, 18 January 1984, The Thorn Birds: 3 xi.
72. Annual Broadcasting Audience Share 1976–1984, BBC History Project.
73. BBC RAPIC A1083 TWPR, 18 January 1984, xi p. 19. Stephen Hearst, special adviser to the director-general and Brian Wenham, director of programmes, Television.
74. BBC RAPIC A1083 TWPR, 'Future policy for the television service', internal discussion paper by Victor Marmion, 1 December 1983.
75. Ibid., p. 2.
76. Interview, Nigel Pope.
77. The BBC had an income of around £700 million, and the ITV companies £1 billion.
78. Interviews, Nigel Pope and Keith Anderson.
79. BBC RAPIC A1083 TWPR, 5 June 1985, minute 144. Anne Laking said there was still considerable audience loyalty but the 'zapper' was now beginning to erode this.
80. BBC RAPIC A1083 TWPR, 18 January 1984, The Thorn Birds: 3 xi Brian Wenham.
81. Adapted from R9/162/1 'Drama Series and Serials: Audience Loyalty Quarter 4 1983', unpublished internal report by Alison Cann.
82. Interview, Alan Hart.
83. Advertisement in The Lady's Companion, 1849, for the first edition of Household Words. Quoted in the introduction to A. Lohri, Household Words, University of Toronto Press, 1975, p. 4.
84. Elizabeth Gaskell, Lizzie Leigh, part 1, in Household Words, 1850. Also collected in Mrs Gaskell, Collected Short Stories, Routledge, London, 1978, pp. 49–76.
85. BBC RAPIC A4284 Eastenders Part 1, 1 November 1984 to 31 December 1987. Memo, 5 December 1985, from Pam Reiss (Manager Output Continuous Services) to Michael Grade (CBBC1), Bill Cotton (MDTel), Brian Wenham (DPTel).
86. EastEnders, Witness Seminar.

CHAPTER 12: SMILEY'S REAL PEOPLE

This chapter was informed by a Witness Seminar on BBC engineering held at Wood Norton.

1. ARKive interview, Desmond Morris.
2. Maxwell Knight, A Cuckoo in the House, Methuen, London, 1955, p. 7.
3. Anthony Masters, The Man Who Was M, Blackwell, Oxford, 1984, p. 226.
4. See Christopher Andrews's Introduction, in John Currie, The Security Service, 1908–1945, Public Record Office, Kew, 1999, p. 7.
5. Masters, The Man Who Was M, p. 231.
6. L. Mathews and M. Knight, Senses of Animals, Philosophical Library, New York, 1963, p. 13.
7. Interview, Desmond Morris.
8. Formalities Historical 1982–6 Memo, R Stoneham to director, Personnel, 7 February 1984, R 154/9/2.
9. Interview, Mike Hodder.
10. http://www.bbc.co.uk/programmes/panorama (1975).
11. Alban Webb, in Marie Gillespie and Alban Webb, Diasporas and Diplomacy, Routledge, Abingdon, 2012, p. 98.
12. Gerald Mansell, 'Why external broadcasting?', BBC Lunchtime Lectures, 11 March 1976.
13. Interview, John Tusa.
14. R. H. Coase, British Broadcasting, LSE, London, 1950, p. 29.

15. Kingsley-Hall papers, Churchill College, Cambridge.
16. Gerald Mansell, BBC Oral History.
17. Interview, Baqer Moin.
18. N&CA Meeting (non-attributable), 26 June 1979.
19. Interview, Michael Palliser.
20. N&CA, 26 June 1979.
21. Gerald Mansell, BBC Oral History.
22. Peter Hennessy, *The Secret State*, Penguin, London, 2002, pp. 2–3.
23. Interview, Michael Palliser.
24. NAO PRO DFE 4/232, Military Aspects of The Home Defence for the United Kingdom, 1 October 1968.
25. Christopher Andrew and Oleg Gordievsky, *Comrade Kryuchkov's Instructions*, Stanford University Press, 1999, p. 67.
26. Hennessy, *The Secret State*, p. 4.
27. William Millward, in F. H. Hinsley and Alan Stripp (eds), *Codebreakers*, OUP, Oxford, 1993, p. 17.
28. PRO CAB 120/30, PV (57) 12.
29. Interview, Bryce McCririck.
30. Interview, Phil Laven.
31. Seminar on Engineering.
32. Interview, Phil Laven.
33. Ibid.
34. Seminar on Engineering.
35. David Loyn, *Butcher and Bolt*, Random House, London, 2010, p. 155.
36. BOG, 6 March 1975, 150.
37. Direct Broadcasting by Satellite Policy 1977–1980, RAPIC D113-6-1.
38. Interview, Phil Laven.
39. Interview, Michael Checkland.
40. Formalities – Historical 1982–86, Memo R Stoneham to director, personnel, 7 February 1984, R154/9/2.
41. Hennessy, *The Secret State*, p. 123.
42. John le Carré, *Tinker Tailor Soldier Spy*, Hodder and Stoughton, London, 1974, p. 28.
43. Interview, Kate Adie.
44. Interview, Stephen Claypole.
45. Mark Hollingsworth and Richard Norton-Taylor, *Blacklist*, Hogarth Press, London, 1988, p. 120.
46. Formalities – General Correspondence, Memo from Mr Cruttwell to GEO, 17 June 1940, R154/11/1.
47. Ibid., Memo Mr Cruttwell to Mr Jardine Brown, 8 August 1940, R154/11/1.
48. See Jeffrey Richelson, in R. Jeffreys-Jones and C. Andrew (eds), *Eternal Vigilance*, Frank Cass, London, 1997, p. 99.
49. Interview, Paul Bonner.
50. Ibid.
51. Interview, Denis Forman.
52. BOG, 5 September 1985, 303(a).
53. Formalities – Historical 1982–6, Memo R Stoneham to director, Personnel, 7 February 1984, R154/9/2.
54. NAO PRO KV4/121, Memo 'B' to 'DSS', 20 December 1933.
55. NAO PRO KV4/121, Memo 'B', 14 March 1934.
56. NAO PRO KV4/121, Memo 'B', 23 March 1934.

57. NAO PRO KV4/121, Memo 'B' to 'DSS', 6 July 1934.
58. NAO TNA PRO KV4/ 121, Memo signed U.G.W.K., 3 April 1935.
59. Staff policy – Security 'College' Clearances Policy 1940–47, Memo GEO to WSA, 10 September 1940, R49/618.
60. Memo Mr Cruttwell to GEO, 30 September 1940, R49/618.
61. Formalities – General Correspondence Memo Box 500 to R Jardine Brown BBC, 25 January 1941, R154/11/1.
62. Formalities – General Correspondence record of a telephone conversation between R Jardine Brown BBC and Captains Strong and Cumming MI5, 7 February 1941, R154/11/1.
63. NAO PRO KV 4/36, Memo 'The Examination of Credentials', DDG Security Service, June 1942.
64. NAO TNA PRO KV4/ 121, note signed Roger H Hollis, 5 August 1940.
65. Formalities – Historical 1950–82, R154/9/1.
66. Ibid., Memo HHP/KS (Box 500) to Tothill BBC, 6 February 1959, R154/9/1.
67. Ibid., BBC News Formalities to Box 500, 21 March 1979, R154/9/1.
68. Ibid.
69. Formalities – Historical 1950–82, Record of a meeting between JH Arkell DSA and Sir Roger Hollis, Box 500, 30 July 1959, R154/9/1.
70. Ibid., Memo DSA to CSTA, 25 April 1960, R154/9/1.
71. Ibid., Hollis to Arkell, 28 June 1960, R154/9/1.
72. Ibid., letter RH to Sir CC, 26 July 1960, R154/9/1.
73. Ibid., statement of BBC position, 14 July 1960, R154/9/1.
74. Ibid., HCG to Arkell, 23 December 1960, R154/9/1.
75. Ibid., OJ Whitley to Box 500, 3 March 1961, R154/9/1.
76. Ibid., Memo GM Lewis Miss to CSTA, 3 May 1961, and his handwritten comments to her, 4 May 1961, R154/9/1.
77. Memo director, Administration JH Arkell to Mr Berry, 1 March 1968, and attached brief, R154/13/1.
78. Security – Vetting of Staff, Note PH Scott to director-general, 25 May 1977, D453–008.
79. Formalities – Historical 1950–82, special duties, 5 July 1977, R154/9/1.
80. Ibid., Note by John Priest, 15 March 1978, R154/9/1.
81. Security – Vetting of Staff, Letter M Swann to PM, 31 January 1980, D453–008.
82. Interview, Mike Hodder.
83. Security – Vetting of Staff, Memo R Stonham SpA to DPA, 30 November 1983, D453–008.
84. Interview, Mike Hodder.
85. Free Communications Group, *In Place of Management*, 1979.
86. Interview, Michael Darlow.
87. Interview, Isabel Hilton. Security – Vetting of Staff, Memo R Rowland C Management Development and Appointments to HID, 26 February 1985, D453–008.
88. Security – Vetting of Staff, Letter Isabel Hilton to Roger Johnson 14 November 1985; Roger Johnson to Isabel Hilton, 2 December 1985, D453–008.
89. Patrick Hill, 'BBC and MI5 – governors didn't know', *Standard*, 19 August 1985.
90. Security – Vetting of Staff, SU/8033/I SWB, 19 August 1985, monitoring report, D453–008.
91. TVWPR, 21 August 1985, 216; RWPRB, 21 August 1985, 172.
92. Security – Vetting of Staff, TVWPR, 11 September 1985, 243, D453–008.
93. Security – Vetting of Staff, Letter Christopher Martin to Tony Hearn, 9 December 1986, D453–008.

94. John le Carré, Introduction to B. Page, D. Leigh and P. Knightley, *Philby*, André Deutsch, London, 1968, p. 27.
95. Ibid., p. 37.
96. Jonathan Powell, BBC interview.
97. *Tinker Tailor Soldier Spy* – Producers File 1977–82, T65/38/1, Letter from David Cornwell to Alec Guinness, 27 February 1978.
98. Ibid. Letter from Alec Guinness to David Cornwell, 2 March 1978.
99. Ibid. Letter from David Cornwell to Alec Guinness, 3 March 1978.
100. Interview, Jonathan Powell.
101. *Tinker Tailor Soldier Spy* – Producers File 1977–82, T65/38/1, Conversation between David Cornwell and Austin Spriggs, p. 5.
102. BOM, 27 September 1982, 769.
103. Interview, Andrew Roos, from *Salon*, 1996, reprinted in Mathew Bruccoli (ed.), *Conversations with John le Carré*, University of Mississippi Press, Jackson, 2004, p. 143.
104. Interview, Jonathan Powell.
105. Ibid.

CHAPTER 13: ENDGAME

1. Interview, Mark Damazer.
2. Ben Pimlott, reprinted in *Frustrate Their Knavish Tricks*, HarperCollins, London, 1994, p. 298.
3. Interview, Marmaduke Hussey.
4. Interview, David Holmes.
5. Interview, Patricia Hodgson.
6. John Tusa, unpublished diary.
7. Interview, Michael Grade.
8. Interview, Mark Tulley.
9. Interview, Joan Bakewell.
10. David Holmes, BBC Oral History.
11. Michael Checkland, Seminar.
12. Interview, Ros Sloboda.
13. Interview, Douglas Hurd.
14. John Cole, 'The Archangel Gabriel as DG wouldn't be acceptable to all party leaders', *The Listener*, 5 February 1987, p. 6.
15. John Campbell, *Iron Lady*, Jonathan Cape, London, 2003, p. 157.
16. Information from Michael Bunce.
17. BBC History Seminar.
18. Interview, David Holmes.
19. Interview, David Barlow.
20. David Barlow, BBC Oral History.
21. Interview, Peter Ibbotson.
22. Interview, Glenn del Medico.
23. Interview, Peter Ibbotson.
24. http://news.bbc.co.uk/2/hi/uk_news/politics/1485089.stm.
25. Interview, Patricia Hodgson.
26. Interview, Lord Deben (John Gummer).
27. Interview, Alasdair Milne.
28. BOG 6.2.1984 74(a).

29. Interview, Alex Gerlis.
30. Interview, Peter Ibbotson.
31. Interview, Alan Protheroe.
32. BOG 16.10.1986 319 director-general's report.
33. Interview, John Birt.
34. Interview, Patricia Hodgson.
35. Interview, Alex Gerlis.
36. Interview, Peter Ibbotson.
37. Interview, Alasdair Milne.
38. Frank Gillard, BBC Oral History; interview, Alan Protheroe.
39. Interview, Michael Cole.
40. Interview, Michael Grade.
41. Interview, Alasdair Milne.
42. (State papers) NI. SPB/34/ 93/02, Broadcasting and Television, 27 September 1979.
43. Interview, Austin Hunter.
44. Interview, Alasdair Milne.
45. BOM Strictly Confidential 7.8.1984 BOM (85) 435–436.
46. See Jean Seaton, *The Hidden Wiring*, 20th Century British History, Part VI, 2013, pp. 212–35.
47. David Barlow, BBC Oral History.
48. Interview, David Holmes.
49. Interview, Alwyn Roberts.
50. Ibid.
51. Interview, Leon Brittan.
52. BOG19/9/85 318 (c).
53. Interview, Allan Little.
54. Interview, Ian Curteis.
55. BOG 13/11/86 360 (d).
56. Interviews, Sir Bernard Ingham and Brian Griffiths.
57. Sam Brittan speaking at 'The Peacock Legacy' conference, Aberystwyth University, 2005.
58. Birt and Jay, 1975, 1975a.
59. Campbell, *Iron Lady*, p. 157.
60. Sir Alan had written on orchestras and music.
61. R78/3532 D215–025–001 Finance the BBC Committee (Peacock) Policy, Meeting BOG and BOM, 14 November 1985; memo S Hearst to Alasdair Milne, 5 December 1985.
62. HO FIN 86 0244/0002/001 'Broadcasting and Wireless Telegraphy BBC Peacock Report', Minute D Hurd to M Thatcher, 11 June 1986 (hereafter HO FIN 86 0244/0002/001).
63. Interview, Janet Morgan.
64. Interview, Peter Ibbotson.
65. Brian Wenham could only offer the defence that Milne was 'a man given to few words'. Wenham, BBC Oral History interview.
66. BM (86) 26 Final Supplementary Evidence to the Peacock Committee, 14 February 1986.
67. 'They were rather uncivil to me. I stood on the quality of our programmes – which I had complete confidence in.' Interview, Alasdair Milne.
68. R44/1403/1 Peacock Committee, background information and BBC Comments, Address by the Director-general of the BBC to the Peacock Committee's Conference on Financing the BBC, 28 November 1985.

69. His committee included Patricia Hodgson, Geoff Buck, the BBC's resourceful director of Finance, Phil Laven, a wily political engineer, Stephen Hearst, former controller of Radio 3 and head of the 'Future Policy Unit', and Janet Morgan, a well-connected political fixer.
70. Brian Wenham, BBC Oral History.
71. Interview, Paddy Barwise.
72. R78/3532 Finance the BBC Committee (Peacock) Policy, Joint Board of Governors and Board of Management meeting on the BBC submission to Peacock, 14 November 1985.
73. Interview, Michael Checkland.
74. Interview, Sam Brittan.
75. Patricia Hodgson, BBC Oral History.
76. Interview, John McCormick.
77. Interview, Marmaduke Hussey.
78. Ibid.
79. BOG 16/10/86 319 Director-general's Report.
80. BOG 30/10/86 340 Director-general's Report.
81. Norman Tebbit, *Upwardly Mobile*, Futura, London, 1991, p. 339.
82. BBC and Libya: Bias and Balance T66/95/2.1986.
83. Interview, Kate Adie.
84. Ibid.
85. Interview, Patricia Hodgson.
86. John Tusa, unpublished diary.
87. Alasdair Milne, unpublished diary, 10 December 1986.
88. Interview, Alasdair Milne. In 1987 Milne's salary was £81,780. This would be worth £198,912.64 in 2015, according to the Bank of England inflation calculator.
89. Interview, Tim Orchard.
90. Letters in private papers of Alasdair Milne.
91. Interview, John Birt.

ACKNOWLEDGEMENTS

IN AUGUST 1939 VIRGINIA WOOLF wrote in her diary, 'I have been thinking about censors. How visionary figures admonish us... All books now seem to me surrounded by a circle of invisible censors.' She was talking about the hesitations that stay the writing hand. Her response to the challenge of evading censors was playful and deceptive. If she exposed her real feelings towards her parents in *To the Lighthouse* (while carefully protecting their identities), in *Orlando* – a camp, bravura portrait of her lover Vita Sackville-West – she artfully effaced her feelings in what appears to be a fiction, even while it is based on an intimate friend. Censors, it seems, are part of the writing game.

When writing about the BBC – a large, self-absorbed, carnivorous beast – some might suspect that external invigilators, bristling with injunctions about sensitive issues, would hover anxiously over the enterprise. But although the BBC asked me to write this history, no one has ever stopped me exploring any field within it. On the contrary, cupboard doors have been flung open and the Corporation has helped me in every way – but never interfered. There may be much that I ought to have done that has been left undone, but the shape of the enquiries and the eventual judgements are entirely my own responsibility.

However, Woolf was highlighting the invidious role of our internal regulators. They have been pesky – although it is only possible to keep them in their place if they are identified. They have been concerned with courtesy: people who have striven for the BBC (even if it ended up treating them badly – or they feel they failed, or indeed were part of a problem) were marked by the Corporation. They had a devotion to the idea of the BBC that seemed to give even the most ruthless BBC mogul a splinter of selfless perspective. Being given such stories has been a privilege. But the regulators have also imposed a responsibility that seems unusual. In most academic work the duty is to the argument, but here there was a perceptible added obligation to the values of the institution, requiring a harsh, not necessarily comfortable independence, which has had to be struggled for.

It was challenging to attempt to meet the BBC's ideals of hard impartiality. Yet this is, in a way, the biography of an institution. In the end all that can be done is to tell a story as accurately and in as many-sided and nuanced a way as possible: the conclusions are no doubt partial, but not casual. I have also anguished (whether effectively or not is for others to judge) about being true to the larger picture of the BBC. It is how the BBC cares about making difficult decisions that is so intriguing and so consequential. I recall thinking that I needed to put my head in a washing machine to try and rinse out my prejudices. I am bound to have failed. My only defence is that I have been very hungry to understand how it functioned, how people inside and *outside* the BBC saw things, how things they could not at the time see clearly influenced outcomes.

The research for this book was funded by a major Arts and Humanities Research Council grant, a British Academy award and a priceless, personal, year's Leverhulme fellowship. This funding means that the work has launched a bunch of impressive academic careers, and I am most grateful for it.

This is, of course, *a* history of the BBC, not *the* history, and I am deeply aware that other scholars would have carved (and will carve) a different story from the archives. My first debt is to Lord Briggs – Asa. I was set the daunting task of carrying forward the story from his own groundbreaking histories of the BBC, work that I fell on as a young scholar. Asa, who has met almost every BBC director-general right back to Lord Reith, has been warmly encouraging throughout. My oldest sparring partners, Professors James Curran and Stephen Barnett, have been a source of new ideas. Sir David Cannadine and Professors Nick Garnham, David Hendy, Paddy Scannel and Miles Taylor all helped me in many ways. Dr Alban Webb, whose own history of the World Service, *London Calling*, is invaluable, has been a humane sounding board. My wonderful department at the University of Westminster, Professors Jeanette Steemers, David Gauntlett, Peter Goodwin and Rosie Thomas among them, have been a stimulating launch pad for thinking. David Goodhart is a restless intellect who has posed important problems in ways that have assisted me. My thinking about the media has been sharpened by colleagues at the Reuters Institute for the Study of Journalism in Oxford (especially John Lloyd and Timothy Garton-Ash), my work with Full Fact, and the intellectual clarity allied to sheer guts of Martin Moore at the Media Standards Trust. And running the Orwell Prize has been a roller-coaster education.

Dame Jenny Abramsky, Mark Adair, Professor Christopher Andrews, Lord Bew, Humphrey Burton, Andrew Coleman, Sir Lawrence Freedman, Lord Hennessy, Sir Nicholas Kenyon, Pat Loughery, Valerie Nazareth and Sir John Tusa all read drafts of the book and helped me find my bearings in difficult new areas. Jenny Hartley – whose company makes thinking an elixir – spent days thoughtfully grappling with the structure of the book with me. Sir Paul Fox took me out for an inspiring lunch when the project started, read the whole draft, made many comments, and marked the end with another joyful lunch. I am immensely grateful to all of them for their interest and help.

This book is the work of a team of teams. Bastions toppled as Dr Anthony McNicholas bore down on them wielding FOIs, patience and curiosity. Professor Suzanne Franks brought her energy and insider grown-up-ness to the research. Dr Heather Sutherland and Daniel Day became scholars working on it. Dr Kirstin Scoog and Anne Baker (who has been a constant support) did extra research for me.

Then there was a BBC team: Chris Graham (now the Information Commissioner) relaunched the idea of the history before I was involved; it was taken up by Justin Phillips; and then Robin Reynolds was tirelessly helpful. Mark Adair and the BBC in Northern Ireland were soberingly helpful and welcoming. John Escolme was cheerfully persistent in finding material. Robert Seatter, the head of BBC History, has been strategic and imaginative about the role of the BBC's past in its present, and has supported the project and me personally with warmth and intelligence.

My understanding of the Corporation has been illuminated by conversations with people in charge of the BBC as the farrago of events has rolled on. Mark Damazer, Richard Sambrook, Jessica Cecil, Helen Boaden, Mark Thompson and others, and Nicholas Kroll, Michael Williams and Diane Coyle at the BBC Trust have let me see the BBC 'mind' at work. It was always the best of interesting fun to talk with Lord Patten, robust, wily and civilised.

I was guided at the start by a conversation with Sir Michael Checkland. I may not have come to the conclusions that he expected, but he is a hero of this book. The story is also concerned with people like Alasdair Milne, who believed in the BBC, but who perhaps tragically could do little more than defend the idea. Later, guardians like Lord Birt, who imagined a new compact between the Corporation and the nation, and Patricia Hodgson, whose insights are always penetrating, had to retrieve a future for the BBC. People who disagree about everything unite in a devotion to the institution.

The most important part of the BBC team has been the staff at the BBC written archive – a treasure house of the distilled thinking of an unusually literate institution, applying principles across every aspect of our national life and international affairs. Jackie Kavanagh, the former head of the archive, has always been kind and intuitive about the records that were in her care, and her successor James Codd and their staff have been tirelessly helpful: the whole project has depended on their deep understanding of the BBC's inner life of papers. Chris Westcott, the head of BBC Monitoring, has added a great deal.

However, this book has always tried to put thinking *in* the BBC in the context of thinking *about* the BBC from outside. For this it needed access to government papers. Sir John Gieve was generously instrumental from the Home Office, and former cabinet secretaries Lord O'Donnell and Lord Butler supported the project. Sue Owen at DFID helped. Tessa Stirling and her staff in the Cabinet Office made the work possible.

The Bodleian Library (and Graham C. Greene) helped me with Sir Hugh Greene's papers; Andrew Riley at Churchill College Archive was a vital source of advice about the papers there; Paul Bonner, the late historian of independent broadcasting, was unstinting in his help; and Suzanne Bardgett at the Imperial War Museum helped in many other ways. The Mary Whitehouse papers at Essex University and the Swann papers at Edinburgh University were invaluable.

Then there has been the Profile team. I am so proud to be published by such an agile, interesting, class act, and Andrew Franklin, sharp and lovely, and the delightful Paul Forty have been very important in making it a better book. I owe a particular debt to Ned Pennant-Rae, who triumphantly submitted the edited manuscript while in harbour in Boston for two hours during a sailing trip. I depended on him more than he knows.

Catherine Crowther, John and Katherine Gieve, Suzanne Franks and John Bowers, Carin Pimlott, Rosaleen Hughes and Nick Butler all lent me charming houses to write in. Gillian Darley, Michael Horowitz, Jane Haynes and many friends have supported me. Penelope Lively has offered a model of grace and intelligence.

Above all, David Loyn brought the standards of his own fastidious, deeply felt reporting and a brisk, no-nonsense adventuring which lifted my spirits and helped my work in every possible way. His sons Tom, Christopher and Jamie Loyn have brought new interests bounding into my life.

My sons Daniel, Nathaniel and Seth Pimlott have kept steady step beside me through everything – my clever, mordant mainstays. Everything I do is for them. It is sad that Ben missed seeing their vaunting lives, but I am rapt watching their large, decent, thrilling stories unfurl.

* * *

This is a book about the BBC, made possible by the Corporation's archives, given a liveliness by the testimony of hundreds of people who worked for it, and grounded in the programmes it made. As much of it was written in a kind of monastic solitude in distant places, BBC Radio 4, Radio 3 and the World Service were often my only companions, lighting up my life with their streams of engaged ideas. I am a BBC enthusiast, but I have strenuously attempted to implement its own demanding standards of independence. Political interference is a threat to the BBC, but I hope I have also shown how politicians have their own legitimate needs in difficult times. We expect the BBC to reflect us – but to be better than we are. As one of the great practical agents of delight and enlightenment, it needs to confront us with truths, but also to propose wild, imaginative alternatives. Dealing as it does with a tough period, the book attempts to locate the Corporation in our national life and as part of our place in the world. The BBC is a peerless institution: one that expresses and shapes our national temperament. It is envied all over the world. I always imagine it as a fragile golden bowl handed from generation to generation. We ought to cherish it and ask it to be bolder, because in so doing we care for ourselves.

* * *

I am most grateful to the following who agreed to be interviewed for the history:

Dame Jenny Abramsky • Mark Adair • Kate Adie • Juliet Alexander • Dave Allen • Keith Anderson • Christopher Andrews • Mike Appleton • Dickie Arbiter • Lord Armstrong • Neal Ascherson • Sir David Attenborough • James Arnold Baker • Joan Bakewell • Lady Balfour • Sir Brian Barder • David Barlow • Edward Barnes • Lord Barnett • Paddy Barwise • Dick Bates • Patrick Bateson • Biddy Baxter • Susan Belbin • Lord Bew • Antonia Bird • Lord Birt • Sir Kenneth Bloomfield • Roger Bolton • Lesley Bonham Carter • Paul Bonner • Sue Bonner • Richard Briers • Lord Briggs • Clare Brigstocke • Sir Sam Brittan • Richard Brock • Michael Buerk • Humphrey Burton • Tony Burton • Tony Byers • Sir Anthony Campbell • Sarah Caplin • Susanna Capon • George Carey • Anna Carragher • Jessica Cecil • Sandra Chalmers • Toni Charlton • Sir Michael Checkland • Sir John Chilcot • Stephen Claypole • Jenny Clayton • Michael Cockerell • Samantha Cohen • John Cole • Michael Cole • Andrew Coleman • Sir Frank Cooper • Cathy Corcoran • Sir Bill Cotton • Paddy Coulter • Chris Cramer • Catherine Crowther • Ian Curteis • Christopher Cviic • Mark Damazar • Michael Darlow • Susan Davies • John Howard Davies • Nicholas Deakin • Lord Debden • Glenn del Medico • Jonathan Dimbleby • Andrew Ehrenberg • Jane Ellison • David Elstein • Sally Feldman • George Fischer • Sir Dennis Forman • Dame Liz Forgan • John Foster • Sir Paul Fox • Robert Fox • Suzanne Franks • John Fray • Tim Gardam • Alex Gerlis • Colin Gilbert • Jimmy Gilbert • Peter Gill • Peter Goodchild • Nik Gowing • Lord Grade • Christopher Graham • Graham C. Green • Lord Griffiths • Patsy Grigg • Libby Grimshaw • Gareth Gwenlan • Julie Hadwin • Brian Hanrahan • Christine Hardwick • Robert Harris • Alan Hart • Rosemary Harthill • Robert Hazel • Tony Hearn • Stephen Hearst • Margaret Heffernan • Thena Heshel • Ashley Hill • Frances Hill • Isabel Hilton • Mike Hodder • Dame Patricia Hodgson • Christopher Hogwood • Angela Holdsworth • Corinne Hollingworth • David Holmes • Baroness Howe • Rosaleen Hughes • Austin Hunter • Lord Hurd • Lord Hussey • Peter Ibbotson • Sir Bernard Ingham • Lord Janvrin • Peter Jay • Steve Jones • Sir Nicholas Kenyon • Wesley Kerr • Francesca Kirby-Green • Chris Langton • Roger Laughton • Phil Laven • Tony Lennon • Alan Little • Yvonne Littlewood • Roy Lockett • Pat Loughrey • Andy Love • David Loyn •

Sue MacGregor • Lord Mason • John McCormick • Bryce McCrirrick • Leonard Miall • Caroline Millington • Alasdair Milne • Kirsty Milne • Ruairidh Milne • Seamus Milne • Eddie Mirzoeff • Baqer Moin • John Moreton • Gerry Morrissey • Dennis Murray • Barbara Myers • Graham Mytton • Sara Nathan • Ron Neil • Sir David Nicholas • Fran O'Brien • Meryl O'Keefe • Ron O'Rourke • Giles Oakely • Tim Orchard • Sir Michael Palliser • Baroness Park • Bryon Parkin • Lord Patten • Helen Pennant-Rea • Geoffrey Perkins • Stephen Plaistow • Peter Plouvier • Jon Plowman • Robert Ponsonby • Nigel Pope • Jonathan Powell (drama) • Jonathan (Nicholas) Powell (No. 10) • Alan Protheroe • Stuart Purvis • Sir Timothy Raison • Dame Esther Rantzen • Sir Malcolm Rifkind • Alwyn Roberts • Lord Rogers • Peter Rosier • Penelope Russell-Smith • Mike Salisbury • Naomi Sargant • John Seaman • Olivia Seligman • Colin Shaw • John Shirley • Susannah Simons • John Simpson • Monica Sims • Ros Sloboda • Anthony Smith • Michael Starks • Fraser Steele • Charles Stewart • Paul Stone • Bella Szombati • Andrew Taussig • Cliff Taylor • Peter Taylor • Duncan Thomas • Mark Thompson • Roy Tipping • Ken Trodd • Susan Tully • Sir Mark Tully • Sir John Tusa • Ellie Updale • Simon Walker • Robin Walsh • David Wedgwood Benn • Sir Charles Wheeler • Joy Whitby • Hugh Whitemore • Arnold Whittal • Stephen Whittle • John Wilkinson • Edward Williams • Gwyneth Williams • Lord Williams • Cheryl Anne Wilson • Michael Wooldridge • Will Wyatt • Alan Yentob • Lord Young

Blaen Pant and Islington
October 2014

INDEX